CONTENTS

How to use this book v

Introduction to Financial and Management Accounting 1

SECTION ONE

Chapter 1 Documents of trade 12

Chapter 2 Double entry book-keeping 25

Chapter 3 Preparation of final accounts 33

Chapter 4 Preparation of final accounts – adjustments 56

Chapter 5 The preparation of manufacturing accounts 96

Chapter 6 Partnerships 111

Chapter 7 Admission of a new partner 133

Chapter 8 The accounts of limited companies 146

Chapter 9 Accounts of not-for-profit organisations 174

Chapter 10 Analysis and interpretation of accounts 191

Chapter 11 Trial balance and the correction of errors 226

Chapter 12 Bank reconciliation statements 241

Chapter 13 Accounting Standards 247

SECTION TWO

Chapter 14 Classification of costs 252

Chapter 15 Inventory control procedures 256

CONTENTS

Chapter 16 Pricing stock issues 265

Chapter 17 Labour costs 281

Chapter 18 Overhead analysis 292

Chapter 19 Job costing 320

Chapter 20 Service costing 330

Chapter 21 Process costing 339

Chapter 22 Break-even analysis 358

Chapter 23 Marginal costing for decision making 373

Chapter 24 Budgetary control and 394
preparation of budgets

Chapter 25 Information Technology in Accounting 422

Chapter 26 Spreadsheets in Accounting 425

INDEX 433

HIGHER and INTERMEDIATE 2

Accounting

Anne M. Stewart

Hodder Gibson

A MEMBER OF THE HODDER HEADLINE GROUP

The Publishers would like to thank the following for permission to reproduce copyright material:

Acknowledgements
The office building on the front cover is the only commercially used Grade-A listed building in Scotland. The famous Art Deco building near Glasgow Airport was saved from demolition by Graham Technology, a global software solutions and service provider, where sound accounting practices – as in any successful business – are essential. Renovation work on the building went on between 2000 and 2004 with help from Historic Scotland and Scottish Enterprise. More details at www.grahamtechnology.com.

Every effort has been made to trace all copyright holders, but if any have been inadvertently overlooked the Publishers will be pleased to make the necessary arrangements at the first opportunity.

Although every effort has been made to ensure that website addresses are correct at time of going to press, Hodder Gibson cannot be held responsible for the content of any website mentioned in this book. It is sometimes possible to find a relocated web page by typing in the address of the home page for a website in the URL window of your browser.

Hodder Headline's policy is to use papers that are natural, renewable and recyclable products and made from wood grown in sustainable forests. The logging and manufacturing processes are expected to conform to the environmental regulations of the country of origin.

If the CD is missing from this package, please contact us on 0141 848 1609 or at hoddergibson@hodder.co.uk, advising where and when you purchased the book.

Orders: please contact Bookpoint Ltd, 130 Milton Park, Abingdon, Oxon OX14 4SB. Telephone: (44) 01235 827720. Fax: (44) 01235 400454. Lines are open 9.00 – 5.00, Monday to Saturday, with a 24-hour message answering service. Visit our website at www.hoddereducation.co.uk. Hodder Gibson can be contacted direct on: Tel: 0141 848 1609; Fax: 0141 889 6315; email: hoddergibson@hodder.co.uk

© Anne Stewart 2006
First published in 2006 by
Hodder Gibson, an imprint of Hodder Education,
a member of the Hodder Headline Group
2a Christie Street
Paisley PA1 1NB

Impression number   5 4 3 2 1
Year   2010 2009 2008 2007 2006

Cover photo by ImageState/Alamy
Illustrations by DC Graphic Design Limited, Swanley Village, Kent.
Typeset in 10.5pt ITC Century Light by DC Graphic Design Limited, Swanley Village, Kent.
Printed and bound in Great Britain by Martins The Printers, Berwick-upon-Tweed.

A catalogue record for this title is available from the British Library

ISBN-10: 0-340-90607-3
ISBN-13: 978-0-340-90607-1

How to use this book

This book contains all you need for complete coverage of Intermediate 2 and Higher Accounting. Chapters 1 to 13 cover Financial Accounting, and Chapters 14 to 26 cover Management Accounting. All the material for both Intermediate 2 and Higher is covered in the book. Material which is only needed for Intermediate 2 is indicated using this icon: and material which is only needed for the Higher is indicated using this icon: .
Material which is needed for both Intermediate 2 and Higher is indicated using this icon .

If you are going to be successful in your accounting work, you will need to spend time practising the techniques required for the varying aspects of financial analysis and reporting. Each chapter includes a comprehensive collection of examples, Tasks and Worksheets. The examples are used to demonstrate procedures, and in most cases, the procedures are broken down into specific steps, with explanatory notes. Follow the examples step-by-step and make sure you understand each part of the process.

Most examples are followed immediately by Tasks. These Tasks will build on the learning presented in the examples, and you should work through the Tasks carefully to ensure you understand the various processes involved. The Tasks are usually quite short pieces of work. Most chapters include a number of Worksheets, which are larger pieces of work. You should work through the Worksheets when you see the instruction **Now do Worksheet 1** in the text in the book. The Worksheets are provided on the CD-ROM as Adobe Acrobat files. You can either print them yourself, or your teacher may provide them as hand-outs.

The solutions to the Tasks and Worksheets are also provided on the CD-ROM. Avoid the temptation to look at the solutions before you attempt the Tasks and Worksheets, but use the solutions to help with any problems you are having and to check your work.

Introduction to Financial and Management Accounting

This Introduction will help you

☆ **understand what accounting is**

☆ **identify the people and organisations interested in accounting information, and understand the different ways they use different types of information**

☆ **distinguish clearly between the role of the Financial Accountant and the Management Accountant**

☆ **understand the different types of work that Financial and Management Accountants perform**

☆ **understand some of the deficiencies of Financial Accounting as a tool for control**

The concept of accounting

A student beginning the study of accounting often finds it difficult to understand the concept of accounting. Their lack of understanding of the way the business world works and the need for detailed record keeping contributes to their initial difficulty.

However, they should be aware that every day they actually do some accounting. When they receive their pocket money, birthday money or the wage from a part time job they make decisions on whether to save or to spend the money. In most cases they alone make these decisions.

They may keep records through their bank account or simply keep a list of what they have spent their money on.

If they wish to buy something in particular they need to check how much money they have before making the purchase, or they may save for the purchase or get into debt by borrowing money from their parents.

If they are continually short of money they may have to explain this to their parents.

Accounting for the business world involves the enterprise in a number of processes:

- **Identifying and recording information**. A garage will identify and record details of car sold, fuel sold or repairs carried out.
- **Classifying and measuring**. The garage will group car sales, fuel sales, repair income, cars purchased, fuel purchased or spare parts purchased for repairs, and total them for the trading period.
- **Communicating and explaining** the results of identifying, recording, classifying and measuring to those parties interested in the accounts of the business enterprise.

Who is interested in accounting information?

There are a large number of individuals, groups, organisations and legal bodies interested in the accounting records of a business enterprise as shown in Figure Int.1.

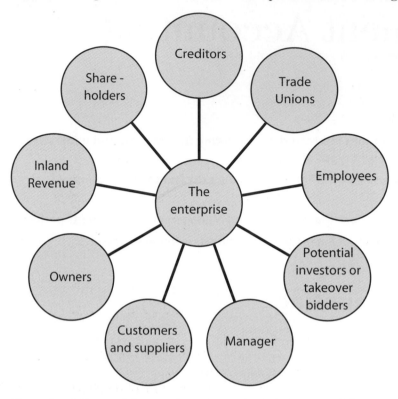

Figure Int.1 Some of the people and organisations interested in accounting information

What are they interested in?

Different groups of people and organisations are interested in different types of information, for different reasons.

Creditors

Creditors are people (or business organisations) who are owed money by a business. They may be owed money because they have lent money (banks) or because they have sold goods or services to the business but have not yet been paid. There are three groups: creditors, bankers and debenture holders.

Creditors, who are interested in:

- whether enough current assets are available to pay current liabilities;
- the make-up of the current assets and estimated actual ability to pay debts;
- the priority of claims on assets in the event of the company failing;
- earnings records, possible future expansion or contraction;
- the policy and calibre of management.

Bankers, who are interested in:

- the purpose and length of loan;
- the company's plans for the repayment of the loan;
- the company's profit trends - is it satisfactory?
- the bank's position if the company fails;
- the calibre and policy of management.

Debenture Holders, who are interested in:

- the ability of the company to pay the interest promptly;
- the ability of the company to re-pay the loan promptly;
- their security if the firm goes into liquidation.

Shareholders

Shareholders are individual people, other businesses or financial institutions who own a share of the company. Shareholders can own very small amounts of the company, or they might own very large portions of the company.

Existing shareholders, who are interested in:

- proposed dividends.

Small potential investors, are interested in:

- profits trends and sales over recent years;
- expansion forecasts in the particular industry;
- yield on investment compared with yields from alternative forms of investment;
- the ease with which dividends can be paid from profits earned;
- the probable certainty of future payments at the same or higher levels of dividend currently reported;
- the calibre and policies of management.

Large potential investors, who are interested in:

- proposed dividends;
- profits trends and sales over recent years;
- expansion forecasts in the particular industry;
- yield on investment compared with yields from alternative forms of investment;
- the ease with which dividends can be paid from profits earned;
- probable certainty of future payments at the same or higher levels of dividend currently reported;
- calibre and policies of management;
- growth prospects of the business enterprise consistent with financial stability.

Inland Revenue

The Inland Revenue is interested in the firm's accounts for tax purposes, to ensure that the firm pays the correct amount of tax.

Employee's representatives

In most businesses, staff will be represented by some kind of staff body, which might be a branch of a national trade union, or a staff association. Employee's representatives are interested in:

- dividends being paid in light of wage claims;
- if profit sharing takes place – the amount due to employees;
- the employee wage increase compared with salaries and bonuses of management and directors.

Takeover bidders

Takeover bidders are usually a large company wishing to diversify or buy competing companies. They are interested in the:

- real value of the assets of the company compared with the Balance Sheet value (depreciation, stock valuation);
- financial and dividend policies of the directors and their effect on shareholders loyalty;
- Stock Exchange price of shares compared with the Balance Sheet valuation and the real value;
- existence of assets which would release large cash profits if sold – valuable land and buildings;
- existence of large cash balances or short-term loans disclosing excess liquidity and therefore under-utilisation of resources.

Managers and owners

Managers and owners are interested in:

- whether the business is selling enough to cover its overheads and to make a profit;
- how much the business owes and is owed;
- how much profit the business is making;
- the effects on the financial position of the enterprise of decisions taken during the financial year;
- how well the business is doing in comparison to competitors;
- how well the business is doing compared to previous years.

What are Financial and Management Accounting?

There are many different branches of accounting. This textbook looks at the two main areas of Financial and Management Accounting.

Take a look at the different types of accountancy jobs advertised in the newspapers, or search the web to discover just how many different branches of accounting there are – Financial Accountants, Management Accountants, Cost Accountants, Financial Services Accountants, Corporate Accountant, Project Accountant etc.

Financial Accounting

Financial Accounting is concerned mainly with the recording function (called book-keeping) and the drafting of final accounts for different kinds of organisation. It deals with the legal requirements, for example complying with the Companies Acts, or keeping an account of a customer's legal indebtedness.

With companies, the final accounts represent the account given to the shareholders, by their directors, of the running of the company during a particular year. It is a statement of the directors' stewardship of the company.

Stewardship means that the business must account to the owners for the activities carried out in their name. These accounts are also given to other interested bodies such as the firm's bankers, creditors, employee representatives, and the Inspector of Taxes.

Financial Accounting is necessary from the legal point of view but it is not an ideal system for controlling and planning the activities of a firm.

Financial Accounting has deficiencies:

- It deals with operations which have already occurred (historical costing). You can control what is happening or about to happen, but you cannot change what has already happened.
- It is concerned with the whole firm. A firm may manufacture and sell 3 distinct products at a yearly profit of £100,000, but this does not tell us whether all 3 products are making a profit or which product(s) make a loss.

Management Accounting

Management Accounting is the branch of accounting which addresses the deficiencies in Financial Accounting. The Institute of Cost and Management Accountants (ICMA) defines Management Accounting as the provision of information required by management for such purposes as:

1 Formulation of policies

2 Planning and controlling the future activities of the enterprise

3 Decision-taking on alternative courses of action

4 Disclosure of policies to shareholders and employees

5 Safeguarding of assets

The above purposes involve management in working to ensure that:

- long-term policy planning takes place so that objectives are met;
- short-term plans are prepared (such as budgets) to meet the objectives;
- actual transactions are recorded;
- actual performance is monitored against projected performance and corrective action is taken when necessary;
- finance is obtained and controlled;
- systems and operations are reported on and reviewed.

Before it is possible to draw up a plan in financial terms the firm must know the costs of all the various operations of the business and the study of these costs for accounting purposes is called **Cost Accounting**.

Cost Accounting is the division of Management Accounting which establishes budgets, cost of operations, processes, departments or products, compares them with actual costs and analyses the variances, profitability or the social use of funds.

Cost Accounting supplies the basic factual information on which management accountancy builds its presentation of planning and control. Cost Accounting aids management in the following ways:

1 Establishing costs for various jobs, operations or processes.

2 Comparing actual costs with budgeted costs.

3 Indicating to management where losses, inefficiencies or wastage are occurring and indicating what corrective action may be taken.

4 Preparing and costing alternative options and indicating which option would be the most profitable.

5 Serving as a basis for price and profit determination.

6 Providing comparative cost data for different periods of time and varying volumes of production.

A system of cost and management accountancy should not be imposed on a business. It should evolve from a careful consideration of the business itself and its special needs.

The aim should be to make the costing system as simple as possible to operate and acceptable to the accountancy staff. To be of any value it must product results promptly.

Certain conditions are essential for the success of a costing system:

● An efficient method of stores and stock control must exist.
● A well-designed wages procedure must exist which includes the method of charging labour costs to production.
● There must be a sound system for the collection of all indirect expenses and the subsequent charging of these expenses to products or service departments.
● The cost and financial accounting systems should be integrated.
● Standardised printed forms should be used wherever possible.
● The status of the Cost Accountant should be clearly defined along with their responsibilities and authority.

Comparison of Financial and Cost Accounts

The profit statement below shows the overall financial position of J Brown at the end of the financial year.

Profit Statement of J Brown
for year ended 31 December Year 1

	£	£
Sales		60,000
Less Costs		
Materials	30,000	
Wages	14,000	
Production overheads	4,000	
Administration overheads	4,000	
Selling and Distribution	2,000	54,000
Net Profit		6,000

It shows an overall profit of £6,000 but using management accounting we can look more closely at the income and costs of each product sold by Brown.

Product Profit and Loss Statement
for year ended 31 December Year 1

Product	A	B	C	Total
	£	£	£	£
Materials	7,400	13,000	9,600	30,000
Wages	5,000	6,000	3,000	14,000
Production overheads	1,200	1,800	1,000	4,000
Administration overheads	1,600	1,000	1,400	4,000
Selling and Distribution	1,000	500	500	2,000
TOTAL COSTS	16,200	22,300	15,500	54,000
Sales	22,200	17,320	20,480	60,000
Profit/(Loss)	6,000	(4,980)	4,980	6,000

From the cost statement we can see that Product B is making a loss and management should investigate:

- its costs and look for savings;
- its selling price with the possibility of raising prices;
- whether to eliminate product B from their range;
- whether to continue production and use B as a loss leader.

What's the difference between Financial and Management Accounting?

The objectives of Financial and Management Accounting differ in the following ways:

Financial Accounting

1   Financial accounts are a **legal requirement** which must comply with law particularly for a plc.

2   The accounts present a **historical record** of the affairs of the enterprise.

3   The accounts are for **external** purposes, available to shareholders, creditors, bankers etc.

4   Financial accounts must comply with the **Statement of Principles** laid down by the professional bodies.

5   Financial accounts show the **stewardship** of the organisation and the **accountability** of management for properties held for others.

6   The accounts provide **information** on inputs and outputs for decision-making purposes.

7   Information given in the audited accounts is given in broad categories and is **unsuitable** for planning, control and decision-making.

Management Accounting

1   The accounts are not for publication – they are used **internally**.

2   The accounts provide **recent**, **current** and **future** estimates of what is or will be happening, and are not a historic record.

3   The accounts report information useful to **internal** management.

4   It is **not essential** to comply with concepts and conventions.

5   Heads of departments are **accountable** for results.

6   Large amounts of **information** can be used in decision-making.

7   More detailed information is needed and often this is needed more quickly than the financial accounting records could provide.

Advantages of Management Accounting

In terms of actually running a business, there are a number of reasons why Management Accounting is important.

Cost ascertainment: This is necessary for pricing purposes and determining profitability of different units. It helps show areas where cost reductions are possible.

Control of current operations: Comparison of actual with forecasted costs allows the analysis of variances showing causes and responsibility. It enables remedial action to be taken.

Decision making: In the short term, it can help with decisions such as whether the firm should make or buy a component, or accept or reject a particular contract. In the long term, it allows the firm to carry out investment appraisal and allows them to decide whether to purchase fixed assets.

Organisation: The preparation of budgets fixes the responsibility for the achievement of these budgets. Budgets must be accepted by departments as achievable.

Planning: This allows the firm to fix objectives and plan for the future.

Task 1

1 State the three processes involved in accounting.

2 Choose three of the parties interested in the accounts of a business enterprise and state what they are particularly interested in finding out from the accounts.

3 Explain what Financial Accounting involves.

4 Explain what Management Accounting involves.

5 Compare and contrast Financial and Management Accounting.

Now do Worksheet Int. 1

SECTION ONE

Financial Accounting

Chapter 1 Documents of trade

Chapter 2 Double entry book-keeping

Chapter 3 Preparation of final accounts

Chapter 4 Preparation of final accounts – adjustments

Chapter 5 The preparation of manufacturing accounts

Chapter 6 Partnerships

Chapter 7 Admission of a new partner

Chapter 8 The accounts of limited companies

Chapter 9 Accounts of not-for-profit organisations

Chapter 10 Analysis and interpretation of accounts

Chapter 11 Trial balance and correction of errors

Chapter 12 Bank reconciliation statements

Chapter 13 Accounting Standards

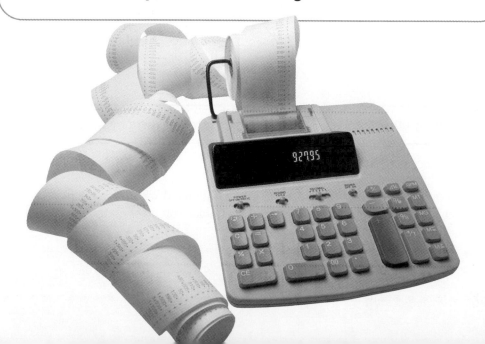

Documents of trade

Intermediate 2 Level Outcomes: ▶

 This chapter includes material from Int 2 level Financial Accounting Outcome 1
☆ **Explain the functions of the different business documents used in the buying, selling and payment process.**

Business transactions

A business transaction occurs when goods or services are provided. Transactions can be of two types:

- **Cash** transaction: the goods are purchased and paid for at the same time.
- **Credit** transaction: the goods are purchased and are paid for at a later date.

All business documents are used as records but only some of them are used by the accounts department.

The document trail

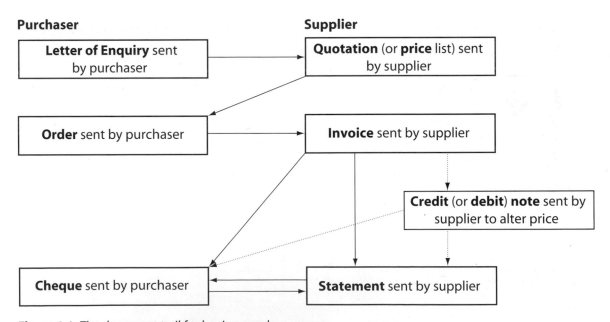

Figure 1.1 The document trail for buying goods

Figure 1.1 shows the documents which are commonly used when one business buys goods from another business. Each document has a particular role in the buying process.

Letter of Enquiry

Bill and Ben operate a garden centre and need a new supplier for garden tools. They send out a **Letter of Enquiry** to a number of possible suppliers, stating:

- what they want;
- what grade/quality;
- how many;
- when the delivery is needed;
- where it is to be delivered to.

Quotation

Interested suppliers send back either a **quotation** or, alternatively a **catalogue** (or **price list**) together with details of any discounts available and carriage/delivery charges.

Bill and Ben will look through these and decide which supplier to place the order with. When they have decided, they will use an order form to place their order.

Order form

The **order form** will give the following details:

- order number (for reference purposes);
- date order was sent;
- quantity of goods required;
- description of goods required;
- catalogue numbers of such goods;
- prices agreed;
- date on which the goods are required;
- place of delivery

The order form is sent to the supplier by the buyer. It may have several copies for use by the various departments involved in the purchasing process.

Bill and Ben's Garden Centre
32 High Street
Anytown
AT33 9EE

Tel: 013723233 VAT Reg No 000/3333/1111
Fax: 013723233
Website: *Email:*
www.intouch.bus.uk Sales@billandben.co.uk

ORDER FORM
To: Gardens Direct plc Official Order No: 7/216
    23 Braemar Street
    Newtown
    NT6 7KK Date: 31 March Year 1

Please supply:

Qty	Description	Cat No	Unit Price	Total
3	Stainless steel forks	SS2	£50.00	£150.00
6	Large wheel barrows	WB45	£30.00	£180.00
Total Value of Order				£330.00

Delivery required : Delivery Address:
End April Year 1 As above

Signed: *Ben Wilson*

Figure 1.2 Order form showing quantities of goods purchased, purchase prices, and dates ordered

Invoice

An **invoice** is a detailed list of the goods purchased and is sent by the seller to the buyer when the goods are despatched. Several copies of the invoice will be prepared at same time and used in different ways:

- the buyer (customer) receives the original;
- a copy is kept by the seller (supplier) to record the transaction in their ledger accounts;
- other departments in the business will receive a copy of the invoice (such as stores and accounts);
- other copies may be used as an Advice Note (forwarded to the buyer), or Delivery Note (sent with the goods).

Each invoice will have the following information:

- name and address of the supplier and purchaser;
- date;
- order number (for reference purposes);
- invoice number;
- details of goods being sent, including catalogue no/reference no, quantity supplied, description, unit price and total price for the quantity, details of any trade discount;
- VAT if any;
- total amount due from the customer;
- terms applicable, whether cash discount is offered for prompt payment.

Gardens Direct plc
23 Braemar Street
Newtown
NT6 7KK

Invoice

Reg No 8888/4444/5555
Email: gardensdirect@onemail.co.uk

Tel: 018582 22
Fax: 017852 44

Your Order No: 7/216

Invoice No: 78/933

To: Bill and Ben's Garden Centre
32 High Street
Anytown
AT33 9EE

Date: 15 April Year 1

Qty	Description	Cat No	Unit Price	Total
3	Stainless steel forks	SS2	£50.00	£150.00
6	Large wheel barrows	WB45	£30.00	£180.00
				£330.00
Less: Trade Discount at 20%				£66.00
NET GOODS VALUE				£264.00
VAT				£43.89
TOTAL VALUE OF INVOICE				£307.89

Terms Nett: 5% within one month

Figure 1.3 Invoice showing quantities of goods sold and invoice prices before and after discount

To calculate the invoice price, Gardens Direct would have to take into consideration any trade discount and/or cash discount offered and VAT to be added.

What is discount?

A **discount** is a reduction in the price of goods. Details of discounts given or available will appear on the invoice. The two types of discount offered are **trade** discount and **cash** discount.

Trade discount

Trade discount is a reduction on the price of the goods being sold and is offered by the seller to the buyer because the buyer is:

- in the same trade;
- and/or buying in bulk.

Trade discount is usually expressed as a percentage and is deducted from the purchase price of the goods. In the invoice Gardens Direct are allowing Bill and Ben's Garden Centre **20% trade discount** off the cost of the goods they are purchasing.

This amounts to 20% of £330 = £66.

Bill and Ben's Garden Centre will pay £330 – £66 = £264 for the goods. This is known as the **net goods value**.

Cash discount

Cash discount is a discount offered by the supplier to encourage their customers to pay promptly – usually within the month. The offer of cash discount affects the way in which VAT is calculated and added to the cost of the goods.

Bill and Ben's Garden Centre are being offered **5% cash discount** if they pay promptly. This is indicated by the **Terms Nett** shown at the bottom of the invoice.

What is Value Added Tax?

Value Added Tax is a tax levied by the Government and is added to the value of most goods and services provided by suppliers. It is calculated on the lowest possible price to be paid for the goods:

The lowest possible price may be:

- cost price;
- cost price less trade discount;
- cost price less cash discount;
- cost price less trade and cash discounts.

Calculation of VAT

Value Added Tax is currently levied at the rate of 17.5% and is added by the supplier to the **net goods value** to calculate the **invoice price** of the goods being sold. The supplier acts as a tax collector on behalf of the Government. At regular intervals the supplier will offset the VAT collected against the VAT paid and either send or receive a cheque from the Government for the amount.

Example 1 Simple VAT calculation

If no type of discount is offered VAT is calculated on the **cost price** of the goods to calculate the amount due to be paid by the customer:

Cost price of goods	£1,000
Add VAT at 17.5%	£175
Total amount due	£1,175

The following formula is used to calculate the VAT to be charged on the goods sold:

VAT = Goods sold × 17.5%

This is then added to the cost price to give the total amount due.

Task 1

Copy and complete the following table to show the VAT calculation and invoice price payable for the following goods

Cost price	VAT charged at 17.5%	Invoice price
£800		
£2,400		
£3,800		
£4,260		
£5,320		

Example 2 VAT calculation including trade discount

When trade discount is offered, VAT is calculated on the goods price less the trade discount.

Calculate the discount to find the net goods value (NGV), then calculate the VAT charged on the NGV and add the VAT to the NGV to find the invoice price.

Cost of goods	£1,000
Less 20% trade discount (20% of £1,000)	£200
VAT charged on net goods value	£800
Add VAT at 17.5% (£800 × 17.5%)	£140
Invoice price	£940

Task 2

Copy and complete the following table to show the VAT calculation and invoice price payable for the following goods.

Cost price	Trade Discount %	Trade Discount amount	Net Goods Value	VAT 17.5%	Invoice price
£600	20%				
£1,500	15%				
£3,200	10%				
£5,480	20%				
£8,264	25%				
£10,000	20%				

Example 3 VAT calculation where only cash discount is offered

When cash discount is offered, VAT is calculated on the goods price less the cash discount. Remember VAT is always calculated on the lowest possible price.

However the cash discount will only be given if the invoice is paid within the time stated. This means that the price of goods on the invoice will be cost price plus VAT.

Cost price of goods	£1,000.00
Less 10% cash discount (10% of £1,000)	£100.00
VAT charged on lowest possible price	£900.00
Add VAT at 17.5% (£900 × 17.5%)	£157.50
Invoice price	£1,157.50

The amount due on the invoice will be the original cost of goods plus the VAT:

Cost of goods	£1,000.00
Add VAT	£157.50
Invoice price	£1,157.50

Task 3

Copy and complete the following table to show the VAT calculation and total cost payable for the following goods.

Cost price	Cash discount %	Cash discount amount	Discounted price (cost - cash discount)	VAT on discounted price 17.5%	Invoice price (Cost price + VAT)
£6,000	20%				
£750	25%				
£4,000	40%				
£8,500	20%				
£6,200	30%				

Example 4   Where both trade and cash discount are allowed

When trade and cash discount are allowed VAT is calculated on the lowest price the customer could pay. Calculate the discounts first and then calculate the VAT on the lowest possible price.

Cost price of goods	£1,000.00
Less 10% trade discount (10% of £1,000)	£100.00
Goods net of trade discount	£900.00
Less 10% cash discount offered (10% of £900)	£90.00
Lowest possible price (used to calculate VAT)	£810.00
Add VAT at 17.5% (£810 × 17.5%)	£141.75

The price on the invoice for the goods will be the net goods value (after the trade discount, but not the cash discount) plus the VAT:

Net Goods Value	£900.00
Add VAT @ 17.5%	£141.75
Invoice price	£1,041.75

Task 4

Copy and complete the following table to show the VAT calculation and invoice price payable for the following goods.

Cost Price	Trade Discount %	Trade Discount amount	Goods net of Trade Discount	Cash Discount %	Cash Discount offered	VAT charged on cost less both discounts	VAT at 17.5%	Invoice price (Cost less Trade Discount + VAT)
£7,500	20%			5%				
£14,500	10%			10%				
£25,000	25%			10%				
£400	20%			12.5%				
£6,300	30%			10%				
£8,000	50%			10%				
£600	50%			10%				

Credit note

Once an invoice has been sent it cannot be changed. If an error is discovered the supplier will send the buyer a **credit note**. The supplier will also keep a copy to record the details in their ledger accounts.

A credit note will be issued if:

- the supplier has made a mistake and charged too much;
- the goods were damaged on delivery and have been returned and no replacement goods have been sent in their place;
- the wrong or unsuitable goods have been supplied and have been returned by the purchaser;
- a charge has been made for the packing cases/pallets/crates and these have been emptied and returned by the customer.

A credit note is also used as evidence that goods have been returned and is an acknowledgement that the returned goods have been received. Credit notes *reduce* the amount due by the buyer.

As credit notes contain the same information as an invoice they are often **printed in red** to distinguish them from other documents.

The credit note is made out by the seller and sent to the buyer and will show the following information:

- name and address of the supplier;
- name and address of the buyer;
- date;
- invoice number (for reference purposes);
- full details (reference no., quantity, description and reason) for goods being returned;
- unit price and total price for the quantity;
- details of trade discount;
- VAT if any;

- terms applicable, whether cash discount is offered for prompt payment;
- total value of credit note.

Any discounts offered on the invoice will also have to be applied to the credit note so that the purchaser is being credited with the amount they paid for the goods.

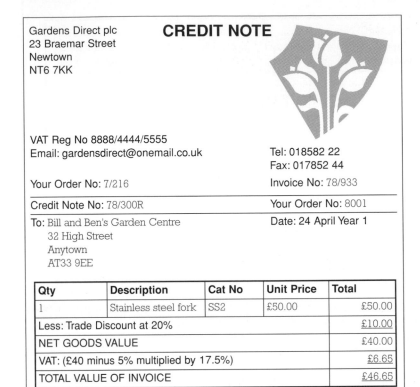

Gardens Direct plc
23 Braemar Street
Newtown
NT6 7KK

CREDIT NOTE

VAT Reg No 8888/4444/5555
Email: gardensdirect@onemail.co.uk

Tel: 018582 22
Fax: 017852 44

Your Order No: 7/216

Invoice No: 78/933

Credit Note No: 78/300R

Your Order No: 8001

To: Bill and Ben's Garden Centre
32 High Street
Anytown
AT33 9EE

Date: 24 April Year 1

Qty	Description	Cat No	Unit Price	Total
1	Stainless steel fork	SS2	£50.00	£50.00
Less: Trade Discount at 20%				£10.00
NET GOODS VALUE				£40.00
VAT: (£40 minus 5% multiplied by 17.5%)				£6.65
TOTAL VALUE OF INVOICE				£46.65

Terms: 5% if paid within one month

Figure 1.4 Credit note showing amount to be credited back to the purchaser after returning goods

If there has been an undercharge or error on the invoice the seller will send a **debit note** to the buyer. It contains the same information as the credit note but **increases** the amount of the original invoice.

Statement of account

At the end of the month the seller of the goods will send out a document called a **statement of account**. A statement of account shows a summary of transactions which have taken place for a given period of time (usually one month). This allows the buyer to pay for his goods at the end of each month rather than write out a cheque for each individual invoice.

The statement of account will show:

- any amount unpaid from previous statement (the balance at the start of the month/period);
- all transactions that took place in a particular month together with the document numbers;
- sales and returns;
- payments made;
- amounts which *increase* the amount the buyer owes the seller, (i.e. all invoices issued since last statement) (**Debit** column);

- amounts which *decrease* the amount the buyer owes (i.e. all credit notes issued and payments made by the buyer since last statement) (**Credit** column);
- balance outstanding (owing) at the end of the month.

The statement of account is a copy of the ledger account in the seller's ledger.

STATEMENT

Gardens Direct plc
23 Braemar Street
Newtown
NT6 7KK

VAT Reg No 8888/4444/5555
Email: gardensdirect@onemail.co.uk

Tel: 018582 22
Fax: 017852 44

To: Bill and Ben's Garden Centre
    32 High Street
    Anytown
    AT33 9EE

Date: 30 April Year 1

Date	Details	Debit £	Credit £	Balance £
Year 1				
April 1	Balance b/f	351.45		351.45
April 5	Invoice No: 78/855 (Sales)	610.55		962.00
April 12	Invoice No 78/933 (Sales)	307.89		1,269.89
April 16	Credit Note No: 78/R155 (Sales Returns)		117.54	1,152.35
April 18	Cheque (No 384874)		345.45	806.90
	Discount		6.00	800.90
April 22	Invoice No 78/984 (Sales)	239.56		1,040.46
April 24	Credit Note No: 78/300R(Sales Returns)		46.65	993.81

Figure 1.5 Statement of Account with details of transactions (purchases, payments and credit notes)

Amounts **owed** for **credit sales** to Gardens Direct plc by Bill and Ben's Garden Centre are shown in the column headed **Debit**.

Amounts **paid** or **returned** by Bill and Ben's Garden Centre are shown in the column headed **Credit**.

The **total amount owed** by Bill and Ben's Garden Centre is the last figure in the **Balance** column.

Items in the **debit** column will **increase** the balance

Items in the **credit** column will **decrease** the balance

Paying for goods and services

Receipts

A **receipt** is evidence that a payment has been made. The payment may be made in cash, by cheques or credit card. The seller of the goods will give a receipt as evidence that payment has been made to the buyer of the goods.

Receipt No:	Gardens Direct plc 23 Braemar Street	
345R	Newtown NT6 7KK	
RECEIPT	Date: ... 18 April 2006	
Received from: Bill and Ben's Garden Centre		

Amount Received	Cash	Cheque
in full settlement of amount due Signature: *R Hamilton*	£ 365.00	£

Figure 1.6 Receipt showing amount received in payment of an Invoice or Statement of Account

Cash sale till receipts

When a cash sale is made the good are handed over to the customer and paid for at the same time a till receipt is issued as evidence that a payment has been received for the goods.

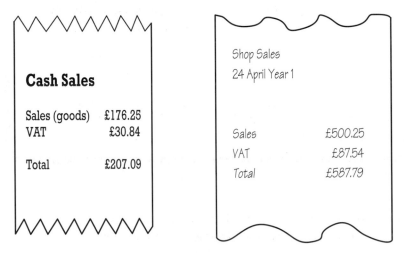

Cash Sales

Sales (goods)	£176.25
VAT	£30.84
Total	£207.09

Shop Sales
24 April Year 1

Sales	£500.25
VAT	£87.54
Total	£587.79

Figure 1.7 Examples of cash receipts

Credit/debit card

Individual customer may pay for their goods from Bill and Ben's Garden Centre by credit or debit cards. Paying by debit card means that the amount is electronically transferred from the customer's bank account to the account to the supplier.

Cheque and cheque counterfoil

Most business enterprises will settle their accounts by preparing a cheque. This is a written order to their bank to pay to the person named on the cheque the amount written on the cheque. When writing a cheque great care must be taken to ensure that it is written clearly with no errors. NO space should be left on the cheque where an unscrupulous person could alter the amount.

Cheques are valid for 6 months. The bank will not cash the cheque after 6 months.

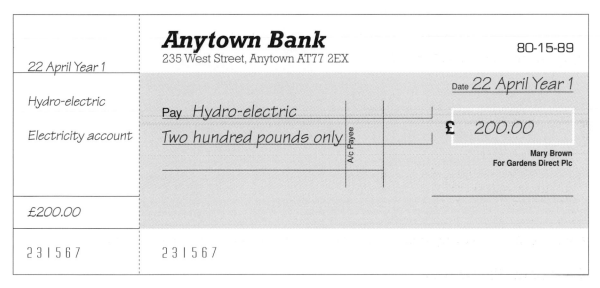

22 April Year 1	**Anytown Bank** 235 West Street, Anytown AT77 2EX	80-15-89
Hydro-electric	Date 22 April Year 1	
Electricity account	Pay Hydro-electric	£ 200.00
	Two hundred pounds only A/c Payee	Mary Brown For Gardens Direct Plc
£200.00		
2 3 1 5 6 7	2 3 1 5 6 7	

Figure 1.8 A cheque, showing the person (or business) the cheque is being paid to, the amount being paid, and the date of payment

A cheque is made up of two parts: the **counterfoil** which is kept by the person paying the amount as evidence of payment and the actual **cheque** which is given to the creditor.

> There are 3 parties to a cheque:
>
> - The drawee is the name of the bank where the account is held – Anytown Bank
> - The drawer is the firm signing the cheque – Mary Brown, Gardens Direct
> - The payee is the person the cheque is being paid to – Hydro Electric

Dishonoured Cheque

A **dishonoured cheque** is one which the bank has refused to pay when it has been given to them. The dishonoured cheque is returned to the payee – the person named on the cheque.

There are several reasons why a cheque may be dishonoured:

- the cheque is stale (more than 6 months old);
- the cheque is dated in the future (post-dated);
- there are errors on the cheque (for example, words and figures differ);
- the writing on the cheque may be illegible;
- no signature;
- there are no funds in the drawer's account.

Now do Worksheet 1.1

Double entry book-keeping

Intermediate 2 Level Outcomes:

 This chapter includes material from Int 2 level Financial Accounting Outcome 2

☆ **Prepare appropriate ledger accounts from completed business documents or a list using double entry book-keeping principles.**

☆ **Check the accuracy of ledger accounts using methods which are consistent with double entry book-keeping principles.**

What is double entry book-keeping?

This chapter gives a brief overview of double entry book-keeping. Book-keeping is an art which developed hundreds of years ago. Merchants and traders kept a book where the details of the amounts owed or owing, the value of assets etc were kept. This book was called a **ledger**. Each page in the ledger was called an account because it told the story or 'gave an account' of what happened to the value of the asset, liability, income, expense, capital or drawings being recorded on that page.

The three basic aims of book-keeping are to:

1   Record financial transactions in a consistent and orderly way.

2   Show the financial position of the firm:
  ● what the firm owes;
  ● what is owed to the firm;
  ● the value of the assets;
  ● the value of the liabilities;
  ● the capital or net worth of the owner.

3   Produce net figures which can be used to calculate the profit or the loss from the business activities.

Accounting transactions are written up from the original documents discussed in the previous chapter such as invoices, credit and debit notes, cheques and receipts. Some businesses will record these in **books of original entry**, called **sales day book**, or **purchases day book**. The entries in the books of original entry are then **posted** to the ledger. Posting simply means transferring the amounts to the ledger accounts.

Every transaction a firm undertakes has two effects on the business and on the ledger accounts of the firm. For example:

● If a firm purchases goods to resell for £10,000 by cheque, the value of the goods purchased will **increase** by £10,000 and the value of the bank will **decrease** by £10,000.

The double entry system of book-keeping requires every business transaction to be entered into two separate ledger accounts. The rule to follow for double entry book keeping is simply:

> For every debit entry there will be a corresponding credit entry of equivalent value.

The terms **debit** and **credit** refer to the debit column and the credit column of the ledger account.

What does a ledger account look like?

There are two styles of ledger account, the **T-Account** and the **Running Balance Account**. We are going to use the running balance style of account. You may be familiar with this if you have a Bank or Building Society account and receive regular statements.

An account is shown below with the columns numbered. We are going to use the following example to show how the information is recorded in the account.

10 January Paid rent by cheque of £500

Name of Account – **Rent account**				
Date	Details	Dr	Cr	Balance
Column 1	Column 2	Column 3	Column 4	Column 5

The name of the asset, expense, liability etc is written at the top of the account and the columns are used as follows:

Column	Information recorded in the columns of the account
1 **Date**	The date of the transaction using the following style: **Jan 10**
2 **Details**	The name of the other ledger account involved in the transaction: **Bank**
3 **Debit** (Dr)	The amount to be debited to this account: **£500 in the Rent account**
4 **Credit** (Cr)	The amount to be credited to this account: **In the Bank account - £500**
5 **Balance**	The **balance** on the account – this is the **difference** between the total of the **debit entries** and the total of the **credit entries** in the account. The balance is recalculated each time an entry is made in the account. As this is the first entry in the **Rent account**, the balance would be £500 in the **Balance** column.

Some people like to write beside the actual balance the type of balance the account has – **Dr** for **debit** or **Cr** for **credit**.

Transactions need to be recorded in a consistent manner if the information contained in the ledger accounts is to be of use to the business. To help with this, there are three separate categories of accounts and there are rules established for each type of account:

Type of account:	Description of this type of account:
REAL accounts	Accounts of assets – these are tangible items the enterprise owns and can be seen and touched, such as buildings, bank, motor vehicles etc. They appear in the **Balance Sheet**.
PERSONAL accounts	Accounts of all the **people** or **firms** the business deals with i.e. our **debtors** (a firm or person who owes us money), and **creditors** (a firm or person we owe money to). These will also appear in the **Balance Sheet**.
NOMINAL accounts (collecting accounts)	Collecting accounts which records the total **expenses** paid and any **incomes** received during a period, such as accounts for rent and rates, telephone bill, light and heat, rent received, discount received purchases, sales. These will appear in the **Trading** and **Profit and Loss Accounts** at the end of the year.

The different types of account have rules for recording transactions. These rules are linked to the assets, liabilities, expenses, drawings and capital of the enterprise.

Type of Ledger Account:	Rule for entry:	
REAL accounts	Debit	INCREASES in the value of assets
	Credit	DECREASES in the value of assets
PERSONAL accounts	Debit	the RECEIVER of goods or money
	Credit	the GIVER of goods or money
NOMINAL accounts	Debit	LOSSES and EXPENSES
	Credit	GAINS and INCOMES

The above can be summarised as follows:

Debit increases in assets, expenses drawings,	Credit decreases in assets expenses drawings
Credit increases in capital revenue or liabilities	Debit decreases in capital, revenue or liabilities

And the rule can be further summarised as follows:

> **Debit** the account **receiving** value.
>
> **Credit** the account **giving** value.

FINANCIAL ACCOUNTING

Recording transaction in ledger accounts

Transactions may be either **cash** or **credit** transactions:

Cash transactions	Credit transactions
Payment takes place at the time the goods or services are bought or sold *either* by cash or cheque.	Goods or services are bought or sold 'on credit' or 'on account'. No payment is made at the time the goods/services are obtained, and payment is made later. Usually a firm will allow you a credit period (often one month) to settle your account. If you take longer, very often you will have to pay interest.

The first transaction which occurs is when a business starts up. Normally this will be when the owner of the business pays into the bank the capital – money being invested in the business. This information needs to be recorded in the ledger accounts of the firm.

Third Eye Enterprises ledger accounts

On 1 January you start up your own business called Third Eye Enterprises and put £50,000 into a business bank account.

To make the entries in the account you need to decide:

- the names of the accounts involved in the transaction;
- the type/category of account;
- the type of entry to be made in each account.

The money is being paid into the bank, so you will obviously need to open a bank account. You will keep records of the amounts you pay into the account and withdraw from this account.

The money has been paid in by the owner of the business and the account which shows how much the owner has contributed to the business is called the **capital account**. In accounting terms, the bank account is referred to as **bank**. It is an asset and under the rules given earlier, it is a **real** account.

The rule is to **debit** the real account when the asset **increases** in value.

The **capital account** is the owner's account and can therefore be classed as a **personal account** and a **creditor's account** (because the business owes the owner the amount they have invested in the business).

The rule is to **credit** a creditor's account because he has **given** money.

When recording a transaction in the ledger ask yourself the following questions and complete the table which will help you to decide on the ledger account entries:

In which accounts are the entries to be made?	What type of accounts are they?	Do accounts increase or decrease?	Are accounts debited or credited?
Bank	Real	Increase	Debit
Capital	Personal – creditor	Increases	Credit

It is often easier to decide on one of the accounts and the type of entry. For example, **Bank** is an asset account and it is increasing therefore the rule is to **debit** the account. The entry in the other account must complete the double entry so we must **credit** the **capital account**.

The following entries will be made in the ledger accounts:

Bank Account

Date	Details	Debit	Credit	Balance	
Jan 1	Capital	50,000		50,000	Dr

Capital Account

Date	Details	Debit	Credit	Balance	
Jan 1	Bank		50,000	50,000	Cr

On 3 January Third Eye Enterprises buys premises for £25,000, paying by cheque.

Use the table below to help you decide what entries have to be made:

In which accounts are the entries to be made?	What type of accounts are they?	Do accounts increase or decrease?	Are accounts debited or credited?
Premises	Real	Increase	Debit
Bank	Real	Decrease	Credit

Bank Account

Date	Details	Debit	Credit	Balance	
Jan 1	Capital	50,000		50,000	Dr
3	Premises		25,000	25,000*	Dr

Premises Account

Date	Details	Debit	Credit	Balance	
Jan 3	Bank	25,000		25,000	Dr

* The Bank balance needs to be recalculated. Before purchasing the premises there was £50,000 in the debit column, representing the money on deposit at the bank. A credit entry was made when the premises were purchased. This reduces the Bank balance. The new balance is £50,000 – £25,000 = £25,000. This figure is shown in the balance column. The balance in the bank account is still debit because the total of the debit column is greater that the total of the credit column.

On 5 January Third Eye Enterprises buys fixtures and fittings for £5,000, paying by cheque:

In which accounts are the entries to be made?	What type of accounts are they?	Do accounts increase or decrease?	Are accounts debited or credited?
Fixtures and Fittings	Real	Increase	Debit
Bank	Real	Decrease	Credit

Bank Account

Date	Details	Debit	Credit	Balance	
Jan 1	Capital	50,000		50,000	Dr
3	Premises		25,000	25,000	Dr
5	**Fixtures and Fittings**		**5,000**	**20,000**	**Dr**

Fixtures and Fittings Account

Date	Details	Debit	Credit	Balance	
Jan 5	**Bank**	**5,000**		**5,000**	**Dr**

Note: Only one account is kept for each asset, person and expense, but the payment for the premises and fixtures and fittings is recorded in **one** Bank account.

On 7 January Third Eye Enterprises purchases goods for £3,000, on credit from Robert Browning:

In which accounts are the entries to be made?	What type of accounts are they?	Do accounts increase or decrease?	Are accounts debited or credited?
Purchases	Nominal	Increase	Debit
Robert Browning	Personal-creditor	Increase	Credit

Purchases Account

Date	Details	Debit	Credit	Balance	
Jan 7	**Robert Browning**	**3,000**		**3,000**	**Dr**

Robert Browning's Account

Date	Details	Debit	Credit	Balance	
Jan 7	**Purchases**		**3,000**	**3,000**	**Dr**

On 10 January Third Eye Enterprises paid rates of £300, by cheque:

In which accounts are the entries to be made?	What type of accounts are they?	Do accounts increase or decrease?	Are accounts debited or credited?
Bank	Real	Decreases	Credit
Rates	Nominal	Increases	Debit

Bank Account

Date	Details	Debit	Credit	Balance	
Jan 1	Capital	50,000		50,000	Dr
3	Premises		25,000	25,000	Dr
5	Fixtures and Fittings		5,000	20,000	Dr
10	**Rates**		**300**	**19,700**	**Dr**

Rates Account

Date	Details	Debit	Credit	Balance	
Jan 10	**Bank**	**300**		**300**	**Dr**

On 12 January Third Eye Enterprises sold goods on credit to Argyll plc worth £500:

In which accounts are the entries to be made?	What type of accounts are they?	Do accounts increase or decrease?	Are accounts debited or credited?
Argyll plc	Personal Debtor	Increases	Debit
Sales	Nominal	Increases	Credit

Argyll plc Account

Date	Details	Debit	Credit	Balance	
Jan 12	**Sales**	**500**		**500**	**Dr**

Sales Account

Date	Details	Debit	Credit	Balance	
Jan 12	**Argyll plc**		**500**	**500**	**Cr**

At the end of the period the arithmetical accuracy of the entries in the ledger accounts can be checked by preparing a **Trial Balance**. The Trial Balance is a list of all the accounts which have a debit or credit balance on them on that date. If an account has a debit balance the amount is entered in the debit column of the Trial Balance, and if an account has a credit balance it is entered in the credit column of the Trial Balance.

After all the ledger accounts have been listed the debit and credit columns are totalled. If they agree, it can be assumed that the Trial Balance is arithmetically correct.

Trial Balance of Third Eye Enterprise		
as at 12 January Year 1		
	Dr £	Cr £
Bank	19,700	
Sales		500
Argyll plc	500	
Rates	300	
Robert Browning		3,000
Purchases	3,000	
Fixtures	5,000	
Premises	25,000	
Capital		50,000
	53,500	53,500

Capital and revenue expenditure

Purchases made by an enterprise can be classed as either **capital** or **revenue expenditure**.

Capital expenditure occurs when an enterprise buys fixed assets such as premises, furniture, fittings, motor vehicles etc.

Revenue expenditure is spending on purchasing goods for resale or paying other expenses such as rent, rates, insurance, etc

When using the information contained in the ledger to prepare the **Trading** and **Profit and Loss Accounts** it is very important that capital expenditure is recorded in its separate asset accounts and not in the purchases account.

If the wrong type of expenditure is deducted from sales this will affect the profits.

 ## Now do Worksheets 2.1 and 2.2

Preparation of final accounts

Intermediate 2 Level Outcomes:

This chapter includes material from Int 2 level Financial Accounting Outcome 4

☆ **Complete partially prepared final accounts of an organisation consistent with financial accounting practice.**

☆ **Complete a partially prepared balance sheet of an organisation consistent with financial accounting practice.**

Higher Level Outcomes:

This chapter includes material from Higher level Financial Accounting Outcome 1

☆ **Complete partially prepared final accounts of an organisation consistent with financial accounting practice.**

☆ **Complete a partially prepared balance sheet of an organisation consistent with financial accounting practice.**

The purpose of final accounts

The final accounts of any business organisation are prepared at the end of the financial year to allow the firm to assess the overall performance of the business and to assist the management in the way they run and plan their activities. The final accounts work on a number of levels. Firstly, they calculate the profit or loss from a years trading activities, and allow the comparison of the actual results with planned results. Secondly, they assist with the forward planning of the business and will provide information in order to obtain loan capital from the bank or private/public investors. Thirdly, the final accounts will show the financial position to a prospective buyer or partner, and finally they are needed for accurate and reliable tax returns.

Final accounts of different business organisations consist of:

*   **Trading** and **Profit and Loss Accounts** for trading concerns - sole traders, partnerships and public limited companies (plcs);
*   **Balance Sheet** for sole traders, partnerships and plcs;
*   **Manufacturing Accounts** in the case of a manufacturing concern;
*   **Appropriation Accounts** for partnerships or plcs.

In this chapter, we're going to look at Trading and Profit and Loss Accounts, and Balance Sheets. Manufacturing Accounts are dealt with in Chapter 5, and Appropriation Accounts are dealt with in Chapter 6 (Partnerships) and Chapter 8 (plcs).

Preparing the Trading and Profit and Loss Accounts

The figures used in the preparation of **Trading** and **Profit and Loss Accounts** are taken from the **Trial Balance**. This is a list of all the accounts in the ledger which have a balance at the end of the financial year. The Trial Balance figures are adjusted to show any increases or decreases in expenses due to accruals or prepayments, provisions etc.

An accrual is an expense which should have been paid during the current financial year but which still has to be paid at the end of the year. An example may be an electricity account which still has to be paid at the end of the financial year for the electricity used during the current financial year.

A prepayment is an amount paid during the current financial year for the next financial year. Sometimes it is referred to as **paid in advance**. For example, insurance premiums are usually paid yearly and some portion may be paid in advance for the following year.

A provision is an amount of profit retained in the business to meet an expected loss. However, it's important to recognize that provisions are **not** sums of money. The most common provisions you will meet are provisions for **depreciation** and for **doubtful debts**.

Trading Account

The **Trading Account** shows the profit or loss made from purchasing goods at one price (**the cost price**) and selling them at a higher price (**the selling price**). Unless the business is a manufacturing concern the Trading Account will be the first final account prepared for a business organisation.

Elements of the Trading Account

The following items will form part of the trading account:

Item	What it is
Sales (or **Turnover**)	**Sales** is the name given to the value of the goods **sold** during the trading period. The sales can be either for **cash** or on **credit.** The sales figure is the first figure entered in the Trading Account. (The cash and credit sales figures may be shown separately in the Trading Account.) **Sales** are also known as **Turnover**.
Sales returns	**Sales returns** is the value of the goods sold which are subsequently returned by the customer for some reason. It may be that they have been damaged, wrongly supplied, or are not up to specification.
The **net sales** value must be shown and this is calculated by the following: **Net sales or (Turnover) = Sales - Sales returns**	
Cost of goods sold	In the next line of the Trading Account we make a statement that we are going to calculate the **cost of goods sold**.

Item	What it is
Cost of goods sold is calculated from:	
Stock at beginning	The value of the goods in our stockroom at the beginning of the financial year, known as the **opening stock**. No matter what happens during the year nothing will alter this figure. We then add our **net purchases** to this figure.
Purchases	This is the value of the goods bought during the year for resale. Purchases may be for cash or on credit. From this we deduct the **purchase returns** to calculate **net purchases**.
Purchase returns	This represents the value of goods we have returned to our suppliers during the year because they were faulty, damaged or wrongly supplied.
Net purchases = Purchases – Purchase returns	
Carriage Inwards	This is the cost of having our purchases delivered to our stores. This figure is added to our net purchases figure because it increases the cost of these purchases and consequently the cost of goods sold.
Cost of goods available for sale = Stock + (Purchases – Purchase returns) + Carriage inwards From the cost of goods available for sale we deduct the stock at the end of the period.	
Stock at end	This represents the value of goods we have not sold during the financial year. These are the goods left in our stockroom which will be used at the start of the next financial year.
Cost of goods sold = Cost of goods available for sale – Stock at end	
Other trading expenses	Sometimes you must include other expenses relating to the purchase and sale of goods. The most common items are warehouse costs, rent and rates and wages of storemen. These other trading expenses are added to the **Cost of goods sold** and represent the **Cost of Sales**. *Look out for this in examination questions.*
Cost of Sales = Cost of goods sold + other trading expenses	
Gross profit	This is the result of deducting the **cost of good sold** or the **cost of sales** from the **net sales** or turnover.
Gross profit = Net sales – Cost of goods sold	

Layout of a Trading Account

Every Trading Account contains the same elements whether you are preparing it for a small sole trader or partnership or the internal accounts of a large plc.

Example 1 Preparing a Trading Account

From the following information, extracted from the Trial Balance and notes, prepare the Trading Account of C & D Designs for the year ended 31 December Year 1.

Trial Balance as at 31 December Year 1	Dr £	Cr £
Stock 1 January Year 1	2,500	
Sales		20,250
Sales returns	250	
Purchases	6,300	
Purchase returns		300
Carriage inwards	500	
Warehouse rent	1,000	

Note: Closing stock amounted to £3,500

Debit balances in the Trial Balance for items in the Trading Account represent **expenses** of trading. **Credit** balances represent gains or **incomes** to the business.

STEP 1 – Set up the heading and columns for the Trading Account

Trading Account C & D Designs For year ended 31 December Year 1			
	£	£	£

It is important to note that the heading must be shown as **for the year ended** as the firm is reporting on what has happened during the financial year. This is known as **historical accounting**.

The Trading Account requires you to use 3 money columns. The first 2 columns are used for the calculation of subsidiary figures, and the end money column shows the most important figures for the firm. In the case of the Trading Account, these will be **net sales**, **cost of goods sold** and the **gross profit**.

STEP 2 – Calculate the **net sales**

Net sales = Sales – Sales returns

Trading Account C & D Designs For year ended 31 December Year 1	£	£	£
Sales		20,250	
Less Sales Returns		250	20,000

continued ➤

Example 1 Preparing a Trading Account continued

STEP 3 – Calculate the **Cost of goods sold** during the year

Cost of goods sold = Cost of goods available for sale – Closing stock
Cost of goods available for sale = Stock + (Purchases – Purchase Returns)
+ Carriage Inwards

Trading Account C & D Designs For year ended 31 December Year 1	£	£	£
Sales		20,250	
Less Sales returns		250	20,000
Less **Cost of goods sold**			
Stock 1 January Year 1		2,500	
Add **Purchases**	6,300		
Less **Purchase Returns**	300	6,000	
Add **Carriage inwards**		500	
		9,000	
Less **Stock 31 December Year 1**		3,500	
Cost of goods sold		5,500	

STEP 4 – Calculate **Cost of Sales**

Add the **Warehouse rent** to the **Cost of goods sold**.

Trading Account C & D Designs For year ended 31 December Year 1	£	£	£
Sales		20,250	
Less Sales returns		250	20,000
Less Cost of goods sold			
Stock 1 January Year 1		2,500	
Add Purchases	6,300		
Less Purchase returns	300	6,000	
Add Carriage inwards		500	
		9,000	
Less Stock 31 December Year 1		3,500	
Cost of goods sold		5,500	
Add **Warehouse rent**		1,000	
Cost of sales			6,500

continued ➤

FINANCIAL ACCOUNTING

Example 1 Preparing a Trading Account continued

STEP 5 – Calculate the **gross profit**

Gross profit = Net sales – Cost of sales

Trading Account C & D Designs For year ended 31 December Year 1	£	£	£
Sales		20,250	
Less Sales Returns		250	20,000
Less Cost of goods sold			
Stock 1 January Year 1		2,500	
Add Purchases	6,300		
Less Purchase Returns	300	6,000	
Add Carriage inwards		500	
		9,000	
Less Stock 31 December Year 1		3,500	
Cost of goods sold		5,500	
Add Warehouse rent		1,000	
Cost of sales			6,500
Gross profit			**13,500**

Points to note when preparing Trading Accounts:

- **Sales returns** are also known as **returns inwards**.

- **Purchase returns** are also know as **returns outwards**.

- If there is no expense for carriage inwards, or warehouse costs then these items would be omitted from the Trading Account.

- Only make entries in the accounts for actual items of expenditure.

Task 1

Trading Accounts

1   From the following information prepare the Trading Account of J Wilson for the year ended 31 December Year 1:

Sales £27,500; Purchases £15,350; Sales Returns £250; Purchase Returns £50; Stock at 1 January Year 1 £1,750; Stock at 31 December Year 1 £1,950; Carriage inwards £100.

continued ➤

2 From the following prepare the Trading Account of R Smith for the year ended 31 December Year 1:

Stock at 1 January Year 1 £1,275; Stock at 31 December Year 1 £3,250; Sales £75,350; Purchases £46,400; Sales Returns £1,260; Purchase Returns £1,425; Carriage inwards £200; Storeman's wages £500.

3 From the following prepare the Trading Account of R Smith and J Brown for the year ended 31 December Year 1:

Stock at 1 January Year 1 £2,400; Stock at 31 December Year 1 £3,250; Credit Sales £125,600 Cash Sales £35,200; Purchases £72,400; Sales Returns £2,450; Purchase Returns £1,475; Carriage inwards £50.

4 From the following prepare the Trading Account of R Simpson plc for the year ended 31 December Year 1:

Stock at 1 January Year 1 £3,750; Stock at 31 December Year 1 £4,300; Sales £68,550; Purchases £33,640; Sales Returns £1,250; Purchase Returns £640; Warehousing costs £200; Carriage inwards £400.

5 At December 31 Year 1 the Trial Balance of S Scott contained the following items:

Stock 1 January Year 1	£2,870
Purchases	£7,390
Sale	£7,490
Returns Outwards	£390
Returns Inwards	£90
Carriage Inward	£450
Warehouse rates	£400

Scott's Stock at 31 December Year 1 was valued at £4,350.

6 From the following information prepare the Trading Account of CGL Ltd for the year ended 31 December Year 1:

Stock at 1 January Year 1 £4,100; Credit Sales £75,000 Cash Sales £37,500; Purchases £83,200; Sales Returns £4,750; Carriage inwards £2,000; Warehouse rent and rates £5,000.Purchase Returns £2,300; Stock at 31 December Year 1 £4,900.

Profit and Loss Account

After the **gross profit** has been calculated in the **Trading Account** it is transferred to the **Profit and Loss Account** where any additional income will be added and all the current year's expenses deducted. The resulting figure is called the **net profit.**

Additions to the gross profit	These are other items of income the enterprise has received this year from sources other than the buying and selling of goods. For example: • commission received by the firm for selling goods on behalf of another firm; • rent received if they sub-let part of their premises; • discount received from suppliers for paying their accounts promptly; • debts previously written off as bad debts, recovered from a debtor who eventually pays what he owes; • decrease in provision for doubtful debts (more of this later). The Total Net Income for the period can now be calculated.
Total net income = Gross profit + Additional income	

Less expenses	The total expenses or overheads of running the business for the year will be listed, totalled and then deducted from the total net income.
	There are a large number of items which may appear in the **less expenses** section of the **Profit and Loss Account**, including: rates, insurance, depreciation of office equipment, salaries, electricity, carriage outwards, salesmen's salaries and commission, delivery van expenses, depreciation of delivery vans, bad debts, interest on loans, bank charges, provisions for doubtful debts, etc.
Net profit	The **net profit** can now be calculated by deducting the total expenses from the **gross profit** and other incomes.
Net profit = Gross profit + Additional income – Expenses	

Example 2 Preparing a Profit and Loss Account

From the information extracted from the Trial Balance as at 31 December Year 1 prepare the Profit and Loss Account.

Trial Balance as at 31 December Year 1	£ Dr	£ Cr
Bad Debts recovered		250
Discounts received		500
Commission received		1,500
Rent and rates	1,500	
Insurance	150	
Postages and telephone	300	
Depreciation of office equipment	200	
Salaries	3,000	
Commission on sales paid	500	
Carriage outwards	450	
Depreciation on delivery vans	1,200	
Bank charges	150	
Interest on loan	1,000	

Gross Profit calculated in Example 1 was £13,500.

For the **Profit and Loss Account**, items in the **debit** column of the **Trial Balance** are losses and expenses will be **deducted** from the **Gross Profit**. Items in the **credit** column represent gains to the business and will be **added** to the **Gross Profit**.

Usually you will be completing the Profit and Loss Account immediately after the Trading Account. However, sometimes you will be given the gross profit figure and simply be asked to prepare the Profit and Loss Account, as in this example.

continued ➤

Example 2 Preparing a Profit and Loss Account continued

STEP 1 – Set-up the **Profit and Loss Account** and enter the **gross profit**

The layout is the same as the Trading Account, only the heading is different.

Profit and Loss Account C & D Designs For year ended 31 December Year 1	£	£	£
Gross profit			13,500

STEP 2 – Add incomes received and total them

Profit and Loss Account C & D Designs For year ended 31 December Year 1	£	£	£
Gross Profit			13,500
Add Income			
Bad debts recovered		250	
Discounts received		500	
Commission received		1,500	2,250
			15,750

STEP 3 – Deduct all expenses for the year to calculate the **net profit**

Profit and Loss Account C & D Designs For year ended 31 December Year 1	£	£	£
Gross profit			13,500
Add Income			
Bad debts recovered		250	
Discounts received		500	
Commission received		1,500	2,250
			15,750
Less Expenses			
Rent and rates		1,500	
Insurance		150	
Postages and telephone		300	
Depreciation of office equipment		200	
Salaries		3,000	
Commission on sales		500	
Carriage outwards		450	
Depreciation on delivery vans		1,200	
Bank charges		150	
Interest on loan		1,000	8,450
Net profit			7,300

continued ➤

FINANCIAL ACCOUNTING

Example 2 Preparing a Profit and Loss Account continued

The **Net Profit** is the reward to the owner for running the business. In the case of a sole trader it will belong solely to him, in a partnership it will be shared between the partners and in a plc it will affect the dividends of the shareholders.

>>> Task 2

Profit and Loss Accounts

1 From the following information prepare the Profit and Loss section of the Trading and Profit and Loss Accounts of J Smith for the year ended 31 December Year 1:

Gross profit £25,750; Rent and rates £500; Insurance £200; Postages £50; Depreciation of motor vehicles £2,000; Advertising £1,000 and Carriage outwards £300; Discount received 500.

Note: Carriage outwards is the cost of delivering your sales to your customers. It is a selling expense and is recorded in the Profit and Loss Account.

2 From the following information prepare the Profit and Loss section of the Trading and Profit and Loss Accounts of J Wilson for the year ended 31 December Year 1:

Gross profit £65,000; Discount received £500; Carriage outwards £450; Depreciation of equipment £600; Bad debts £500; Bank charges £150; Delivery van expenses £500 and Commission received £500.

3 From the following information prepare the Profit and Loss section of the Trading and Profit and Loss Accounts of J Brown for the year ended 31 December Year 1:

Gross profit £28,500; Commission received £675; Bad debts recovered £100; Rent received £2,500; Depreciation of furniture £300; Repairs and maintenance £5,000; Electricity £300; Rates £300; Insurance £240; Carriage outwards £400; Depreciation of delivery vans £1,500; Bank charges £50; Interest on loan £150 and Bad debts £350.

4 From the following information prepare the Profit and Loss section of the Trading and Profit and Loss Accounts of T Smith for the year ended 31 December Year 1:

Gross profit £35,000; Commission received £500; Rent received £3,000; Depreciation of furniture £1300; Repairs and maintenance 2,500; Electricity £2,000; Rates £800; Insurance £1,240; Carriage outwards £200; Depreciation of delivery vans £1,000; Bank charges £25; Interest on loan £250 and Bad debts £100.

5 From the following information prepare the Profit and Loss section of the Trading and Profit and Loss Accounts of Lee for the year ended 31 December Year 1:

Gross profit £50,500; Commission received £1,675; Bad debts recovered £500; Rent received £4,500; Depreciation of furniture £1,300; Repairs and maintenance £9,000; Electricity £2,300; Rates £2,000; Insurance £1,240; Carriage outwards £1,400; Depreciation of delivery vans £2,500; Advertising £150; Interest on overdraft £1,150 and bad debts £350.

Combined Trading and Profit and Loss Accounts

Normally the Trading and Profit and Loss Accounts are prepared as one combined account. If you had been asked to prepare the Trading and Profit and Loss Account of C & D Designs in Examples 1 and 2, the same steps would have been followed, except that at STEP 1 the heading would have been:

> **Trading and Profit and Loss Account C & D Designs**
> **For year ended 31 December Year 1**

And the account would have looked like this:

C & D Designs Trading and Profit and Loss Account For year ended 31 December Year 1	£	£	£
Sales		20,250	
Less Sales returns		250	20,000
Less Cost of goods sold			
Stock 1 January Year 1		2,500	
Add Purchases	6,300		
Less Purchase returns	300	6,000	
Add Carriage inwards		500	
		9,000	
Less Stock 31 December Year 1		3,500	
Cost of goods sold		5,500	
Add Warehouse rent		1,000	
Cost of sales			6,500
Gross profit			13,500
Add Income			
Bad debts recovered		250	
Discounts received		500	
Commission received		1,500	2,250
			15,750
Less Expenses			
Rent and rates		1,500	
Insurance		150	
Postages and telephone		300	
Depreciation of office equipment		200	
Salaries		3,000	
Commission on sales		500	
Carriage outwards		450	
Depreciation on delivery vans		1,200	
Bank charges		150	
Interest on loan		1,000	8,450
Net profit			7,300

FINANCIAL ACCOUNTING

You must also remember that we wish to calculate the profit or loss for the period. Sometimes the expenses will exceed the gross profit, in which case the enterprise will have made a net loss.

Task 3

Trading and Profit and Loss Accounts

Before beginning to tackle a combined exercise it is a good idea to consider each item and decide in which part of the Trading and Profit and Loss Account it will be entered. Write T beside a Trading Account item and P for the Profit and Loss. Question 1 has been completed for you.

1 From the following information prepare the Trading and Profit and Loss Accounts of Connel Enterprises for the year ended 31 December Year 1.

Stock 1 January Year 1	£2,500 T
Carriage inwards	£400 T
Carriage outwards	£500 P
Rent and rates	£1,000 P
Commission received	£1,500 P
Bad debts recovered	£200 P
Purchases	£10,000 T
Sales	£65,500 T
Returns outwards	£500 T
Returns inwards	£100 T
Depreciation of machinery	£1,500 P
Insurance	£2,500 P
Interest on loan	£1,000 P
Bad debts	£500 P
Stock 31 December Year 1	£2,000 T

2 From the following information prepare the Trading and Profit and Loss Accounts of Taynuilt Traders for the year ended 31 December Year 1.

Stock 1 January Year 1	£5,000
Purchases	£37,000
Sales	£165,500
Purchase returns	£1,000
Sales returns	£500
Carriage in	£2,400
Carriage outwards	£1,500

continued ➤

Rent and rates	£3,000
Commission received	£500
Bad debts recovered	£500
Electricity	£1,600
Advertising	£400
Depreciation of machinery	£3,500
Insurance	£1,500
Interest on loan	£1,200
Bad debts	£500
Stock 31 December Year 1	£7,000

3 From the following information prepare the Trading and Profit and Loss Accounts of Duror Dynamics for the year ended 31 December Year 1.

Stock 1 January Year 1	£7,000
Purchases	£48,000
Sales	£200,000
Purchase returns	£2,500
Sales returns	£800
Carriage in	£1,200
Carriage outwards	£3,000
Rent and rates	£6,500
Commission paid	£1,000
Bad debts recovered	£500
Electricity	£2,600
Advertising	£800
Depreciation of machinery	£7,500
Insurance	£3,000
Interest on loan	£2,400
Bad debts	£1,000
Stock 31 December Year 1	£5,000

continued ➣

4 From the following Trial Balance extract prepare the Trading and Profit and Loss Accounts of Dalmally Traders for the year ended 31 December Year 1.

	Dr £	Cr £
Stock 1 January Year 1	5,000	
Purchases	67,500	
Sales		325,500
Purchase returns		3,000
Sales returns	500	
Carriage in	3,500	
Carriage outwards	2,100	
Rent and rates	3,600	
Commission paid	300	
Bad debts recovered		200
Electricity	2,500	
Advertising	500	
Depreciation of machinery	2,000	
Insurance	2,400	
Interest on loan	2,500	
Bad debts	200	

Stock at 31 December Year 1 amounted to £7,000.

Note: Losses and expenses are listed in the debit column, gains in the credit column.

Balance Sheet

The last section of the final accounts to be prepared is the **Balance Sheet**. This is a statement, **not an account**, prepared at the end of the financial year stating the value of the assets, liabilities and capital of the firm or organisation.

Assets

Assets are divided into two classes, **fixed assets** and **current assets**, which will have debit balances in the Trial Balance.

Fixed assets

Fixed assets are items owned by the business, and which will remain in the business for a long period – more than one year. These assets are not primarily purchased for sale.

They provide the infrastructure which allows the business to continue to operate. If any of these assets are sold and not replaced the business may not be able to continue to operate.

Fixed assets are reduced in value over time by means of **depreciation**. Examples of fixed assets are premises, plant and machinery, motor vehicles, fixtures and fittings, office equipment etc.

Current assets

Current assets are items owned by the business which will be kept for less than one year. Their value changes from day to day and they have a relatively short life. These assets are primarily for conversion into cash.

Examples of current assets include prepayments, stocks of goods, stationery or raw materials, work in progress, debtors, bank and cash.

Current assets of the enterprise are listed in the Balance Sheet in the **order of liquidity**. The asset which takes the longest to turn into cash is listed first.

The current assets should be listed as follows:

- **Prepayments**. Expenses paid in the current financial year which will benefit the following financial year (such as insurance).
- **Stock**. Raw materials, work in progress or finished goods which the business owns at the end of the financial year.
- **Debtors**. Enterprises which owe the business money for goods purchased on credit and which have not yet been paid.
- **Bank**. The balance in the bank account on that date.
- **Cash**. The amount held within the business either in the safe, till or cash box in the form of cash.

Liabilities

Liabilities can be divided into three groups and will have credit balances in the Trial Balance.

Current liabilities

Current liabilities are items owed by the enterprise which will be paid off in the near future and certainly within one year.

Examples of current liabilities include accruals, creditors, VAT, dividends due, debenture interest due, bank overdraft etc.

These items are not listed in any particular order, although they can be listed in the order of priority for payment if the firm became bankrupt:

- **Accruals**. Amounts due to be paid at the end of the year for goods or services received.
- **Creditors**. Amounts owed by the enterprise for goods purchased on credit during the year
- **VAT**. The balance owed to, or by, HM Customs and Excise for VAT. The figure is the net result of deducting VAT paid by the enterprise from the VAT collected by the enterprise from its customers. VAT can be either a credit balance (current liability) or a debit balance (current asset)
- **Bank overdraft**. Occurs when a firm withdraws more money from the bank than they have deposited. This could be due to a temporary cash flow problem.

Long term liabilities

Long term liabilities are long term debts to the business and will take more than one year to pay off. Examples of long term liabilities are a Building Society or Commercial Bank loan, or Finance House Agreement for purchases of specific fixed assets, for example purchase of machinery, mortgages etc.

Capital

Capital represents the money provided by the owner of the business to start and run it. This figure is sometimes referred to as the **net worth** of the firm – what the business would be worth to the owner(s) once all the liabilities have been paid off.

The capital of the enterprise can be increased by net profit or reduced by drawings.

From the Balance Sheet the following figures can be calculated:

Working capital	This represents the liquid resources of the enterprise and is calculated as follows: **Current assets – current liabilities**
Net assets/Capital employed	This is the **total value of the assets** of the enterprise less the **current liabilities**. It indicates the value of the capital employed by the business enterprise. The **capital employed** in the firm must be financed by either the owners of the business or lenders to the business.

Example 3 Preparing the Balance Sheet

The following balances have been taken from the ledger of Kintallin Manufacturers for the year ended 31 December Year 1:

	Dr	Cr
	£000s	£000s
Premises	500	
Plant and machinery	250	
Motor vehicles	10	
Provision for depreciation: • Plant and machinery • Motor vehicles		200 3
Stock	10	
Debtors	23	
Bank	14	
Cash	1	
Prepayments - Rent	2	
Accruals – Wages		1
Creditors		23
VAT		2

continued ➢

Example 3 Preparing the Balance Sheet continued

	Dr	Cr
	£000s	£000s
Building society loan		50
Capital		450
Net profit		131
Drawings	50	

Remember assets appear in the debit column and liabilities in the credit column of the Trial Balance.

STEP 1 – Head up the Balance Sheet

The date for the Balance Sheet will be shown 'as at' because it will only be correct on that particular date. More debts may be incurred, or cash received from debtors. These will change their values in the Balance Sheet. Three money columns will be needed to record the values.

Kintallin Manufacturers Balance Sheet as at 31 December Year 1			
	£000	£000	£000

STEP 2 – Enter the **fixed assets** of the enterprise

This is the first section of the Balance Sheet to be completed.

Fixed assets must be shown at their *true and fair* value. The **cost**, **total** or **aggregate depreciation**, and **net book value** of the fixed assets must appear in the Balance Sheet.

The three money columns are headed up as shown below:

Kintallin Manufacturers Balance Sheet as 31 December Year 1			
	£000	£000	£000
FIXED ASSETS	Cost	Aggregate Depreciation	Net Book Value
Premises	500		500
Plant and machinery	250	200	50
Motor Vehicles	10	3	7
	760	203	557

All 3 columns are totalled. The **cost** and **aggregate depreciation** figures will not be used in the rest of the Balance Sheet therefore a line is drawn under them to show they are no longer used. The **net book value** (NBV) will be used to calculate the **capital employed**.

continued ➢

Example 3 Preparing the Balance Sheet continued

STEP 3 – Enter the **current assets** into the Balance Sheet and total them

*Remember these need to be listed in the **order of liquidity**. Prepayments, Stock, Debtors, Bank, Cash. To help remember you could use the mnemonic* primary school dinners beat chips.

Kintallin Manufacturers Balance Sheet as at 31 December Year 1			
	£000	£000	£000
FIXED ASSETS	Cost	Aggregate Depreciation	Net Book Value
Premises	500		500
Plant and machinery	250	200	50
Motor vehicles	10	3	7
	760	203	557
CURRENT ASSETS			
Prepayments – Rent	2		
Stock	10		
Debtors	23		
Bank	14		
Cash	1	50	

STEP 4 – Enter the **current liabilities** into the Balance Sheet and total them

Kintallin Manufacturers Balance Sheet as at 31 December Year 1			
	£000	£000	£000
FIXED ASSETS	Cost	Aggregate Depreciation	Net Book Value
Premises	500		500
Plant and machinery	250	200	50
Motor vehicles	10	3	7
	760	203	557
CURRENT ASSETS			
Prepayments – Rent	2		
Stock	10		
Debtors	23		
Bank	14		
Cash	1	50	

continued ➤

Example 3 Preparing the Balance Sheet continued

Kintallin Manufacturers Balance Sheet as at 31 December Year 1	£000	£000	£000
CURRENT LIABILITIES			
Accruals – Wages	1		
Creditors	23		
VAT	2	26	

STEP 5 – Calculate the **working capital** and **net assets**

Working capital = Current assets – Current liabilities

Net assets = Fixed assets + Working capital – Current liabilities

Kintallin Manufacturers Balance Sheet as at 31 December Year 1	£000	£000	£000
FIXED ASSETS	Cost	Aggregate Depreciation	Net Book Value
Premises	500		500
Plant and machinery	250	200	50
Motor vehicles	10	3	7
	760	203	557
CURRENT ASSETS			
Prepayments – Rent	2		
Stock	10		
Debtors	23		
Bank	14		
Cash	1	50	
CURRENT LIABILITIES			
Accruals – Wages	1		
Creditors	23		
VAT	2	26	24
Capital employed			581

continued ➤

Example 3 Preparing the Balance Sheet continued

STEP 6 – Deduct **long term liabilities** from the **net assets**

Kintallin Manufacturers Balance Sheet as at 31 December Year 1			
	£000	£000	£000
FIXED ASSETS	Cost	Aggregate Depreciation	Net Book Value
Premises	500		500
Plant and machinery	250	200	50
Motor vehicles	10	3	7
	760	203	557
CURRENT ASSETS			
Prepayments – Rent	2		
Stock	10		
Debtors	23		
Bank	14		
Cash	1	50	
CURRENT LIABILITIES			
Accruals – Wages	1		
Creditors	23		
VAT	2	26	24
Capital employed			581
Less long term liabilities			
Building Society loan			50
NET WORTH			531

The **net worth** figure represent the value of the assets actually owned by the proprietors of the business – the owners equity.

STEP 7 – Complete the **Financed by** section of the balance sheet

This shows how the owner's share of the business has been financed. The figures will include the opening capital, profits made by the business and drawings from the business.

continued ➤

Example 3 Preparing the Balance Sheet continued

Kintallin Manufacturers Balance Sheet as at 31 December Year 1			
	£000	**£000**	**£000**
FIXED ASSETS	Cost	Aggregate Depreciation	Net Book Value
Premises	500		500
Plant and machinery	250	200	50
Motor vehicles	10	3	7
	760	203	557
CURRENT ASSETS			
Prepayments – Rent	2		
Stock	10		
Debtors	23		
Bank	14		
Cash	1	50	
CURRENT LIABILITIES			
Accruals – Wages	1		
Creditors	23		
VAT	2	26	24
NET ASSETS			581
Less Long term liabilities			
Building Society loan			50
NET WORTH			531
Financed by:			
Capital at the start	450		
Add Net Profit	131	581	
Less Drawings		50	531

Balance Sheet equations

Financial accounting is based on a very simple idea called the **Balance Sheet equation**.

The fact that all the assets of an organisation must be financed either from the capital invested by the owner or by loans to the firm gives rise to the first Balance Sheet equation:

Assets = Liabilities

For Kintallin Manufacturers:

Assets = £607,000 and **Liabilities** = £607,000

This equation can be further expanded using the subtotals from the Balance Sheet:

(Fixed assets + Current assets) = (Current liabilities + long term liabilities + Capital)

The figures for Kintallin Manufacturers would be:

(£557,000 + £50,000) = (£26,000 + £50,000 + £531,000)

*The fact that the **total assets** will always **equal** the **total liabilities** of the enterprise can be used to calculate missing figures from the Balance Sheet.*

This owners share or **net worth** of the business can be calculated from Balance Sheet figures:

Assets – Liabilities = Capital

£607,000 – £76,000 = £531,000

Task 4

1   From the following information prepare the Balance Sheet of J Smith on 31 May Year 1.

Premises (cost)	£21,200
Furniture and fittings (cost)	£5,500
Motor vehicles (cost)	£15,000
Provision for depreciation: • Furniture and fittings • Motor vehicles	£1,000 £2,500
Stock	£3,000
Debtors	£2,680
Bank	£1,510
Cash	£200
Capital at start	£28,390
Net profit for year	£12,500
Drawings for year	£2,700
Creditors (Cr)	£1,400
VAT (Cr)	£1,000
Bank loan	£5,000

continued ➤

2 From the following information prepare the Balance Sheet of R Simpson on 31 December Year 1.

Stock	£6,550
Debtors	£7,200
Bank	£8,120
Cash	£400
Capital at start	£34,960
Net profit for year	£11,560
Drawings for year	£3,900
Creditors	£4,800
VAT (Cr)	£2,100
Loan from I Wilson (5 years)	£10,000
Shop premises (cost)	£20,000
Furniture and fittings (cost)	£3,750
Delivery vans (cost)	£18,500
Provision for depreciation: • Furniture and fittings • Delivery vans	£1,500 £3,500

 *Now do Worksheets 3.1 and 3.2*

Preparation of final accounts – adjustments

Intermediate 2 Level Outcomes: ⠀⠀▶

This chapter includes material from Int 2 level Financial Accounting Outcome 4

☆ **Complete partially prepared final accounts of an organisation consistent with financial accounting practice.**

☆ **Complete a partially prepared balance sheet of an organisation consistent with financial accounting practice.**

Higher Level Outcomes: ⠀⠀▶

This chapter includes material from Higher level Financial Accounting Outcome 1

☆ **Complete partially prepared final accounts of an organisation consistent with financial accounting practice.**

☆ **Complete a partially prepared balance sheet of an organisation consistent with financial accounting practice.**

Accruals and prepayments

When preparing final accounts you must ensure that:

1 Every Trading and Profit and Loss Account is accurately prepared and shows the correct profit for every period. To do this you must make sure that all the Profit and Loss Accounts in the ledger include all amounts which **should have been paid** out and which **should have been received**.

2 The Balance Sheet must give a *true and fair* view of the affairs of the business by showing the assets at their true value.

When preparing financial statements, accountants apply a series of rules or accounting concepts developed over a period of time to ensure the relevance and reliability, of the information being presented.

The accruals or the matching concept

The **Accruals/Matching** concept states that income should be recognised and charged to the **Trading** and **Profit and Loss Accounts** in the year it is earned, not received.

The Accruals/Matching concept is applied when preparing final accounts.

You may have to carry out the following adjustments when preparing a set of final accounts for exam purposes.

Adjustments to final accounts may include:

1 prepayments at start and end of year;

2 accruals at start and end of year;

3 provisions for doubtful debts;

4 depreciation and/or appreciation of assets.

Prepayments

A **prepayment** is an amount paid in advance for a service or item still to be received. Prepayments are current assets of the firm because the firm still has to receive the service they have paid for.

Example 1

The financial year ends on 31 December Year 1. The insurance account shows the annual insurance payments made during the current financial year for motor vehicles and buildings purchased on those dates:

Insurance Account					
Date	Details	Dr	Cr	Balance	
Mar 1	Bank (Motor Vehicle A)	240		240	Dr
Apr 1	Bank (Motor Vehicle B)	240		480	Dr
July 1	Bank (Motor Vehicle C)	360		840	Dr
Oct 1	Bank (Buildings)	1,800	1,010	2,640	Dr

As each insurance payment is for one year and the financial year is from 1 January to 31 December Year 1 it is clear that some of the insurance payments made will cover the vehicles and buildings owned by the firm for Year 2.

The insurance expense incurred for Year 1 must be calculated and entered in the Profit and Loss Account for Year 1.

The payments are shown on the calendar below:

Insurance payments for Year 1												
Insurance for:	J	F	M	A	M	J	J	A	S	O	N	D
Vehicle A												
Vehicle B												
Vehicle C												
Buildings												

continued ➤

The shaded areas in the diagram on the previous page show the period for which the insurance has been paid in the current financial year. The amounts to be charged against the profits for insurance can now be calculated using the following formula:

Example 1 continued

Insurance amount paid ÷ 12 months × number of months insurance paid for in current year.

Vehicle A: 10 months insurance =	£240 ÷ 12 × 10 =	£200
Vehicle B: 9 months insurance =	£240 ÷ 12 × 9 =	£180
Vehicle C: 6 months insurance =	£360 ÷ 12 × 6 =	£180
Buildings: 3 months insurance =	£1,800 ÷ 12 × 3 =	£450
Total insurance paid		**£1,010**

The total amount paid for insurance relating to Year 1 has been calculated and will be entered into the less expenses section of the Profit and Loss Account.

Profit and Loss Account For year ended 31 December Year 1		
	£	£
Gross profit		42,500
Less Expenses		
Insurance	1,010	

The credit entry to be made in the insurance account for this transfer to the Profit and Loss Account is shown below:

Insurance Account					
Date	Details	Dr	Cr	Balance	
Mar 1	Bank (Motor Vehicle A)	240		240	Dr
Apr 1	Bank (Motor Vehicle B)	240		480	Dr
July 1	Bank (Motor Vehicle C)	360		840	Dr
Oct 1	Bank (Buildings)	1,800		2,640	Dr
Dec 31	Profit and Loss		1,010	1,630	Dr

The prepayments for Year 2 are calculated by deducting the insurance amount charged for Year 1 from the total insurance amounts paid.

This calculation is shown below for each individual insurance premium paid:

	Vehicle A	Vehicle B	Vehicle C	Buildings	Total
	£	£	£	£	£
Insurance for year	240	240	360	1,800	2,640
Charged for Year 1	200	180	180	450	1,010
Prepaid for Year 2	40	60	180	1,350	1,630

continued ➤

Example 1 continued

Total insurance prepaid = £1,630

This prepaid amount appears in the current assets section of the Balance Sheet:

Balance Sheet extract Year 1	
Current Assets	
Prepayments – insurance	£1,630

For some examination questions you may be required to show the ledger accounts. However, when preparing final accounts for an enterprise the working notes shown above will usually be sufficient.

Task 1

Part c) of the question is optional for Higher students (but is strongly recommended).

Prepayments at year end

1   The following figures appear in the Trial Balance of R Brown as at 31 December Year 1.

	£
Rent	750
Rates	500
Insurance	1,500
Interest on loan	1,200

The following amounts have been prepaid for Year 2:

Rent	£200
Rates	£50
Insurance	£150
Interest on Loan	£300

You are required to:

a)   calculate the amount of each expenses to be charged against the Year 1 profits;

b)   calculate the total prepayments to be entered in the Balance Sheet at the end of Year 1;

c)   show the ledger account for each expense showing the transfer to the Profit and Loss Account.

continued ➤

2   T D Productions purchased new machinery on 1 July Year 1 and paid the annual insurance premium of $1,200 on that date. Their financial year ends on 30 September Year 1.

You are required to:

a) calculate the insurance to be charged against the year's profits;

b) calculate the amount prepaid for the following year;

c) prepare the insurance account clearly showing the transfer to the Profit and Loss Account.

3   The following figures appear in the Trial Balance of C White as at 31 December Year 1.

	$
Rent paid	1,500
Rates	1,200
Insurance	2,400

The following amounts have been prepaid for the following year:

Rent	$300
Rates	$100
Insurance	$200

You are required to:

a) calculate the amount of each expenses to be charged against the Year 1 profits;

b) calculate the total prepayments to be entered in the Balance Sheet at the end of Year 1

c) show the ledger account for each expense clearly showing the transfer to the Profit and Loss Account.

4   During the year ended 31 December Year 1 Brian Askew made the following payments for rates:

1 January - $300
1 April - $300
1 July - $300
1 October - $300
29 December - $300

You are required to:

a) calculate the amount to be entered in the Profit and Loss Account for the year ended 31 December Year 1;

b) calculate the prepayment to be shown in the Balance Sheet;

c) prepare the rates account clearly showing the transferred amount.

continued ➤

5 Greengage and Smith's rent is £600 per quarter. During the year ended 31 December Year 1 they made payments to their landlord on 5 January, 29 March, 27 June, 24 September and 18 December for £600 each time.

You are required to:

a) calculate the amount to be transferred to the Profit and Loss Account

b) state the prepayment entered in the Balance Sheet on 31 December Year 1.

c) show the rent account for the year clearly showing the transfer to the Profit and Loss Account.

Prepayments at the start of the financial year

If the profit figure for the current financial year is adjusted for prepayments at the end of that financial year then the following year an adjustment must be made to its profit for the prepaid amount at the start of the year.

In Example 1, the amount calculated for insurance prepaid at the end of Year 1 was £1,630. The calendar for Year 2 for insurance payments will show:

INSURANCE PAYMENTS – Year 2												
Insurance for:	J	F	M	A	M	J	J	A	S	O	N	D
Vehicle A												
Vehicle B												
Vehicle C												
Buildings												

The shaded areas represent the amounts paid during the last financial year, Year 1, which relate to insurance for this financial year, Year 2. These amounts will be charged against the profit earned in Year 2.

The following payments were made for the period **up to** 31 December Year 2 for insurance of vehicles and buildings:

> £100 paid for Vehicle A **until** 31 December Year 2
> £135 paid for Vehicle B **until** 31 December Year 2
> £180 paid for Vehicle C **until** 31 December Year 2
> £600 paid for Buildings **until** 31 December Year 2

To calculate the total insurance costs for Year 2 to be charged against the profits the prepayments at the start are added to the amounts paid for the remainder of the year:

	Vehicle A £	Vehicle B £	Vehicle C £	Buildings £
Amount prepaid at start	40	60	180	1,350
Paid for Year 2	100	135	180	600
Charges for Year 2	140	195	360	1,950

Obviously with insurance payments, 12 months insurance will have been paid during Year 2 and there will be prepayments at the end of Year 2 for Year 3.

The treatment of prepayments can be summarised in Example 2.

Example 2

At the start of Year 2, £300 rent had been prepaid, £1,200 is paid during the year and of that £1,200 paid, £400 has been prepaid for Year 3.

To calculate the amount to be charged for rent for the current year:

Rent prepaid at start Year 1	£300	
Add Paid during Year 1	£1,200	
	£1,500	
Less Prepaid at end Year 1	£400	This figure appears in the Balance Sheet.
Rent charge for current year	£1,100	This figure appears in the Profit and Loss Account.

In most cases in examinations you will be asked to adjust Trial Balance figures for prepayments and include the appropriate figures in the Profit and Loss Account and Balance Sheet. You must ensure that full working notes are shown as above.

Task 2

Prepayments at start and end of year

1   From the following information prepare the Profit and Loss Account of J Smith & Sons for year ended 31 December Year 2.

Expense	Paid during year	Prepaid at start of year	Prepaid at end of year
	£	£	£
Stationery	500	50	10
Rent	6,000	300	500
Insurance	1,200	100	500
Rates	3,400	1,000	200
Salaries	10,000	300	0

The gross profit for the year was £35,700.

In addition you are required to show the rent account at the end of the year clearly showing the transfer to the Profit and Loss Account.

continued ➤

2 During the financial year ended 31 December Year 1 the following annual payments were made:

1 April Year 1   Insurance of premises £2,400
1 July Year 1   Rates of £600
1 October Year 1   Motor vehicle insurance £1,800

a) Calculate the amounts to be charged in the Profit and Loss Account.

b) Show the motor vehicle insurance account at the end of the financial year.

Now do Worksheet 4.1

Accruals

An **accrual** is an amount due to be paid at the end of the financial year for an item or service already received or used.

The amount due to be paid is added to the actual amount paid and then entered into the Profit and Loss Account. This is an example of the **matching concept**.

The amount still due to be paid at the end of the year is shown in the Balance Sheet as a **current liability**.

Example 3 Accruals at the end of the financial year

During the financial year John Brown and Sons had paid their workforce £4,950 wages. At the end of the financial year they calculated that they owed their workforce £350 for wages from the last pay day to the end of the financial year.

	£	
Wages paid	4,950	
Add Wages due	350	This figure is entered in the Balance Sheet.
Wages chargeable to Profit and Loss Account	5,300	This figure is charged in the Profit and Loss Account.

Wages Account

Date	Details	Dr	Cr	Balance	
Dec 31	Bank	4,950		4,950	Dr
Dec 31	Profit and Loss		5,300	350	Cr

Note that the balance in the wages account changes from debit to credit showing that this is a liability.

Task 3

Accruals at the end of the year

1 During the financial year ending 31 December Year 1 Allan Enterprises made the following payments:

Wages	£10,250
Electricity	£2,200
Rent	£1,200
Interest on loan	£900

At the end of the financial year the following amounts were due to be paid:

Wages	£250
Electricity	£200
Rent	£1,200
Interest on loan	£90

a) Calculate the amounts to be charged against profits for the above expenses.

b) State the total amount for accruals to be shown in the Balance Sheet.

c) Prepare the ledger accounts for each expense.

2 From the following information prepare the Profit and Loss Account of Timson Travels Ltd for year ended 31 December Year 1.

Expense	Paid during year	Due to be paid at the end of the year
	£	£
Stationery	250	50
Rent	3,000	300
Insurance	600	100
Rates	1,700	500
Salaries	10,000	800

Gross profit for the year amounted to £52,000

In addition prepare the ledger account for each expense clearly showing the transfer to the Profit and Loss Account.

 Now do Worksheet 4.2

Accruals at the start of the financial year

 As with prepayments there may be accruals at the start of the year - amounts which were owed for the last financial year. These payments will be made at the start of the next financial year and will be included in the total figure shown in the ledger account for the wages paid during the current financial year

The amount due for last year has already been included in the final accounts of the previous year and was matched against last year's income. To calculate the expense amount for the current financial year the amount accrued for the previous year should be deducted from the expense amount paid.

Example 4

During Year 2 Boyd Bros paid £6,250 for wages. Included in this amount is £350 which was paid for wages owed for Year 1. Calculate the wages to be charged to the Profit and Loss Account for year ended 31 December Year 2.

	£
Wages paid Year 2	6,250
Less Wages owed Year 1	350
Profit and Loss	5,900

The ledger account would appear as follows:

Wages Account

Date	Details	Dr	Cr	Balance	
Jan 1	Balance		350	350	Cr
Dec 31	Bank	6,250		5,900	Dr
Dec 31	Profit and Loss		5,900	nil	

The situation can arise where an expenses item is accrued at the start and at the end of the financial year and the expenses paid amount will require to be adjusted for the both accruals.

Example 5

Morrison Bros provide you with the following information regarding amounts paid for rates during the year ended 31 December Year 2.

Included in the rates paid amount of £3,900 is £600 which was accrued at the start of the financial year. At the end of the financial year £400 has still to be paid.

Calculation of rates to be charged for year ended 31 December Year 2:

	£
Rates paid	3,900
Less Accrued for Year 1	600
	3,300
Add Accrued Year 2	400
Rates for Year 2	3,700

continued ➤

Side text: FINANCIAL ACCOUNTING

Example 5 continued

The rates account is shown below:

Rates Account					
Date	Details	Dr	Cr	Balance	
Jan 1	Balance		600	600	Cr
Dec 31	Bank	3,900		3,300	Dr
Dec 31	Profit and Loss		3,700	400	Cr

Task 4

Accruals at the start of the year

1 a) From the following information calculate the amount to be charged in the Profit and Loss Account for the following:

ITEM	Amount paid during year	Amount accrued at start of year
	£	£
Wages	10,500	500
Rent	6,000	300
Rates	3,400	100
Salaries	10,000	300

The gross profit for the year was £49,500. On 1 January Year 1, the following amounts were due for Year 2:

- Insurance £200
- Rates £200

You are required to prepare the:

b) Profit and Loss Account for the year ended 31 December Year 2;

c) Ledger accounts for rent and wages.

2 On 1 January Year 1, the following amounts were due to be paid: Insurance £500; Rates £50. During the financial year ended 31 December Year 1 the following payments were made:

- Insurance of premises £2,400
- Rates of £600
- Motor vehicle insurance £1,800

continued ➤

In addition a bank loan of £5,000 was received on 1 July. Interest is payable at the rate of 10% per annum, no interest has been paid. At the end of Year 2, the following amounts were outstanding:

- Insurance £300
- Rates £200

You are required to:

a) calculate the amounts to be charged in the Profit and Loss Account for each expense;

b) calculate the total accruals which would be shown in the Balance Sheet as at 31 December Year 2;

c) prepare the ledger account for insurance for Year end 31 December Year 2.

Now do Worksheet 4.3

The treatment of accruals and prepayments can be summed up in Figure 4.1.

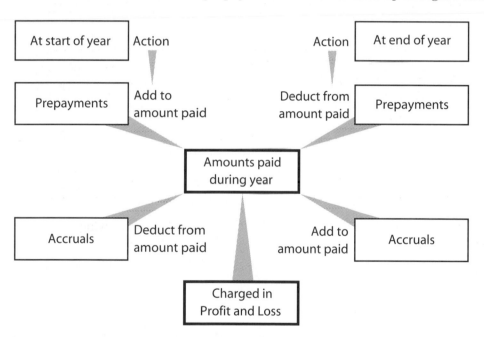

Figure 4.1 Treatment of accruals and prepayments

Bad debts and provision for doubtful debts

At the end of the financial year the accountant should look at the list of debtors and decide if any of these debtors are unlikely to pay the amounts owed to the firm. If there are any such debtors the amount owed should be considered as a **bad debt** and should be written off and charged against the profit in the Profit and Loss Account for the year.

Once this is done the debtors figure may still not give a *true and fair* view of the debtors of the firm since there may still be some debtors who might not be able to pay their debts.

A good accountant **always anticipates** a loss to the firm and never anticipates a profit. This is very much in line with the principles of the **prudence concept**. This states that it is better to understate the profit or the value of an asset rather than overstate them. The actual figure

for bad debts for the year is written off in the **less expenses** section of the Profit and Loss Account.

Example 6

Fred Smith owed us £500 and we received a letter on 20 October saying he was unable to pay and we should consider his debt to be bad.

STEP 1 – Close off Smith's account in the ledger

This is done by crediting his account with the amount owed and debiting the **bad debts account**. This account will collect details of all the bad debts which have occurred during the current financial year.

Fred Smith's Account					
Date	Details	Dr	Cr	Balance	
Feb 1	Sales	500		500	Dr
Oct 10	Bad debts		500	nil	

Bad Debts Account					
Date	Details	Dr	Cr	Balance	
May 3	B Robertson	100		100	Dr
June 4	L Graham	50		150	Dr
Aug 3	B Stewart	120		270	Dr
Oct 10	**Fred Smith**	500		770	Dr

STEP 2 – Transfer the total bad debts to the profit and loss account

Bad Debts Account					
Date	Details	Dr	Cr	Balance	
May 3	B Robertson	100		100	Dr
June 4	L Graham	50		150	Dr
Aug 3	B Stewart	120		270	Dr
Oct 10	**Fred Smith**	500		770	Dr
Dec 31	**Profit and Loss**		770	nil	

Profit and Loss Account Extract		
Gross Profit		25,000
Less Expenses		
Bad debts	770	

Note: The bad debts amount is always written off in the Profit and Loss Account of the enterprise.

Task 5

Bad debts written off

1   John Brown runs a small wholesale hardware supply business. On 6 February he sold goods on credit to Home and Hardware worth £375. On 5 November he received a lawyer's letter saying Home and Hardware had been declared bankrupt and that no payment would be made for the debt outstanding.

Prepare the ledger accounts for Home and Hardware and the bad debts account at the end of the year.

2   Stuart Green manufactures decorative flower pots for sale to garden centres. The Happy Bloom Garden Centre purchased pots on credit on 3 March for £200 and on 1 April for £500. By the end of the financial year no payment had been received for either amount and Green decides to write off these debts as bad.

Prepare the ledger accounts for The Happy Bloom Garden Centre and the bad debts account for the year ended 31 December Year 1.

3   Alistair Wylie manufactures reproduction furniture for sale to hotels. During the year Wylie sold on credit to the Holmfirth Hotels, a chain of hotels furniture suppliers worth £10,000. By the end of the financial year no payment had been received and Wylie decides to write off the amount as a bad debt.

   a) Prepare the ledger accounts for Holmfirth Hotels and the Bad Debts account at the end of the year.

   b) Show the transfer of Bad Debts to the Profit and Loss Account for the bad debts.

4   R Smith, who owes your firm £300 dies tragically in a road accident. It is decided to write off his debt as bad.

Show the entries in the ledger accounts and in the Profit and Loss Account to record this fact.

Partial bad debts

Sometimes the whole amount of a debt may not be bad. This occurs when the debtor is able to pay some of the debt, the rest being written off as bad. The amount paid is termed a **premium**.

Example 7

On 23 January Julie Roger sold goods on credit to Wilson and Green worth £2,500. On 20 September she receive a letter stating that Wilson and Green had been declared bankrupt and would only be able to pay 50% of the amount owed.

STEP 1 – Calculate the amount paid by Wilson and Green and enter the amount in the ledger account

Amount to be received = amount owed × percentage paid
$$= £2,500 \times 50\% = £1,250$$

continued ➤

Example 7 continued

Wilson and Green's Account

Date	Details	Dr	Cr	Balance	
Jan 23	Sales	2,500			Dr
Sept 20	Bank		1,250	1,250	Dr

STEP 2 – Write off the remainder of the amount as bad

Wilson and Green's Account

Date	Details	Dr	Cr	Balance	
Jan 23	Sales	2,500			Dr
Sept 20	Bank		1,250	1,250	Dr
Sept 20	**Bad debts**		1,250	nil	

Bad Debts Account

Date	Details	Dr	Cr	Balance	
Sept 20	Wilson and Green	1,250		1,250	Dr

Task 6

Premium paid on doubtful debts

1. Julie and Shazia operate a wholesale floristry business. During January, they sold flowers on credit to Livewire Decor, worth $3,000. On 16 June they receive a letter informing them that Livewire Decor had been declared bankrupt and that they would only receive 20p in the $ for amounts owed.

    a) Calculate the amount they will receive from Livewire Decor.

    b) Prepare the ledger accounts for Livewire Decor and the bad debts account at the end of the year.

    c) Show the entries in the Profit and Loss Account for the bad debts.

2. Moore and Mathieson operate a chain of furniture shops. On 1 June they obtained a contract from Le Fleur to supply dining room tables and chairs for their newly refurbished restaurant worth $25,000. Le Fleur paid $10,000 on 1 July and $2,000 on 2 August. On 28 November they receive a letter stating that Le Fleur had been made bankrupt and that they would receive 25p in the $ for amounts still outstanding.

    a) Calculate the amount they will receive from Le Fleur

    b) Prepare the ledger accounts for Le Fleur and the bad debts account at the end of the year.

    c) Show the entries in the Profit and Loss Account for the bad debts.

Now do Worksheet 4.4

Bad debts recovered

Some people declared bankrupt will do everything possible to clear their debts. Some even pay back bad debts years after the accounts were closed. Any debts previously written off as bad and subsequently recovered are added to the gross profit in the Profit and Loss Account. In the ledger some record must be made to show the payment of the bad debt previously written off.

Example 8

Rob Drummond was declared bankrupt on 1 June Year 1 owing Richard Mackay £500. On 3 August Year 3, Mackay received a cheque from Drummond for the full amount.

STEP 1 – Open a new account for Drummond

The amount paid is debited in the bank account and credited in Drummond's Account.

Bank Account					
Date	Details	Dr	Cr	Balance	
Aug 3	Rob Drummond	500		500	Dr

Rob Drummond's Account					
Date	Details	Dr	Cr	Balance	
Aug 3	Bank		500	500	Cr

STEP 2 – Close Drummond's account by transferring to **bad debts recovered account**

Rob Drummond's Account					
Date	Details	Dr	Cr	Balance	
Aug 3	Bank		500	500	Cr
Aug 3	Bad debts recovered	500		nil	

Bad Debts Recovered Account					
Date	Details	Dr	Cr	Balance	
Aug 3	Rob Drummond		500	500	Cr

STEP 3 – Transfer figures to Profit and Loss Account at year end

Bad Debts Recovered Account					
Date	Details	Dr	Cr	Balance	
Aug 3	Rob Drummond		500	500	Cr
Dec 31	Profit and Loss	500		nil	

continued ➤

FINANCIAL ACCOUNTING

Example 8 continued

Profit and Loss Account extract for year ended 31 December Year 1		
Gross Profit		25,000
Add Income		
Add Bad debts recovered	500	

Task 7

Bad debts recovered

1 M Lister, a former director of a liquidated private company, wishes to settle the debts of the company, although he has no personal liability at law. On April 10 he sends you a cheque for £450, being payment of one quarter of the debt owed.

Show the entries in the Profit and Loss Account at the end of the current year to record this transaction. The debt was previously written off as bad 2 years ago.

2 During the financial year ended 31 December Year 3 R and G Manufacturers receives a cheque from G Grier for £300 for a debt previously written off as bad.

Show the entries in the Profit and Loss Account and the ledger accounts to record this payment.

3 On 2 July Year 2 D MacInnes & Sons receive a cheque from K Lennon for £400. This amount had been written off as bad in the previous year.

Show the entries in the Profit and Loss Account and the ledger accounts to record this payment.

4 During the financial year ended 30 June Year 2, A Andrews wrote off the debt of B Baker as bad. On 28 June Year 4, Andrews received a cheque from Baker for £250 in settlement of the debt.

Show the entries in the Profit and Loss Account and the ledger accounts to record this payment.

5 During the financial year ended 31 December Year 2, Jones wrote off £200 debts as bad. He later received a cheque from R Thomson for £200 being an amount previously written off as bad.

Show the entries in the Profit and Loss Account and the ledger accounts to record this payment.

Provision for doubtful debts

Following the principles of the prudence concept some business enterprises may decide to make provisions for any loss which might occur. This is called **creating a provision**.

Creating a provision **does not** result in actual cash being set aside but entails the retention of resources within the business by reducing the profit available to the owner, partners or shareholders. The provision is deducted from the gross profit.

The provision for doubtful debts figure can be calculated as a percentage of the actual total debtors at the end of the year. Alternatively, a total debtors schedule is drawn up to show the total amounts owed to the enterprise and the length of time they have been outstanding. The provision might be based on the older debts.

In the first year the total provision is written off to the Profit and Loss Account. In subsequent years the difference between last year's figure and this year's new figure is written off to the Profit and Loss Account.

The provision for doubtful debts will be deducted from the debtors figure in the Balance Sheet to show them at a *true and fair* view. Again the prudence concept being applied.

Example 9

John Smith's debtors at 31 December Year 1 amount to £10,000. He decides to create a provision for doubtful debts of 5%.

STEP 1 – Creating a new provision for doubtful debts

The information required for this in examination questions is the total debtors figure at the end of the financial year and the percentage provision.

Provision for doubtful debts = 5% of £10,000 = £500.

STEP 2 – Record the accounting entries in the provision account

A new account will be opened for provision for doubtful debts.

Note: Provision accounts have credit balances as they normally represent decreases in assets.

Provision for Doubtful Debts Account					
Date	Details	Dr	Cr	Balance	
Dec 31	Profit and Loss		500	500	Cr

STEP 3 – Record the provision in the Profit and Loss Account

Profit and Loss Account Extract		
Gross profit		25,000
Less Expenses		
Provision for doubtful debts	500	

continued ➤

Example 9 continued

STEP 4 – Show the effect on the Balance Sheet

Balance Sheet Extract			
Current assets			
Debtors	10,000		
Less Provision for doubtful debts	500	9,500	

The debtors appear in the Balance Sheet at their *true and fair* value – what we think they will pay.

Adjusting the provision for doubtful debts for subsequent years

The provision for subsequent years may be more or less than the previous year. If the new provision is **less than** the previous year the difference is **added** back to the gross profit, but if the figure is **more than** the previous year the difference is **deducted** from the gross profit at the end of the year.

Example 10

J Smith begins business in Year 1. At the end of this year he calculates that 5% of his debtors will be bad and decides to create a provision for doubtful debts for Year 2 based on his debtors figure at the end of the Year 1 of £5,000.

Over the next three years he maintains the same percentage figure as the provision for doubtful debts. In the table below is shown the total debtors at the end of each year.

Year	Provision for doubtful debts %	Total Debtors at year end £
Year 1	5	5,000
Year 2	5	7,500
Year 3	5	6,000

STEP 1 – Calculate provision for doubtful debts at end of Year 1 and open the provision account

This amount is 5% of the debtors figure at the end of the financial year. No provision figure exists therefore the whole amount will be deducted from the gross profit in the Profit and Loss Account.

Provision for doubtful debts end Year 1 = 5% of £5,000 = £250

Provision for Doubtful Debts Account					
Date	Details	Dr	Cr	Balance	
Year 1 Dec 31	Profit and Loss		250	250	Cr

continued ➤

Example 10 continued

STEP 2 – Enter the provision in the Profit and Loss Account and Balance Sheet

J Smith Profit and Loss Account Extract – Year 1	£	£
Gross profit		40,000
Less Expenses		
Provision for doubtful debts	250	

Balance Sheet Extract	£	£	
Current assets			
Debtors	5,000		
Less Provision for doubtful debts	250	4,750	

STEP 3 – Calculate the change in provision at the end of Year 2.

Provision for doubtful debts end Year 2 = 5% of £7,500 = £375

The change is calculated by comparing the provision for Year 1 with that of year 2.

Year 1 Provision for doubtful debts   = £250

Year 2 Provision for doubtful debts   = £375

Increase in provision for doubtful debts = £125

This increase is the amount which will appear in the Profit and Loss Account and is deducted from the gross profit.

STEP 4 – Show the provision for doubtful debts at end of Year 2

Provision for Doubtful Debts Account					
Date	**Details**	**Dr**	**Cr**	**Balance**	
Year 1 Dec 31	Profit and Loss		250	250	Cr
Year 2 Dec 31	**Profit and Loss**		125	375	

continued ➤

Example 10 continued

STEP 5 – Show the Profit and Loss Account and Balance Sheet extract at end of Year 2

J Smith Profit and Loss Account Extract – Year 2	£	£
Gross profit		55,000
Less Expenses		
Increase in provision for doubtful debts	125	

Balance Sheet Extract	£	£	£
Current assets			
Debtors	7,500		7,500
Less Provision for doubtful debts	375*	7,125	375*

* However, note that it is the **full amount** (the total provision for the forthcoming year) of the provision for doubtful debts which is deducted in the Balance Sheet

Some students worry about only entering the change in the provision for doubtful debts and not the whole amount. There is already a retained amount of profit for doubtful debts, so we are simply recording the increase.

Steps 3, 4 and 5 will be repeated for end of Year 3

STEP 3 (Year 3) – Calculate the change in provision at the end of Year 3

Provision for doubtful debts end of Year 3 = 5% of £6,000 = £300

The change is calculated by comparing the provision for Year 2 with that of Year 3

Year 2 Provision for doubtful debts =   £375
Year 3 Provision for doubtful debts =   £300
Decrease in provision for doubtful debts =   £75

This decrease is the amount which will appear in the Profit and Loss Account

The decrease means we do not need to retain as much of our doubtful debt resources for Year 3 as we did in Year 2.

STEP 4 (Year 3) – Show the provision for doubtful debts at end of Year 3

Provision for Doubtful Debts Account					
Date	Details	Dr	Cr	Balance	
Year 1 Dec 31	Profit and Loss		250	250	Cr
Year 2 Dec 31	Profit and Loss		125	375	Cr
Year 3 Dec 31	**Profit and Loss**	**75**		**300**	**Cr**

continued ➤

Example 10 continued

STEP 5 (Year 3) – Show the Profit and Loss Account and Balance Sheet extract at end of Year 3

The decrease in the provision for doubtful debts will be added back to the gross profit in the Profit and Loss Account, increasing the profit available to the owners.

J Smith Profit and Loss Account Extract – Year 3	£	£	£
Gross profit			60,000
Add Income			
Increase in provision for doubtful debts			75
			60,075

Balance Sheet Extract	£		£
Current assets			
Debtors	6,000		
Less provision for doubtful debts	300*	5,700	

* Again note that it is the **full provision** for Year 3 which is deducted from the **debtors** figure in the Balance Sheet.

Summary: Dealing with provision or doubtful debts

New provision	• Calculate the amount of the provision.
	• Open and credit **provision account**.
	• Deduct from **gross profit** in **Profit and Loss Account**.
	• Deduct whole provision from **debtors** in **Balance Sheet**
Increase in provision	• Calculate new provision for the year.
	• Calculate **increase** in provision = **previous provision** – **new provision**.
	• **Deduct** increase in provision from **gross profit** in **Profit and Loss Account**
	• Deduct **whole new** provision from **debtors** in **Balance Sheet**.
Decrease in provision	• Calculate new provision for the year.
	• Calculate **decrease** in provision= **previous provision** – **new provision**.
	• **Add** decrease in provision to **gross profit** in **Profit and Loss Account**.
	• Deduct **whole** new provision from **debtors** in **Balance Sheet**.

Remember that in most cases you will be adjusting figures from the Trial Balance for inclusion in Profit and Loss and Balance Sheets of an enterprise.

Task 8

Provision for doubtful debts

1   At 31 December Year 1 a firm's debtors amounted to £35,000 and at 31 December Year 2 £37,500. It is the firm's practice to have a bad debt provision of 5% of the debtors at the end of each year. Calculate Profit and Loss Account extracts for the Year 1 and Year 2.

2   The following figures have been extracted from the ledger accounts of J Brown and Co on 31 December Year 1:

Debtors   £5,000
Provision for doubtful debts   £200
Bad debts   £300

For Year 2, the provision for doubtful debts is to be 6% of debtors.

You are required to:

a)   calculate the increase/decrease in provision for doubtful debts.

b)   show the Profit and Loss Account entries for provision and bad debts.

c)   show the Balance Sheet extract for Debtors.

  Now do Worksheet 4.5

Provision for depreciation of fixed assets

Fixed assets have been defined as long-term assets, owned by the business, for use in the business and not for resale. When a fixed asset is purchased the firm has made an investment known as **capital expenditure**.

Fixed assets have a finite life and fall in value over this lifetime. This fall in value is known as **depreciation**. Depreciation is the reduction in the value of an asset due to fair wear and tear or obsolescence.

Assets depreciate through:

1   **Use** – as an asset is used, its value decreases.

2   **Fair wear and tear** – use of machinery or vehicles or exposure to the elements.

3   **Time** – with the passage of time the asset decreases in value. For example, the value of the lease on a property will decrease with the passage of time.

4   **Obsolescence** – caused by technical advances or changes in fashion. For example, the huge strides in computer technology reduces the value of computers purchased even one year ago.

As the fixed asset loses value, its value must be decreased in the books of the business by writing off the reduction to a provision for depreciation account.

The purpose of writing off depreciation is not to write down the asset to its value at the balance sheet date but to spread the net cost of the asset over its estimated life. **Net cost** can be defined as the **cost of the asset** less its **scrap value**.

Although depreciation is a deduction from profits it **does not** give rise to an allocation of cash into a fund for the replacement of the asset. This would only happen if an actual sinking fund was set up and a cash amount equal to the reduction in the asset value was transferred to this fund at the end of the year.

The underlying principles for depreciation can be summarised as follows:

1   Every year should carry a proper share of expenses. Only if a year carries its full share of losses can the true profit figure be achieved.

2   Losses should be evenly spread over the lifetime of the asset.

3   Assets must be correctly valued on the Balance Sheet, giving a *true and fair* view of the business.

The actual amount charged for depreciation over the lifetime of the asset is simply guesswork, based on experience. Only when the asset is sold can the accuracy of these guesses be confirmed.

Depreciation and the Companies Acts

The Companies Acts requires companies to show the assets of the firm *at cost less the total depreciation to date*. This means that a prospective investor can see the actual value of the assets of the business and he can determine whether his proposed investment is wise.

As a result of this, the fixed asset accounts in the ledger only show the cost of the asset or the purchase or sale of the asset. The reduction in value is shown in the provision for depreciation accounts.

Methods of depreciating assets

Straight line method or equal instalment method

The **straight line** method of depreciation is where the same amount of depreciation is written off the value of the asset each year. It is also known as the **equal instalment** method. Examples of assets depreciated by this method are furniture, fittings, plant and machinery, etc.

Calculation of annual depreciation

To calculate the depreciation to be charged annually, the accountant will deduct the scrap value of the asset from the cost of the asset, and divide the result by the estimated life of the asset.

$$\textbf{Annual Depreciation} = \frac{\textbf{cost of asset} - \textbf{scrap value}}{\textbf{estimated life of asset}}$$

Example 11

On 1 January Year 1 Brown Bros purchase plant and machinery for £228,000. After 10 years its scrap value is estimated to be £5,000. Calculate the annual depreciation.

STEP 1 – Calculate the annual depreciation of the plant and machinery

$$\text{Annual Depreciation} = \frac{£228,000 - £5,000}{10 \text{ years}}$$

$$= \frac{£223,000}{10 \text{ years}} = £22,300$$

Show the plant and machinery account, the provision for depreciation of plant and machinery, Profit and Loss Accounts and Balance Sheet extracts at the end of the first 3 years of the asset's life.

STEP 2 – Open fixed asset and provision ledger accounts

Plant and Machinery Account					
Date	Details	Dr	Cr	Balance	
Year 1 Jan 1	Bank	228,000		228,000	Dr

Provision for Depreciation of Plant and Machinery Account					
Date	Details	Dr	Cr	Balance	
Year 1 Dec 31	Profit and Loss		22,300	22,300	Cr

The plant and machinery accounts shows the cost of the asset and the provision account shows the amount written off the value of the asset due to fair wear and tear during the year.

STEP 3 – Enter the provision for depreciation of plant and machinery in the Profit and Loss Account

Profit and Loss Account For year ended 31 December Year 1	£	£	£
Gross profit			165,000
Less Expenses			
Provision for depreciation: • Plant and Machinery		22,300	

continued ➤

Example 11 continued

STEP 4 – Make the Balance Sheet entries for Year 1

Balance Sheet as at 31 December Year 1			
	£	£	£
FIXED ASSETS	Cost	Aggregate Depreciation	Net Book Value
Plant and Machinery	228,000	22,300	205,700

STEP 5 – Show the ledger entries for Year 2

The plant and machinery account remains unchanged at the end of Year 2, because we are maintaining the asset at cost in the ledger account

The provision for depreciation account will show an additional £22,300 being provided for the loss in value of the fixed asset.

Plant and Machinery Account					
Date	Details	Dr	Cr	Balance	
Year 1 Jan 1	Bank	228,000		228,000	Dr

Provision for Depreciation of Plant and Machinery Account					
Date	Details	Dr	Cr	Balance	
Year 1 Dec 31	Profit and Loss		22,300	22,300	Cr
Year 2 Dec 31	Profit and Loss		22,300	44,600	Cr

STEP 6 – Show the entries in the final accounts

Profit and Loss Account For year ended 31 December Year 2	£	£	£
Gross profit			250,000
Less Expenses			
Provision for depreciation: • Plant and Machinery		22,300	

Note that only the depreciation **charged against profits for Year 2** is deducted from the gross profit in the Profit and Loss Account.

Balance Sheet as at 31 December Year 2			
	£	£	£
FIXED ASSETS	Cost	Aggregate Depreciation	Net Book Value
Plant and Machinery	228,000	44,600	183,400

Note that the **total depreciation to date** (Year 1 + Year 2) is deducted from the cost of the asset in the Balance Sheet. This is the balance of the provision for depreciation account.

continued ➤

Example 11 continued

STEP 7 – Show the ledger account entries for Year 3

The plant and machinery account remains unchanged at the end of Year 3, because we are maintaining the asset at cost in the ledger account.

The provision for depreciation account at the end of Year 3 will show another £22,300 being provided for the loss in value of the fixed asset.

Plant and Machinery Account					
Date	**Details**	**Dr**	**Cr**	**Balance**	
Year 1 Jan 1	Bank	228,000		228,000	Dr

Provision for Depreciation of Plant and Machinery Account					
Date	**Details**	**Dr**	**Cr**	**Balance**	
Year 1 Dec 31	Profit and Loss		22,300	22,300	Cr
Year 2 Dec 31	Profit and Loss		22,300	44,600	Cr
Year 3 Dec 31	**Profit and Loss**		**22,300**	**66,900**	**Cr**

STEP 8 – Show the final account entries for Year 3

Profit and Loss Account **For year ended 31 December Year 3**	**£**	**£**	**£**
Gross profit			190,000
Less **Expenses**			
Provision for depreciation: • **Plant and Machinery**		22,300	

Note that only the depreciation **charged against profits for Year 3** is deducted from the gross profit in the Profit and Loss Account.

Balance Sheet as at 31 December Year 3			
	£	**£**	**£**
FIXED ASSETS	Cost	Aggregate Depreciation	Net Book Value
Plant and Machinery	228,000	**66,900**	**161,1000**

Note that the **total depreciation to date** (Year 1 + Year 2 + Year 3) is deducted from the cost of the asset in the Balance Sheet. This is the balance of the provision for depreciation account

In examination questions you will normally be asked to calculate the provision for depreciation for the current financial year. Ledger accounts will not normally be necessary.

I2 H

Task 9

Provision for depreciation – Straight line method

1 From the following information calculate the annual depreciation to be charged against the profits of L Yule for the following fixed assets purchased on 1 January Year 1. Yule uses the straight line method of depreciation.

Asset	Cost £	Estimated Life	Residual/Scrap Value £
Machinery	200,000	5 years	20,000
Fixtures and Fittings	42,000	4 years	2,000
Office Equipment	20,000	3 years	2,000

2 Albert plc purchase new machinery for £250,000 on 1 January Year 1. The machine will be replaced after 7 years at which time the residual value of the machine is estimated to £40,000. Albert uses the straight line method of depreciation.

a) calculate the annual depreciation to be charged for Years 1, 2 and 3.

b) show the ledger accounts for machinery, and provision for depreciation of machinery for Years 1, 2 and 3.

c) show the Profit and Loss and Balance Sheet extract for Year 3.

3 Alan Lamb purchased office equipment for £8,500. He estimates the life of the asset will be 5 years after which it will have a residual value of £500. Lamb uses the straight line method of depreciation.

Copy and complete the table:

Year	Cost £	Charge to Profit and Loss A/c £	Aggregate Depreciation £	Net Book Value £
1				
2				
3				
4				
5				

4 Kennedy plc purchase new plant and machinery for £500,000. They decide to write 20% off the cost of the assets as a provision for depreciation each year.

You are required to:

a) calculate the annual provision for depreciation.

b) show the ledger accounts for plant and machinery and the provision for depreciation of plant and machinery for Years 1, 2 and 3.

c) show the Profit and Loss Account and Balance Sheet extract for Year 2.

continued ➢

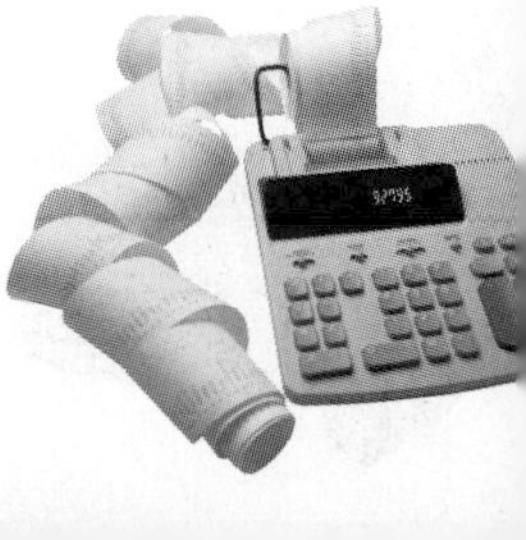

5. From the following information calculate the annual depreciation to be charged against the profits of McKiernan, Smith and Smith for the following fixed assets purchased on 1 January Year 1. They use the straight line method of depreciation.

Asset	Cost £	Annual Provision for Depreciation
Machinery	200,000	20%
Fixtures and Fittings	42,000	10%
Office Equipment	20,000	10%

You are required to show:

a) the annual charge for depreciation for each of the above assets.

b) the Profit and Loss Account extract for Year 3.

c) the Balance Sheet extract for Year 3.

Amortization of leases

A lease on property is usually granted for a specific number of years. The value of the lease decreases by a fixed fraction annually. Amortization is simply a special case of the straight line or equal instalment method of depreciation.

Calculation of amortization of lease

The amount the lease decreases in value each year is called the amortization charge and can be calculated as follows:

$$\text{Annual decrease in value} = \frac{\textbf{original cost of lease}}{\textbf{lifetime of lease}}$$

Example 12

J Brown purchases a 10 year lease for £100,000. Calculate the annual amortization charge.

$$\text{Amortization charge} = \frac{£100,000}{10 \text{ years}} = £10,000 \text{ per annum}$$

The £10,000 will be **deducted** from the **gross profit** in the Profit and Loss Account and the value of the lease will be **decreased** in the Balance Sheet.

Task 10

Amortization of lease

1   Smithson and Sons negotiated a 10 year lease for factory premises from Property-hire plc. The lease cost £250,000.

Calculate the annual amortisation to be charged against profits.

2   Caster plc wishes to expand their business but is unable to purchase land to build a new factory. They negotiate the lease of a factory from Factory Properties plc for 20 years at the cost of £300,000.

Calculate the annual amortisation of the lease to be charged against profits.

3   Alpha Cars wishes to expand their business and decide to take a 25 year lease costing £100,000 on a garage from Church Properties.

Calculate the annual amortisation of the lease to be charged against profits.

4   Brian Jones wishes to run his own restaurant and arranges a 10 year lease on a suitable building costing £50,000.

Calculate the annual amortisation of the lease to be charged against profits.

5   Queen and Sons negotiated a 25 year lease on a warehouse property from Gladstone Properties plc. The lease cost £500,000.

Calculate the annual amortisation to be charged against profits.

Advantages of straight line method of depreciation

1   Straightforward and easy to calculate.
2   Easy method to understand.
3   The asset is written off over a definite period of time to its predicted value.
4   The valuation of the asset appearing on the Balance Sheet each year is reasonably fair, and complies with the requirements of the Companies Acts in most cases.

Disadvantages of straight line method of depreciation

1   When a new asset is purchased or an existing asset is sold the depreciation must be recalculated.
2   The charge to the Profit and Loss Account increases over the years because of the increased repair and maintenance costs of the asset.
3   There is no provision for the replacement of the asset at the end of its life.

The criticisms in 1 and 2 are overcome by the use of the **diminishing balance** method of depreciation, which is the second method of depreciation to be discussed.

Diminishing balance method of depreciation

With the **diminishing balance** (or **reducing balance**) method of depreciation a **fixed percentage** is calculated on the written down (book value) value of the asset each year.

The depreciation written off is transferred to the provision for depreciation account each year and the asset is maintained in the asset account at its historic cost (where the historic cost is the original cost price of the asset).

Example 13

Fixtures and fittings cost £5,000 on 1 January Year 1 and it is decided that these assets will be depreciated at a rate of 10% per annum on the written down value.

STEP 1 – Calculate the provision for depreciation for Year 1

For year 1 the provision for depreciation will be based on the cost of the asset.

Provision for depreciation = Cost × percentage depreciation.
$$= £5,000 × 10\% = £500$$

The accounting entries in the ledger accounts for the fixtures and fittings and provision accounts are shown below.

Fixtures and Fittings Account					
Date	Details	Dr	Cr	Balance	
Year 1 Jan 1	Bank	5,000		5,000	Dr

Provision for Depreciation of Fixtures and Fittings Account					
Date	Details	Dr	Cr	Balance	
Year 1 Dec 31	Profit and Loss		500	500	Cr

The Profit and Loss Account and Balance Sheet entries are shown below.

C Brown Profit and Loss Account For year ended 31 December Year 1	£	£	£
Gross profit			65,210
Less Expenses			
Provision for depreciation: • Fixtures and Fittings		500	

C Brown Balance Sheet as at 31 December Year 1	£	£	£
FIXED ASSETS	Cost	Aggregate Depreciation	Net Book Value
Fixtures and Fittings	5,000	500	4,500

continued ≻

Example 13 continued

STEP 2 – Calculate the net book value of the asset at the end of Year 2

The provision for depreciation for year 2 will be calculated on the **written down** or **net book value** of the asset at the end of Year 1. This figure will be the net book value shown in the Balance Sheet.

In examination questions you will be provided with the cost of the asset and the provision for depreciation written off, to date, on the asset.

Net book value = Cost of asset – provision for depreciation.

The net book value of the fixtures and fittings at the end of year 1 was:

Net book value = £5,000 – £500
= £4,500.

STEP 3 – Calculate the provision for depreciation of the fixtures and fittings for year 2

Provision for depreciation = Net book value × depreciation percentage
= £4,500 × 10%
= £450

STEP 4 – Record the entries in the ledger account and final accounts

Provision for Depreciation of Fixtures and Fittings Account						
Date	Details		Dr	Cr	Balance	
Year 1 Dec 31	Profit and Loss			500	500	Cr
Year 2 Dec 31	**Profit and Loss**			450	950	Cr

The Profit and Loss Account and Balance Sheet entries are shown below.

C Brown Profit and Loss Account For year ended 31 December Year 2	£	£	£
Gross profit			75,000
Less **Expenses**			
Provision for depreciation: • **Fixtures and Fittings**		450	

C Brown Balance Sheet as at 31 December Year 2	£		£		£
FIXED ASSETS	Cost		Aggregate Depreciation		Net Book Value
Fixtures and Fittings	5,000		950		4,050

The provision for depreciation would continue to be written off the net book value of the asset when the diminishing balance method of depreciation is used.

continued ➤

Example 13 continued

The following table shows the depreciation to be written off on the first 5 years of the asset's life.

Year of life	Cost of asset £	Depreciation Calculation	Actual Depreciation charged to P & L A/c each year £	Book value at year end £
Year 1	5,000	10% of £5,000.00	500.00	4,500.00
Year 2	5,000	10% of £4,500.00	450.00	4,050.00
Year 3	5,000	10% of £4,050.00	405.00	3,645.00
Year 4	5,000	10% of £3,645.00	364.50	3,280.50
Year 5	5,000	10% of £3,280.50	328.05	2,952.45

Task 11

Provision for depreciation – Diminishing balance method

1   The following assets are owned by L Lennox. On 31 December Year 2 he depreciates them using the diminishing balance method.

Calculate the charge for depreciation in the Profit and Loss Account at the end of year 2.

Asset	Cost £	Percentage Depreciation	Provision for Depreciation to date £
Motor vehicles	35,000	25%	9,500
Office equipment	12,500	20%	2,000
Plant and machinery	150,000	10%	35,000

2   The flowing balances were extracted from the ledger accounts of Miller & Weir on 31 December Year 2 before the completion of the final accounts.

Premises	£100,000
Delivery van	£50,000
Computer equipment	£15,000
Office furniture	£8,000
Provision for depreciation • Delivery van • Computer equipment • Office furniture	£12,000 £3,000 £2,000

continued ➤

Miller & Weir depreciates fixed assets at the following rate using the diminishing balance method.

Delivery van	25%
Computer equipment	30%
Office furniture	10%

Calculate the amount to be charged against this years profit for the provision for depreciation of each asset and show the fixed asset section of the Balance Sheet at 31 December Year 2.

3 The following information was taken from the Trial Balance of Benton & Co on 30 June Year 1 prior to the preparation of the final accounts.

Premises	£75,000	
Motor vehicles	£36,000	
Office furniture	£23,000	
Provision for depreciation • Motor vehicles • Office furniture		£8,500 £3,200

Benton & Co depreciate their assets using the diminishing balance method. Depreciation is provided for on the rate of 20% for motor vehicles and 15% for office furniture.

a) Calculate the depreciation charge for the year.

b) Show the entries for depreciation in the Profit and Loss Account extract and the fixed assets section of the Balance Sheet on 30 June Year 2

Advantages of the diminishing balance method

1 It is straightforward and recalculations are not required with the purchase or sale of an asset.

2 The charge against profits is more evenly spread over the life of the asset since the diminishing charge for depreciation is offset against increased charges for repairs

3 With the exception of assets with short lives, it clearly shows that for many assets, the annual loss in value is greatest in the first few years of their lives.

Disadvantages of the diminishing balance method

1 The percentage figure to be deducted each year can be difficult to calculate (although there is an acceptable formula).

2 For assets with a short life, the percentage figure is so high that is becomes ridiculous. For example, an asset with a short of life of 2 years would require to be written off by 99% to remove it from the books.

3 There is no provision for the replacement of the asset.

Revaluation of assets method of depreciation

Sometimes it is impossible to treat a particular asset using the above methods. For example, in farm accounting a herd account cannot be depreciated in the regular way. Each animal the farmer owns will have to be valued separately (appraised) at the end of his financial year.

Another example of this would be loose tools used in a factory where these are physically counted and a value placed on them.

Using the revaluation of assets method, the value placed on the asset at the end of the year is compared with the value at the beginning of the financial year and the difference is calculated and transferred to the Profit and Loss Account.

Summary of book-keeping entries required for provisions for depreciation

1   **When the asset is purchased:**
    Debit the asset account with the value of the asset.
    Credit the account which shows the method of purchase - Cash, Bank Creditor.

    Note: The only time you will make any other entry in the asset account is when the asset is sold or you make an additional purchase.

2   **At the end of the first year**
    Calculate the depreciation to be charged on the asset, then:
    credit the provision for depreciation account.

3   **Transfer to the Profit and Loss Account the depreciation charged for the year.**

    We do this by deducting the year's depreciation from the gross profit.

Sale of assets

As fixed assets get old they lose their value because:

- repairs become more frequent resulting in higher costs and the possibility of lost production while the machine is being repaired;
- the machine becomes obsolete, or new machinery may cut the cost of production.

When this happens the enterprise will usually sell the old machine and buy a new model.

When the old machine is sold there are 3 accounting possibilities:

- the machine may be sold at its existing book value;
- the machine may be sold at a price higher than its existing value;
- the machine may be sold at price lower than its existing book value.

The enterprise needs to calculate the profit or loss on the sale of the asset and record this in the final accounts of the enterprise. The amount of the provision for depreciation is a 'guesstimate' of how much the asset has lost its value over the lifetime of the asset. This amount is only confirmed when the actual asset is sold.

Example 14

James Smith purchased a machine on 1 January Year 1 for £50,000 by cheque. He decided to depreciate the asset using the straight line method by £5,000 per annum. On 1 January Year 4 he sells the asset for £4,000.

Calculate the profit or loss on the sale of the asset

STEP 1 – Record the purchase of the asset in the machinery account

Machinery Account					
Date	Details	Dr	Cr	Balance	
Year 1 Jan 1	Bank	50,000		50,000	Dr

STEP 2 – Calculate the Depreciation provided for on the machine

Provision for Depreciation of Machinery					
Date	Details	Dr	Cr	Balance	
Year 1 Dec 31	Profit and Loss		5,000	5,000	Cr
Year 2 Dec 31	Profit and Loss		5,000	10,000	Cr
Year 3 Dec 31	Profit and Loss		5,000	15,000	Cr

Depreciation provided for on machinery is recorded in the provision account and the Profit and Loss Account at the end of each financial year

STEP 3 – Transfer the cost and provision for depreciation figures to a sale of asset account

Machinery Account					
Date	Details	Dr	Cr	Balance	
Year 1 Jan 1	Bank	50,000		50,000	Dr
Year 4 Jan 1	Sale of Asset		50,000	nil	Dr

Provision for Depreciation of Machinery					
Date	Details	Dr	Cr	Balance	
Year 1 Dec 31	Profit and Loss		5,000	5,000	Cr
Year 2 Dec 31	Profit and Loss		5,000	10,000	Cr
Year 3 Dec 31	Profit and Loss		5,000	15,000	Cr
Year 4 Jan 1	Sale of Asset	15,000		nil	

continued ➤

Example 14   continued

Sale of Asset – Machinery Account					
Date	Details	Dr	Cr	Balance	
Year 4 Jan 1	**Machinery Account**	50,000		50,000	Dr
Year 4 Jan 1	**Provision for Depreciation**		15,000	35,000	Dr

The £35,000 represents the net book value of the asset, or what the owner thinks the asset is worth.

STEP 4 – Asset sold at its net book value

If the asset is sold at its **net book value** of £35,000 no profit or loss will have been made on the sale of the asset

Sale of Asset – Machinery Account					
Date	Details	Dr	Cr	Balance	
Year 4 Jan 1	Machinery Account	50,000		50,000	Dr
Year 4 Jan 1	Provision for Depreciation		15,000	35,000	Dr
Year 4 Jan 1	**Bank**		35,000	**Nil**	

Record the sale of the asset in the ledger account. Debit the bank account and credit the sale of asset account.

STEP 5 – Asset sold at more than its net book value

The machinery was sold for £37,500. This is more than the net book value, so it has been sold for a profit.

Sale of Asset – Machinery Account					
Date	Details	Dr	Cr	Balance	
Year 4 Jan 1	Machinery Account	50,000		50,000	Dr
Year 4 Jan 1	Provision for Depreciation		15,000	35,000	Dr
Year 4 Jan 1	Bank		37,500	2,500	Cr
Year 4 Jan 1	**Profit and Loss Account**	2,500		**nil**	

continued ➢

Example 14 continued

The profit made on the sale of the asset is a gain to the business and should be added to the gross profit figure in the Profit and Loss Account.

Profit and Loss Account Extract Year 4			
	£	£	£
Gross Profit			30,000
Add Income			
Profit on sale of machinery			2,500
			32,500

STEP 6 – Asset sold at less than its net book value

The machinery was sold for £33,000. This is less than its net book value, so it has been sold at a loss.

Sale of Asset – Machinery Account					
Date	Details	Dr	Cr	Balance	
Year 4 Jan 1	Machinery Account	50,000		50,000	Dr
Year 4 Jan 1	Provision for Depreciation		15,000	35,000	Dr
Year 4 Jan 1	Bank		33,000	2,000	Dr
Year 4 Jan 1	**Profit and Loss Account**		**2,000**	**nil**	

The deficit on the sale of the asset is a loss to the business and should be deducted from the gross profit figure in the Profit and Loss Account.

Profit and Loss Account Extract Year 4			
	£	£	£
Gross Profit			30,000
Less Expenses			
Loss on sale of machinery			2,000
			28,000

continued ➤

Example 14 continued

It may not be necessary to show the ledger accounts to calculate the profit or loss on the sale of an asset. This can be set out in a statement and the same information shown above in the accounts could be recorded as follows:

	Sold at Net Book Value £	Sold at a profit £	Sold at a loss £
Cost of machinery	50,000	50,000	50,000
Less Provision for depreciation	15,000	15,000	15,000
Net Book Value	35,000	35,000	35,000
Selling price	35,000	37,500	33,000
Profit/(Loss) on sale of machinery	0	2,500	(2,000)

Task 12

Able plc keeps the following asset register for motor vehicles owned by the firm and uses the straight line method of depreciation.

Vehicle	Date purchased	Cost	Annual Depreciation	Date sold	Amount received
1	1 Jan Year 1	£25,000	10% cost	1 Jan Year 3	£19,500
2	1 Jan Year 1	£30,000	10% cost	1 Jan Year 5	£16,500
3	1 July Year 3	£28,500	5% cost	1 Jan Year 6	£24,000
4	1 Jan Year 4	£40,000	10% cost	1 July Year 7	£30,000
5	1 Jan Year 8	£25,000	25% cost	1 July Year 9	£7,000

From the above information calculate the profit or loss on the sale of each vehicle

In the question above the straight line method of depreciation has been used. Some firms prefer to depreciate their assets using the diminishing balance method.

Example 15

On 1 January Year 1 Robert Smith purchased computer equipment for £10,000. He provides for depreciation at the rate of 25% of the diminishing balance. At the end of Year 2 he sells the computer equipment for £4,500.

Calculate the profit or loss on sale of the asset.

continued ➤

Example 15 continued

STEP 1 – Calculate the annual depreciation provided for on the computer equipment

Year 1
Depreciation = 25% of cost
= 25% of £10,000
= £2,500

Year 2
Depreciations = 25% × (cost – aggregate depreciation)
= 25% × (£10,000 – £2,500)
= £1,875

STEP 2 – Calculate the aggregate depreciation

Depreciation for Year 1 + Year 2 = £2,500 + £1,875
= £4,375

STEP 3 – Calculate the profit or loss on sale of computers

Cost	£10,000
Less Aggregate depreciation	£4,375
Net Book Value	£5,625
Less Selling Price	£4,500
Loss on sale of asset	£1,125

Task 13

Beta plc keeps the following asset register for delivery vans owned by the firm and uses the diminishing balance method of depreciation.

Delivery Van	Date purchased	Cost	Annual Depreciation Rate Diminishing balance	Date sold	Amount received
1	1 Jan Year 1	£50,000	25%	1 Jan Year 3	£28,000
2	1 Jan Year 1	£40,000	20%	1 Jan Year 3	£25,000
3	1 July Year 2	£30,000	15%	1 Jan Year 5	£22,000
4	1 Jan Year 3	£25,000	10%	1 July Year 4	£23,000
5	1 Jan Year 4	£25,000	25%	1 July Year 7	£5,000

From the above information calculate the profit or loss on the sale of each vehicle

Now do Worksheets 4.6 and 4.7

The preparation of manufacturing accounts

Intermediate 2 Level Outcomes:

I2

This chapter includes material from Int 2 level Financial Accounting Outcome 4

☆ **Complete partially prepared manufacturing and trading accounts for an organisation consistent with financial accounting practice.**

Higher Level Outcomes:

H

This chapter includes material from Higher level Financial Accounting Outcome 1

☆ **Complete partially prepared manufacturing and trading accounts for an organisation consistent with financial accounting practice.**

Manufacturing costs and accounts

I2
H

Manufacturing concerns are businesses which actually make products. The products made may be completed in the factory requiring no further processing or they may be sets of components which can be assembled in the factory into finished products or sold to other manufacturers as part of other products.

Examples of manufacturing concerns are white goods such as washing machines and freezers, and everything from computers and cars to furniture and light bulbs.

Any business organisation which is involved in a manufacturing or production process should prepare a **Manufacturing Account**. The Manufacturing Account is used to show:

- the cost of the goods manufactured;
- the profit (or unusually the loss) on the manufacturing process.

Types of costs shown in a Manufacturing Account

A manufacturer needs to distinguish clearly between the different types of costs incurred and the manufacturing account reflects this. Costs are divided into 2 types – **direct** costs and **indirect** costs.

Direct costs are those costs incurred which can be identified with the items being produced – they are part of the actual item being made. These costs include:

- **Direct materials** These are the materials actually used in production, such as flour in bread, cloth in a shirt or hops in brewing.
- **Direct wages** These are the wages of the workforce actually engaged in the manufacturing process, such as the wages of sewing machine operator, baker or brewer.

- **Direct expenses** These will consist of expenses which vary directly with the output and can be related directly to the units manufactured. The expenses can range from royalties on licensed production to the cost of gas for baking ovens and power to drive the machinery.

Indirect costs are not directly linked to the manufacturing processes, but are incurred by other processes which are necessary to enable the production process to be carried out. These expenses are classified as **overheads**. Examples include factory light and heat, storeman's wages, factory manager's salary, the rent, rates, insurance, repairs, and upkeep of the factory. They are often referred to as the **factory overheads**.

You may also see the terms **fixed** and **variable costs** being used. **Fixed costs** are costs which remain more or less constant irrespective of changes in the volume of production. They do not alter **in the short term** even when the level of production changes. For example, the rent of the factory will remain the same from month to month regardless of the level of output. **Fixed cost** is another name for an **indirect cost** or **overhead**.

Variable costs are costs which vary directly with the level of output. For example if a clothing manufacturer uses 2 metres of material to make one cushion cover, then 10 cushion covers would take 20 metres of material, 20 cushion covers would take 40 metres of material. **Variable cost** is another name for **direct cost**.

Preparation of the Manufacturing Account

The Manufacturing Account is prepared in 3 sections: the **prime cost**, the **manufacturing overheads**, and the **stock of work-in-progress**.

Prime cost of manufacture

Prime cost means first cost, and refers to the variable or direct costs. Within the prime cost section of the Manufacturing Account several different calculations are performed.

The manufacturer will need to know the cost of:

- raw materials used;
- direct labour;
- direct expenses.

These three expenses added together are the prime cost of manufacture

Calculation of the prime cost of manufacture is carried out in 3 separate steps:

- calculation of **raw materials** consumed;
- calculation of **direct labour costs**;
- calculation of **direct overheads**.

Calculation of cost of raw materials consumed

Raw materials can be one of the most important components of the overall costs, particularly for high-value materials. Changes in the costs of raw materials, as a result of changing prices, can have a significant impact on the overall profitability of a product.

Example 1

AB plc, a manufacturing concern, provides you with the following information and asks you to calculate the cost of raw materials used in production.

Opening stock	£2,000
Purchase of raw materials	£10,000
Materials returned to supplier	£500
Carriage inwards on raw materials	£200
Closing stock	£2,500

You will be familiar with calculating the cost of goods sold from the Trading Account and if you look carefully the same elements will appear, but for raw materials (opening stock, purchases, returns, carriage inwards and closing stock). The calculation is the same and is set out as follows:

Cost of raw materials consumed:	£	£
Opening stock		2,000
Add Purchases	10,000	
Add Carriage inwards	200	
	10,200	
Less Purchase returns	500	9,700
		11,700
Less Closing stock		2,500
Cost of raw materials consumed		9,200

Task 1

Calculate the cost of raw materials consumed by the following firms. Use the layout above to set out your answer.

	AB plc £	BC plc £	CD plc £	DE plc £	EF plc £
Raw materials					
Opening stock	10,000	5,000	8,000	12,000	35,000
Closing stock	9,000	6,500	9,300	11,200	32,500
Purchases	75,000	45,000	125,000	78,000	90,000
Carriage inwards	500	2,300	4,500	1,000	800
Purchase returns	2,500	3,000	8,500	2,000	4,500

Calculation of direct labour costs

As with most enterprises, a manufacturing concern needs to keep a close check on its labour costs.

Example 2

AB plc, a manufacturing concern, provides you with the following information and asks you to calculate the **cost of direct labour** used in production.

	£
Direct wages paid	£75,000
Direct wages accrued	£3,500

When calculating the cost of direct labour for the Manufacturing Account any accruals or prepayments of labour must be included. Remember an accrual is an amount due to be paid.

The labour cost to be included in the prime cost section of the Manufacturing Account will be:

Labour cost = direct wages paid + direct wages accrued at year end
= £75,000 + £3,500
= £78,500

 Task 2

Calculate the cost of direct labour for the following firms.

	AB plc £	BC plc £	CD plc £	DE plc £	EF plc £
Wages paid	100,000	76,900	38,400	120,200	42,000
Wages due at 31 Dec	8,700	5,200	1,300	12,300	4,300
Direct labour					

Calculation of the cost of direct expenses

Although they are sometimes harder to see, it is essential to account for all the direct expenses incurred in a manufacturing process.

Example 3

AB plc, a manufacturing concern, provides you with the following information and asks you to calculate the direct expense costs for the year.

Direct power	£12,500
Royalties	£3,000
Hire of special machine	£12,000

These costs should be shown separately in the prime cost section of the Manufacturing Account.

continued ➤

Example 3 continued

Direct expenses are the third component of the direct costs which make up the prime cost of manufacture. They include all the costs which are not either labour or materials costs. In this case, the direct expenses are simply the sum of the three items listed:

Direct expenses:	
Direct power	£12,500
Royalties	£3,000
Hire of special machine	£12,000
Total	**£27,500**

These costs, along with direct labour are entered in the Manufacturing Account and are added to the cost of raw materials consumed to calculate the prime cost of manufacture.

Task 3

Calculate the cost of direct expenses for the following firms.

	AB plc £	BC plc £	CD plc £	DE plc £	EF plc £
Direct Expenses					
Direct Power	20,000	15,000	9,000	15,000	67,000
Hire of machine			2,500		
Royalties	1,200		900	1,300	4,550

Addition of all costs into prime costs

When the individual components of raw materials, direct labour costs and direct expenses have been calculated, these figures need to be collated in the prime cost statement section of the Manufacturing Account.

AB plc
Manufacturing Account for year ended 31 December Year 1

Cost of raw materials consumed:	£	£	£
Opening stock		2,000	
Add Purchases	10,000		
Add Carriage inwards	200		
	10,200		
Less Purchase returns	500	9,700	
		11,700	
Less Closing stock		2,500	
Cost of raw materials consumed		9,200	

AB plc Manufacturing Account for year ended 31 December Year 1	£	£	£
Add Direct labour (75,000 + 3,500)		78,500	
Add other direct expenses			
Direct power	12,500		
Hire of machine	3,000		
Royalties	12,000	27,500	
Prime Cost of Manufacture			115,200

All workings must be shown for calculations included in financial statements. You can either have a separate note or you can show the calculations in brackets beside the figure, as shown above for direct labour.

Manufacturing overheads

Manufacturing overheads are the second set of costs required for the Manufacturing Accounts. **Manufacturing overheads** are also known as the **factory overheads**, **fixed costs** or **indirect costs** – 3 names for the same cost.

Manufacturing overheads are costs which cannot be directly identified in the manufactured product but are incurred by the factory as a whole. For example, factory rent and rates, factory manager's salary, heat and light, depreciation of factory machinery, factory repairs, indirect material, loose tools.

Example 4

AB plc, a manufacturing concern, provides you with the following information and asks you to calculate the manufacturing overhead cost for the year

	£
Rent and rates	5,000
Rent due at 31 December Year 1	1,000
Factory repairs	4,000
Factory insurance	3,250
Factory insurance prepaid at 31 December Year 1	250
Depreciation of machinery	3,000

Any adjustments for accruals and prepayments will have to be made to the above figures before inclusion in the Manufacturing Account.

Prime Cost of Manufacture			115,200
Add Factory overheads			
Rent and rates (5,000 + 1,000)		6,000	
Factory repairs		4,000	
Factory insurance (3,250 – 250)		3,000	
Depreciation of machinery		3,000	16,000
			131,200

FINANCIAL ACCOUNTING

The **prime cost** of manufacture and the **factory overheads** are added together and equal the **total manufacturing cost incurred**. However this is not the total cost of manufacture as we still have to deal with **work-in-progress**, which is the third section of the Manufacturing Account.

Stock of work-in-progress

Stock of **work-in-progress** is the third set of costs required for the Manufacturing Account. Stock of work-in-progress represents the value of the partly completed work in the factory at the start and end of the financial year.

Work at the start of the financial year will be completed and its costs included in the manufacturing account and the units in the good output. Work-in-progress at the end of the year will be carried forward to the following year's manufacture and therefore its cost must be deducted from the cost of manufacture.

Example 5

At the end of the year AB plc, informs you that the stock of work-in-progress at the start and end of the year was as follows:

	£
Stock of work-in-progress at 1 January Year 1	3,200
Stock of work-in-progress at 31 December Year 1	2,600

Depreciation of machinery		3,000	16,000
			131,200
Add Work-in-progress at 1 January Year 1			3,200
			134,400
Less Work-in-progress at 31 December Year 1			2,600
Manufacturing cost of production			131,800

Example 6

The following list of balances were taken from the ledger accounts of R MacTavish plc, a manufacturer of plastic chairs, for the year ended 31 December Year 1.

	£000*
Stock of raw materials – 1 January	25
Stock of work-in-progress – 1 January	10
Raw materials purchased	105
Purchase returns of raw materials	5
Carriage on raw materials	8
Direct manufacturing wages	22
Direct manufacturing wages due	3
Manufacturing royalties	8
Direct power	10
Factory lighting	6
Factory rent and rates	10
Rates due	1
Depreciation of machinery	5
Factory repairs	3
Factory manager's salary	12
Stock of raw materials – 31 December	23
Stock of work-In-progress – 31 December	9

* In this example the zeros for thousands are omitted. Many of the questions you will be asked to answer will appear this way.

STEP 1 – Calculate the prime cost of manufacture and enter into the account

Remember this is completed in 3 steps:

- Calculation of raw materials consumed;
- Calculation of direct labour costs;
- Calculation of direct expenses.

The cost of goods manufactured or produced is then calculated and transferred to the Trading Account of the manufacturing concern.

The Manufacturing Account will appear as follows:

continued ➤

Example 6 continued

R MacTavish plc Manufacturing Account for year ended 31 December Year 1	£000s	£000s	£000s
Cost of raw materials consumed			
Opening stock raw materials		25	
Add Purchases raw materials	105		
Add Carriage inwards	8		
	113		
Less Purchase returns of raw materials	5	108	
		133	
Less closing stock raw materials		23	110
Add direct costs			
Manufacturing wages (22 + 3)		25	
Manufacturing royalties		8	
Direct power		10	43
Prime Cost of Manufacture			153

STEP 2 – Calculate factory overheads

Remember to adjust for accruals and prepayments.

Add Factory Overheads			
Factory lighting		6	
Factory rent and rates (10 – 1)		9	
Depreciation of machinery		5	
Factory repairs		3	
Factory manager's salary		12	35
			188

STEP 3 – Adjust for work-in-progress to calculate manufacturing cost of production

			188
Add Work-in-progress 1 January Year 1			10
			198
Less Work-in-progress 31 December Year 1			9
Manufacturing Cost of Production			189

Now do Worksheet 5.1

Transferring manufacturing costs into the Trading Account

The next stage in calculating trading profits for a manufacturing concern is to transfer the manufacturing costs into the Trading Account.

The finished goods will be transferred from the factory into the warehouse ready for sale and the manufacturing cost of production will be transferred into the Trading Account.

Included in the Trading Account will be the expenses incurred in storing the finished goods prior to sale. These are known as **warehouse expenses**. Sometimes this general term will be used, but at other times individual expenses will be allocated to the Trading Account as part of the warehousing costs. These expenses will include indirect wages, rent, insurance etc of the warehouse.

The manufacturing cost of production will be transferred into the Trading Account at the cost figure.

Example 7

R MacTavish plc provide you with the following information relating to their trading activities during year 1:

	£000
Stock of finished goods 1 January Year 1	20
Purchase of finished goods	30
Sales	420
Stock of finished goods at 31 December Year 1	35
Warehouse expenses	15

We know from the Manufacturing Account that the manufacturing cost of production was £189,000.

You are already familiar with Trading Accounts. What you need to learn is how to transfer the cost of the manufactured goods into the Trading Account.

Head up the Trading Account in the normal way:

R MacTavish plc **Trading Account for year ended 31 December Year 1**	£000	£000	£000
Sales			420
Less Cost of goods sold			
Opening stock of finished goods	20		
Add Purchases of finished goods	30		
***Add* Manufacturing Cost of Production**	**189**	239	
Less Closing stock of finished goods		35	
Cost of goods sold		204	
Add Warehouse expenses		15	219
Gross Profit			201

continued ➤

Task 4

From the following information prepare the Trading Accounts of the following manufacturing concerns to calculate their gross profit for the year ended 31 December Year 1.

	AB plc £000s	BC plc £000s	CD plc £000s	DE plc £000s	EF plc £000s
Sales	200	176	139	86	93
Stocks of finished goods:					
Opening stock	20	17	9	13	10
Closing stock	18	19	11	10	8
Purchase of finished goods	20	13	0	16	9
Warehouse expenses	20	10	8	9	11
Manufacturing Cost of Production	100	80	50	40	30

Sharing of overhead expenses between factory, warehouse and office

Within the factory building there will be a warehouse to store finished goods and there may be administrative offices. The cost of heat, rent, rates, insurance etc of the warehouse and office is not a manufacturing expense and the total should not be included as a manufacturing cost. These expenses should be charged for the warehouse in the Trading Account, and for the office in the Profit and Loss Account.

As only one figure is normally given for shared expenses, the amounts to be charged to manufacturing costs and against the profits in the Profit and Loss Account will have to be calculated. This is usually calculated on a ratio or percentage basis.

Example 8

The rent for the year of £6,000 is to be apportioned between the factory, warehouse and the office in the ratio of 3:2:1.

To calculate the amount to be charged add the 3 ratios together:
    Total = 3 + 2 +1 = 6:

Then divide the rent by the total = 6,000 ÷ 6
                    = £1,000

For the factory, to calculate the cost for rent, multiply £1,000 × 3:
    Amount to be charged = £1,000 × 3 = £3,000

For the warehouse, the cost is £1,000 × 2:
    Amount to be charged = £1,000 × 2 = £2,000

continued ➤

Example 8   continued

For the office, the cost is £1,000 × 1:
   Amount to be charged = £1,000 × 1 = £1,000

The factory rent will be ³⁄₆ (or ½) of £6,000   = £3,000

The warehouse rent will be ²⁄₆ (or ⅓) of £6,000   = £2,000

The office rent will be ⅙ of £6,000 = £1,000   = £1,000

Always check that the total of the apportionments agrees with total expenses to be divided between the various cost centres. Expenses may also be divided between the factory, the warehouse and the office on a percentage basis.

Example 9

Insurance costs of £2,000 for the year are to be split as follows: 60% charged against the factory, 25% to the warehouse and 15% charged against the office.

Factory insurance will be 60% of £2,000   = £1,200
Warehouse insurance will be 25% of £2,000 =   £500
Office insurance will be 15% of £2,000   =   £300

Remember you may have to adjust the expenses figure for accruals and prepayments **before dividing** the total expenses for the year between the factory and the office.

Task 5

1   Calculate the figures to be included in the Manufacturing Account and Profit and Loss Account of XYZ Manufacturing plc if expenses are to be apportioned between the factory, warehouse and the office using the basis shown:

	Rent and Rates	Building Insurance	Heat and Light
Expense amount	£15,000	£25,000	£8,000
Factory	½	50%	75%
Warehouse	¼	30%	15%
Office	¼	20%	10%

continued ➤

2 Calculate the figures to be included in the Manufacturing Account and Profit and Loss Account of Consul Manufacturing plc if expenses are to be apportioned between the factory, warehouse and the office using the basis shown:

	Building Insurance	Building Repairs	Rent
Expense amount	£24,000	£5,000	£36,000
Factory	½	60%	½
Warehouse	¼	25%	⅜
Office	¼	15%	⅛

3 Calculate the figures to be included in the Manufacturing Account and Profit and Loss Account of Zepher plc if expenses are to be apportioned between the factory, warehouse and the office using the basis shown:

	Insurance	Heat and Light	Rent and Rates
Expense amount	£6,000	£8,000	£60,000
Factory	60%	⅗	80%
Warehouse	25%	⅕	15%
Office	15%	⅕	5%

4 Calculate the figures to be included in the Manufacturing Account and Profit and Loss Account of Ford plc if expenses are to be apportioned between the factory, warehouse and the office using the following basis:

	Insurance	Heat and Light	Indirect Wages	Rent and Rates
Expense amount	£5,000	£12,000	£18,000	£20,000
Factory	55%	⅝	50%	60%
Office	25%	⅛	10%	10%
Warehouse	20%	¼	40%	30%

5 Calculate the figures to be included in the Manufacturing Account and Profit and Loss Account of Morris plc if expenses are to be apportioned between the factory, warehouse and the office using the following basis:

	Insurance	Rates	Indirect Wages
Expense amount	£15,000	£8,000	£40,000
Factory	⅔	50%	35%
Office	⅙	15%	25%
Warehouse	⅙	35%	40%

 *Now do Worksheet 5.2*

Manufacturing cost per unit

Some manufacturing concerns like to produce additional information from their Manufacturing Accounts in order to compare the results from one year to another or their results with competitors. One very useful additional piece of information is the **cost per unit of output**.

Example 10

School Direct plc produced 200,000 plastic school chairs at a total cost of £400,000. What is the cost per unit of output?

Cost per chair = manufacturing costs ÷ chairs produced
$$= £400,000 ÷ 50,000 \text{ chairs}$$
$$= £8 \text{ per chair}$$

Profit on manufacture

Some manufacturing concerns like to compare their cost of manufacture with the wholesale cost of their output. They do this to see whether it has been more or less profitable to manufacture the product rather than purchase the items and sell them on.

The enterprise will calculate the profit on manufacture by comparing the cost of manufacture with the wholesale cost of buying the same product.

Example 11

The work-in-progress and manufacturing cost of productions section of the Manufacturing Account is shown below. The enterprise could purchase the same quantity of goods from another manufacturer at a wholesale cost of £250,000. In order to make a useful comparison, it is necessary to calculate the profit on manufacture.

Profit on manufacture = wholesale cost of output – manufacturing cost of output
$$= £250,000 – £189,000$$
$$= £61,000$$

The profit figure is added to the manufacturing cost of output in the Manufacturing Account and the wholesale cost of the output is shown.

R MacTavish plc	
	£000s
	188
Add Work-in-progress 1 Jan Year 1	10
	198
Less Work-in-progress 31 Dec Year 1	9
Manufacturing Cost of Production	189
Profit on Manufacture	61
Wholesale cost of output	250

FINANCIAL ACCOUNTING

Task 6

From the following information calculate the profit on manufacture for the following firms.

	AB plc £	BC plc £	CD plc £	DE plc £	EF plc £
Manufacturing Cost of Production	50,000	26,900	32,300	123,600	500,500
Wholesale Cost of Output	90,000	56,300	47,500	250,000	806,000

For each enterprise state the amount to be transferred to the Trading Account.

Transfer to the Trading and Profit and Loss Accounts

Where a profit is calculated on manufacture the wholesale cost of output figure is transferred to the Trading Account and any profit on manufacture is added to the gross profit from the Trading Account. This will increase the cost of goods sold, reducing the gross profit, however the profit on manufacture will be added to the gross profit, increasing profits.

Trading Account of ABC plc for year ended 31 December Year 1	£	£	£
Sales			420
Less Cost of goods sold			
Opening stock of finished goods	20		
Add Purchases of finished goods	30		
Add Wholesale cost of output	250	300	
Less Closing stock of finished goods		35	
Cost of goods sold			335
Gross Profit			85
Add Profit on Manufacture			61
			146
Less Expenses			

 Now do Worksheets 5.3 and 5.4

Partnerships

What is a partnership?

A partnership is a form of business enterprise. The 1890 Partnership Act defines a partnership as *the relation which subsists between persons carrying on a business in common with a view of profit.*

Examples of partnerships are solicitors, accountants, architects, surveyors, estate agents, dentists, doctors as well as small business concerns such as plumbers and joiners. Partnerships can be formed for almost any purpose.

Partnerships are assumed to exist where the partners actually share profits and losses proportionately, even though there may not be a written partnership agreement signed between the partners. The minimum number required to form a partnership is two and the maximum is 20, although there can be exceptions, such as solicitors and accountants.

There is no legal obligation for a written agreement to be drawn up when a partnership is formed but this is advisable. Where no agreement is drawn up then the partners are protected by Section 24 of the Partnership Act 1890 which states:

- All partners are entitled to contribute equally to the capital of the firm.
- Profits and losses of the partnership are to be shared equally by the partners.
- No interest is payable on capital invested but if a partner lends money to the partnership then that partner is entitled to interest on the loan at a rate of 5% per annum.
  (Note: This interest is a charge against the profits in the Profit and Loss Account.)
- The accounts of the partnership must be freely available to all partners.
- No partner may have a salary.
- No new partner may be introduced without the prior agreement of all existing partners.

- Any disagreements by the partners can be settled by majority vote. However, there are certain matters which must be settled by all partners agreeing.
- All partners have the right to take part in the management of the partnership.

Partnership agreement

It is usually better for Partners to draw up their own partnership agreement, rather than use Section 24 of the 1890 Partnership Act when forming a partnership. It should be drawn up in writing and should include details of:

- the amount of capital each partner is to contribute and whether capital is fixed or not;
- how profits and losses, including capital profits and losses, are to be shared;
- the amount each partner is to be allowed to withdraw (drawings) from the partnership;
- whether interest, and how much, is to be allowed on the partners' capital invested;
- whether interest, and how much, is to be charged on partners' drawings;
- whether or not a partner is to be allowed a salary. (Sometimes one partner will carry out more work in the business than the others and it may be agreed to pay him a salary. This can often happen with a junior partner);

In most cases like a sole trader the liability of a partner for the debts of the partnership is unlimited unless a partner is classed as a limited partner of the partnership under the Limited Liability Partnership Act 2000.

Limited partners

Under the Limited Partnership Act of 1907 a partnership may register with the Registrar of Companies to allow one or more partners to become a **limited partner**. A limited partner is one who contributes capital in the form of money or property to the partnership but who is not responsible for any of the debts of the partnership over the amount they have invested in the partnership.

Limited liability means that if the partnership fails, the **limited partner** would only loose the amount invested in the partnership, whereas a **general partner** could also lose personal possessions such as their home, car, etc, which could be sold to pay partnership debts.

Where a limited partner exists in a partnership, one or more one of the other partners must be classed as a general partner. These partners have unlimited liability.

Limited partners may not:

- withdraw or receive back any part of the capital they have invested in the business during the lifetime of the partnership;
- take part in the management of the partnership;
- make contracts on behalf of the partnership.

Limited Liability Partnership Act 2000

A partnership formed under the Limited Liability Partnership Act must register with the Registrar of Companies in Edinburgh in Scotland, Cardiff in Wales and London in England and lodge an incorporation document.

In many ways a limited liability partnership is like that of a company. Members have the advantage of limited liability, but with the more flexible structure of management than the traditional partnership.

This type of partnership has an unlimited membership capacity but requires a minimum of 2 members who will have signed the incorporation document.

Partners are advised to draw up a partnership agreement similar to that of a traditional partnership. If no agreement is drawn up the conditions set out in the Act will apply to any disputes or disagreements. New members can be admitted to the partnership with the agreement of the other partners.

Like a company, the partnership is a separate legal entity and can make contracts. It must lodge its audited accounts with the Registrar of Companies.

A successful sole trader may decide that the only way for his business to continue to grow is to take on a partner to help with the running of the business.

Partnerships have several advantages and disadvantages over a sole trader business.

Advantages of partnerships

- Relatively easy to form. There are no legal formalities to follow unless there is a limited partner or it is formed under the Limited Liability Partnership Act 2000.
- Partners can specialise in one area of the business. For example, one accountant may specialise in tax and another in auditing accounts.
- More capital will be available to the partnership.
- The workload of the partnership can be spread allowing partners to take holidays without the business being affected.
- Decision making is shared.
- A partnership might find it easier to raise funds in the form of a loan as they tend to be a bigger business than a sole trader.

Disadvantages of partnerships

- There are more people to share in the profits (and possible losses) of the business.
- General partners have unlimited liability.
- Disagreements can occur as to the direction the business should take.
- Decisions made by one partner are binding on all the partners
- A partnership will need to be dissolved if one partner dies
- Partners can be sued since the partnership is unincorporated.

Task 1

1   What is a partnership?

2   List six items which should be included in a partnership agreement.

3   List three advantages and three disadvantages of forming a partnership

4   Explain the term *limited partner*.

5   State one advantage of being a limited partner

6   What are the restrictions placed on a limited partner.

7   Explain the term *general partner*.

8   Outline the significance of the Limited Liability Partnership Act 2000 to the formation of partnerships.

Accounting for partnerships

Like a sole trader a partnership will keep ledger accounts and prepare Trading Accounts, Profit and Loss Accounts and Balances Sheets at the end of the financial year.

In addition to the Trading and Profit and Loss Accounts, a partnership will prepare an Appropriation Account, and keep separate capital, drawings and current accounts.

Capital Accounts

A sole trader's investment in his business is shown in his capital account. In a partnership each partner will have his own capital account showing the amount he/she has invested in the business at the start of the partnership. Normally no other entry will be made in the capital account unless the partner is bringing in more capital, withdrawing capital or the partnership is re-valued on the admission of a new partner.

Drawings accounts

The drawings account shows the withdrawals of cash or other assets (such as stock) made by the partners during the year. At the end of the financial year the drawings amount will be transferred to the current account of the appropriate partner.

Current accounts

Partners' investments in their business are fixed, so a separate ledger account is kept to show the income and drawings for each partner. This information is kept in the partner's current accounts. These accounts record for each partner the share of profit, interest paid or charged, salaries paid and drawings. They are kept separate from the partner's capital account which remains static.

Profit and Loss Appropriation Account

Partnerships need to calculate their gross and net profits in the same way as a sole trader. The net profit is then shared between the partners according to the partnership agreement. The account which shows this sharing of the net profits is called the Profit and Loss Appropriation Account.

Example 1

Andrew and David started business as a partnership with capitals of £30,000 and £20,000 respectively. Their partnership agreement states that:

- Profits will be shared between Andrew and David in the ratio of 3:2.
- David is to receive a salary of £10,000 per annum.
- During the year Andrew withdrew from the partnership £20,000 and David £12,000.

At the end of Year 1 they have made a net profit of £50,000.

You are required to prepare the Appropriation Account for the year ended 31 December Year 1.

STEP 1 – Set out the Appropriation Account format and enter the net profit

Profit and Loss Appropriation Account of Andrew and David For year ended 31 December Year 1			
	£	£	£
Net Profit	**50,000**	**50,000**	**50,000**

STEP 2 – Add any sources of income to the partnership

In this example there is no other source of income, but if interest was charged on drawings it would be added to the net profit at this point.

STEP 3 – Deduct the appropriations of profit outlined in the partnership agreement

These would be any salary or interest on capital being paid to the partners. The figure left after the partnership agreement deductions have been made is called the **residual profit**. The amount to be shared between the partners according to their profit sharing ratios.

Profit and Loss Appropriation Account of Andrew and David For year ended 31 December Year 1			
	£	£	£
Net Profit			50,000
Less **Appropriations**			
Salary – David			10,000
Residual Profit			40,000

continued ➤

FINANCIAL ACCOUNTING

Example 1 continued

STEP 4 – Share residual profit between partners in their profit-sharing ratios and enter into the Appropriation Account

The residual profit is the amount available for division between the partners after the terms of the partnership agreement has been met.

Profit sharing ratios:

Andrew	3
David	2
Total	5

This means that Andrew is to receive 3/5 of the residual profit and David 2/5.

Andrew receives 3/5 of £40,000   = £24,000
David receives 2/5 of £40,000   = £16,000

Profit and Loss Appropriation Account of Andrew and David For year ended 31 December Year 1		
	£	£
Net Profit		50,000
Less Appropriations		
Salary – David		<u>10,000</u>
Residual Profit		40,000
Share of Profits:		
Andrew	**24,000**	
David	**<u>16,000</u>**	**<u>40,000</u>**

All profits are shared between the partners. There will be no balance of profits carried forward to the next financial year.

The figures in the Appropriation Account are then transferred to the current account.

STEP 5 – Transfer of salary and profits to the current accounts

You will need to open a current account for each partner. Any amount a partner is due to receive will be **credited** to the **current account**, any amount they are due to pay to the partnership or have already withdrawn from it will be **debited**.

Andrew's Current Account					
Date	Details	Dr	Cr	Balance	
Dec 31	Share of profit		24,000	24,000	Cr

continued ➤

Example 1 continued

David's Current Account

Date	Details	Dr	Cr	Balance	
Dec 31	Salary		10,000	10,000	Cr
Dec 31	Share of profit		16,000	26,000	Cr

STEP 6 – Transferring drawings to the current account

The drawings made by each partner throughout the year are recorded in a drawings account. At the end of the year, the total of the **drawings account** is transferred to the **current account** of each partner.

The drawings accounts for Andrew and David are shown below:

Andrew's Drawings Account

Date	Details	Dr	Cr	Balance	
Dec 31	Balance	20,000		20,000	Dr
Dec 31	Current Account		20,000	nil	

David's Drawings Account

Date	Details	Dr	Cr	Balance	
Dec 31	Balance	12,000		12,000	Dr
Dec 31	Current Account		12,000	nil	

The drawings accounts are closed off by transferring the total to the current accounts.

Andrew's Current Account

Date	Details	Dr	Cr	Balance	
Dec 31	Share of profit		24,000	24,000	Cr
Dec 31	Drawings	20,000		4,000	Cr

David's Current Account

Date	Details	Dr	Cr	Balance	
Dec 31	Salary		10,000	10,000	Cr
Dec 31	Share of profit		16,000	26,000	Cr
Dec 31	Drawings	12,000		14,000	Cr

The final balances on the current accounts show how much the partner is entitled to withdraw from the partnership without affecting his capital. The balances will appear in the **financed by** section of the partner's balance sheet.

Task 2

From the following information prepare the following accounts for each partnership, on 31 December Year 1:

1 Profit and Loss Appropriation Account

2 Drawings accounts

3 Current accounts

	Profit sharing ratios	Partner's Drawings £	Salary £	Net Profit £
Partnership A & B Net Profit				25,000
A	3	8,000		
B	2	6,000	5,000	
Partnership C & D Net Profit				38,000
C	2	12,500	8,000	
D	1	6,250		
Partnership E & F Net Profit				32,500
E	1	7,200		
F	1	6,900	9,000	
Partnership G & H Net Profit				36,000
G	3	18,200		
H	1	5,900	6,000	
Partnership I & J Net Profit				72,000
I	5	25,300	8,000	
J	3	19,900		

Interest on capital

Partnership agreements often state that the partners are to receive interest on their capital invested. This is often the case where partners invest different amounts. It acts as a reward for the partner who has contributed the most capital.

The **interest on capital** will be deducted in the **Appropriation Account** before the calculation of the share of profits.

Example 2

Richard and Gwen are in partnership sharing their profits and losses in proportion to capital invested. Their partnership agreements states that interest on capital is to be allowed at 5% per annum. They provide you with the following additional information at the end of Year 1.

Capital: Richard £75,000, Gwen £25,000
Drawings: Richard £12,500, Gwen £3,400
Net Profit: £60,000
Salary: Gwen £6,500.

Prepare the Appropriation Account, current accounts and drawings accounts of the partners.

STEPS 1–3 – Open the Appropriation Account, enter net profit and salary

Profit and Loss Appropriation Account of Richard and Gwen For year ended 31 December Year 1			
	£	£	£
Net Profit			**60,000**
Less **Appropriations**			
Salary – Gwen		**6,500**	

STEP 4 – Calculate interest on capital and enter into the Appropriation Account

Interest on capital is to be allowed at 5% of capital invested.

The working notes for the interest on capital calculations can be shown in brackets instead of separate working notes. This can save valuable time in an examination.

Profit and Loss Appropriation Account of Richard and Gwen For year ended 31 December Year 1			
	£	£	£
Net Profit			60,000
Less Appropriations			
Salary – Gwen		6,500	
Interest on Capital			
Richard (5% of £75,000)	3,750		
Gwen (5% of £25,000)	1,250	5,000	

continued ➤

Example 2 continued

STEP 5 – Calculate residual profit and share between the partners

Profit and Loss Appropriation Account of Richard and Gwen For year ended 31 December Year 1			
	£	£	£
Net Profit			60,000
Less Appropriations			
Salary – Gwen		6,500	
Interest on Capital			
Richard (5% of £75,000)	3,750		
Gwen (5% of £25,000)	1,250	5,000	11,500
Residual Profit			**48,500**
Share of Profits			
Richard (¾ of £48,500)		36,375	
Gwen (¼ of £48,500)		12,125	48,500

Richard and Gwen share profits in proportion to their capital invested. You need to calculate the ratio:

Richard	£75,000
Gwen	£25,000
Total	£100,000

They will receive the following proportions:

Richard	£75,000/£100,000
Gwen	£25,000/£100,000

These figures need to be reduced to more manageable fractions or converted to percentages.

Richard	¾ or 75%
Gwen	¼ or 25%

STEP 6 – Transfer the appropriations and share of profit to the current accounts

Richard's Current Account					
Date	Details	Dr	Cr	Balance	
Dec 31	Interest on Capital		3,750	3,750	Cr
Dec 31	Share of profit		36,375	40,125	

continued ➤

Example 2 continued

Gwen's Current Account

Date	Details	Dr	Cr	Balance	
Dec 31	Salary		6,500	6,500	Cr
Dec 31	Interest on capital		1,250	7,750	
Dec 31	Share of profit		12,125	19,875	Cr

STEP 7 – Transfer the drawings from the drawings account to the current account

Richard's Drawings Account

Date	Details	Dr	Cr	Balance	
Dec 31	Balance	12,500		12,500	Dr
Dec 31	Current Account		12,500	nil	

Gwen's Drawings Account

Date	Details	Dr	Cr	Balance	
Dec 31	Balance	3,400		12,000	Dr
Dec 31	Current Account		3,400	nil	

Richard's Current Account

Date	Details	Dr	Cr	Balance	
Dec 31	Interest on Capital		3,750	3,750	Cr
Dec 31	Share of profit		36,375	40,125	
Dec 31	Drawings	12,500		27,625	Cr

Gwen's Current Account

Date	Details	Dr	Cr	Balance	
Dec 31	Salary		6,500	6,500	Cr
Dec 31	Interest on capital		1,250	7,750	
Dec 31	Share of profit		12,125	19,875	Cr
Dec 31	Drawings	3,400		16,475	Cr

Current account balances

Current accounts will not always have credit balances. Sometimes the partner will have withdrawn more from the partnership than he was entitled to. In this event the balance on the current account will be a debit balance.

If a partnership has existed for several years there may already be a balance on the current accounts of the partners. If the balance is credit this represent money the partner was entitled to withdraw from the business in the previous year which has been left in the business. If the balance is debit this indicates that the partner withdrew more from the business than his entitlement, so he owes the partnership the amount of the debit balance.

Task 3

From the following information prepare the following accounts for each partnership and partner, on 31 December Year 1:

1 Profit and Loss Appropriation Account

2 Drawings accounts

3 Current accounts

	Capital	Profit sharing ratios	Interest on Capital	Partner's Drawings £	Salary £	Net Profit £
Partnership Alan & Eileen Net Profit						40,000
Alan	30,000	Proportion to capital	5%	9,000		
Eileen	20,000			8,000	12,000	
Partnership Carol & Matthew Net Profit						60,000
Carol	60,000	2	6%	10,000	14,000	
Matthew	30,000	1		8,500		
Partnership Graham & Morven Net Profit						75,000
Morven	50,000	1	5%	7,200		
Graham	50,000	1		6,900	10,000	
Partnership Robin & Mark Net Profit						78,000
Robin	75,000	3	5%	10,000		
Mark	25,000	1		7,500	18,000	
Partnership George & Val Net Profit						45,000
George	50,000	5	7%	16,700	12,000	
Val	30,000	3		13,500		

Additions to net profit in Appropriation Account

Interest on drawings

Partner's drawing can be in the form of cash, stock or other benefits (such as house decoration carried out by the firm's own workers). Some partnership agreements will allow for interest to be charged on drawings. This is often done to restrict the drawings made by each partner. Any interest charged on drawings is a gain to the partnership and will be added to the **net profit** in the **appropriation account**. Interest charged on drawings is debited in the current account.

Example 3

Wilson and Whyte are in partnership. Their net profit for the year ended 31 December Year 2 was £58,000. Their partnership agreement includes these conditions:

1 Opening balances on the current accounts are: Wilson £500 Dr and Whyte £600 Cr.

2 Interest is charged on drawings at the rate of 3% per annum. Wilson withdrew £28,000 during the year and Whyte £35,000.

3 Interest is allowed on capital at the rate of 5% pa. Wilson has invested £20,000 in the partnership and Whyte £30,000.

4 A salary of £5,000 will be paid to Wilson.

5 Any remaining profit is to be shared in the proportion to capital invested.

You are required to prepare the following accounts:

a) Appropriation Account for the year ended 31 December Year 2

b) Current accounts

c) Drawings account

STEP 1 – Set up the Appropriation Account and enter the net profit

Wilson and Whyte Profit and Loss Appropriation Account For year ended 31 December Year 2			
	£	£	£
Net Profit			58,000

continued ➤

Example 3 continued

STEP 2 – Calculate the interest charged on drawings and add to the net profit

Working notes for this calculation can be shown in the Appropriation Account.

Wilson and Whyte Profit and Loss Appropriation Account For year ended 31 December Year 2			
	£	£	£
Net Profit			58,000
Add Interest on Drawings			
Wilson (3% of £28,000)		840	
Whyte (3% of £35,000)		1,050	1,890
			59,890

STEP 3 – Complete the remainder of the Appropriation Account

Wilson and Whyte Profit and Loss Appropriation Account For year ended 31 December Year 2			
	£	£	£
Net Profit			58,000
Add Interest on Drawings			
Wilson (3% of £28,000)		840	
Whyte (3% of £35,000)		1,050	1,890
			59,890
Less Appropriations			
Interest on capital:			
Wilson (5% of £20,000)	1,000		
Whyte (5% of £30,000)	1,500	2,500	
Salary – Wilson		5,000	7,500
Residual Profit			52,390
Share of Profits:			
Wilson (2/5 of £52,390)		20,956	
Whyte (3/5 of £52,390)		31,434	52,390

continued ➤

Example 3 continued

STEP 4 – Prepare the current and drawings accounts and transfer appropriations of profits to them

As the partnership has been operating for some time there are already balances on the current accounts from the start of the financial year.

Wilson's Current Account

Date	Details	Dr	Cr	Balance	
Jan 1	Balance	500		500	Dr
Dec 31	**Interest on Capital**		1,000	500	Cr
Dec 31	**Salary**		5,000	5,500	Cr
Dec 31	**Share of profit**		20,956	26,456	Cr
Dec 31	**Interest on Drawings**	840		25,616	Cr
Dec 31	**Drawings**	28,000		2,384	Dr

Whyte's Current Account

Date	Details	Dr	Cr	Balance	
Jan 1	Balance		600	600	Cr
Dec 31	**Interest on capital**		1,500	2,100	Cr
Dec 31	**Share of profit**		31,434	33,534	Cr
Dec 31	**Interest on Drawings**	1,050		32,484	Cr
Dec 31	**Drawings**	35,000		2,516	Dr

By the end of the financial year both partners have withdrawn more from the business than they were entitled to. The partners may have to discuss their drawings policy!

Wilson's Drawings Account

Date	Details	Dr	Cr	Balance	
Dec 31	Balance	28,000		28,000	Dr
Dec 31	**Current Account**		28,000	nil	

Whyte's Drawings Account

Date	Details	Dr	Cr	Balance	
Dec 31	Balance	35,000		35,000	Dr
Dec 31	**Current Account**		35,000	nil	

Partner's loan

Rather than increase the amount of capital invested in the partnership a partner may decide to provide additional funds in the form of a loan. The partner will receive an agreed amount of interest. This loan will be shown as a long-term liability in the Balance Sheet of the partnership. The interest paid on the loan is a legitimate charge against profits and will appear in the Profit and Loss Account as would a loan from the bank.

Example 4

MacIver and Turner are in partnership sharing profits and losses equally. MacIver has lent the partnership £10,000 and is to receive 5% interest. Net profit before interest on the loan amounted to £56,900.

STEP 1 – Calculate the interest on the loan

Interest on loan = 5% of £10,000 = £500

STEP 2 – Calculate the profit available for appropriation.

Profit available = Net profit (before interest on loan) – Interest on loan

£56,900 – £500 = £56,400

This can be shown in the Appropriation Account in the following way:

MacIver and Turner Profit and Loss Appropriation Account For year ended 31 December Year 1			
	£	£	£
Net Profit (before interest on loan)			56,900
Less Interest on loan			**500**
			56,400

STEP 3 – Enter the loan interest into MacIver's current account

MacIver's Current Account					
Date	Details	Dr	Cr	Balance	
Dec 31	Loan Interest		500	500	Cr

The remainder of the Apprpriate Account would be completed as before.

Example 5 continued

STEP 1 – Prepare the fixed assets section of the Balance Sheet

You are already quite familiar with this area of accounting study.

Smith and Jones
Balance Sheet as at 31 December Year 1

FIXED ASSETS	Cost £	Aggregate Depreciation £	Net Book Value £
Premises	50,000	–	50,000
Fixtures and fittings	20,000	5,000	15,000
Motor vehicles	10,000	5,000	5,000
	80,000	10,000	70,000

STEP 2 – Calculate the working capital

Smith and Jones
Balance Sheet as at 31 December Year 1

FIXED ASSETS	Cost £	Aggregate Depreciation £	Net Book Value £
Premises	50,000	–	50,000
Fixtures and fittings	20,000	5,000	15,000
Motor vehicles	10,000	5,000	5,000
	80,000	10,000	70,000
Add Working capital			
CURRENT ASSETS			
Rent prepaid	200		
Stock	2,500		
Debtors	9,500		
Bank	5,000		
Cash	500	17,700	
Less CURRENT LIABILITIES			
Creditors	3,500		
VAT	1,000		
Accrual - Wages due	200	4,700	13,000
			83,000

*This is the **current assets – current liabilities** section of the Balance Sheet.*

continued ➤

FINANCIAL ACCOUNTING

Example 5 continued

STEP 3 – Deduct long-term liabilities

Smith and Jones
Balance Sheet as at 31 December Year 1

FIXED ASSETS	Cost £	Aggregate Depreciation £	Net Book Value £
Premises	50,000	-	50,000
Fixtures and fittings	20,000	5,000	15,000
Motor vehicles	10,000	5,000	5,000
	80,000	10,000	70,000
Add Working capital			
CURRENT ASSETS			
Rent prepaid	200		
Stock	2,500		
Debtors	9,500		
Bank	5,000		
Cash	500	17,700	
Less CURRENT LIABILITIES			
Creditors	3,500		
VAT	1,000		
Accrual - Wages due	200	4,700	13,000
			83,000
Less **LONG-TERM LIABILITIES**			
Building Society Loan		15,000	
Loan from Smith		5,000	20,000
Capital employed			63,000

STEP 4 – Prepare the finances by section of the Balance Sheet

This is slightly different from a sole trader, in that the capital accounts of the partners will remain the same figure unless additional capital is introduced. The changes to each partner's worth in the business is recorded in the current account figures.

continued ➤

Example 5 continued

Smith and Jones Balance Sheet as at 31 December Year 1			
FIXED ASSETS	Cost £	Aggregate Depreciation £	Net Book Value £
Premises	50,000	–	50,000
Fixtures and fittings	20,000	5,000	15,000
Motor vehicles	10,000	5,000	5,000
	80,000	10,000	70,000
Add Working capital			
CURRENT ASSETS			
Rent prepaid	200		
Stock	2,500		
Debtors	9,500		
Bank	5,000		
Cash	500	17,700	
Less CURRENT LIABILITIES			
Creditors	3,500		
VAT	1,000		
Accrual - Wages due	200	4,700	13,000
			83,000
Less LONG-TERM LIABILITIES			
Building Society Loan		15,000	
Loan from Smith		5,000	20,000
Capital employed			63,000
Financed by:			
Capital accounts			
Smith		30,000	
Jones		20,000	50,000
Current accounts			
Smith*		(200)	
Jones		13,200	13,000
			63,000

* Smith's current account balance is **debit**. This figure is deducted from Jones current account balance to show the net current account balances in the Balance Sheet.

Note. *The balances used for the current account figures will be the ones you calculated at the end of the year after appropriations and additions and deductions have been made to any opening balance.*

continued ➤

Task 5

From the following list of balances prepare the Balance Sheet of Tom and Jack for the year ended 31 December Year 1.

	£
Premises at cost	30,000
Furniture at cost	8,000
Motor vehicles at cost	2,000
Provision for depreciation:	
Furniture	800
Motor vehicles	200
Stock	4,200
Debtors	3,200
Provision for doubtful debts	200
Bank	5,000
Cash	500
Prepayments	500
Creditors	2,500
VAT (Cr)	350
Accruals	200
Building Society Mortgage	10,000
Capital Accounts:	
Tom	15,000
Jack	10,000
Current Accounts:	
Tom	10,150
Jack	4,000

Now do Worksheets 6.2

Now do Worksheets 6.3 and 6.4

CHAPTER 7

Admission of a new partner

Goodwill and the admission of a new partner

Goodwill is an intangible asset which may arise from the reputation of the business, the article sold, the personality of the proprietor, monopoly, trade marks, customer loyalty or a favourable locality. The term has received various legal definitions:

- nothing more than the probability that the old customers will resort to the old place;
- the benefit arising from connection and reputation;
- the cash value of a firm's good name.

If a firm has been in existence for some time and the owner(s) want to sell the business, or bring in another partner, they may be able to obtain more than the asset value of the business, by selling it as a going concern.

As Goodwill is an intangible asset it will be prudent for the partners to write off the value of Goodwill over a relatively short time.

Valuation of Goodwill

The Goodwill attached may need to be valued on the death of an existing partner, the admission of a new partner, or on the sale of the business. No general rule applies to the calculation of the value of Goodwill. It can be based on several years average operating profits before partnership salaries, interest on capital etc have been deducted, or it may be the average of the 'super profits' (profits achieved over a certain figure).

FINANCIAL ACCOUNTING

Example 1

MacKay and Thompson have been in partnership for 20 years sharing profits and losses equally. They decide to admit MacDonald into the partnership. MacDonald will bring in £50,000 cash.

Goodwill is to be valued as the average of the last 5 years profits.

Profits

Year	Profits £
1	22,500
2	25,700
3	32,500
4	36,500
5	34,700
5 year total	**151,900**

Calculate the Goodwill

Goodwill $= \text{Total Profits} \div 5$
$= £151,900 \div 5 = £30,380$

Goodwill will appear in the accounts of a business enterprise if:

- it has been purchased;
- it has been necessary to raise Goodwill in connection with the admission of a new partner;
- a partner has died and the partnership is being dissolved when it is necessary to calculate the partner's share of Goodwill to pay to his dependents;
- a partner retires.

Task 1

From the following information calculate the Goodwill to be created on admission of a new partner for the following partnerships.

Year	A & B Profits £	C & D Profits £	E & F Profits £	G & H Profits £	I & J Profits £
1	30,200	42,000	35,000	75,000	120,000
2	32,500	45,000	40,000	95,000	130,000
3	35,750	48,000	41,500	100,000	129,000
4	40,000	47,500	45,000	99,500	130,000
5	42,200	45,300	48,700	102,000	128,000

Admission of new partners

It is usual to charge an incoming partner a premium for Goodwill. The new partner may:

1. Pay a premium for the Goodwill directly to the existing partners, with no record being made in the firm's books. This is a disadvantage to the incoming partner as no record of his purchase of Goodwill appears in the firm's accounts.

2. A Goodwill account is opened and debited with the Goodwill, the existing partner's accounts being credited in their current profit sharing ratios with the Goodwill. No actual payment is made for the Goodwill. When this occurs the partners may decide that the Goodwill created is to be written off the capitals of the new partners in their new profit sharing ratios.

3. The premium 'paid' for the Goodwill by the incoming partner is retained in the business, the sum being debited to the Goodwill account and credited to the partner's capital accounts in their profit sharing ratios.

4. The premium paid for Goodwill is entered in the accounts and withdrawn, in cash, by the partners immediately.

5. An agreed amount of cash is withdrawn by the old partners (Cr cash account) and charged to the Goodwill account (Dr Goodwill).

In most questions you will be asked to complete for the admission of a new partner. Method 2 is the one most commonly used.

Revaluation of the partnership assets on admission of new partner

When a new partner is introduced the old partnership ceases to exist. Therefore, any capital gains made up to that date must be credited to the old partner's capital accounts in their existing profit sharing ratios. Any Goodwill built up by the old partners must also be credited to them in their profit sharing ratios.

Example 2

Richard and Andrew have invested £150,000 and £50,000 respectively in their business sharing profits and losses in proportion to capital. On 1 May they have the following assets and liabilities:

- Property   £40,000
- Motor vehicles   £5,000
- Office equipment   £4,000
- Debtors   £50,000
- Creditors   £20,000

They decide to admit Sarah as a partner. She will bring in capital of £15,000 and a motor vehicle worth £8,000. They agree to revalue the assets of the partnership as follows:

- Freehold property   £50,000
- Motor vehicles   £3,000
- Office equipment   £2,000
- A provision for doubtful debts of £2,000 is to be created

continued ➤

FINANCIAL ACCOUNTING

Example 2 continued

Goodwill is to be valued at £20,000 and this is to be credited to the existing partners in their profit sharing ratio. The Goodwill will then be written off the capital accounts of the new partners in their new profit sharing ratios. Sarah is to receive a 20% share of the profits. Richard and Andrew are to continue to share profits in their existing profit sharing ratios.

To record the admission of Sarah into the partnership:

STEP 1 – Record the revaluation of the assets

Ledger accounts will already exist for the assets being re-valued.

Debit the **asset** account with **increases** in value.

Credit the **asset** account with **decreases** in value.

Freehold Property Account					
Date	Details	Dr	Cr	Balance	
May 1	Balance	40,000		40,000	Dr
May 1	**Revaluation**	**10,000**		**50,000**	**Dr**

Motor Vehicle Account					
Date	Details	Dr	Cr	Balance	
May 1	Balance	5,000		5,000	Dr
May 1	**Revaluation**		**2,000**	**3,000**	

Office Equipment Account					
Date	Details	Dr	Cr	Balance	
May 1	Balance	4,000		4,000	Dr
May 1	**Revaluation**		**2,000**	**2,000**	

Debtors Accounts					
Date	Details	Dr	Cr	Balance	
May 1	Balance	50,000		50,000	Dr

As no Provision for doubtful debts exists this will have to be created.

Provision for Doubtful Debts					
Date	Details	Dr	Cr	Balance	
May 1	**Revaluation**		**2,000**	**2,000**	**Dr**

continued ➤

Example 2 continued

STEP 2 – Credit existing partners with their share of Goodwill

Debit the **Goodwill** account.

Credit the existing partners' **capital accounts** with their share.

Goodwill Account					
Date	Details	Dr	Cr	Balance	
May 1	Richard (¾ × 20,000)	15,000		15,000	Dr
May 1	Andrew (¼ × 20,000)	5,000		5,000	Dr

Richard's Capital Account					
Date	Details	Dr	Cr	Balance	
May 1	Balance		150,000	50,000	Cr
May 1	Goodwill		15,000	165,000	Cr

Andrew's Capital Account					
Date	Details	Dr	Cr	Balance	
May 1	Balance		50,000	50,000	Cr
May 1	Goodwill		5,000	55,000	Cr

STEP 3 – Open revaluation account and record increases/decreases in the value of the assets

Credit increases in value of asset.

Debit decreases in value of asset.

Revaluation Account					
Date	Details	Dr	Cr	Balance	
May 1	Freehold property		10,000	10,000	Cr
	Motor vehicles	2,000		8,000	Cr
	Office equipment	2,000		6,000	Cr
	Provision for doubtful debts	2,000		4,000	Cr

- If the **revaluation account** has a **debit** balance this means that there has been a **reduction** in the net assets value of the existing partnership. There has been a **loss** on revaluation. This loss must be deducted from the existing partners' capital figures.

- The more usual case is that there will be a **credit** balance on the **revaluation account** showing an **increase** in the net asset value of the partnership. This is a **profit** on revaluation.

continued ➤

Example 2 continued

STEP 4 – Calculate the share of profit or loss on revaluation for each partner and enter into their capital accounts

The revaluation account will be close off by transferring the profits to the capital accounts of the existing partners. The existing partners share their profits or losses equally.

Share of profit on revaluation = Profit on revaluation × profit sharing ratio

Richard's share of profit on revaluation:

£4,000 × 75% = £3,000

Andrew's share of profit on revaluation:

£4,000 × 25% = £1,000

Revaluation Account					
Date	**Details**	**Dr**	**Cr**	**Balance**	
May 1	Freehold property		10,000	10,000	Cr
	Motor vehicles	2,000		8,000	Cr
	Office equipment	2,000		6,000	Cr
	Provision for doubtful debts	2,000		4,000	Cr
	Richard's Capital	**3,000**		**1,000**	**Cr**
	Andrew's Capital	**1,000**		**nil**	

Richard's Capital Account					
Date	**Details**	**Dr**	**Cr**	**Balance**	
May 1	Balance		150,000	150,000	Cr
May 1	Goodwill		15,000	165,000	Cr
May 1	**Revaluation profit**		**3,000**	**168,000**	Cr

Andrew's Capital Account					
Date	**Details**	**Dr**	**Cr**	**Balance**	
May 1	Balance		50,000	50,000	Cr
May 1	Goodwill		5,000	55,000	Cr
May 1	**Revaluation profit**		**1,000**	**56,000**	Cr

STEP 5 – Record the admission of Sarah into the partnership

This will involve recording the capital and assets brought into the business by Sarah:

- **Debit** bank and motor vehicles
- **Credit** capital

continued ➤

Example 2 continued

Sometimes a new partner will bring fixed assets into the business. Sarah is bringing into the business money and an asset in the form of a motor vehicle. The motor vehicle account must show this new asset.

Sarah's Capital Account						
Date	**Details**		**Dr**	**Cr**	**Balance**	
May 1	Bank			15,000	15,000	Cr
May 1	Motor Vehicle			8,000	23,000	Cr

Motor Vehicle Account						
Date	**Details**		**Dr**	**Cr**	**Balance**	
May 1	Balance		5,000		5,000	Dr
May 1	Revaluation			2,000	3,000	Dr
May 1	Capital – Sarah		8,000		11,000	Dr

Bank Account						
Date	**Details**		**Dr**	**Cr**	**Balance**	
May 1	Capital – Sarah		15,000		15,000	Dr

STEP 6 – Calculate the Goodwill to be written off the partners' capital accounts

The Goodwill is to be written off using the partners' new profit-sharing ratios:

- Sarah's profit sharing ratio is 20%;

- Richard and Andrew are to continue to share the remainder of the profit in their same profit sharing ratios of 75% and 25% (Richard continues to receive 3 times as much as Andrew).

To calculate the Goodwill to be written off the partners' capital accounts, start with Sarah. She is to be debited with 20% of the Goodwill created:

Sarah's share of Goodwill = 20% of £20,000 = £4,000

Richard and Andrew are to share the remainder of the Goodwill. The remainder of the Goodwill is:

£20,000 – £4,000 = £16,000
Richard's share of Goodwill = 75% of £16,000 = £12,000
Andrew's share of Goodwill = 25% of £16,000 = £4,000

When sharing profits between the partners you would calculate their share using the same method as above.

continued ➤

Example 2 continued

STEP 7 – Adjust the capital accounts and close off the Goodwill account

Each partners' capital account will be debited with their share of Goodwill and the Goodwill account will be closed by crediting it with each partners' share.

Goodwill Account

Date	Details	Dr	Cr	Balance	
May 1	Richard	10,000		10,000	Dr
May 1	Andrew	10,000		20,000	Dr
May 1	**Capital – Richard**		**12,000**	**8,000**	**Dr**
May 1	**Capital – Andrew**		**4,000**	**4,000**	**Dr**
May 1	**Capital – Sarah**		**4,000**	**nil**	

Richard's Capital Account

Date	Details	Dr	Cr	Balance	
May 1	Balance		150,000	150,000	Cr
May 1	Goodwill		15,000	165,000	Cr
May 1	Revaluation profit		3,000	168,000	Cr
May 1	**Goodwill (written off)**	**12,000**		**156,000**	**Cr**

Andrew's Capital Account

Date	Details	Dr	Cr	Balance	
May 1	Balance		50,000	50,000	Cr
May 1	Goodwill		5,000	55,000	Cr
May 1	Revaluation profit		1,000	56,000	Cr
May 1	**Goodwill (written off)**	**4,000**		**52,000**	**Cr**

Sarah's Capital Account

Date	Details	Dr	Cr	Balance	
May 1	Bank		15,000	15,000	Cr
May 1	Motor Vehicle		8,000	23,000	Cr
May 1	**Goodwill (written off)**	**4,000**		**19,000**	**Cr**

The new partnership can then begin trading.

Sometime a question will ask for the recalculation of the profit sharing ratios to be used in future.

continued ➤

Example 2 continued

Calculation of Profit Sharing Ratios:

- Sarah is to receive 20%
- Richard is to receive 75% of (100% – 20%)
  = 75% of 80% = 60%
- Andrew is to receive 25% of (100% – 20%)
  = 25% of 80% = 20%

The new profit sharing ratios will be:

- Richard: 60%
- Andrew: 20%
- Sarah: 20%

Task 2

Calculation of new profit sharing ratios

For each of the partnerships below calculate the new profit sharing ratios.

1 Mary and Anne are in partnership sharing profits and losses in the ratio of 3:2. They admit Lesley as a partner. Lesley is to receive ⅙ of the profits and Mary and Anne will continue to share their profits and losses in the original profit sharing ratios.

2 John and James are in partnership sharing profits and losses equally. They admit Tom as a partner. Tom is to receive 20% of the profits and John and James will continue to share their profits and losses in the original profit sharing ratios.

3 Gale and Alex are in partnership sharing profits and losses in the ratio 3:1. They admit Gordon as a partner. Gordon is to receive ⅕ of the profits and Gale and Alex will continue to share their profits and losses in the original profit sharing ratios.

4 Haley and David are in partnership sharing profits and losses in the ratio 80%:20%. They admit Fred as a partner. Fred is to receive 10% of the profits and Haley and David will continue to share their profits and losses in the original profit sharing ratios.

5 Rusty and Paddy are in partnership sharing profits and losses in the ratio ¾:¼ They admit Shuna as a partner. Shuna is to receive ⅕ of the profits and Rusty and Paddy will continue to share their profits and losses in the original profit sharing ratio

Preparing the asset ledger accounts and revaluation account is time consuming in exams. You will often be asked simply to calculate the partner's share of profit or loss on revaluation, the Goodwill and to show capital accounts of the new partners.

Example 3

Stuart and Debbie have each invested £50,000 in their business. They share profits and losses equally. On 1 August they have the following assets and liabilities:

- Property   £30,000
- Furniture and fittings £10,000
- Stock   £3,500
- Debtors   £8,000
- Creditors   £5,000

They decide to admit Eileen as a partner. She will bring in capital of £30,000 and a motor vehicle worth £10,000. They agree to revalue the assets of the partnership as follows:

- Property   £50,000
- Furniture and fittings £8,000
- Stock   £3,000
- A provision for doubtful debts of £100 is to be created

Goodwill is agreed at £15,000 and this is to be credited to the existing partners in their profit sharing ratio. The Goodwill will then be written off the capital accounts of the new partners in their new profit sharing ratios.

Eileen is to receive a 20% share of the profits. Stuart and Debbie are to continue to share profits in their existing profit sharing ratios.

From the above information you are required to:

a)   Calculate the profit or loss on revaluation;

b)   Calculate the Goodwill shared by existing partners;

c)   Show the partner's capital account on admission, taking account of Goodwill written off;

d)   Calculate the new profit sharing ratios of the partners.

STEP 1 – Prepare a table to showing asset values and changes and profit or loss on revaluation

Asset	Value £	Re-valued at £	Change in value +/- £
Property	30,000	50,000	+20,000
Furniture and fittings	10,000	8,000	-2,000
Stock	3,500	3,000	-500
Debtors	8,000	7,900	-100
Profit on revaluation			+17,400

continued ➤

Example 3 continued

To calculate the profit or loss on revaluation, compare the original value and new value. The difference will be entered in the **changes in value** column. The net figure from this column will represent the profit (+) or loss (-) in revaluation.

STEP 2 – Calculate share of profit on revaluation for each partner

Stuart and Debbie share profits and losses equally, so:

- Stuart's share is 50% of £17,400 = £8,700
- Debbie's share is 50 % of £17,400 = £8,700

STEP 3 – Calculate Stuart and Debbie's share of Goodwill

Stuart's Capital Account					
Date	Details	Dr	Cr	Balance	
Aug 1	Balance		50,000	50,000	Cr
Aug 1	Revaluation profit		8,700	58,700	Cr
Aug 1	Goodwill		7,500	66,200	Cr

Debbie's Capital Account					
Date	Details	Dr	Cr	Balance	
Aug 1	Balance		50,000	50,000	Cr
Aug 1	Revaluation profit		8,700	58,700	Cr
Aug 1	Goodwill		7,500	66,200	Cr

Eileen's Capital Account					
Date	Details	Dr	Cr	Balance	
Aug 1	Bank		30,000	30,000	Cr
Aug 1	Motor Vehicle		10,000	40,000	Cr

- Stuart's share of Goodwill = 50% of £15,000 = £7,500
- Debbie's share of Goodwill = 50% of £15,000 = £7,500

continued ➤

Example 3 continued

STEP 4 – Prepare the capital accounts of all partners

Stuart's Capital Account					
Date	**Details**	**Dr**	**Cr**	**Balance**	
Aug 1	Balance		50,000	50,000	Cr
Aug 1	Revaluation profit		8,700	58,700	Cr
Aug 1	Goodwill		7,500	66,200	Cr
Aug 1	**Goodwill (written off)**	**6,000**		**60,200**	

STEP 5 – Close the Goodwill account

The Goodwill is to be written off all three partners' capital accounts in their new profit sharing ratios.

Calculation of Goodwill to be written off each partner's capital account:

- Eileen's share = 20% of £15,000 = £3,000
- Stuart's share = 50% of (£15,000 – £3,000) = £6,000
- Debbie's share = 50% of (£15,000 – £3,000) = £6,000

STEP 6 – Calculation of new profit sharing ratios

- Eileen's share = 20%
- Stuart's share: 50% of (100% – 20%) = 40%
- Debbie's share: 50% of (100% – 20% = 40%

Debbie's Capital Account					
Date	**Details**	**Dr**	**Cr**	**Balance**	
Aug 1	Balance		50,000	50,000	Cr
Aug 1	Revaluation profit		8,700	58,700	Cr
Aug 1	Goodwill		7,500	66,200	Cr
Aug 1	**Goodwill (written off)**	**6,000**		**60,200**	Cr

Eileen's Capital Account					
Date	**Details**	**Dr**	**Cr**	**Balance**	
Aug 1	Bank		30,000	30,000	Cr
Aug 1	Motor Vehicle		10,000	40,000	Cr
Aug 1	**Goodwill (written off)**	**3,000**		**37,000**	Cr

Task 3

1 Explain the accounting term **Goodwill**.

2 Describe the business attributes which are thought to give rise to Goodwill.

3 Explain when Goodwill will be valued by a partnership.

4 Explain two methods of calculating a value for Goodwill.

5 Describe three ways in which Goodwill may be treated in the accounts of a business enterprise.

 Now do Worksheet 7.1

FINANCIAL ACCOUNTING

CHAPTER 8

The accounts of limited companies

Intermediate 2 Level Outcomes: ▪▪▪➡

This chapter includes material from Int 2 level Financial Accounting Outcome 4

☆ **Explain the key features which distinguish different types of business organisations.**

☆ **Complete partially prepared final accounts of an organisation consistent with financial accounting practices.**

☆ **Complete partially prepared balance sheets of an organisation consistent with financial accounting practices.**

Higher Level Outcomes: ▪▪▪➡

This chapter includes material from Higher level Financial Accounting Outcome 1

H

☆ **Discuss the formation, funding, management, control and the reporting procedures of an organisation.**

☆ **Complete partially prepared final accounts of organisations consistent with financial accounting practice.**

☆ **Complete partially prepared balance sheets for an organisation consistent with financial accounting practice.**

I2
H

What is a limited company?

The setting up and running of a limited company is governed by the Companies Act of 1985. This is a consolidation of previous Companies Acts of 1948, 1967, 1976, 1980 and 1981.

A limited company is a type of business organisation authorised by Act of Parliament whose capital is contributed by members purchasing shares and who have the privilege of limited liability.

Limited liability means that the shareholders are only liable for the debts of the company up to the amount of their shareholding or the amount they have agreed to contribute. They are not liable for the company's debts beyond that sum.

Limited companies are the only practicable way of collecting the vast sums of capital required for the huge business ventures of the modern world.

There are two different types of limited company; private limited companies and public limited companies.

Private limited company

Features of a private limited company include:

- The company name ends in the word **limited**.
- The company cannot issue shares to the general public and shares can only be sold with the agreement of the other shareholders. A shareholder wishing to sell their shares may find it difficult to do so.
- The minimum number of directors is one and there is no age limit for members.
- Private limited companies are often family businesses with the family members or close friends being the shareholders.
- Control of the company cannot be lost to outsiders as the other members of the company must agree for shares to be sold.
- The business is a legal entity and can continue even if one or more of the shareholders dies.
- There are fewer regulations governing the running of the private limited company compared with a public limited company.
- Small and medium companies need not file full accounts and the accounts they do file need not comply fully with accounting standards.
- Shareholders receive dividends.
- Financial information must be filed with the Registrar of Public Companies. This will then be available to customers and competitors.

Public limited company

Features of a public limited company include:

- The company name ends in the word **public limited company** or **plc**.
- The plc is a separate legal entity which can make contracts, own assets, employ people, sue and be sued in its own right.
- The plc must have a minimum of £50,000 share capital.
- It has continuity of existence even if its shareholders change.
- It is run by a Board of Directors who are elected at the Annual General Meeting.
- A Chairperson is in charge of the Board of Directors.
- Shares in the company can be sold openly on the Stock Exchange.
- Shareholders have limited liability and are only liable for the amount of their shareholding or the amount they have agreed to pay for shares.
- The accounts of the plc must be lodged with the Registrar of Public Companies and are published.
- The plc will pay Corporation Tax on profits.
- There is a separation between shareholders and management who run the company.
- Shareholders receive dividends.
- The plc can make a rights issue of shares.
- Outsiders can take over ownership of the plc if they can purchase 50% of the shares.

Formation of a plc

The formation of a plc can be a very expensive process and will include the following steps:

1   The capital structure of the plc will be decided. The price to be paid will depend on whether an existing business is to be purchased, the assets to be purchased, the cost of formation and the working capital required.

2   The promoters will then approach financiers with a view to underwriting the issue of shares. Underwriting means that any unsold shares in the company will be purchased by the underwriting financiers.

3   Solicitors prepares any contract documents and lodge with the Registrar of Companies the following:

   ● Application for Registration signed by a minimum of 7 persons;
   ● Memorandum of Association;
   ● Articles of Association.

4   At this stage, a Certificate of Incorporation is issued which allows the company to start trading.

5   The Prospectus, giving details of the company, is then issued to possible investors, and filed with the Registrar

6   After the public have subscribed for the shares of the company (a minimum of 25% of the share value must be received from shareholders), the Registrar will then issue a Certificate to Commence Business and the public limited company can begin trading and its shares can be quoted on the Stock Exchange.

The Memorandum of Association

The 1985 Companies Act states that certain details must be included in the **Memorandum of Association**. This document discloses the conditions which govern the company's relationship with the outside world and will contain the following clauses:

1   The name of the company with the words **public limited company**.

2   A statement that the company is registered in Scotland or England.

3   The objects of the company and the range of its activities.

4   A statement that the members' liability is limited.

5   The amount of the authorised share capital and details of its make-up.

6   A declaration made by the first members undertaking to take up at least one share each in the company. This is called the **Association clause**.

The Articles of Association

The **Articles of Association** is a key document which sets out the rules that governs the internal running of the company and contain:

1   The rules regulating the issue of capital, transfer and forfeiture of shares.

2   The rules governing the holding of shareholders meetings: Annual, Ordinary and Extraordinary.

3   The procedure for keeping and auditing accounts.

4   The powers and duties of Directors including the length of time they can serve before re-election.

5   The rights of shareholders.

Procedure for issuing shares

A prospectus is a document issued to the general public and financial organisations inviting them to apply to purchase shares in the public limited company. The shares are usually paid for in instalments. For example, a firm selling shares at one pound each may receive the amount in several instalments, such as:

- 50p per share paid when the application is made;
- 25p per share when the allotment is made;
- 25p per share on first and final call.

The setting up of and the selling of shares in a plc is a very expensive business. The expenses incurred in this are called **preliminary and issue expenses**, also known as **formation expenses**. Often a firm will employ the services of underwriters to sell the shares for them and who will agree to purchase any unsold shares in the plc. These preliminary and issue expenses are written off the profits of the plc during the first year.

Shares can be sold:

- at **Par** – sold at their face value (their nominal value). For example, a £1 share sold for £1.
- at a **Premium** – sold for more than their face value. For example, a £1 share sold for £1.50.

Classes of shares

There are different classes of share which can be issued but the most common are **ordinary shares**, **preference shares** and **deferred** (or **founder**) **shares**.

Ordinary shares

Features of ordinary shares:

- These are the most common type of share.
- These shares have no fixed rate of dividend and only receive their dividend after all previous claims have been met.
- They are sometimes referred to as the **equity** of the company and are said to be the riskiest form of shareholding.
- If no founder or deferred shares exist ordinary shareholders are entitled to share in the remaining undistributed profits of the company.
- They carry the voting rights of the company and risk losing all if the company is wound up.

In the Balance Sheet of a plc under the heading **issued capital** details of the ordinary shares would be shown as follows:

200,000 Ordinary shares of £1 each fully paid.

Preference shares

Preference shares can be issued as **cumulative preference shares**, **non-cumulative preference shares** and **participating preference shares**.

Features of preference shares:

- Shareholders receive a fixed rate of dividend.
- They receive their dividend before ordinary shareholders.
- They have no voting rights, unless dividends are in arrears.
- If the plc is wound up, preference shareholders will have priority on receiving their shareholding compared with ordinary shareholders.

FINANCIAL ACCOUNTING

Cumulative preference shares

Features of cumulative preference shares:

- These shareholders receive a fixed rate of dividend every year before the ordinary shareholders are paid.
- If profits are insufficient to allow full payment of their dividend in one year the arrears will be carried forward to the next year when they will be paid before any other dividend is declared on other shares.
- These shareholders have no voting rights unless the payment of dividend is in arrears.

Non-cumulative preference shares

Features of non-cumulative preference shares:

- These shares are similar to cumulative preference shares except that they do not carry the right for any arrears in dividend from the previous year to be made up.
- They usually carry no voting rights unless the dividend is 6 months in arrears.

Cumulative and non-cumulative preference shares are usually entitled to priority in repayment of share capital in the event of the winding up of the company.

Participating preference shares

Features of participating preference shares include:

- In addition to a fixed rate of dividend a bonus dividend is paid after the deferred and ordinary shareholders have been paid a certain percentage dividend.
- They may also have priority in the repayment of share capital in the event of the winding up of the company.
- They carry no voting rights.

In the Balance Sheet of a plc under the heading **Issued Capital** details of the preference shares would be shown as follows:

500,000 7% Preference shares of £1 each fully paid

Preference shareholders receive a 7% return on the shares they own as their dividend.

Deferred or founder shares

Features of deferred or founder shares:

- As the name suggests these are the shares of the founders or management of the company.
- They are entitled to a dividend only after all other classes of shares have received their share of the profits.

Share premium

A **share premium** is a **capital reserve** which is created when shares are sold for more than their face value. For example, if a £1 share was sold for £1.50, the extra 50p per share would represent the share premium.

These reserves can only be used for financing the issue of bonus shares, writing off any discount on shares sold, and financing the redemption of ordinary shares.

Issues of new shares

Sometimes a plc will issue new shares. This can be done in response to a particularly successful year or in order to generate new additional capital for the company. New shares can be issued as a bonus issue or rights issue to their shareholders.

Bonus shares (or scrip Issue)

If a company has had a particularly successful year or their reserves have been built up so that the issued capital is out of proportion to the capital employed the plc may decide to issue **bonus shares** to the existing ordinary shareholders.

- The shareholders make no payment for these shares which are usually issued in a ratio according to their shareholding, so one bonus share might be issued for every five held, for example.
- The reserves of the plc are used to finance the issue of the bonus shares.
- The issued share capital will be increased and the reserves decreased by the amount of the bonus issue.
- The shareholder may sell these shares on the Stock Exchange and realise the bonus in cash.

Rights issue

If a plc wishes to raise additional capital it may decide to make a **rights issue** to existing shareholders:

- Shareholders are offered the right to purchase additional shares in the company at a discounted price.
- The rights issue is normally made in proportion to existing shareholding, similar to the issue of bonus shares.
- This right to purchase shares at a discount can be sold on the open market if the shareholder does not wish to purchase the additional shares in the plc.

Raising capital for a plc

Shares are only one way for plcs to raise capital. In addition to the issue of shares a plc can raise capital from a variety of other sources and most big plcs will use some (or even all) of these sources.

Loans to the plc

Plcs can seek loans in the form of **debentures** and **mortgages**.

Debentures

A plc can raise capital by issuing **debentures** to the general public. A debenture holder does not take as many risks, with his own capital, as a shareholder does.

Features of debentures:

- Debentures are loans to the company and are not as risky an investment as shares.
- They receive a fixed rate of interest annually, chargeable against the profits.
- Interest is paid whether the plc is making a profit or loss.
- Debentures will be redeemed (bought back) on a certain date.

FINANCIAL ACCOUNTING

- A debenture (fixed or mortgage debenture) may be secured on specific assets of the plc (such as land and buildings). If the firm goes into liquidation the money raised from the sale of the assets will be used to pay off the debenture holders before any of the shareholders.
- A debenture not secured on an asset of the plc is called a floating or naked debenture.
- Debenture holders have no voting rights.

Other sources of finance available to a plc

Bank overdraft

An **overdraft** is a loan to the company made when the bank allows the plc to withdraw more money than the have in their account. This is a fairly short term type of finance.

Trade creditors

Trade creditors arise when the plc purchases goods on credit and pays for them at a later date. Care must be taken to ensure that these debts are paid off quickly.

Leasing

Instead of purchasing fixed assets the plc can decide to hire, rent or **lease** the fixed assets over a specific period of time. A fixed amount will be paid each month for the hire of the asset. Part of the leasing agreement usually includes the maintenance of the fixed assets. This type of agreement can solve cash flow problems which may occur should the plc try to purchase the fixed asset.

Government and European Union grants

There are a large number of grants and loans available from the Government, European Union or local authorities. In order to qualify the business must secure or create employment.

Mortgage

A **mortgage** is a long-term loan to the company and is generally used to purchase premises or land. The mortgage may be secured on the land or buildings. Mortgages tend to be repaid over a long period of time, usually 20-25 years. The advantage of a mortgage is that the interest rate tends to be fairly low compared to a commercial loan from a bank or financial institution.

Hire purchase

Hire purchase is often used when an enterprise wishes to purchase plant and machinery or vehicles. The hire purchase agreement requires a fixed amount to be paid the remainder paid art regular intervals.

Factoring

Factoring may occur if a plc is having trouble collecting its debts. It may decide to use a factor to collect them. The factor will either pay the outstanding invoices less a fee to the plc, or collect the debts on behalf of the company and pay the amount outstanding less a fee to the plc. Whichever method is chosen the plc benefits in that they receive immediate finance from their debts.

Venture capital

If a business is new or speculative they may have trouble raising money from the normal sources such as banks. A **venture capitalist** is someone who is prepared to risk their capital by investing in this speculative business. Venture capitals may attract funds from financial institutions and business angels. A **business angel** is a person or institution who invests in business because they believe they have the potential to become successful.

Provisions and reserves

Provisions or reserves are **not** sums of money but resources retained within the business from the profits earned during the financial year.

Provisions are charges against profits and appear in the profit and loss account. They are resources set aside to cover an expected loss. A provision is either:

- An amount written off by way of providing for depreciation or reduction in the value of an asset.
- An amount retained to provide for any liability or loss which is likely to be incurred.
- An amount retained for any liability which is certain to occur.

The most common examples of provisions are:

- Depreciation of fixed assets and provision for doubtful debts.
- Other provisions include provision for deferred repairs.

Reserves are not charges against profits but an appropriation of profit. Reserves can be either capital reserves or revenue reserves.

Capital reserves arise from profits which have **not** been accumulated from the normal trading activities of the enterprise and include:

- **Share premium** where shares are sold above face value.
- **Revaluation reserves** created where assets such as land and buildings have appreciated in value. The increase in value is debited to the asset account and credited to a revaluation reserve.
- **Capital redemption reserve** which arises when shares are bought back from shareholders.

These reserves are not available for distribution to shareholders in the form of dividends but can be used to finance the bonus issue of shares to existing shareholders

Revenue reserves arise from the trading activities of the business enterprise. Unlike a partnership or sole trader a plc may retain some of their profits each year. They may use these in years where profits are poor to equalise the dividends paid to their shareholders.

Capital of a plc

There are many variations in the description of the share capital of a plc.

Authorised capital is the amount of capital which can be issued by the plc as stated in the Memorandum of Association. For example:

1,000,000 Ordinary share of £1 each
500,000 7% Preference shares of £1 each

Issued capital is the part of the authorised capital which has been issued to the public and which has been fully or partly paid. From the example above, the shares might be divided between partly and fully-paid shares:

500,000 Ordinary shares of £1 each fully paid
250,000 7% Preference shares of £1 each fully paid

or

500,000 Ordinary shares of £1 each partly paid
250,000 7% Preference shares of £1 each partly paid

Called-up capital is the amount of money which the shareholders have been required to pay. A company may not necessarily require the full amount at once on the shares it has issued, and therefore calls up only what it needs.

Paid-up capital is the amount of called-up capital that has actually been paid by the shareholders. Occasionally a shareholder fails to pay an amount due when the call is made. This amount owing is called a **call in arrears**. No dividend will be paid on shares where calls are in arrears.

Final accounts of a public limited company

Under the 1985 Companies Act every company must specify to the Registrar of Companies on a special form the date called the **Accounting Reference Date** when the final accounts will be prepared and submitted to the Registrar and to the members of the company. Accounts of plcs must be published and differ from those prepared for internal accounting purposes. The published accounts must be modified by the accountants to comply with the regulations.

The preparation of the final accounts of a plc must comply with the provisions laid down in the Company Act of 1985 and with the standards set by the Accounting Standard Board. Any changes in the method of preparation of the final accounts from one year to the next must be noted in the published accounts of the plc.

The final accounts of a plc are similar in structure to that of a partnership and sole trader. The main difference occurs in the Balance Sheet because of the different capital structure

The following final accounts must be prepared:

- Manufacturing Account – if the plc is a manufacturing concern
- Trading and Profit and Loss Account
- Profit and Loss Appropriation Account
- Balance Sheet

The internal Manufacturing, Trading and Profit and Loss Accounts of a plc will be prepared in much the same way as a sole trader or partnership. The only real difference is the size of the business enterprise. Like a partnership the plc will prepare a Profit and Loss Appropriation Account to show how the profits made are to be distributed.

Profit and Loss Appropriation Account

The Profit and Loss Appropriation Account will start with the net profit before taxation.

Taxation

Like a sole trader or a partner a plc will be required to pay tax on their profits. Sole traders and partners will pay personal income tax. This tax is **not** recorded in the accounts of the business enterprise.

A plc is required by law to pay **Corporation Tax** on their annual profits. Their accountants will estimate how much tax is to be paid on the profits earned each year. This amount will be deducted from the net profit before tax in the Appropriation Account and reduces the amount available for dividends to the shareholders. The rate for Corporation Tax is set by the Chancellor of the Exchequer in his annual budget.

Shareholder's dividends

Each shareholder hopes to receive an appropriation of profit in the form of a dividend at the end of each year. The Directors of the plc decide annually:

- whether or not dividends are to be paid to all shareholders;
- the percentage dividend to be paid to ordinary shareholders;
- the amount of profit to be retained in the profit and loss account.

Unlike a partnership where all the profit is appropriated it is quite normal for the Appropriation Account to have a balance at the end of one year to be carried forward to the next.

Dividend payments

Dividends paid to shareholders are normally made in two payments. The first dividend is often paid half-way through the financial year and is called an **interim** dividend. The second dividend, called the **final** dividend, is declared by the directors at the end of the financial year and agreed by the shareholders at the Annual General Meeting. This amount will normally appear in the **current liabilities** section of the Balance Sheet as it has still to be paid to the shareholders at the end of the financial year.

Calculation of dividends

Preference share dividend

Preference shareholders receive a fixed rate of dividend each year.

Example 1

ABC plc's capital structure includes the issue of 100,000 7% Preference shares of £1 each fully paid.

The dividend due for the year is calculated using the following formula:

$$\text{Dividend due} = \text{Value of shares} \times \text{dividend rate}$$
$$= \pounds100,000 \times 7\%$$
$$= \pounds7,000$$

Task 1

Calculate the annual dividend to be paid to the Preference shareholders of the following plcs.

Plc	Value of Preference Shares	Dividend rate
A plc	100,000	5%
B plc	250,000	10%
C plc	400,000	6%
D plc	500,000	9%
E plc	1,000,000	6%

Example 2

DEF plc's capital structure includes the issue of 250,000 5% Preference shares of £1 each fully paid. It is the policy of DEF plc to make an interim payment of half the amount due to Preference shareholders half way through the financial year.

The interim dividend is calculated using the following formula:

Interim dividend = Value of shares × dividend rate × ½
= 250,000 × 5% × ½
= £6,250

The total dividend for the year will be:

£250,000 × 5% = £12,500.

This means that at the end of the financial year £6,250 will still have to be paid. This will be termed the **final dividend**. The interim dividend paid need not be half the amount due, but can be any amount the plc decides.

Task 2

Complete the following table to show the interim dividend paid, the final dividend due and the total dividend for the year if each plc decides make an interim payment of half the dividend due to Preference shareholders.

Plc	Value of Preference Shares	Dividend rate	Interim dividend paid	Total dividend for year	Final dividend due
Alpha plc	200,000	6%			
Beta plc	500,000	5%			
Gamma plc	50,000	9%			
Delta plc	300,000	8%			
Epsilon plc	750,000	7%			

Ordinary share dividend

Ordinary shareholders receive a variable rate of dividend each year depending on how profitable the company has been.

Example 3

ABC plc's capital structure includes the issue of 500,000 Ordinary shares of £1 each fully paid. It was agreed at the Annual General Meeting that Ordinary shareholders would receive a 5% dividend for the year.

The dividend due for the year is calculated using the following formula:

Dividend due = Value of shares × dividend rate declared
= £500,000 × 5%
= £25,000

Task 3

Calculate the annual dividend to be paid to the Ordinary shareholder of the following plcs.

Plc	Value of Ordinary Shares	Dividend Rate declared
A plc	500,000	6%
B plc	400,000	10%
C plc	450,000	8%
D plc	250,000	7%
E plc	800,000	12%

Example 4

DEF plc's capital structure includes the issue of 500,000 Ordinary shares of £1 each fully paid. It is the policy of DEF plc to make an interim payment during the year to the Ordinary shareholders. This amount may be a percentage of the share capital or an amount per ordinary share.

The interim dividend is calculated using the following formulae:

Percentage Method	Rate Per Share Method
The plc decides to pay the Ordinary shareholders an interim dividend of 2%.	The plc decides to pay the Ordinary shareholders an interim dividend of 2p per share.
Dividend = Value of shares × dividend rate = £500,000 × 2% = £10,000	Dividend = Number of shares × amount per share = 500,000 × 2p = £10,000

continued ➤

FINANCIAL ACCOUNTING

Example 4 continued

At the end of the financial year the plc declares the amount of the final dividend which will be paid to the Ordinary shareholders. They may say that a final divided of 7% or 7p per share is to be paid.

The dividend due to be paid to the Ordinary shareholders will be calculated as follows:

Percentage Method	Rate Per Share Method

A final dividend of 7% is to be paid.
 	
Dividend = Value of shares × dividend rate
      = £500,000 × 7%
      = £35,000
	A final dividend of 7p per share is to be paid.
	
	Dividend = Number of shares × amount per share
	      = 500,000 × 7p
	      = £35,000

The total dividend paid to the Ordinary shareholders will be:

Dividend payment	Percentage method	Rate per share method
Interim dividend paid	£10,000	£10,000
Final dividend to be paid	£35,000	£35,000
Total dividend for year	£45,000	£45,000

Or they may say that a total dividend for the year of 7% or 7p per share is to be paid.

The total dividend for the year must be calculated:

Percentage Method	Rate Per Share Method

A total dividend of 7% is to be paid.
 	
Dividend = Value of shares × dividend rate
      = £500,000 × 7%
      = £35,000
	A total dividend of 7p per share is to be paid.
	
	Dividend = Number of shares × amount per share
	      = 50,000 × 7p
	      = £35,000

The Ordinary shareholders have already received part of this amount as an interim dividend. To calculate the final dividend due to them the interim payment must be deducted from the total dividend due.

	Percentage Method	Rate Per Share Method
Total dividend for year	£35,000	£35,000
Less Interim dividend paid	£10,000	£10,000
Final dividend to be paid	£25,000	£25,000

Task 4

Prepare a table to show the interim, final and total dividend amounts due to be paid to the shareholders in each of the following plcs.

Plc	Value of Ordinary Share Capital	Interim dividend	Final dividend due	Total dividend for year

You are provided with the following information relating to the interim, final dividend and total amounts to be paid to the shareholders in each company.

Plc	Value of Ordinary Share Capital	Interim dividend	Final dividend due	Total dividend for year
Alpha plc	200,000	3p per share		10p per share
Beta plc	500,000	3p per share	4p per share	
Gamma plc	50,000	4%	5%	
Delta plc	300,000	3%		9%
Epsilon plc	750,000	?	8%	12%

It should be noted that dividends will only be calculated on the value of the paid-up or partly called capital. If a plc has not asked the shareholder to pay the full amount due then dividends will only be calculated on the amount actually paid. This will apply to both Ordinary and Preference shares.

Example 5

Anderson plc has issued 200,000 Ordinary shares with a face value of £1. To date they has only asked the shareholders to pay 75p of the face value.

The value of the Ordinary share capital received is:

Ordinary share capital = 200,000 × 75p
= £150,000

At the end of the financial year they declare a dividend of 10%.

The total dividend to be paid will be:

£150,000 × 10% = £15,000

Task 5

The following companies have issued shares of £1, each which have been partly paid.

Calculate the total dividend to be paid for each class of share.

Plc	Type of share	Number of shares of £1 each	Share Capital called up	Dividend declared
White plc	Ordinary	100,000	75p	5%
Black plc	6% Preference	50,000	50p	
Green plc	Ordinary	200,000	50p	8%
Brown plc	9% Preference	20,000	80p	
Grey plc	Ordinary	250,000	25p	7%

Preparation of Appropriation Account

Example 6

Smith plc has issued the following shares:

100,000 Ordinary shares of £1 each fully paid, and;
50,000 8% Preference shares fully paid.

During the year ended 31 December Year 1 they made a net profit before tax of £100,000 and the balance on the Profit and Loss Appropriation Account amounted to £24,000 on 1 January Year 1.

The Directors decide to:

- provide for Corporation Tax of £25,000.
- pay the Preference dividend in full.
- pay a total dividend to the Ordinary shareholders of 10%.

From the above information prepare the Profit and Loss Appropriation Account of Smith plc for the year ended 31 December Year 1.

STEP 1 – Set up the Profit and Loss Appropriation Account

Smith plc Profit and Loss Appropriation Account For year ended 31 December Year 1		
	£	£

STEP 2 – Enter the net profit before tax and deduct Corporation Tax

Smith plc Profit and Loss Appropriation Account For year ended 31 December Year 1		
	£	£
Net Profit before tax		100,000
Less Corporation Tax		25,000
Net Profit after tax		25,000

continued ➢

Example 6 continued

STEP 3 – Calculate Preference and Ordinary dividends due and enter into the Appropriation Account

Preference Share Dividends due	Ordinary Share Dividends due
8% × £50,000 = £4,000	10% × £100,000 = £10,000

Smith plc Profit and Loss Appropriation Account For year ended 31 December Year 1		
	£	£
Net Profit before tax		100,000
Less Corporation Tax		25,000
Net Profit after tax		75,000
Less **Appropriations**		
Dividends proposed:		
Preference Dividends due	4,000	
Ordinary Dividend due	10,000	14,000

STEP 4 – Calculate the balance of retained profit for the year and the final balance on the Profit and Loss Appropriation Account

Smith plc Profit and Loss Appropriation Account For year ended 31 December Year 1		
	£	£
Net Profit before tax		100,000
Less Corporation Tax		25,000
Net Profit after tax		75,000
Less Appropriations		
Dividends proposed:		
Preference Dividends due	4,000	
Ordinary Dividend due	10,000	14,000
Retained Profit for the year		61,000
Retained Profit b/f		24,000
Retained Profit c/f		85,000

The dividends due to be paid by the plc will appear as current liabilities in the Balance Sheet. The retained profit brought forward (shown as **Retained Profit b/f**) is the profit from the previous year held in the Profit and Loss Appropriation Account. The retained profit carried forward (**shown as Retained Profit c/f**) will appear in the Capital and Revenue Reserves in the Balance Sheet.

Task 6

1 Prepare the Appropriation Account of A plc from the following information. Issued share capital of the plc is 60,000 Ordinary shares of £1 each and 20,000 10% Preference shares.

On December 31 Year 1 it was ascertained that the company had made a net profit of £42,000, before tax, and that there was a balance of retained profits from last year of £3,500. The Directors decided to:

- provide for Corporation Tax of £10,000;
- pay the Preference shareholders in full;
- pay a dividend of 12% to the Ordinary shareholders.

2 Prepare the Appropriation Account of B plc from the following information. The issued share capital amounts to 90,000 Ordinary shares of £1 each and 20,000 8% Preference shares all of which have been issued and are fully paid.

On December 31 Year 1 it was ascertained that the company had made a net profit of £70,000, before tax, and that a balance of undistributed profits from last year amounted to £4,500. The Directors decided to:

- provide for Corporation Tax of £10,000;
- pay the Preference shareholders in full;
- pay a dividend of 10% to the Ordinary shareholders.

3 Prepare the Appropriation Account of C plc from the following information. The issued capital of the company is 280,000 £1 Ordinary shares and 20,000 8% Preference shares all of which have been fully paid.

During the financial year ended 31 December Year 1 the company made a net profit of £90,000. A balance of undistributed profits from last year amounted to £10,000. The Directors decided to:

- provide £20,000 for Corporation Tax;
- pay the Preference shareholders in full;
- propose to pay a total dividend of 8% on the Ordinary shareholders

Example 7

Jones plc has issued the following shares:

200,000 Ordinary shares of £1 each fully paid, and;
80,000 8% Preference shares fully paid.

During the year ended 31 December Year 1 they made a net profit before tax of £90,000 and the balance on the Profit and Loss Appropriation Account amounted to £10,000.

During the year they made dividend payments to the Ordinary shareholders of £10,000 and paid half the Preference dividend.

continued ➤

Example 7 continued

The Directors decide:

- to provide for Corporation Tax of £25,000;
- to pay the Preference dividend in full;
- to pay a final dividend to the Ordinary shareholders of 10%.

From the above information prepare the Profit and Loss Appropriation Account of Smith plc for the year ended 31 December Year 1.

STEP 1 – Set up the Profit and Loss Appropriation Account

Smith plc Profit and Loss Appropriation Account For year ended 31 December Year 1			
	£	£	£

STEP 2 – Enter the net profit before tax and deduct Corporation Tax

Smith plc Profit and Loss Appropriation Account For year ended 31 December Year 1		
	£	£
Net Profit before tax		90,000
Less Corporation Tax		25,000
Net Profit after tax		65,000

STEP 3 – Calculate interim and final Preference and Ordinary dividends and enter into the Appropriation Account

Dividend calculations:

Interim Preference Share Dividends		Interim Ordinary Share Dividends	
8% × £80,000 × ½ = £3,200		= £10,000	
Final Preference Dividend Proposed		**Final Ordinary Share Dividend Proposed**	
8% × £80,000 × ½ = £3,200		10% × 200,000 = £20,000	
Total Preference Dividend Paid		**Total Ordinary Share dividend paid**	
Interim	£3,200	Interim	£10,000
Final	£3,200	Final	£20,000
Total	£6,400	Total	£30,000

In exercises where data is provided in a Trial Balance the dividend figures shown there represent the interim dividends paid. They are treated in exactly the same way in the Appropriation Account as the dividends calculated above.

continued ➤

Example 7 continued

Jones plc Profit and Loss Appropriation Account
For year ended 31 December Year 1

	£	£	£
Net Profit before tax			90,000
Less Corporation Tax			25,000
Net Profit after tax			65,000
Less **Appropriations**			
Dividends paid and proposed:			
Preference Dividends:			
Interim	3,200		
Final	3,200	6,400	
Ordinary Dividend:			
Interim	10,000		
Final	20,000	30,000	36,400

STEP 4 – Calculate the balance of retained profit for the year and the final balance on the Profit and Loss Appropriation Account

Jones plc Profit and Loss Appropriation Account
For year ended 31 December Year 1

	£	£	£
Net Profit before tax			90,000
Less Corporation Tax			25,000
Net Profit after tax			65,000
Less Appropriations			
Dividends paid and proposed:			
Preference Dividends:			
Interim	3,200		
Final	3,200	6,400	
Ordinary Dividend:			
Interim	10,000		
Final	20,000	30,000	36,400
Retained profit for year			28,600
Retained profit b/f			10,000
Retained profit			38,600

The dividends due to be paid by the plc will appear as current liabilities in the Balance Sheet and the **Retained Profit c/f** will appear in the capital and revenue reserve in the Balance Sheet.

continued ➤

Task 7

1   Prepare the Appropriation Account of Alpha plc from the following information.
Issued share capital of the plc is 120,000 Ordinary shares of £1 each and 50,000
10% Preference shares.

On December 31 Year 1 it was ascertained that the company had:

- made a net profit of £100,000, before tax;
- a balance of retained profits from last year of £25,000;
- paid an interim dividend to Ordinary shareholders of 2p per share;
- paid Preference shareholders half their share dividend.

The Directors decided to:

- provide for Corporation Tax of £25,000;
- pay the Preference shareholders in full;
- pay a final dividend of 10p per share to the Ordinary shareholders.

2   Prepare the Appropriation Account of Beta plc from the following information.
The issued share capital amounts to 120,000 Ordinary shares of £1 each and 50,000
6% Preference shares all of which have been issued and are fully paid.

On December 31 Year 1 it was ascertained that the company had

- made a net profit of £120,000, before tax;
- a balance of retained profits from last year of £5,000;
- paid an interim dividend to Ordinary shareholders of 4% share;
- paid an interim payment of £1,000 to the Preference shareholders.

The Directors decided to:

- provide for Corporation Tax of £30,000;
- pay the Preference shareholders in full;
- pay the Ordinary shareholders a total dividend of 12%.

3   Prepare the Appropriation Account of Carron plc from the following information.
The issued share capital of the company is 200,000 £1 Ordinary shares and 50,000
7% Preference shares all of which have been fully paid

During the financial year ended 31 December Year 1 the company made a net profit
of £100,000. A balance of undistributed profits from last year amounted to £10,000.
An interim dividends of 5% was paid to the Ordinary shareholders and 2% to
Preference shareholders.

The Directors decided to:

- provide £25,000 for Corporation Tax;
- pay the Preference shareholders in full;
- propose to pay a **total** dividend of 12% on the Ordinary shareholders.

continued ➤

4 Prepare the Appropriation Account of Dingwall plc from the following information. The issued share capital of the company is 500,000 Ordinary shares of £1 each (of which 75p has been called up) and 300,000 9% Preference shares, all of which have been issued and fully paid.

A net profit of £275,000, before tax, had been made during the financial year ended 31 March Year 2. A balance of undistributed profits from last year amounted to £30,000. The Directors resolved to:

- provide for Corporation tax of £75,000;
- pay the Preference shareholders in full;
- recommend a final 15% dividend on the Ordinary shares.

5 Prepare the Appropriation Account of West plc from the following information. The issued share capital of the company is 300,000 Ordinary shares of £1 each (of which 50p has been called up) and 100,000 50p 9% Preference shares all of which have been issued and fully paid.

A net profit of £120,000, before tax, had been made during the financial year ended 31 October Year 2. A balance of undistributed profits from last year amounted to £10,000. An interim dividend was paid to the Preference shareholders of £1,500.

The Directors resolved to:

- provide for Corporation Tax of £75,000;
- pay the Preference shareholders in full;
- recommend a final 15% dividend on the Ordinary shares.

Balance sheets of public limited companies

Balance sheets are an essential part of the legal framework required for the regulation of plcs, and they form part of the annual submissions to Companies House. Balance Sheets must always be signed by a Director of the company, and depending on the size of the company, they may need to be assessed by an independent auditor. There are strict rules concerning the way in which Balance Sheets are submitted, and if submissions are incorrect or late, the company can be fined. It is therefore essential that Balance Sheets are properly prepared!

Example 8

From the following list of balances prepare the Balance Sheet of Wilson plc for the year ended 31 December Year 1

	£000s
Goodwill	10
Patents and trademarks	230
Premises at cost	640
Plant and machinery at cost	250
Motor vehicles at cost	225
Investments (market valued £40,000)	30

continued >

Example 8 continued

	£000s
Provision for Depreciation:	
• Plant and machinery	150
• Motor vehicles	30
Provision for doubtful debts	20
Prepayments	5
Stock	85
Net Debtors	63
Bank	150
Cash	14
Creditors	22
Preference dividend due	5
Ordinary dividend due	25
Corporation Tax	20
Accruals	5
8% Debentures (Year 10-12)	100
300,000 Ordinary Share of £1 each fully paid	300
100,000 8% Preference shares of £1 each fully paid	100
Share premium	100
Revaluation reserve	75
Profit and Loss Account	750

STEP 1 – Identify the items to be included in the fixed assets and investments section of the Balance Sheet.

The fixed assets section of the balance sheet is set out in much the same way as that of a sole trader or partnership. The assets should be listed in their order of permanence beginning with the fixed assets.

However for a plc, Balance Sheet fixed assets are divided into 3 sections:

- **Intangible assets** which includes goodwill, patents and trademarks. These are assets which have no physical substance but do have a value to the plc.

- **Tangible assets** are items such as premises and plant machinery, vehicles and equipment. Tangible assets must be shown at cost price and net book value.

- **Investments** are items such as long term investments in shares in other companies. These investments will be shown at cost in the Balance Sheet but will have a note about their current market value.

continued ➤

FINANCIAL ACCOUNTING

Example 8 continued

Balance Sheet of Wilson plc as at 31 December Year 1				
Fixed Assets	£000	£000	£000	£000
Intangible Assets				
Goodwill				10
Patents and trademarks				230
				240
Tangible Assets	*Cost*	*Aggregate Depreciation*	*Net Book Value*	
Premises	640		640	
Plant and machinery	250	150	100	
Motor Vehicles	225	30	195	
	1,115	180	935	935
Investments (valued at £40,000)				30

STEP 2 – Identify the current assets and list them in the Balance Sheet

The current assets of a plc are very similar to those of a sole trader and partnership and will include items such as prepayments, stock, debtors, bank, and cash.

Balance Sheet of Wilson plc as at 31 December Year 1				
Fixed Assets	£000	£000	£000	£000
Intangible Assets				
Goodwill				10
Patents and trademarks				230
				240
Tangible Assets	*Cost*	*Aggregate Depreciation*	*Net Book Value*	
Premises	640		640	
Plant and machinery	250	150	100	
Motor vehicles	225	30	195	
	1,115	180		935
Investments (valued at £40,000)				30
Current Assets				
Prepayments		5		
Stock		105		
Debtors*		23		
Bank		150		
Cash		14	297	

* Debtors less provision for doubtful debts (43 – 20) = 23.

continued ➢

Example 8 continued

STEP 3 – Identify the current liabilities and enter these in the Balance Sheet then calculate the working capital and capital employed

In addition to creditors and VAT, the current liabilities will include any dividends or Corporation Tax still to be paid.

Note: *The omissions of dividends and Corporation Tax due are one of the most common errors made by students when preparing the Balance Sheet of a plc. Remember:*

- **Working capital** *is the* **current assets – current liabilities**
- **Capital employed** *represents* **total assets – current liabilities**

Balance Sheet of Wilson plc as at 31 December Year 1				
Fixed Assets	£000	£000	£000	£000
Intangible Assets				
Goodwill				10
Patents and trademarks				230
				240
Tangible Assets	Cost	Aggregate Depreciation	Net Book Value	
Premises	640		640	
Plant and machinery	250	150	100	
Motor vehicles	225	30	195	
	1,115	180		935
Investments (valued at £40,000)				30
Current Assets				
Prepayments		5		
Stock		105		
Debtors*		23		
Bank		150		
Cash		14	297	
Current Liabilities				
Creditors		22		
Accruals		5		
Preference Dividend due		5		
Ordinary dividend due		25		
Corporation tax		20	77	
				220
Capital Employed				1,425

continued ➤

Example 8 continued

STEP 4 – Calculate the shareholder's interest in the plc

Any long-term loan the plc has arranged will be deducted from the capital employed in the enterprise to show the value of the net assets financed by the shareholders from shares and reserves.

Balance Sheet of Wilson plc as at 31 December Year 1			
Fixed Assets	£000	£000	£000	£000
Intangible Assets				
Goodwill				10
Patents and trademarks				<u>230</u>
				240
Tangible Assets	*Cost*	*Aggregate Depreciation*	*Net Book Value*	
Premises	640		640	
Plant and machinery	250	150	100	
Motor vehicles	<u>225</u>	<u>30</u>	<u>195</u>	
	<u>1,115</u>	<u>180</u>	935	935
Investments (valued at £40,000)				30
Current assets				
Prepayments		5		
Stock		105		
Debtors		23		
Bank		150		
Cash		<u>14</u>	297	
Current Liabilities				
Creditors		22		
Accruals		5		
Preference Dividend due		5		
Ordinary dividend due		25		
Corporation tax		<u>20</u>	<u>77</u>	
				220
Capital Employed				1,425
Less Long-term Liabilities				
8% Debentures (Year 10-12)				<u>100</u>
Net Assets				**<u>1,325</u>**

continued ➤

Example 8 continued

STEP 5 – Prepare the liabilities section of the Balance Sheet

The **liabilities** section of the Balance Sheet will appear underneath the **assets** section in a columnar style balance sheet.

As the Balance Sheet is being prepared for internal use there is no need to show the value of the authorised capital.

This section begins with the issued capital of the plc. The number, class and value of shares issued must be shown.

Financed by	£000s	£000s	£000s	£000s
Issued Capital				
300,000 £1 Ordinary Shares			300	
100,000 8% £1 Preference Shares			<u>100</u>	400

STEP 6 – Identify and enter the capital and revenue reserves of the plc

These reserves belong to the ordinary shareholders as they are made up from retained profits and the revaluation of assets

Financed by	£000s	£000s	£000s	£000s
Issued Capital				
300,000 £1 Ordinary Shares			300	
100,000 8% £1 Preference Shares			<u>100</u>	400
Capital and Revenue Reserves				
Share Premium			100	
Revaluation Reserve			75	
Profit and Loss Account			<u>750</u>	<u>925</u>
Shareholder's interest				<u>1,325</u>

The shareholder's interest total should agree with the net assets invested in the enterprise.

Task 8

1 From the following information prepare the Balance Sheet of MacIver plc for the year ended 31 March Year 3.

	£000s
Patents	15
Premises at cost	200
Machinery at cost	100
Trade Investments (market valued £70,000)	100
Provision for Depreciation • Machinery	25
Provision for doubtful debts	10
Stock	52
Debtors	38
Bank	42
Creditors	16
Cash	14
Ordinary dividend due	14
Corporation Tax due	20
Accruals	2
Mortgage	40
200,000 Ordinary Shares of £1 each fully paid	200
Share premium	100
Profit and Loss Account	124

continued ➤

2 From the following information prepare the Balance Sheet of Alpha plc for the year ended 31 October Year 2.

	£000s
Goodwill	50
Premises at cost	500
Equipment at cost	120
Motor vehicles at cost	100
Investments (market valued £100,000)	80
Provision for Depreciation ● Equipment ● Motor vehicles	60 20
Provision for doubtful debts	10
Prepayments	3
Stock	20
Debtors	25
Bank	60
Cash	5
Creditors and VAT	28
Preference dividend due	10
Ordinary dividend due	12
Corporation Tax due	25
Accruals	3
Mortgage	75
400,000 Ordinary shares of £1 each fully paid	400
50,000 8% Preference shares of £1 each fully paid	50
Share premium	75
Revaluation reserve	95
Profit and Loss Account	100

 *Now do Worksheets 8.1 and 8.4*

 Now do Worksheets 8.2 and 8.3

Accounts of not-for-profit organisations

Intermediate 2 Level Outcomes: ▮▮▶

This chapter includes material from Int 2 level Financial Accounting Outcome 4

☆ **Explain the key features which distinguish different types of business organisations.**

☆ **Complete partially prepared final accounts of organisations consistent with financial accounting practice.**

Higher Level Outcomes: ▮▮▶

This chapter includes material from Higher level Financial Accounting Outcome 1

☆ **Discuss the formation, funding, management, control and the reporting procedures of an organisation.**

☆ **Complete partially prepared final accounts of organisations consistent with financial accounting practice.**

Running a not-for-profit organisation

Clubs and non-profit making organisations have some interest other than making a profit. They use their funds to promote the interests of their members. These clubs can be quite large, such as golf clubs, health clubs, and squash clubs, or fairly small organisations like youth or drama clubs. As with public limited companies a report of where the funds have come from and how they are spent, must be given to the club members annually.

The club is run by a **committee** which is elected annually at the Annual General Meeting. Office bearers – President, Chairperson, Secretary and Treasurer will be elected at the Annual General Meeting or from within the committee elected at the Annual General Meeting.

The **Treasurer** is responsible for the financial running of the club and will perform similar duties to that of an accountant in a profit-making organisation. The Treasurer will collect subscriptions from the club members and pay the bills during the year. At the end of the financial year the final accounts of the club will be prepared for presentation to the club members at the Annual General Meeting.

Sources of finance for a club

The club will not sell a product in the same way a business enterprise does. It will provide facilities for its members to further their interests. The activities of the club will be financed from a variety of sources.

- **Subscriptions** Each year the members of the club will pay a subscription which will entitle them to use the facilities of the club. The subscriptions will not normally provide sufficient money for the club to operate. Other sources of income will be required.
- **Revenue from the sale of food and refreshments** If the club is large they may operate a bar or café which will generate profits for the club. A separate account will kept for this activity and a Trading and Profit and Loss Account prepared at the end of the financial year.
- **Donations** The club may receive donations from businesses in its area or from existing and former club members.
- **Fund-raising activities** Clubs and societies often run fund-raising events to help finance the club. It is common for them to hold raffles, dances, and sponsored events to increase the income of the club or to raise money for a specific project.
- **Loans** A club may borrow money from a bank or other financial institution. (For example, they may get a Building Society Mortgage to finance an extension to a clubroom.)
- **Grants** If the club wishes to improve its facilities it may apply for and be given a grant by the Local Authority, Sports Council or Lottery.

Treatment of life membership fees

Most membership fees are paid on an annual basis and do not need any special treatment, However, some club or society constitutions allow members to purchase life membership of the club. They will pay a substantial lump sum and will not be required to pay any annual subscriptions thereafter.

These fees can be dealt with in two ways:

1 The fee is transferred to a life membership account with a bank or building society. The interest earned on this account is treated as annual income.

2 The Committee may decide on an arbitrary figure, say 25 years, for the writing-off of the life membership fee into the income and expenditure account. Each year 1/25 of the amount is transferred from the account into income. In addition to this, interest earned from the investments of the life membership fee will also be included in income.

The basic principles which underlie the record-keeping of a profit organisation will apply to that of a club or non-profit making organisation.

Accounts of a non-profit making organisation

A club or society will prepare the following accounts during and at the end of the year.

- Bank or Cash Account
- Receipts and Payments Account
- Income and Expenditure Account
- Balance Sheet

Cash/Bank account

The Treasurer will keep a **Cash/Bank account** which will detail all monies received and paid out by the club during the financial year.

Bank Account					
Date	Details	Dr	Cr	Balance	
April 1	Balance			4,300	Dr
April 2	Subscriptions	120		4,420	Dr
April 4	Subscriptions	350		4,770	Dr
April 5	Subscriptions	650		5,420	Dr
April 5	Hydro Electric		230	5,190	Dr
April 6	Locker fees	160		5,350	Dr
April 9	Rates		1,200	4,150	Dr

This account may have analysis columns added to record the totals for each source of income or expenditure.

Bank Account								
Date	Details	Dr	Cr	Balance	Subscriptions	Locker Fees	Fuel and Power	Rates
April 1	Balance			4,300				
April 2	Subscriptions	120		4,420	120			
April 4	Subscriptions	350		4,770	350			
April 5	Subscriptions	650		5,420	650			
April 5	Hydro Electric		230	5,190			230	
April 6	Locker fees	160		5,350		160		
April 30	Rates		1,200	4,150				1,200
Totals					1,120	160	230	1,200

At the end of the year each source of receipts and payment will be totalled and transferred to a Receipts and Payments Account.

Features of Receipts and Payments Accounts

The Receipts and Payments Account will:

- show **actual** amounts received and **actual** amounts paid during the financial period;
- not distinguish between capital and revenue incomes and expenditure;
- not show details of any accruals and prepayments;
- not show details of any assets or liabilities owned or owed by the club or society.

Example 1

Use the information given in the analysed bank account to prepare a Receipts and Payments Account.

STEP 1 – Set up the receipts and payments account and insert the opening balance

Anytime Squash Club Receipts and Payments Account For year ended 30 April Year		
	£	£
Opening Balance		4,300

STEP 2 – List the various receipts, total and add to opening balance

Anytime Squash Club Receipts and Payments Account For year ended 30 April Year		
	£	£
Opening Balance		4,300
Add Receipts		
Subscriptions	1,120	
Locker fees	160	1,280
		5,580

STEP 3 – List the payments and deduct from the total cash available to calculate the closing balance

Anytime Squash Club Receipts and Payments Account For year ended 30 April Year		
	£	£
Opening Balance		4,300
Add Receipts		
Subscriptions	1,120	
Locker fees	160	1,280
		5,580
Less Expenditure		
Electricity	1,200	
Rates	230	1,430
Closing Balance		4,150

The closing balance will be included in the Balance Sheet of the club.

FINANCIAL ACCOUNTING

Now do Worksheet 9.1

Income and Expenditure Accounts

The **Income and Expenditure Account** is similar to that of the **Profit and Loss Account** of sole traders, partnerships and limited companies in that it shows transactions such as payments of expenses, receipts of incomes, depreciation, accruals and prepayments.

The members of the club will not be particularly interested in the details of the incomes and expenses but in the profits or losses of the activities like dances, raffles, and the bar. The Treasurer will offset the expenses against the incomes of the various fundraising activities and simply show the profits or losses in the income and expenditure.

If the income of the club is greater than the expenditure the club will have a made a **surplus** of income over expenditure. If the expenditure is greater than the income the club will have made a **deficit** of income over expenditure.

As with a Profit and Loss Account, capital expenditure **will not** appear in the Income and Expenditure Account.

Example 2

Winton Sports club was started on 1 January Year 1 with a donation of £1,860.

The following Receipts and Payments Account has been prepared by the Treasurer of the Winton Sports Club at the end of Year 1

Receipts and Payments Account For year ended 31 December Year 1		
	£	£
Opening Balance b/f		1,860
Add Receipts		
Subscriptions received	6,100	
Bar sales	22,000	
Dance ticket sales	6,500	
Bank loan	101,000	
Total receipts		**135,600**
Less Payments		
Competition expenses	930	
Secretary's expenses	450	
Travel expenses	3,000	
Rates and insurance	1,125	
General expenses	360	
Bar steward's wages	3,840	
Dance expenses	2,100	
Purchase of bar stocks	16,050	

continued ➤

Example 2 continued

Receipts and Payments Account For year ended 31 December Year 1		
	£	£
Purchase of new equipment	2,400	30,255
Closing Balance c/f		**105,345**

On 31 December the following additional information was available:

- Subscriptions due from members for Year 1 amounted to £1,050, and £500 has been prepaid for Year 2;

- Rates due to be paid £100;

- Bar stocks amounted to £1,800;

- Creditors for the bar £1,650;

Depreciation of equipment is to be charged at 5% of cost per annum.

You are asked to prepare the Income and Expenditure Account from the above information.

STEP 1 – Prepare the headings and columns for the Income and Expenditure Account

Winton Sports Club Income and Expenditure Account For year ended 31 December Year 1			
	£	£	£
Income			

STEP 2 – Calculate and enter subscriptions for Year 1 and enter into the Income and Expenditure account

Remember amounts appearing in the Receipts and Payment Account have **actually been paid**. However the total may contain amounts paid in advance for next year, and there may still be amounts due to be received for this year. These will be added to the total to calculate the actual income for the period.

For all calculations start with the amounts paid as shown in the Receipts and Payments Account.

Subscriptions received	£6,100
Add Subscription due end Year 1	£1,050
	£7,150
Less Prepaid for Year 2	500
	£6,650

continued ➢

Example 2 continued

Winton Sports Club Income and Expenditure Account For year ended 31 December Year 1	£	£	£
Income			
Subscriptions		6,650	

Other sources of income need to be calculated. The normal method is to calculate the net profit or loss for any activity and enter this figure into the Income and Expenditure Account.

STEP 3 – Calculate profit/loss from the bar

This is achieved by preparing a Trading and Profit and Loss Account for the bar. This is exactly the same as any Trading and Profit and Loss account.

Bar Trading and Profit and Loss Account For year ended 31 December Year 1	£	£	£
Sales			22,000
Less Cost of goods sold			
Purchases*		17,700	
Less Closing stock		1,800	15,900
Gross profit			6,100
Less expenses			
Bar Steward's wages			3,840
Net profit			2,260

Note there is no opening stock for the bar as this is the first year of the club's activities.

***Bar Purchases** The actual value of stock purchased for the bar needs to be calculated. Remember and take into account any amounts still to be paid for purchases (i.e. Bar Creditors):

Purchases	16,050
Add Bar creditors	1,650
Total Purchases	17,700

The profit on the bar is entered in the Incomes section of the Income and Expenditure Account.

continued ➤

Example 2 continued

Winton Sports Club Income and Expenditure Account For year ended 31 December Year 1	£	£	£
Income			
Subscriptions		6,650	
Profit from bar		**4,260**	

STEP 4 – Calculate profit/loss from the dance

	£
Sale of dance tickets	6,500
Less dance expenses	2,100
Profit from dance	4,400

Winton Sports Club Income and Expenditure Account For year ended 31 December Year 1	£	£	£
Income			
Subscriptions		6,650	
Profit from bar		2,260	
Profit from dance		**4,400**	**13,310**

Total income can now be calculated.

STEP 5 – Calculate and enter expenses into the Income and Expenditure Account

Remember the expenses must be adjusted for accruals and prepayments at the end of the financial year.

Winton Sports Club Income and Expenditure Account For year ended 31 December Year 1	£	£
Income		
Subscriptions	6,650	
Profit from bar	2,260	
Profit from dance	4,400	13,310

continued ➤

Example 2 continued

Winton Sports Club Income and Expenditure Account For year ended 31 December Year 1	£	£
Less Expenses		
Competition expenses	930	
Secretary's expenses	450	
Travel expenses	3,000	
Rates and insurance (Note 1)	1,225	
General expenses	360	
Depreciation of equipment (Note 2)	120	6,085

Note 1

Rate and insurance paid: £1,125
Add rates due to be paid: £100
Total for year: **£1,225**

Note 2

Annual depreciation of equipment = 5% of cost
                = 5% of £2,400
                = **£120**

STEP 6 – Calculate surplus or deficit of income over expenditure

Winton Sports Club Income and Expenditure Account For year ended 31 December Year 1	£	£
Income		
Subscriptions	6,650	
Profit from bar	2,260	
Profit from dance	4,400	13,310
Less Expenses		
Competition expenses	930	
Secretary's expenses	450	
Travel expenses	3,000	
Rates and insurance (Note 1)	1,225	
General expenses	360	
Depreciation of equipment (Note 2)	120	6,085
Surplus of income over expenditure		**7,225**

continued ➤

Example 2 continued

The bank loan is not treated as income but is shown in the Receipts and Payments Account and in the club's Balance Sheet. However, any interest paid on the loan will be shown as an expense.

Any surplus is added to the accumulated fund in the Balance Sheet, and any deficit will be deducted.

More about subscriptions

In calculating subscriptions for the year the prepayments and accruals at the end of the financial year must be considered. In addition you may also need to consider prepayments and accruals at the start of the financial year.

Accruals of subscriptions at the end represent amounts owed to the club and are **current assets**.

Prepayments at the end represent the use of the facilities the club owes the member for the following year. This is considered to be a **current liability**.

Accruals at the start of the financial year represent amounts owed by members for the previous year. These amounts will be deducted from the **subscriptions paid** during the year.

Prepayments at the start of the year represent amounts paid last year for the use of the club facilities this year. This amount will be added to the **subscriptions paid** this year.

Figure 9.1 will help you to calculate the subscriptions for the year.

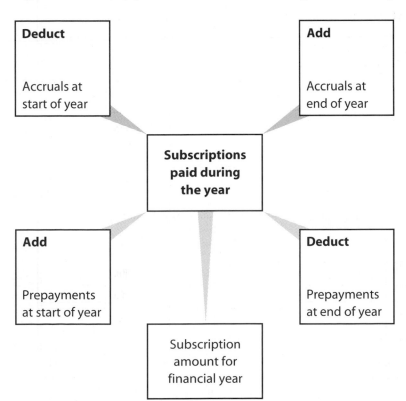

Figure 9.1 How to treat club subscriptions

Task 1

From the following information calculate the subscriptions for the year ended 31 December Year 1.

Subscriptions Received £	Accruals at end of year £	Subscriptions for the year £
3,570	100	
8,400	200	
9,300	600	
10,350	50	
15,300	950	

Task 2

From the following information calculate the subscriptions for the year ended 31 December Year 1.

Subscriptions Received £	Prepayments at end of year £	Subscriptions for the year £
8,300	300	
12,500	600	
1,300	200	
4,590	240	
4,760	150	

Task 3

From the following information calculate the subscriptions for the year ended 31 December Year 1.

Subscriptions Received £	Accruals at start of year £	Subscriptions for the year £
5,690	250	
8,400	700	
5,700	100	
7,800	120	
8,900	400	

Task 6

1   The Zeta Social Club has the following assets and liabilities on 1 January Year 1:

Premises   £100,000
Equipment   £5,000
Cash   £500
Rates due   £500
Bank   £2,000
Subscriptions prepaid   £100
Subscriptions accrued   £150
Bar Stocks   £7,000

Calculate the accumulated fund as at 1 January Year 1.

2   The following are the assets and liabilities of the Table Top Tennis Club at 1 July Year 2.

	£		£
Equipment	250	Printing bill due	20
Subscriptions due	20	Tuck shop stock	300
Electricity due	£50	Repairs to tables due	30
Bank	550	Cash	25

From the above information calculate the value of the accumulated fund on 1 July Year 2.

3   Calculate the Accumulated Fund of the Whitewater Canoe Club from the following balances, taken from the accounts on 1 January Year 3.

	£		£
Equipment	2,250	Subscriptions prepaid	30
Coach hire amount due	400	Canoe trailer	1,500
Bank	400	Cash	75

continued >

4 The Beaver Swimming Club has the following balances on 1 September Year 2.

	£		£
Equipment	500	Mini bus	10,300
Cash	100	Bank	400
Bill for engraving trophies	60	Pool hire due	50
Printing Gala programme due	120		

Calculate the accumulated fund at that date.

5 The Angels Cheerleading Club has the following balances on 1 September Year 2.

	£		£
Equipment	300	Mini bus	10,300
Cash	15	Bank	1,200
Creditors	120	Tuck shop stock	120
Rent and rates due	70	Subscriptions prepaid	30

Calculate the accumulated fund of the club on 1 September Year 2.

Example 4

The following are the list of assets and liabilities at the start and end of the financial year. Prepare the Balance Sheet of the Anytown Cricket Club at the end of the financial year for presentation at the Annual General Meeting.

	1 January Year 2	31 December Year 2
	£	£
Equipment	6,000	8,500
Bar stock	5,000	4,000
Subscriptions due	200	50
Bank	1,200	1,320
Rates due	150	–
Bar creditor		450
Accumulated fund	12,250	13,420
Surplus		1,170

continued ➤

Example 4 continued

STEP 1 – Set-up the Balance Sheet headings

Anytown Cricket Club Balance Sheet as at 31 December Year 2	£	£	£

STEP 2 – Group the fixed and current assets and enter in the Balance Sheet

Anytown Cricket Club Balance Sheet as at 31 December Year 2	£	£	£
Fixed assets			
Equipment			8,500
Current assets			
Stock	4,000		
Subscriptions due	50		
Bank	<u>1,320</u>	5,370	

STEP 3 – Complete **Current Liabilities**

Anytown Cricket Club Balance Sheet as at 31 December Year 2	£	£	£
Fixed assets			
Equipment			8,500
Current assets			
Stock	4,000		
Subscriptions due	50		
Bank	<u>1,320</u>	5,370	
Current liabilities			
Bar creditors		<u>450</u>	<u>4,920</u>
			13,420

continued ➣

Example 4 continued

STEP 4 – Complete the **financed by** section of the club's Balance sheet

When completing this you need to show the accumulated fund at the start of the financial year and add any surplus or deduct any deficit.

Anytown Cricket Club Balance Sheet as at 31 December Year 2	£	£	£
Fixed Assets			
Equipment			8,500
Current assets			
Stock	4,000		
Subscriptions due	50		
Bank	1,320	5,370	
Current liabilities			
Bar creditors		450	4,920
			13,420
Financed by			
Accumulated fund 1 January		12,250	
Add surplus		1,170	13,420

 *Now do Worksheets 9.3 and 9.5*

 Now do Worksheet 9.4

CHAPTER 10

Analysis and interpretation of accounts

Intermediate 2 Level Outcomes:

I2

This chapter includes material from Int 2 level Financial Accounting Outcome 5

☆ **Explain briefly the purpose of accounting ratios.**

☆ **Calculate accounting ratios using correct formulae.**

☆ **Comment on the performance of a business organisation for two consecutive financial periods.**

Higher Level Outcomes:

H

This chapter includes material from Higher level Financial Accounting Outcome 2

☆ **Explain the purpose of accounting ratios and the uses made of these by different stakeholders and users.**

☆ **Calculate accounting ratios using correct formulae.**

☆ **Comment, using either the ratios calculated or provided, on the performance of a business organisation for two consecutive accounting periods or of two similar business organisations for a single accounting period.**

I2

H

Analysing accounts to compare results

We already know that there are a wide range of individuals, groups and organisations who are interested in the accounts of a business enterprise. Stakeholders will have a particular interest in one company. These stakeholders are the owners, manager and employees. They may carry out a ratio analysis of the enterprise's final accounts to make comparisons between:

● past and present financial results;
● their results and the results of a similar business;
● budgeted and actual results.

In order to make the results of the analysis valid they must be carried out in the same way each time. The preparation of final accounts is governed by the Companies Acts and Accounting Standards. These make it easier to compare like with like because the same method of preparing financial statements is being employed from year to year and in many cases from enterprise to enterprise.

In carrying out the ratio analysis of the business enterprise the stakeholders will compare the results in three separate areas:

● Profitability
● Liquidity
● Efficiency

Profitability

Profitability ratios analyse whether the business has met its objectives. Profitability ratios compare the **mark-up**, **gross profit**, **net profit** and **return on capital** of an organisation.

Liquidity

Liquidity ratios assess how easy it is for the enterprise to pay it debts. Liquidity ratios will analyse the **current ratio**, which compares the current assets to the current liabilities and the **acid test ratio** which compares liquid capital (debtors, bank cash, and possibly, short term investments) with current liabilities.

Efficiency

Efficiency ratios give an indication of how well the business enterprise has used its assets and controlled its debts. Efficiency ratios will compare **average stock**, **rate of stock turnover**, **debtors' collection period**, **creditors' payment periods** and the **use of fixed assets**.

Other uses of ratio analysis

Ratio analysis can also be used as a basis for preparing forecasts of future results and to calculate missing figures. For example, if stock was destroyed in a fire, the value of stock destroyed can be calculated using the various ratios.

To learn about the various ratios which can be calculated we are going to look at each element of the final accounts.

Trading Account ratios

Information in the Trading Accounts allows us to calculate the **gross profit percentage** and **mark-up** ratios as **profitability** ratios and the **rate of stock turnover** as an **efficiency** ratio.

Profitability ratios

Gross profit percentage

The **gross profit percentage** is used to calculate what the gross profit is in relation to the sales achieved by the business

The **gross profit percentage** on turnover is calculated using the formula:

$$\text{gross profit percentage} = \frac{\text{Gross profit} \times 100}{\text{Turnover}}$$

(Remember **Turnover** is **Sales – Sales returns**)

Example 1

The following is the Trading Account of F Green for the years ended 31 December Year 1 and Year 2. You can use this information to calculate the gross profit percentage.

Trading Account of R Green for Years Ended 31 December Year 1 and Year 2				
	Year 1		Year 2	
	£	£	£	£
Sales		150,000		200,000
Less cost of goods sold				
Opening stock	15,000		10,000	
Add net purchases	70,000		125,000	
	85,000		135,000	
Less Closing stock	10,000		15,000	
Cost of sales		75,000		120,000
Gross profit		75,000		80,000

F Green's gross profit percentage for each year:

Year 1	Year 2
$\dfrac{£75,000 \times 100}{£150,000} = 50\%$	$\dfrac{£80,000 \times 100}{£200,000} = 40\%$

An interesting trend relating to the gross profit percentage is that if **business trends are steady** the gross profit percentage will be **constant**.

F Green's gross profit percentage has **fallen** by 10% from 50% to 40%. This will need to be investigated.

There are a number of reasons why there may be a fall in the gross profit percentage:

- **Cash losses:** theft of takings or wrong amounts being rung up on the till.
- **Stock losses:** theft of stock by employees or the passing out of stock to friends.
- **Mark downs**: the reduction in price of slow moving or shop soiled items. This may be the result of bad buying and an investigation may show this to be the result of one particular buyer and appropriate action should be taken.
- **Increased purchase price**: these increase could be passed on to the customer, but competition may not allow this.
- **Expenses**: some expenses are incurred in the Trading Account and increases in these will result in a reduction in the gross profit.
- **Incorrect stock valuation**: an overvaluation of stock overstates the profit and gives an artificially high percentage gross profit figure. As this stock then becomes the opening stock for the next period it will artificially inflate the cost of goods sold and result in a lower gross profit percentage in the next year.

Conversely the gross profit percentage may **increase**. A rise in the gross profit percentage is almost always due to increased efficiency.

Task 1

From the following information calculate the gross profit and the gross profit percentage for each of the following firms

	A	B	C	D	E
	£	£	£	£	£
Turnover	250,000	80,000	125,000	50,000	500,000
Cost of goods sold	125,000	60,000	75,000	20,000	375,000
Gross profit					
Gross profit %					

Mark-up

The **mark-up** is the amount by which the cost of goods sold has been increased to achieve the selling price. It is normally expressed as a percentage of the cost of sales.

The **mark-up** is calculated using the formula:

$$\textbf{mark-up} = \frac{\text{Gross profit} \times 100}{\text{Cost of sales}}$$

Example 2

Using the information given in Example 1, calculate F Green's mark-up for the year.

Year 1	Year 2
$\frac{£75,000 \times 100}{£75,000} = 100\%$	$\frac{£80,000 \times 100}{£120,000} = 66\frac{2}{3}\%$

Task 2

From the following information calculate the gross profit and the mark-up percentage for each of the following firms:

	A	B	C	D	E
	£	£	£	£	£
Turnover	250,000	80,000	125,000	50,000	500,000
Cost of goods sold	125,000	60,000	75,000	20,000	375,000
Gross profit					
Mark-up %					

Efficiency ratio

Rate of stock turnover

The rate of stock turnover figure is very important because it is at the point where the stock turns over that the profits are made. We say stock has turned over when it has been sold and is replaced with new stock. The higher the rate of stock turnover the greater should be the profits of the firm.

Rate of stock turnover is expressed as a number followed by the word **times**. For example if the rate of stock turnover was **six times** a year this would mean that the stock had been sold every two months.

The **rate of stock turnover** is calculated using the formula:

Rate of stock turnover = $\dfrac{\text{Cost of goods sold}}{\text{Average stock}}$ = x times

The formula to calculate the average stock is usually:

Average stock = $\dfrac{\text{opening + closing stocks}}{2}$

However if only one stock figure is given in a question that figure is taken as the average stock.

Example 3

Using the information in Example 1, calculate F Green's rate of stock turnover for each year.

Year 1	Year 2
Average stock $=\dfrac{\pounds15,000 + \pounds10,000}{2} = \pounds12,500$	Average stock $=\dfrac{\pounds10,000 + \pounds15,000}{2} = \pounds12,500$
Rate of stock turnover $=\dfrac{\pounds75,000}{\pounds12,500} = 6$ times	Rate of stock turnover $=\dfrac{\pounds120,000}{\pounds12,500} = 9.6$ times

The acceptable rate of stock turnover varies for different business enterprises. Retailers such as supermarkets will be looking to turnover their average stock 24 times in one year whereas a jeweller, selling high value items may be happy with a stock turnover rate of 4-6 times a year.

Occasionally you may be asked to express the rate of stock turnover as a period of time – days, weeks or months. Calculate the number of times the stock has turned over then divide this number into 365, days, 52 weeks or 12 months to calculate the period

The formula for this calculation will be:

Rate of stock turnover = $\dfrac{\text{Cost of goods sold}}{\text{Average stock}}$ = x times

continued ➤

Example 3 continued

Period of time $= \dfrac{\text{Days (or weeks, months)}}{\text{Rate of stock turnover}} = \text{x days (or weeks, months)}$

Green's rate of stock turnover expressed as weeks would be:

Rate of stock turnover	Rate of stock turnover
$= \dfrac{\text{£75,000}}{\text{£12,500}} = 6 \text{ times}$	$= \dfrac{\text{£120,000}}{\text{£12,500}} = 9.6 \text{ times}$
$\text{Period} = \dfrac{52 \text{ weeks}}{6 \text{ times}} = 8.67 \text{ weeks}$	$\text{Period} = \dfrac{52 \text{ weeks}}{9.6 \text{ times}} = 5.42 \text{ weeks}$

Task 3

a) From the following information calculate the average stock and the rate of stock turnover:

Cost of Sales £	Stock at start £	Stock at end £
100,000	25,000	21,000
250,000	35,000	30,000
350,000	47,000	49,000
20,000	5,000	3,000
75,000	13,500	11,500
60,000	18,000	14,500
200,000	29,000	35,000

b) Calculate the stock turnover in weeks for the rates of stock turnover calculated in a).

Task 4

1 A Paxton provides you with the following information for the years ended 31 December Year 1, 2 and 3.

continued ➤

Trading Accounts of A Paxton for Years ended 31 December Year 1, 2 and 3.

	Year 1		Year 2		Year 3	
	£	£	£	£	£	£
Sales		68,000		75,000		82,000
Less Cost of sales						
Opening stock	4,500		5,000		6,500	
Purchases	34,200		36,300		39,000	
	38,700		41,300		45,500	
Less Closing stock	5,000	33,700	6,500	34,800	5,300	40,200
Gross profit		34,300		40,200		41,800

You are required to calculate:

a) Gross profit percentage.

b) Rate of stock turnover.

c) Rate of stock turnover in weeks.

2 For Paxton calculate his mark-up percentage for each year.

3 R Brown provides you with the following information and asks you to calculate his gross profit percentage and rate of stock turnover in months for the financial years ended 30 June Year 1, 2, 3 and 4.

	Year 1	Year 2	Year 3	Year 4
	£	£	£	£
Sales	340,000	220,000	460,000	500,000
Cost of goods sold	170,000	55,000	368,000	300,000
Average stock	21,250	6,875	36,800	25,000

4 For Brown calculate the mark-up percentage for each year.

5 F Kirkwood provides you with the following information and asks you to calculate his gross profit percentage and rate of stock turnover for the financial years ended 31 October Year 1, 2, 3 and 4.

	Year 1	Year 2	Year 3	Year 4
	£	£	£	£
Sales	500,000	540,000	480,000	600,000
Cost of goods sold	200,000	300,000	360,000	210,000
Average Stock	25,000	15,000	20,000	35,000

continued ➤

6 Using the information in Question 5 calculate Kirkwood's mark-up percentage for each year.

7 G Williamson provides you with the following information for the years ended 31 March Years 1, 2 and 3.

Trading Accounts of G Williamson for Years ended 31 March Year 1, 2 and 3						
	Year 1		Year 2		Year 3	
	£000s	£000s	£000s	£000s	£000s	£000s
Sales		160		180		200
Less Cost of sales						
Opening stock	10		14		16	
Purchases	100		130		160	
	110		144		176	
Less Closing stock	14	96	16	128	20	156
Gross profit		64		52		44

You are required to calculate:

a) Gross profit percentage
b) Average stock
c) Rate of stock turnover in days

8 From the information provided in Question 7 calculate Williamson's mark-up for each year.

Profit and Loss account ratios

Information in the profit and loss accounts allows us to calculate the **net profit percentage** as a **profitability** ratio and the **expense ratio** as an **efficiency** ratio.

Profitability ratio

Net profit percentage

The **net profit percentage** ratio indicates how well a business enterprise has controlled their overheads. The **net profit** figure is calculated by deducting the **total expenses** from the **gross profit**. If there is little difference between the gross and net profit percentages this indicates that the business enterprise has low overheads or has been able to control its overheads efficiently.

The net profit percentage on turnover is calculated using the formula:

$$\textbf{Net profit percentage on turnover} = \frac{\text{Net profit} \times 100}{\text{Turnover}}$$

Example 4

This Profit and Loss Account is a continuation from the Trading Account in Example 1. The turnover figures are given below to help with the preparation of the ratios. You can use the information to calculate F Green's net profit for the year.

	Year 1		Year 2	
	£	£	£	£
Turnover		150,000		200,000

The following is the Profit and Loss Account of F Green for the years ended 31 December Year 1 and Year 2.

Profit and Loss Account of R Green for Years Ended 31 December Year 1 and Year 2				
	Year 1		Year 2	
	£	£	£	£
Gross Profit		75,000		80,000
Less expenses				
Administration expenses	15,000		17,000	
Selling expense	4,000		3,800	
Financial expenses	2,000	21,000	2,200	23,000
Net profit		54,000		57,000

F Green's net profit percentage for each year:

Year 1	Year 2
$\dfrac{£54,000 \times 100}{£150,000} = 36\%$	$\dfrac{£57,000 \times 100}{£200,000} = 28.5\%$

Gross profits are carried forward to the Profit and Loss Account where other incomes are added and losses and expenses deducted. The net profit percentage should be fairly constant from year to year and if not an investigation should be carried out.

If the gross profit has remained constant and the net profit percentage has decreased then an explanation should be sought. If the gross profit percentage has remained constant there is clearly nothing wrong with the trading activities of the enterprise. There can therefore be only two explanations for this decrease:

- expenses have increased;
- other incomes/profits have declined, such as a decrease in commission received, rent or commission received etc.

Efficiency ratio

Expense ratios

Expense ratios enable an accountant to compare every expense with the same expense from the previous year. By converting the actual amount paid to a percentage the expenses can be compared on the same basis. The accountant can then see whether they have risen abnormally.

Expense ratios are calculated using the formula:

$$\textbf{Expense ratio} = \frac{\text{Expense} \times 100}{\text{Turnover}}$$

Example 5

Use the information in Example 1 and 4 to calculate F Green's expenses ratios for each year:

Year 1	Year 2
Administration expenses percentage:	Administration expenses percentage:
$\frac{£15,000 \times 100}{£150,000} = 10\%$	$\frac{£17,000 \times 100}{£200,000} = 8.5\%$
Selling expenses:	Selling expenses:
$\frac{£4,000 \times 100}{£150,000} = 2.67\%$	$\frac{3,800 \times 100}{£200,000} = 1.9\%$
Financial expenses percentage:	Financial expenses percentage:
$\frac{£2,000 \times 100}{£150,000} = 1.33\%$	$\frac{2,200 \times 100}{£200,000} = 1.1\%$

From the expense ratio percentages it can be clearly seen that Year 2 is consistently lower, despite the fact that the gross and net profit percentages are also lower than Year 1. Expenses are being controlled more efficiently in Year 2.

 Task 5

Calculate the net profit and expense ratios from the following information for the 4 enterprises all operating in the video rental market:

	Turnover (£)	Net Profit (£)	Administration Expenses (£)	Selling Expenses (£)
Video nights	250,000	100,000	100,000	50,000
Videos-4-u	300,000	150,000	75,000	5,000
Nights-in	75,000	50,000	30,000	20,000
Video Rentals	550,000	350,000	125,000	75,000

Now do Worksheet 10.1

Balance Sheet ratios

The Balance Sheet shows the assets and liabilities of a business enterprise on a particular date, usually the end of the financial year. The Balance Sheet can be analysed to show how efficient the enterprise is at controlling debts, using assets; to show whether it can pay its debts and how profitable it has been for the owner of the business.

The information contained in the Balance Sheet can be used to calculate the **return on capital employed** (**ROCE**) as a profitability ratio, the **current** and **acid test** ratios as Liquidity ratios, and **debtors collection period**, **creditors payment period**, and **turnover to fixed assets** ratios as efficiency ratios.

Profitability ratios

Return on capital employed

Capital employed is a statement of the capital used to provide two classes of assets:

- **Fixed capital** tied up in the **fixed assets** of the enterprise. These are in permanent use in the business forming the framework for running its enterprise.
- **Circulating** or **floating capital** tied up in the **current aassets** which are in the process of being turned over, or circulated, and used in the business to make a profit.

The return on capital employed (ROCE) is the most important ratio calculated by the owner, partners and shareholders of a business enterprise. It compares the profit earned in the year with the capital invested in the business.

A good return on the capital employed is essential to any business organisation. Poor returns may make the owners or partners consider whether it is worthwhile to continue to run the business or to sell it and invest their money elsewhere. Shareholders will also consider whether they should retain or sell shares in a company which is not giving them an adequate dividend because of poor profits. (ROCE can also be expressed as **return on capital invested**.)

There are many different definitions and formulae used to calculate the ROCE. The formula used will depend on the type of business and the circumstances in which you meet the term.

Tasks in this unit will concentrate on two formulae, ROCE for a sole trader, and ROCE for other business organisations.

Return on capital employed for a sole trader

The return on capital employed for a sole trader or partnership is calculated using the formula:

$$\text{Return on capital employed} = \frac{\text{Net profit}}{\text{Capital at start}} \times 100$$

Example 6

Erin Smith started business on 1 March Year investing £50,000. At the end of the financial year the net profit achieved was £12,500.

Smith's return on capital employed is:

$$\text{ROCE} = \frac{£12,500}{£50,000} \times 100 = 25\%$$

This is a good return and a much better return than if Smith had simply deposited the £50,000 in a bank or building society account.

Task 6

From the following information calculate the return on capital employed for each of the sole traders who all operate in the bakery business.

	The Oven Shop	The Pie Shop	Goodies Bakery	Argyle Bakery
Capital at start	£75,000	£100,000	£120,000	£200,000
Net profit for year	£34,000	£10,000	£45,000	£108,000

Comment on how satisfied each business will be with their ROCE.

Return on capital employed for other business organisations

For business organisations other than sole traders, the return on capital employed is calculated using the formula:

$$\text{ROCE} = \frac{\text{Net profit after tax} \times 100\%}{(\text{Fixed assets} + \text{net current assets*}) - \text{long-term liabilities}}$$

* **net current assets** are **current assets – current liabilities**

Example 7

From the following information calculate the return on capital employed of Alpha Enterprises.

Fixed assets	£200,000
Current assets	£52,000
Current liabilities	£35,000
Long-term liabilities	£75,000
Net profit after tax	£50,000

$$\textbf{ROCE} = \frac{£50,000 \times 100\%}{(£200,000 + (£52,000 - £35,000)) - £75,000}$$
$$= 35.2\%$$

This is a good return for the business and Alpha Enterprises is probably happy with it.

Task 7

From the following information calculate the return on capital employed for the following businesses.

	Black Ltd £000s	White Ltd £000s	Grey Ltd £000s	Green Ltd £000s	Brown Ltd £000s
Fixed assets	250	125	90	30	70
Current assets	50	30	10	6	12
Current liabilities	20	10	5	2	4
Long-term liabilities	80	45	25	8	10
Net profit after tax	70	35	12	8	18

Liquidity ratios

An enterprise must have sufficient liquid assets to pay any immediate debts which arise. Liquid assets are those which can be turned into cash very quickly such as short-term investments, stock, debtors and bank. The two ratios used to monitor the liquidity position of a business enterprise are the **current ratio** and the **acid test ratio**.

Current ratio

The current ratio (or **working capital ratio**) focuses on the relationship between the **current assets** and **current liabilities**.

The current ratio is calculated using the formula:

$$\text{Current ratio} = \frac{\text{Current assets}}{\text{Current liabilities}}$$

A enterprise should never allow itself to run short of working capital. This is a very common reason for business failures. If the business purchases too many fixed assets, (called **over-capitalisation**) and then has to borrow money from the bank, (usually 2% above base lending rate), the enterprise will find that much of its profits are being creamed off by the bank in the form of interest, leaving the enterprise unable to earn a fair reward for its efforts.

There is no 'right' figure for the current ratio. The ratio often depends on the type of business the enterprise operates. The current ratio should never fall below 1:1 - for every £1 of current liabilities there should be £1 of current assets available to pay them off. An enterprise would prefer to have a higher current ratio and in general accountants consider 1.5:1 to be acceptable, however, some prefer the safer margin of 2:1.

If a business enterprise has a current ratio less than 1:1 it means that it is in effect insolvent and could be under pressure from its creditors to pay off its debts quickly. A low ratio indicates a lack of working capital and an ability to meet the immediate debts. A high ratio might indicate that too much capital could be tied up in stock or in cash which is not being used to generate income.

Example 8

The following information has been extracted from the balance sheet of Alpha Enterprises for the year ended 31 December Year 2.

	£	£
Current assets		
Stock	16,000	
Debtors	14,000	
Bank	20,000	
Cash	2,000	52,000
Current liabilities		
Creditors	28,000	
VAT	7,000	35,000
Working capital		17,000

Current ratio = $\dfrac{\text{Current assets}}{\text{Current liabilities}}$

$$= \frac{£52,000}{£35,000}$$

$$= 1.49:1$$

This would be considered to be an acceptable ratio by the accountant of Alpha Enterprises.

Task 8

From the following balance sheet extracts calculate the current ratio for each enterprise.

Current Assets	Alpha	Beta	Gamma	Delta	Omega
Stock	25,000	15,000	16,000	22,500	10,500
Debtors	8,000	18,000	19,600	5,400	6,300
Bank	10,000	7,000	5,400	22,300	4,800
Cash	3,000	1,000	500	200	800
Current liabilities					
Creditors	18,000	32,500	24,500	15,300	15,700
VAT	5,000	12,500	6,200	6,500	2,400

Calculate the current ratio for each of the above enterprises and comment on their current liquidity position.

Acid test ratio

The **acid test ratio** is often referred to as the **quick ratio** or **liquid capital ratio** and it is the critical test of solvency. Can the enterprise, with its present cash and debtors, (due to pay within the month) meet the current liabilities? This ratio should be at least 1:1. For every £1 of current liabilities there should be £1 of liquid capital available to pay them.

Sometimes in calculating the acid test ratio readily marketable investments will be added to the quick assets figure.

The acid test ratio is calculated using the formula:

$$\textbf{Acid test ratio} = \frac{\text{Current assets} - \text{stock}}{\text{Current liabilities}}$$

The acid test ratio for Alpha Enterprise would be:

$$\text{Acid test ratio} = \frac{\$52,000 - \$16,000}{\$35,000} = 1.03:1$$

FINANCIAL ACCOUNTING

Task 9

From the following information calculate the acid test ratio for each enterprise.

Current Assets	Alpha	Beta	Gamma	Delta	Omega
Stock	25,000	15,000	16,000	22,500	10,500
Debtors	8,000	18,000	19,600	5,400	6,300
Bank	10,000	7,000	5,400	22,300	4,800
Cash	3,000	1,000	500	200	800
Current liabilities					
Creditors	18,000	32,500	24,500	15,300	15,700
VAT	5,000	12,500	6,200	6,500	2,400

Comment on the acid test liquidity position of each enterprise.

Task 10

Compare the current ratio calculated in Task 8 with the acid test ratio calculated in Task 9 for each of the enterprises.

Identify the reasons why some enterprises have an unacceptable current ratio and/or acid test ratios.

Efficiency ratios

Debtors collection period

The **debtors' collection period** measures the time taken by debtors to pay their debts. It can be expressed in days, weeks or months. It is an indication of how efficient the business enterprises credit control system is operating.

The debtors collection period is calculated using the formula:

$$\textbf{Debtors collection period} = \frac{\text{Average debtors} \times \text{time period*}}{\text{Total credit sales}}$$

*The time period may be days, weeks or months, depending on how the question has been asked. To calculate the number of days, weeks or months credit allowed to the debtors multiply by 365, 52 or 12. Note that you should always round up the period to a whole number of days.

Example 9

Alpha Enterprise supplies you with the following information relating to their debtors and credit sales for the 3 year period ending 31 December Year 5.

Debtors balance on 1 January Year 3 was £18,000.

	Year 3 £	Year 4 £	Year 5 £
Debtors	20,000	22,500	25,000
Credit sales	200,000	180,000	240,000

Use the above information to calculate the length of time we allow our debtors to pay (in days)

$$\text{Debtors collection period} = \frac{\text{Average debtors} \times 365}{\text{Total credit sales}}$$

Year 3

$$\frac{((£18,000 + £20,000)/2) \times 365}{£200,000} = 34.67 \text{ days, rounded up to 35 days}$$

Year 4

$$\frac{((£20,000 + £22,500)/2) \times 365}{£180,000} = 43.1 \text{ days, rounded up to 44 days}$$

Year 5

$$\frac{((£22,500 + £25,000)/2) \times 365}{£240,000} = 36.12 \text{ days, rounded up to 37 days.}$$

Task 11

Beta Enterprise supplies you with the following information relating to their debtors, and credit sales for the 3 year period ending 31 August Year 5.

Debtors at 1 September Year 2 were £16,000.

	Year 3 £	Year 4 £	Year 5 £
Debtors	12,000	12,300	25,000
Credit sales	190,000	180,000	100,000

Calculate the debtors collection period in days it takes for Beta Enterprises debtors to pay.

Creditors payment period

The **creditors payment period** is the length of time it takes the enterprise to pay its creditors. It can also be expressed in days, weeks or months.

The creditors payment period is calculated using the formula:

$$\text{Creditors payment period} = \frac{\text{Average Creditors} \times \text{time period*}}{\text{Total credit sales}}$$

*The time period may be days, weeks or months, depending on how the question has been asked. To calculate the number of days, weeks or months credit allowed to the debtors multiply by 365, 52 or 12. As with the debtors' collection period, the answers must be rounded up to a whole number of days.

Example 10

Alpha Enterprise supplies you with the following information relating to their creditors and credit purchases for the 3 year period ending 31 December Year 5.

Creditor balances on 1 January Year 3 were £12,000.

	Year 3 £	Year 4 £	Year 5 £
Creditors	14,000	12,300	16,000
Credit Purchases	100,000	90,000	120,000

$$\text{Creditors payment period} = \frac{\text{Average creditors} \times 365}{\text{Total credit purchases}}$$

Year 3

$$\frac{((£12,000 + £14,000)/2) \times 365}{£100,000} = 47.45 \text{ days, rounded up to 48 days}$$

Year 4

$$\frac{((£14,000 + £12,300)/2) \times 365}{£90,000} = 53.3 \text{ days, rounded up to 54 days}$$

Year 5

$$\frac{((£12,300 + £16,000)/2) \times 365}{£120,000} = 43.04 \text{ days, rounded up to 44 days.}$$

Alpha Enterprise is taking quite a long time to pay their creditors. Some creditors may object to this and put pressure on Alpha Enterprise. They may stop supplying them with the goods unless they pay faster. Alpha Enterprises are losing out on any cash discounts offered for prompt payment.

Task 12

Delta Enterprise supplies you with the following information relating to their creditors, and credit purchases for the 3 year period ending 31 March Year 5.

Creditors at 1 April Year 2 were £9,000.

	Year 3 £	Year 4 £	Year 5 £
Creditors	6,000	14,000	12,000
Credit Purchases	120,000	130,000	150,000

Calculate the creditors payment period in weeks it takes for Delta Enterprises debtors to pay.

Fixed asset turnover

The **fixed asset turnover** measures how productive the fixed assets employed in the business are at generating sales income or turnover. It will show the sales generated for every £1 of fixed asset employed in the business. An enterprise will be interested in this ratio, particularly if they have recently invested in fixed assets, to see if the increase in fixed assets has been worthwhile and generated an increase in turnover.

This ratio indicates a trend in performance and needs to be considered along with other ratios before effective conclusions can be drawn.

The fixed asset turnover is calculated using the formula:

$$\text{Fixed asset turnover} = \frac{\text{Net turnover}}{\text{Fixed assets at net book value}}$$

Example 11

The following information was extracted from the final accounts of Omega Ltd for the years 1, 2 and 3. Calculate the fixed asset turnover ratio.

	Year 1	Year 2	Year 3
Fixed assets (NBV)	100,000	150,000	140,000
Net turnover	60,000	75,000	80,000

Year 1

$$\text{Fixed asset turnover} = \frac{£60,000}{£100,000} = 0.6:1$$

Year 2

$$\text{Fixed asset turnover} = \frac{£75,000}{£150,000} = 0.5:1$$

Year 3

$$\text{Fixed asset turnover} = \frac{£80,000}{£140,000} = 0.57:1$$

Task 13

The following information was extracted from the final accounts of Zeta Ltd for the Years 1, 2 and 3.

Calculate the fixed asset turnover ratio

	Year 1 £	Year 2 £	Year 3 £
Fixed assets (NBV)	150,000	240,000	380,000
Net turnover	60,000	110,000	190,000

Summary of accounting ratio formulae

Ratio	Formulae
Profitability	
Gross Profit	$\dfrac{\text{Gross Profit} \times 100}{\text{Turnover}}$
Net Profit	$\dfrac{\text{Net Profit} \times 100}{\text{Turnover}}$
Mark-up*	$\dfrac{\text{Gross Profit} \times 100}{\text{Cost of sales}}$
Return on Capital Employed	$\dfrac{\text{Net Profit} \times 100}{\text{Capital at start}}$ *or* $\dfrac{\text{Net Profit after Tax} \times 100\%}{\text{(Fixed Assets + Net Current Assets*)} - \text{Long-term Liabilities}}$
Liquidity	
Current Ratio	$\dfrac{\text{Current Assets}}{\text{Current Liabilities}}$
Acid Test Ratio*	$\dfrac{\text{Current Assets} - \text{Stock}}{\text{Current Liabilities}}$
Efficiency Ratios	
Average Stock	$\dfrac{\text{Opening} + \text{Closing stocks}}{2}$
Rate of Stock Turnover	$\dfrac{\text{Cost of Goods Sold}}{\text{Average Stock}} = \text{times}$ $\dfrac{\text{Days, Weeks, Months}}{\text{Rate of Stock Turnover}}$

continued ➤

Efficiency Ratios	
Expense Ratios	$\dfrac{\text{Expense}}{\text{Turnover}} \times 100$
Debtors' Collection Period	$\dfrac{\text{Average Debtors} \times \text{time period*}}{\text{Total Credit Sales}}$
Creditors' Payment Period	$\dfrac{\text{Average Creditors} \times \text{time period*}}{\text{Total Credit Purchases}}$
Fixed Asset Turnover	$\dfrac{\text{Net Turnover}}{\text{Fixed Assets at net book value}}$

*Examined at Higher only

Task 14

The following is the Trading, Profit and Loss and Balance Sheet of XYZ for the years ended 31 December Year 1, 2 and 3.

	Year 1 £	Year 2 £	Year 3 £
Sales – Cash	100,000	100,000	75,000
Sales – Credit	60,000	60,000	45,000
Total sales	160,000	160,000	120,000
Less Cost of sales	136,000	120,000	96,000
Gross profit	24,000	40,000	24,000
Less Overheads:			
Salaries and wages	12,000	20,000	10,000
Other expenses	7,000	17,000	8,000
Total overheads	19,000	37,000	18,000
Net profit	5,000	3,000	6,000

continued ➤

Balance Sheet 31 December Years 1, 2 and 3			
	Year 1 £	Year 2 £	Year 3 £
Fixed assets			
Land and buildings	12,000	16,000	15,000
Plant and equipment	6,000	5,000	8,000
	18,000	21,000	23,000
Add Working capital			
Current assets			
Stock	9,000	6,000	8,000
Debtors	10,500	7,000	9,500
Bank and cash	15,500	17,500	16,500
	35,000	30,500	34,000
Less Current liabilities			
Creditors	16,000	11,500	11,000
	19,000	19,000	23,000
Capital employed	37,000	40,000	46,000
Financed by			
Capital at start	32,000	37,000	40,000
Add Net profit	5,000	3,000	6,000
Capital at end	37,000	40,000	46,000

Note The stock, debtors and creditors figures shown in the Balance Sheet for each year is equivalent to the average figure for that year.

All purchases are on credit, so use the cost of sales as the credit purchases figure when calculating the creditors payment period.

From the above accounts of XYZ you are required to calculate the following ratios for each year.

a) Gross profit percentage

b) Net profit percentage

c) Stock turnover

d) Total expenses ratio to turnover

e) Return on capital employed

f) Current ratio

g) Fixed asset to turnover

continued ➤

h) Acid test ratio

i) Debtors collection period in months

j) Creditors payment period in months

Your answers should be set out in a table which groups the results for each year under the headings of **profitability**, **liquidity** and **efficiency**.

An example of the table is given here:

Ratio	Year 1	Year 2	Year 3
Profitability			
Liquidity			
Efficiency			

Note You must show full working notes for each calculation.

Now do Worksheet 10.2

Using ratios to prepare estimated statements

In addition to analysing the performance of a business organisation, ratios can be used to prepare forecast statements and to calculate missing figures for inclusion in a set of final accounts.

Using the Gross Profit Ratio

Remember that the Gross Profit figure is calculated using the following formulae:

Gross profit	= Sales – Cost of goods sold
	= £100,000 – £60,000
so Gross profit	= £40,000

Given any two of these components the third can be calculated:

Sales	= Cost of goods sold + profit
	= £60,000 + £40,000
so Sales	= £100,000

Cost of goods sold	= Sales – Profit
	= £100,000 – £40,000
so Cost of goods sold	= £60,000

Task 15

Copy and complete the table.

	Turnover £	Cost of Goods Sold £	Gross Profit £
	300,000		75,000
		120,000	120,000
	90,000		30,000
	150,000	60,000	
		50,000	75,000
	80,000		35,000
		43,500	26,500
	25,000		10,000

Example 12

The expected turnover of J Brown's business is £100,000 and he estimates that his gross profit will be 25% of his **cost of goods sold**. Calculate the gross profit figure.

The gross profit is calculated using the following formula:

$$\textbf{Gross profit} = \frac{\text{Gross profit \% × turnover £}}{\text{Cost of goods sold \% + gross profit \%}}$$

STEP 1 – Consider the information we know

Sales are £100,000 and the gross profit is 25% of his cost of goods sold.

The gross profit amount is calculated as a percentage of the cost of goods sold. When we do not know the actual amount, we substitute 100% to represent the cost of goods sold.

STEP 2 – Calculate the selling price as a percentage of the cost price

The selling price of the goods is then expressed as:

Cost % + Profit % = 100% + 25% = 125%

STEP 3 – Calculate the gross profit

To calculate his gross profit use the following formula:

$$\text{Gross profit} = \frac{\text{Gross profit \% × turnover £}}{\text{Cost of goods sold \% + gross profit \%}}$$

$$= \frac{25\% × £100,000}{100\% + 25\%}$$

$$= £20,000$$

continued ➤

FINANCIAL ACCOUNTING

Example 12 continued

STEP 4 – Check the accuracy of your calculation

To check that the gross profit actually is 25% of the cost of sales:

Turnover	= £100,000
Less Gross profit	= £20,000
Cost of sales	= £80,000

And £20,000 = 25% of £80,000 – the cost of coods sold.

Task 16

Copy and complete the following table

Sales	Cost of Sales	Gross Profit %	Gross Profit £
£100,000		25% of cost of sales	
£250,000	£150,000	?% of cost of sales	£100,000
£350,000		?% cost of sales	£150,000
£20,000	£10,000	?% of cost of sales	
£75,000		20% of cost of sales	
£60,000		20% of cost of sales	
£200,000		25% of cost of sales	

Using the rate of stock turnover and average stock

The **rate of stock turnover = cost of goods sold ÷ average stock** = number of times

If we know two of the components we can calculate the third. If the cost of goods sold is £150,000 and the average stock is £25,000, the rate of stock turnover is:

Cost of goods sold ÷ average stock = number of times
= £150,000 ÷ £25,000 = 6 times

and rearranging to calculate the cost of goods sold:

Average stock × rate of stock turnover = cost of goods sold
= £25,000 × 6 times = £150,000

and rearranging again to calculate the average stock:

Cost of goods sold ÷ rate of stock turnover = average stock
= £150,000 ÷ 6 times = £25,000

(Remember that the average stock is usually opening stock + closing stock ÷ 2)

If we know the average stock and the opening or closing stock we can calculate the missing figure.

Example 13

Green wants to know the value of his opening stock. His average stock for the year was £20,000 and his closing stock is £18,000.

STEP 1 – Calculate the total of the opening and closing stock

To do this we need to know what the total of the stock was before the average was calculated.

Total stock = Average stock × 2
= £20,000 × 2
= £40,000

We know what the closing stock figure is £18,000, so to calculate the opening stock we subtract the closing stock from the total stock:

Opening stock = Total stock – closing stock
= £40,000 – £18,000
= £22,000

The above techniques can be used when preparing an estimated trading account.

Task 17

Calculate the missing figures for the table:

Cost of Goods Sold £	Rate of Turnover	Average Stock(£)	Opening Stock £	Closing Stock £
£75,000		£25,000	£28,000	
	8 times	35,000		46,000
£120,000		30,000	35,000	
	10 times	27,000		34,000
	5 times	36,000	41,500	
£66,900		6,690	8,200	
£240,500	10 times		29,100	
750,000		50,000	49,500	
	5 times	12,300		10,800

Calculating purchases

When preparing an estimated Trading and Profit and Loss Account you may not be given the purchases figure.

Example 14

Jane Wyper provides you with the following information and asks you to prepare her Profit Statement for the year ended 30 April Year 2.

Credit sales	£240,000
Gross profit ratio	40%
Net profit ratio	25%
Rate of stock turnover	8 times
Opening stock	£20,000

STEP 1 – Prepare a template for the Profit Statement, entering figuring already known

Jane Wyper

Profit Statement for year ended 30 April Year 2

	£	£
Sales		240,000
Less Cost of sales		
Opening stock	20,000	
Add Purchases	————	
Less Closing stock	————	
Cost of goods sold		————
Gross profit		
Less expenses		————
Net profit		

STEP 2 – Calculate the gross and net profit figures and enter them into the template

Gross profit = 40% of £240,000 = £96,000
Net profit = 25% of £240,000 = £60,000

continued ➤

Example 14 continued

Jane Wyper

Profit Statement for year ended 30 April Year 2

	£	£
Sales		240,000
Less Cost of sales		
Opening stock	20,000	
Add Purchases	————	
Less Closing stock	————	
Cost of goods sold		————
Gross profit		**96,000**
Less Expenses		————
Net profit		**60,000**

STEP 3 – Calculate and enter the cost of goods sold and the expenses figures into the template

You already know that the **cost of goods sold = sales – gross profit**

   = £240,000 – £96,000 = £144,000

and that the **expenses = gross profit – net profit**

   = £96,000 – £60,000 = £36,000

Jane Wyper

Profit Statement for year ended 30 April Year 2

	£	£
Sales		240,000
Less Cost of sales		
Opening stock	20,000	
Add Purchases	————	
Less Closing stock	————	
Cost of goods sold		**144,000**
Gross profit		96,000
Less Expenses		**36,000**
Net profit		60,000

continued ➤

Example 14 continued

STEP 4 – Calculate the closing stock figure

To calculate the closing stock figure we need to know the average stock figure:

Average stock = Cost of goods sold ÷ rate of stock turnover
= £144,000 ÷ 8 = £18,000

Now calculate the total of the opening and closing stocks:

Average Stock × 2
= £18,000 × 2 = £36,000

To calculate the closing stock:

Closing stock = Total stocks – opening stock
= £36,000 – £20,000 = £16,000

Jane Wyper

Profit Statement for year ended 30 April Year 2

	£	£
Sales		240,000
Less Cost of sales		
Opening stock	20,000	
Add Purchases	———	
Less Closing stock	**16,000**	
Cost of goods sold		144,000
Gross profit		96,000
Less Expenses		36,000
Net profit		60,000

STEP 5 – Calculate the purchases figure

To calculate the purchases figure you need to work backwards through the Trading Account. The cost of goods sold amount is calculated by deducting the closing stock from (opening stock + purchases).

The total of opening stock + purchases can be calculated by adding the closing stock to the cost of coods cold:

= £16,000 + £144,000 = £160,000

This figure represents the cost of goods we had **available for sale** during the year and is the opening stock plus the purchases.

The purchases can now be calculated by deducting the opening stock from the cost of goods **available for sale**

Cost of goods available for sale – opening stock
= £160,000 – £20,000 = £140,000

continued ➤

Example 14 continued

Jane Wyper		
Profit Statement for year ended 30 April Year 2		
	£	£
Sales		240,000
Less Cost of sales		
Opening stock	20,000	
Add purchases	**140,000**	
Cost of goods available for sale	160,000	
Less Closing stock	16,000	
Cost of goods sold		144,000
Gross profit		96,000
Less Expenses		36,000
Net profit		60,000

Task 18

From the following information you are required to prepare Profit Statements for each business enterprise for the year ended 31 May Year 2.

	Alpha Ltd	Beta Ltd	Delta Ltd	Gamma Ltd	Omega Ltd
Credit Sales	£80,000	£300,000	£180,000	£80,000	£90,000
Gross Profit %	25%	45%	35%	25%	50%
Net Profit %	15%	25%	20%	20%	30%
Rate of Stock Turnover	10 times	12 times	8 times	6 times	5 times
Opening Stock	8,000		19,000		7,800
Closing Stock		19,500		10,500	

  Now do Worksheet 10.3

 ***Now do Worksheet 10.4***

Analysing the performance of a business enterprise

Analysing the performance of a business enterprise is probably one of the most difficult areas in accounting for students to become proficient. Candidates may be required to compare the results of a single enterprise for a two year period or to compare the enterprise's results with the industry standard or with that of a competitor.

Analysing the performance of a business enterprise is more than just calculating a set of ratios. It requires an understanding of how these ratios are related.

Example 15

The following are the industry standard ratios and those calculated for James Allan & Sons for the year ended 31 December Year 1 and Year 2

Ratio	Year 1	Year 2
Gross Profit ratio	30%	35%
Net Profit ratio	22%	20%
Mark-up ratio	50%	50%
Return on Capital Employed	15%	18%
Current ratio	1.75:1	2.2:1
Acid test ratio	0.9:1	1.1:1
Expense ratio	8%	15%
Rate of Stock Turnover	6 times	8 times
Turnover to Fixed Assets	1.5:1	2:1
Debtors Collection period	35 days	28 days
Creditors Payment period	30 days	31 days

When comparing performance there are several questions which need to be considered. You need to compare the four **profitability** ratios and consider how they have changed from one year to the next.

You also need to consider the liquidity and efficiency ratios. **Liquidity** ratios indicate how easy it is for the enterprise to pay off its debts. These are a test of the solvency of the enterprise. **Efficiency** ratios allow the enterprise to compare how efficient it is at controlling expenses, selling its goods, collecting debts, paying creditors, and using its fixed assets.

STEP 1 – Compare the mark-up figures. This is a **profitability** ratio.

When comparing mark-up you need to consider the following:

- Has the percentage increased or decreased?
- Is the reason for the increase/decrease the result of a change in price?
- Did the decrease result in more sales?

continued ➤

Example 15   continued

- Did they increase mark-up because there is no competition?
- Is the market such that they can charge a higher price and still sell the same number of goods. (The rate of stock turnover will help to answer this question.)

Allan's mark-up ratio has remained the same for each year. They may not be able to alter it because of market conditions.

STEP 2 – Consider the gross profit ratio. This is a **profitability** ratio.

The gross profit percentage will be linked to the mark-up. When comparing gross profit ratios you need to consider:

- Was the increases/decrease was due to a change in Mark-up?
- Was there an increase in the cost of goods sold not being passed onto their customer?
- Was there a decrease in the cost of goods sold because of bulk buying?
- Was there a change in supplier who offered better discounts and these are not passed onto customers in the form of lower prices.

There was no change in mark-up, but there has been an increase in the gross profit percentage. This could be because of either a change in supplier who offered lower prices, or bulk buying because of increased demand. These lower prices have not being passed onto customers.

STEP 3 – Consider the net profit ratio. This is a **profitability** ratio.

The net profit ratio will be linked to the gross profit and mark-up ratios. If these increase, the net profit ratio will generally increase unless the enterprise is unable to control its expenses efficiently.

When comparing the net profit ratio you need to consider:

- Was the increase/decrease due to a change in mark-up or gross profit ratio?
- Have the enterprise's expenses increased/decreased during the year in relation to turnover? Check the expenses ratio to confirm the reason.
- How efficient is the enterprise at controlling expenses?

The net profit ratio of Allan has decreased in Year 2. This has been brought about by an increase in their expenses. The enterprise has not been able to control its expenses as efficiently in year 2 as it did in year 1.

STEP 4 – Consider the return on capital employed. This is a **profitability** ratio.

Return on capital employed is linked to the net profit, gross profit and mark-up ratio. When comparing return on capital employed you need to consider:

- If the return on capital employed has increased, is it because of increased efficiency, better control of expenses, increased prices?
- If the ROCE decreased, is it because the enterprise is less efficient in controlling expenses?

continued ➤

Example 15 continued

- You may also consider whether the return is acceptable. Could the owner receive the same or a better return by investing the capital in a building society?

STEP 5 – Compare the current (working capital) ratio. This is a **liquidity** ratio.

When considering liquidity you can compare the results for the 2 years but may also need to take into account the accepted norm for the current ratio. Ratios between 1.5:1 and 2:1 are considered acceptable.

You may also need to consider how the debtors' collection period and the creditors payment period and the stock turnover may result in a change in the current ratio.

When comparing the performance you may wish to consider:

- If the ratio has increased is it because of a build up in stock resulting from a reduction in the rate of stock turnover?
- Has the business purchased fixed assets resulting in a shortage of liquid resources?
- Has the ratio decreased because the debtors and bank are lower?
- Have creditors increased because of a slow-down in payment?

Allan's current ratio is within the accepted norm for both years, but Year 2 shows an increase to slightly above the accepted norm.

The rate of stock turnover has increased possibly resulting in less stock being held. The debtors' collection period had decreased showing that our debtors are paying more quickly, therefore the bank may have increased. We are taking approximately the same amount of time to pay off our creditors.

STEP 6 – Compare the acid test ratio. This is a **liquidity** ratio.

The acid test ratio is a more immediate test of liquidity and tests the ability of the enterprise to meet its debts without making any sales.

Again there is a link between the acid test ratio, current ratio stock turnover and debtors' collection and creditors' payment periods. The norm is 1:1. When considering the acid test ratio for any enterprise you need to consider:

- Is there is sufficient cash available to meet their debts?
- If the ratio is lower than 1:1 is the enterprise insolvent?
- If the ratio is higher than 1:1 should the enterprise consider some form of short-term investment?
- If lower it could be that the debtors are taking too long to pay resulting in the enterprise taking longer to pay off its creditors.

Allan's acid test ratio has improved in Year 2. They were in a slightly worrying liquidity position at the end of Year 1 when the ratio was 0.9:1. Looking at the other ratios this improvement may have been brought about by the improvement in the debtors' collection period.

continued ➤

Example 15 continued

STEP 7 – Compare the rate of stock turnover. This is an **efficiency** ratio.

When considering the rate of stock turnover check to see if the mark-up and gross profit ratios have had an effect on sales.

By comparing the rate of stock turnover the enterprise can see how quickly it is selling its goods. Generally speaking the more often the enterprise sells the average stock the higher the gross profit will be.

- If the rate of stock turnover has changed is it because there has been a change in mark-up?
- Has the closing stock figure changed dramatically over the period? If so suggest reasons why.

Allan should be pleased because the rate of stock turnover has increased over the 2 years despite an increase in mark-up. This could be because they are the only supplier of this particular product and can set their own mark-up.

STEP 8 – Compare the expenses ratio. This is an **efficiency** ratio.

The expense ratio shows how efficient the enterprise is at controlling its expenses.

- If the ratio increased, the enterprise is not controlling its expenses as efficiently as before.
- If the ratio has decreased then it is more efficient at controlling its expenses.

Allan's expense ratio has increased by 7%. This means that the enterprise is less efficient at controlling its expenses. They will have to investigate why this has happened and may have to analyse individual expenses to find out where the inefficiencies are. It could be that they have had to increase staff wages because of an industry agreement, or there could have been a huge jump in fuel prices they have not been able to control.

STEP 9 – Compare the debtors' collection period. This is an **efficiency** ratio.

The debtors' collection period indicates how quickly debtors pay their debts. When considering this ratio you need to consider:

- How long it is taking to collect payment from debtors.
- Whether it is in line with the industry standard.
- If the time period increases does the enterprise need a better credit control system?
- What effect on liquidity the period allowed has.
- The dangers of an extended period of time and the possible increase in bad debts.

Allan's debtors' collection period had improved by 7 days. They are more efficient at collecting their debts. This may be the reason for the improved current and acid test ratios.

continued ➤

Example 15 continued

STEP 10 – Compare the creditors' payment period. This is an **efficiency** ratio.

This indicates how long the enterprise is taking to settle its debts. The enterprise will need to consider:

- Whether there has been an increase or decrease in the time period.
- If there has been an increase, what effect will that have on the suppliers – will they continue to supply them?
- If firms press for payment, will this affect the liquidity position of the enterprise?
- Will an increase in the time period taken affect the enterprise's ability to obtain credit from other suppliers?

Allan's credit payment period has remained almost the same (30 days to 31 days). This is within the accepted norm for paying off debts, as they are normally settled within one month.

STEP 11 – Compare the turnover to the fixed assets. This is an **efficiency** ratio.

The ratio of turnover to fixed assets shows how efficiently the enterprise is using its fixed assets. The rate of stock turnover may help to explain why there has been a change in this ratio.

In comparing these figures the enterprise may need to consider:

- If there has been a change, is it because they are using their fixed assets more or less efficiently?
- Has there been an increase in the value of fixed assets over the period resulting in a decrease?
- If fixed assets have increased and sales decreased they need to consider if the expenditure on fixed assets has been worthwhile.

Allan's turnover to fixed assets ratio has improved. This is in line with the increase in stock turnover which indicates an increase in the sales.

The above example is comparing the performance of an enterprise in Year 1 and Year 2. The same sorts of questions need to be asked when comparing one enterprise with another of an enterprises performance with the industry standard.

  Now do Worksheets 10.5 and 10.6

CHAPTER 11

Trial balance and the correction of errors

Intermediate 2 Level Outcomes:

I2

This chapter includes material from Int 2 level Financial Accounting Outcome 3
- ☆ **Identify correctly the type of error and the relevant ledger accounts affected.**
- ☆ **Using double entry book-keeping principles make entries in the appropriate ledger accounts and, where necessary, the suspense account to correct errors.**

Higher Level Outcomes:

H

This chapter includes material from Higher level Financial Accounting Outcome 1
- ☆ **Calculate year end figures and adjust for accounting errors.**

Errors in the Trial Balance

At the end of the financial period a Trial Balance will be extracted from the ledger accounts of the business enterprise to:

- check the arithmetical and double entry accuracy of the accounts;
- provide a summary of the balances on each ledger account;
- provide information for the preparation of the final accounts.

The Trial Balance consists of 2 columns of figures listed under the headings of **debit** and **credit**. It shows the names of all the accounts in the ledger which have a balance on them at that date. **Debit** balances show assets, debtors and expenses and **credit** balances show the liabilities and capital of the business.

If the double entries have been made correctly the total of the debit column and the total of the credit column of the Trial Balance will agree. The Trial Balance is an indication of the arithmetical accuracy of the entries made in the ledger accounts of an enterprise. If the Trial Balance agrees, then on the face of it, the ledger accounts are accurate. But is this the case?

Even although Trial Balance does agree, errors may still have been made in the ledger accounts.

These errors which are not revealed by the Trial Balance can be classified as errors of **original entry**, **omission**, **commission**, **principle**, **compensation**, and **complete reversal**.

Errors of original entry

An error of original entry occurs when a mistake is made in either preparing the original document to record the transaction, such as an invoice or credit note, or when an error is made in transferring a figure from the original document to the ledger accounts.

Example 1

On May 10 ABC plc sent the following credit note to John Smith for goods returned.

Sales	£100.00
VAT	15.00
	£115.00

STEP 1 – Show the ledger accounts with the original entry made to record the credit note

John Smith's Account

Date	Details	Dr	Cr	Balance
May 1	Balance	235.00		235.00
May 10	**Sales returns and VAT**		**115.00**	**120.00**

Sales Returns Account

Date	Details	Dr	Cr	Balance
May 10	**John Smith**	**100.00**		**100.00**

VAT Account

Date	Details	Dr	Cr	Balance
May 10	**John Smith**	**15.00**		**15.00**

As the total of the debit and credit entries agree no difference will be shown by the Trial Balance to indicate an error.

On 30 May the auditor discovered that there had been an error in calculating the VAT amount. VAT should have been £17.50 and not £15.00. A debit note will be issued for the amount of the undercharge.

STEP 2 – Enter the transaction in the appropriate ledger account to correct the error

The error of £2.50 (the difference in the VAT amount) must be entered in the VAT and John Smith's Account.

Credit John Smith's account   £2.50
Debit VAT account   £2.50

continued ➤

Example 1 continued

John Smith's Account				
Date	Details	Dr	Cr	Balance
May 1	Balance	235.00		235.00
May 10	Sales returns and VAT	115.00	115.00	120.00
May 30	**VAT**		**2.50**	**122.50**

VAT Account				
Date	Details	Dr	Cr	Balance
May 10	John Smith	15.00		15.00
May 30	**John Smith**	**2.50**		**17.50**

Example 2

When transferring the goods value of the invoice received from Evans plc on 10 June the accounts clerk of ABC plc transposed two figures. He debited purchases and credited Evans plc with £254 instead of £245. The error was discovered on June 30.

STEP 1 – Show the ledger account entries for Evan plc and purchases

VAT Account				
Date	Details	Dr	Cr	Balance
June 10	**Purchases**		**254**	**254**

VAT Account				
Date	Details	Dr	Cr	Balance
June 10	**Evans plc**	**254**		**254**

As the debit entry equals the credit entry no error will be shown as the Trial Balance would agree.

STEP 2 – Calculate the amount of the error

Figure entered = £254
Actual figure = £245
Difference   =   £9

£9 too much has been entered to Evans plc and the purchases accounts.

continued ➤

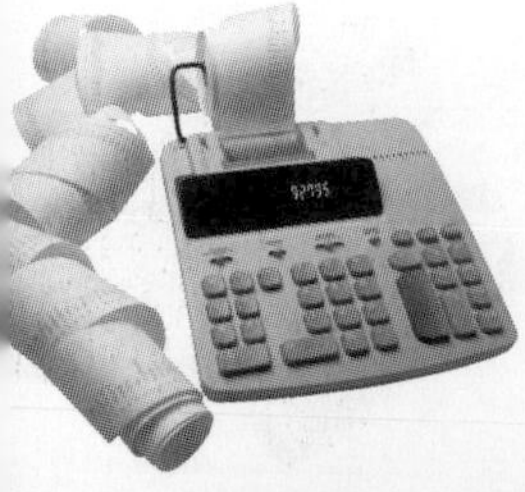

Example 2 continued

STEP 3 – Make the ledger account entries to correct the errors

Evans plc's account needs to be **reduced** by £9. Make a **debit** entry in the **account** for £9.

Purchases account also needs to be **reduced** by £9. Make a **credit** entry in the **purchases account** for £9.

Evans plc Account

Date	Details	Dr	Cr	Balance
June 10	Purchases		254	254
June 30	**Purchases**	9		**245**

Purchases Account

Date	Details	Dr	Cr	Balance
June 10	Evans plc	254		254
June 30	**Evans plc**		9	**245**

> > > ## Task 1

You are working for the auditor of KLJ plc and discover the following ledger account errors:

a) The value of the goods shown on the invoice sent to Allan Wells for £250 was incorrect and should have been £350.

b) It was later discovered that the goods value of a credit note for £400 sent to Wilson Associates should have been £450.

c) A cheque for £5,000 from James Wales plc was recorded in their account and the bank account as £500.

d) An invoice sent to F Smith for £4,350 had been entered in Smith's account and the sales account as £4,550.

e) A cheque paid for Electricity had been entered in the accounts as £428, instead of £842.

Show the ledger entries required to correct the errors.

Note *It may help you also show the original entries in the ledger accounts before the discovery of the errors.*

Errors of omission

Errors of omission occur when a transaction has been completely omitted from the ledger accounts. As no debit or credit entry has been made the Trial Balance will continue to agree.

FINANCIAL ACCOUNTING

Example 3

When tidying the office on June 14 the cleaner found a cheque under the desk from Donaldson plc for £5,000 in full settlement of their account. This cheque had been completely omitted from the ledger accounts of ABC plc. As no entries have been made in the ledger account the Trial Balance will continue to agree.

The following entries will be made to correct the above error.

Bank Account				
Date	**Details**	**Dr**	**Cr**	**Balance**
June 1	Balance	25,000		25,000
June 14	**Donaldson plc**	**5,000**		**30,000**

Donaldson plc Account				
Date	**Details**	**Dr**	**Cr**	**Balance**
June 1	Balance	5,050		5,050
June 14	**Bank**		**5,000**	**50**

 Task 2

You work in the accounts section of Track plc and have been asked to correct the following errors discovered on 30 September.

a) John Smith discovered an invoice, sent by ARC plc, for £500 underneath a folder on his desk.

b) The chequebook had not been passed to the ledger clerk to write up payments made to the following:

   - Alan Wilson Associates for £5,000;

   - Graham plc for £6,500;

   - British Telecom for £250.

c) An invoice from Allan plc for goods purchased by Track plc for £30,200 had been completely omitted from the ledger accounts.

d) J Wilson had paid his account of £400 by cheque in full, but this had not been entered in the ledger accounts of the firm.

Make the necessary entries to correct the above errors.

Errors of commission

An error of commission occurs when an error is made in entering transactions in the ledger accounts, such as debiting J Smith's account instead of T Smith's account. The Trial Balance will not show this error and it may only be noticed when J Smith contacts the firm to say they have received an incorrect statement at the end of the month.

Example 3

An invoice sent on 1 September to K Williamson for £200 was debited to K Williams' account instead of K Williamson's account. Williams contacted your firm on 28 September reporting the error.

STEP 1 – The ledger account of Williams is opened

K Williams' Account				
Date	**Details**	**Dr**	**Cr**	**Balance**
Sept 1	Sales	200		200

STEP 2 – Correct the error in Williams' account and Williamson's account

To cancel the error in K Williams' account credit the account for £200. The other entry will be in the correct account – K Williamson

K Williams' Account				
Date	**Details**	**Dr**	**Cr**	**Balance**
Sept 1	Sales	200		200
Sept 28	**K Williamson**		**200**	**nil**

Williams account now shows that he does not owe anything to the business.

K Williamson's Account				
Date	**Details**	**Dr**	**Cr**	**Balance**
Sept 28	**K Williams**	**200**		**200**

The correct amount of Williamson's debt is shown in his ledger account.

Task 3

You are required to correct the errors made in the ledger accounts of XYZ plc during the month of March. The errors were discovered on 28 March.

a) A cheque received from L Lion for £200 was entered correctly in the bank account but credited to I Lion's account.

b) Goods worth £3,500 sold on credit to Hamilton plc were entered correctly in the sales account but debited to the account of Hamilton Ltd.

c) Goods valued at £500 sold to W Brown had been entered correctly in the sales account but debited to W Browne's account.

d) An account for heating oil of £100 had been debited to the electricity account instead of the fuel account.

Error of principle

An error of principle is made when an entry is made in the wrong type of account. The most common type of this error is when a fixed asset is purchased or sold and entered in the purchases or sales account instead of the fixed asset account.

Example 4

On 7 June John Denver plc purchased a new delivery van on credit from Esquire Vehicles plc for £30,000. This was entered in the purchases account. The purchase of the new motor van is capital expenditure and should have been entered in the fixed asset account of motor vans.

STEP 1 – Show the purchase account

Purchases Account				
Date	Details	Dr	Cr	Balance
June 7	Esquire Vehicles plc	30,000		30,000

STEP 2 – Open the Motor Vans account and correct the entry in the purchases account

Purchases Account				
Date	Details	Dr	Cr	Balance
June 7	Esquire Vehicles plc	30,000		30,000
June 30	**Motor van**		**30,000**	**nil**

Motor Van Account				
Date	Details	Dr	Cr	Balance
June 30	Purchases	30,000		30,000

Task 4

During the month of May the following errors were found in the ledger accounts of KLH plc and corrected on 28 May.

a) A new computer system for controlling the production line was purchased for £16,500. This was entered into the purchases account.

b) Two delivery vans were sold for cost at £9,000. This was entered in the sales account.

continued ➤

c) Repairs to motor vehicles of £900 was entered in the motor vehicles account instead of the vehicle maintenance account.

d) The purchase of goods for resale worth £4,000 had been wrongly entered in the equipment account.

Make the necessary entries in the appropriate ledger accounts to correct the above errors.

Errors of compensation

Errors of compensation occur when two or more errors are made when entering transactions in the ledger accounts which cancel each other.

Example 5

J Smith records his purchase and sales in a spreadsheet and transfers the total to the purchases and sales accounts at the end of each month.

At the end of January £15,300 purchases and £43,200 sales were transferred into the purchases and sales ledger accounts. A few days later, it was discovered there had been an error in the spreadsheet and that the sales figure had been over-added by £2,000 and the purchases figure had also been over-added by £2,000.

STEP 1 – Open both ledger accounts and show the balances transferred

Purchases Account

Date	Details	Dr	Cr	Balance
Jan 30	Creditors	15,300		15,300

Sales Account

Date	Details	Dr	Cr	Balance
Jan 30	Debtors		43,200	43,200

The above accounts show the balances in the 2 ledger accounts.

STEP 2 – Correct the errors

To do this the purchases accounts needs to be **reduced** by £2,000 by means of a **credit** entry and the sales account needs to be **reduced** by £2,000 by means of a **debit** entry.

Purchases Account

Date	Details	Dr	Cr	Balance
Jan 30	Balance	15,300		15,300
Jan 30	**Sales**		**2,000**	**13,300**

continued ➤

Example 5 continued

Sales Account				
Date	Details	Dr	Cr	Balance
Jan 30	Balance		43,200	43,200
Jan 30	**Purchases Account**	**2,000**		**41,200**

Sometimes this type of error will occur because of arithmetical errors in the accounts. This may be referred to as undercasting (means the total is less than it should be) or overcasting (where the totals are greater than they should be).

 Task 5

a) The total value of purchases transferred to the purchases account was £34,200, and the total value of sales transferred to the sales account was £67,400. It was later discovered that the purchases account had been over-added by £2,300 and that the sales account had also been over-added by £2,300.

b) When checking the accounts it was discovered that the sales returns figure had been under-added by £500 and that the sales account had been under-added by £500.

c) Both the sales returns and the purchases returns accounts have been undercast by £50.

d) The cash account balance of £350 had been overcast by £10 and the discount received account balance of £290 had also been overcast by £10.

Show the ledger entries required to correct the errors.

Errors of reversal

An error of complete reversal means that the entries have been made on the wrong sides of the accounts.

Example 6

On January 30 a payment by cheque of £350 to John Smith had been treated as a receipt and debited to the bank account and credited to John Smith's account.

This type of error is a little more difficult to correct. You need to cancel the original entries and then make the correct entry in the account. Effectively you need to make a debit and credit entry for double the amount.

continued ≻

Example 6 continued

STEP 1 – Open the ledger accounts to show the errors

Bank Account

Date	Details	Dr	Cr	Balance
Jan 30	John Smith	350		350

John Smith's Account

Date	Details	Dr	Cr	Balance
Jan 30	Bank		350	350

STEP 2 – Cancel the entries made in the accounts

Do this by entering the same amount in the opposite column.

Bank Account

Date	Details	Dr	Cr	Balance
Jan 30	John Smith (error)	350		350
Jan 30	**John Smith (cancelling error)**		**350**	**nil**

John Smith's Account

Date	Details	Dr	Cr	Balance
Jan 30	Bank (error)		350	350
Jan 30	**Bank (cancelling error)**	**350**		**nil**

STEP 3 – Make the correct entries in the appropriate ledger accounts

Bank Account

Date	Details	Dr	Cr	Balance
Jan 30	John Smith (error)	350		350
Jan 30	John Smith (cancelling error)		350	nil
Jan 30	**John Smith (correct entry)**		**350**	**350**

John Smith's Account

Date	Details	Dr	Cr	Balance
Jan 30	Bank (error)		350	350
Jan 30	Bank (cancelling error)	350		Nil
Jan 30	**Bank (correct entry)**	**350**		**350**

continued ➤

Example 6 continued

Looking carefully at the accounts it can be seen that we have in fact made total debit entries of double the error and total credit entries of double the error to correct.

The account could have been completed as follows:

Bank Account				
Date	Details	Dr	Cr	Balance
Jan 30	John Smith (error)	350		350
Jan 30	**John Smith (cancelling and correcting the error)**		**700**	**350**

John Smith's Account				
Date	Details	Dr	Cr	Balance
Jan 30	Bank (error)		350	350
Jan 30	**Bank (cancelling and correcting error)**	**700**		**350**

Task 6

From the following information correct the errors made in the ledger accounts of T Robin:

a) Sale of goods on credit to K Livingstone for £3,000 had been debited to the sales account and credited to Livingstone's account.

b) Receipt of £200 cash from W Lombard had been debited to his account and credited in the bank.

c) A loan of £3,000 from R Briggs had been credited in the bank account and debited in Brigg's loan account.

d) Goods taken for own use of £900 had been debited to the purchases account and credited to the drawings account.

 Now do Worksheet 11.1

Suspense account and the correction of errors

The **suspense account** is a temporary account created when the Trial Balance fails to agree because of arithmetical or book-keeping errors in the ledger accounts. If the error cannot be immediately discovered the difference between the debit and credit columns of the Trial Balance will be entered into a suspense account and the suspense account will be added to the Trial Balance.

When the errors are discovered the correct entry will be made in the appropriate ledger account and the double entry completed in the suspense account.

Errors which cause the Trial Balance not to agree:

- Omission of one of the double entries. One half of the transaction is entered correctly in the correct ledger account, the other entry is omitted from the other ledger account.
- Two entries were made in either the debit or the credit column of the ledger accounts.
- There has been an error in the casting of an account.
- The wrong figure was entered in one of the ledger accounts, including transposition of figures.
- An account is omitted from the Trial Balance.
- An account is entered on the wrong side of the Trial Balance.

Example 7

On 31 December Year 1 the Trial Balance of XYZ plc failed to agree and a suspense account was opened and the difference of £5,718 was entered on the credit side of the suspense account.

On investigation the following errors were discovered:

- Good purchased by cash for £400 had been credited in the cash account but no entry had been made in the purchases account.

- An invoice for advertising of £500, paid by cheque, had been debited in the advertising account and the bank account.

- The wages account had been overcast by £1,500.

- Repairs to premises costing £46 had been debited to the repairs account as £64 in error.

- The sales account balance of £4,000 had been entered in the Trial Balance as £400.

Correct the errors using the suspense account.

STEP 1 – Open the suspense account

Suspense Account				
Date	Details	Dr	Cr	Balance
Dec 31	Difference in Trial Balance		5,718	5,718

continued ➤

Example 7 continued

STEP 2 – Correction of error of omission of an entry

Good purchased by cash for £400 had been credited in the cash account but not entered in the purchases account.

To correct this error the purchases account needs to be debited with the missing purchases figure, the double entry is completed in the suspense account.

Suspense Account

Date	Details	Dr	Cr	Balance
Dec 31	Difference in Trial Balance		5,718	5,718
Dec 31	**Purchases Account**		**400**	**6,118**

Purchases Account

Date	Details	Dr	Cr	Balance
Dec 31	**Suspense Account**	**400**		**400**

STEP 3 – Correction of two entries made on the same side of the ledger accounts

An invoice for advertising of £500, paid by cheque, had been debited in the advertising account and the bank account. The correct entry should have been to credit the bank account.

To correct the entry in the bank account the amount will need to be doubled to £1,000. The first £500 will cancel the error, and the next £500 will make the correct entry in the bank account.

Suspense Account

Date	Details	Dr	Cr	Balance
Dec 31	Difference in Trial Balance		5,718	5,718
Dec 31	Purchases Account		400	6,118
Dec 31	**Bank Account**	**1,000**		**5,118**

Bank Account

Date	Details	Dr	Cr	Balance
Dec 31	**Suspense Account**		**1,000**	**1,000**

continued ➤

Example 7 continued

STEP 4 – Correction of error of under/overcasting

The wages account had been overcast by £1,500. The wages account balance is too high. To reduce the balance the wages account needs to be credited for the amount of the overcast.

Suspense Account				
Date	**Details**	**Dr**	**Cr**	**Balance**
Dec 31	Difference in Trial Balance		5,718	5,718
Dec 31	Purchases Account		400	6,118
Dec 31	Bank Account	1,000		5,118
Dec 31	**Wages Account**	**1,500**		**3,618**

Wages Account				
Date	**Details**	**Dr**	**Cr**	**Balance**
Dec 31	**Suspense Account**		1,500	1,500

STEP 5 – Correction of an error of transposition

Repairs to premises costing £46 had been debited to the repairs account as £64. Transposition occurs when figures are reversed. In this example a debit entry of **£64** has been made in the repairs account instead of **£46**. The corresponding credit entry has been made correctly in the cash/bank account of £46.

The difference between the amounts is = £64 – £46 = £18.

The debit column is £18 too high. To correct this error a credit entry needs to be made in the Repairs Account and the Suspense Account debited.

Suspense Account				
Date	**Details**	**Dr**	**Cr**	**Balance**
Dec 31	Difference in Trial Balance		5,718	5,718
Dec 31	Purchases Account		400	6,118
Dec 31	Bank Account	1,000		5,118
Dec 31	Wages Account	1,500		3,618
Dec 31	**Repairs Account**	**18**		**3,600**

Repairs Account				
Date	**Details**	**Dr**	**Cr**	**Balance**
Dec 31	**Suspense Account**		18	18

continued ➤

FINANCIAL ACCOUNTING

Example 7 continued

STEP 6 – Correction of error where wrong amount entered in the Trial Balance

The sales account balance of $4,000 had been entered in the Trial Balance as $400. The ledger account is correct but the Trial Balance credit column is too high by $3,600 ($4,000 – $400 = $3,600)

The sales account is correct in the ledger, the error was made in transferring the figure to the Trial Balance. As the Trial Balance is not a ledger account there will be only one entry made in the suspense account to correct the error.

Suspense Account				
Date	**Details**	**Dr**	**Cr**	**Balance**
Dec 31	Difference in Trial Balance		5,718	5,718
Dec 31	Purchases Account		400	6,118
Dec 31	Bank Account	1,000		5,118
Dec 31	Wages Account	1,500		3,618
Dec 31	Repairs Account	18		3,600
Dec 31	**Trial Balance**	**3,600**		**0**

Now do Worksheets 11.2, 11.3 and 11.4

Bank reconciliation statements

Intermediate 2 Level Outcomes: ⏵

This chapter includes material from Int 2 level Financial Accounting Outcome 3

☆ **Identify correctly the type of error and the relevant ledger accounts affected.**

☆ **Using double entry book-keeping principles make entries in the appropriate ledger accounts and, where necessary, the suspense account to correct errors.**

Bank statements

A firm records monies received and monies paid out by cheques in their bank account. Their bank will also keep a record of monies paid into and withdrawn from the firm's bank account held by the bank. At the end of the month the bank sends the enterprise the bank's record of the transactions, from their point of view, in the form of a **bank statement**.

When the bank statement is received from the bank the accountant or chief cashier will check the entries in the bank statement against the entries made in the enterprise's own bank account in their ledger. The balance on the bank account and the bank statement, at the end of the month, rarely agree.

There are four main reasons for this disagreement: **time**, **omissions**, **errors** and **dishonoured cheques**.

Time

As an enterprise pays their accounts or receives cheques from creditors they will almost immediately enter these amounts into the firm's bank account in their ledger. However, there will be a delay in the firm's bank entering the amounts into their record of the firm's bank account. These delays can occur because:

- Cheques/cash received from creditors may be kept by the business for a few days before being deposited in the bank account.
- Cheques paid out by the firm will be sent, by post, to the creditor taking one or two days. The creditor may hold them for a few days more before depositing them into their bank account at their own bank.
- Once cheques are deposited with the bank it will take three working days to clear the cheque. **Clearing** is the term used to describe the process of transferring funds from one bank account to another.
- These time delays may mean that cheques sent by an enterprise may take almost one week to reach their own bank account and be deducted from their account.

Omissions from the bank account

In addition to cheques and cash paid in and cheques withdrawn from the bank account the bank statement may have items in it which have not yet been recorded in the bank account of the enterprise.

- **Standing orders** for certain sums of money to be paid on a regular basis (such as monthly insurance premiums). Standing orders are raised by the enterprise giving an instruction to the bank.
- **Directs debits** arranged so that a creditor can ask the bank for money direct from the enterprise's bank account instead of receiving a cheque. This allows variable amounts to be withdrawn from the firm's bank account for goods purchased, or payments made to the local authority for rates. The enterprise must sign a Direct Debit Mandate giving the creditor power to ask for the money.
- **BACs (Bankers' Automated Clearing System)** sometimes called a **credit transfer** where sums of money are automatically transferred to another bank account, for example wages paid to employees

Errors sometimes occur

Differences which occur between the bank account balance and the bank statement balance caused by an error either made by the book-keeper or by a bank employee.

Dishonoured cheques

A dishonoured cheque is a cheque which the drawer's bank refuses to pay. This may be because:

- there are insufficient funds in the creditor's bank to pay the amount;
- the drawer has instructed the bank to stop payment for some reason;
- an error has been found on the cheque by the bank (for example, the amount on the cheque in words and figures may be different);
- the cheque has not been signed by the drawer or the signature is different from the specimen given to the bank

If a dishonoured cheque is received by the business the amount in their bank account will be greater than the amount shown in the bank statement.

Preparation of a bank reconciliation statement

Items to be entered in the bank reconciliation statement will come from the enterprise's ledger bank account. These can be classified under two headings, **Unpresented cheques** and **Amounts not yet credited**.

Unpresented cheques

Unpresented cheques are cheques written by the enterprise, sent to creditors, which have not yet reached the enterprise's bank account for payment.

Amounts not yet credited

Amounts not yet credited are sometimes called uncleared lodgements and represent amounts deposited by the enterprise which the bank has not yet added to their bank account balance held at the bank when the bank statement was sent out.

Example 1

Compare the bank account and bank statement figures and create the necessary changes to the bank account. You will also need to prepare a bank reconciliation statement.

STEP 1 – Compare the bank account and the bank statement figures

The bank account and the bank statement figures are compared and the common figures are ticked.

ANYTOWN ROYAL BANK

| 123 High Street
ANYTOWN
AG12 6YU | Current Account
ABC Plc

Sheet No 27 |

STATEMENT DATE 31 July Year 1				Account No 667589
Year 1	*Particulars*	*Withdrawn*	*Paid In*	*Balance*
June 30	Balance Forward			5,351.76✓
July 7	047135 Cheque	250.31✓		5,101.45
July 7	047136 Cheque	500.67✓		4,600.78
July 8	047137 Cheque	300.00✓		4,300.78
July 16	Cheque		780.00✓	5,080.78
July	Cheque		50.00✓	5,130.78
July 15	**D/D – Anytown Power plc**	**125.00**		**5,005.78**
July 18	5678 Credit		2,000.00✓	7,005.78
July 19	047139 Cheque	300.57✓		6,705.21
July 21	**BAC – Wages**	**2,300.00**		**4,405.21**
July 27	Cheque		1,800.00✓	6,205.21
July 27	**Credit Transfer – Dividend**		**900.00**	**7,105.21**
July 28	**Credit Transfer – Rates**	**430.00**		**6,675.21**
July 28		Total Withdrawn 4,206.55	Total Paid in 5,530.00	Balance 6,675.21

continued ➤

Example 1 continued

Bank Account

Date	Details	Dr	Cr	Balance
July 1	Balance Forward			5,351.76✓
July 1	J Smith		250.31	5,101.45
July 1	ABC plc		500.67✓	4,600.78
July 5	Wilson plc		300.00✓	4,300.78
July 12	Cash Sales	780.00✓		5,080.78
July 13	A Byers	50.00✓		5,130.78
July 18	Cash Sales	2,000.00✓		7,130.78
July 19	Brown Bros		300.57✓	6,830.21
July 27	Alan Houston plc	1,800.00✓		8,630.21
July 28	Cash Sales	**5,000.00**		13,630.21
July 29	S Carson		**1,300.21**	12,330.00

STEP 2 – Update the bank account in the ledger with the unticked items in the bank statement

Items shown in the withdrawn column of the bank statement are entered in the credit column of the bank account and items in the paid in column will be entered in the debit column of the bank account.

Bank Account

Date	Details	Dr	Cr	Balance
July 1	Balance Forward			5,351.76✓
July 1	J Smith		250.31✓	5,101.45
July 1	ABC plc		500.67✓	4,600.78
July 5	Wilson plc		300.00✓	4,300.78
July 12	Cash Sales	780.00✓		5,080.78
July 13	A Byers	50.00✓		5,130.78
July 18	Cash Sales	2,000.00✓		7,130.78
July 19	Brown Bros		300.57✓	6,830.21
July 27	Alan Houston plc	1,800.00✓		8,630.21
July 28	Cash Sales	**5,000.00**		13,630.21
July 29	S Carson		1,300.21	12,330.00
July 30	**Electricity**		**125.00**	**12,205.00**
July 30	**Wages**		**2.300.00**	**9,905.00**
July 30	**Dividend Received**	**900.00**		**10,805.00**
July 30	**Rates**		**430.00**	**10,375.00**

continued ➤

Example 1 continued

The balance shown is the updated bank account and represents the actual cash at bank that the business enterprise has.

STEP 3 – Start the bank reconciliation statement

Head up the bank reconciliation statement, date it and start the statement with the balance shown on the bank statement

Bank Reconciliation Statement As at 30 July Year 1		
	£	£
Balance as per Bank Statement		6,675.21

STEP 4 – Add items which will increase the amount in the bank account at the bank

These are listed under the heading **Add items not yet credited**.

Bank Reconciliation Statement As at 30 July Year 1		
	£	£
Balance as per Bank Statement		6,675.21
Add **items not yet credited**		
Cash Sales		**5,000.00**
		11,675.21

STEP 5 – Deduct payments made in the enterprise's bank account in the ledger

These are listed under the heading **Unpresented Cheques**.

Bank Reconciliation Statement As at 30 July Year 1		
	£	£
Balance as per Bank Statement		6,675.21
Add amounts not yet credited		
Cash Sales		5,000.00
		11,675.21
Less **Unpresented Cheques**		
S Carson		**1,300.21**

continued ➤

Example 1 continued

STEP 6 – Calculate bank reconciliation statement balance

Bank Reconciliation Statement As at 30 July Year 1	£	£
Balance as per Bank Statement		6,675.21
Add amounts not yet credited		
Cash Sales		<u>5,000.00</u>
		11,675.21
Less **Unpresented Cheques**		
S Carson		<u>1,300.21</u>
To agree with Balance as per corrected Bank Account		**10,375.00**

The balance on the bank reconciliation statement agrees with the updated bank account and shows how much money the firm will have in the bank when the unpresented cheques and items not yet credited are dealt with by the enterprise's bank.

  Now do Worksheets 12.1 and 12.2

CHAPTER 13

Accounting Standards

Higher Level Outcomes ▮▮➡

H ⬇

This chapter includes material from Higher level Financial Accounting Outcome 3
☆ **Explain briefly the purpose of the Statement of Principles.**
☆ **Explain the role of SSAPs and FRSs in recording and reporting financial performance.**

A true and fair view

The accounts produced by any business enterprise should reflect a *true and fair view* of the financial position of that organisation. In order to achieve this true and fair view accountants need to follow a set of rules, referred to as accounting concepts, conventions or principles.

These concepts and frameworks under which accountants work have been developed over a long period of time. In the United Kingdom the Accounting Standards Committee was established in the 1970s and it issued a number of Statements of Standard Accounting Practice (SSAP's).

These included the four basic fundamental concepts of **going concern**, **consistency**, **prudence**, and **accruals and matching**.

Going concern

The concept of **going concern** assumes that the business will carry on trading in the foreseeable future. This affects how assets are valued. As the business will continue to operate the assets can be valued at historical cost. However if the business was to be wound up, the assets would need to be revalued at their possible selling value. In the case of machinery, vehicles, plant etc these values will be lower than their historical cost. Premises or land and buildings on the other hand are likely to realise more than their historical cost.

Consistency

The **consistency** concept states that the accounts of the business enterprise should be prepared on the same basis each year. For example if a fixed asset is depreciated using the straight-line method in the first year, this method should be used in subsequent years. Using the same basis to prepare the final accounts allows comparisons on performance to be made.

Should a business enterprise decide to change its basis of preparing its final accounts it should state this when reporting its final accounts.

Prudence

The concept of **prudence** states that an accountant should always be cautious when reporting the financial position of an organisation. The accountant should:

- never anticipate a profit;
- always provide for any anticipated loss;
- select the lowest value when valuing assets for inclusion in the final accounts.

Accruals and matching concept

The **accruals** concept states that any revenue should be recognised when it is earned and not when it is received. An example of this concept is that of sales. If the financial year ends in June and goods are sold on credit that month the revenue should be included in June's sales figure and in the final accounts of the enterprise, even though the actual money may not be received until July, in the next financial year.

The **matching** concept states that when calculating profit the expenses incurred for the financial year, should be set against that sales revenue for that year.

Avoiding confusion through the use of accounting concepts

The use of these accounting concepts avoids confusion and inconsistencies when preparing the final accounts. Their application enables comparisons to be made between different enterprise's results or the results of the same enterprise from one year to the next.

There are a number of other concepts which are applied when preparing the final accounts of an enterprise:

- **Objectivity**. The final accounts of an enterprise should be objective, not subjective, and based on actual evidence.
- **Business entity**. This states that the financial affairs of the business enterprise should be kept separate from that of the owner. The business is a separate legal entity and personal transactions should be kept separate from those of the business.
- **Historical cost**. This states that the accounting should be based on the original cost of the transaction. Assets should be valued at historical cost (the cost shown on the invoice).
- **Money measurement**. This states that each transaction, asset, liability, and capital should be expressed in monetary terms.
- **Dual aspect**. This states that each transaction has two effects on the accounts of a business enterprise
- **Materiality**. This states that an accountant should not spend time trying to categorise minor business expenses. Instead these could be grouped together under the heading of sundry expenses.
- **Realisation**. This states that revenue should not be recognised until the goods have actually been exchanged.

Since 1990, the body governing the concepts and framework used in the preparation of accounting statements has been the Accounting Standards Board.

The aims of the Accounting Standards Board (ASB) are to establish and improve standards of financial accounting and reporting to the benefit of those preparing, using or auditing accounting statements and to show the stewardship for the financial year or to make decisions based on the accounting information produced.

To achieve their aims, the ASB will:

- establish accounting standards;
- provide a framework to allow others to make judgements in resolving accounting issues;
- issue new standards;
- update or amend existing standards in line with economic developments or any deficiencies identified in current accounting practice;
- address any urgent issues promptly.

In conducting its affairs the ASB follows certain guidelines. These are to:

- **Be objective**. Information produced from the application of accounting standards should be neutral and free from any form of bias which might influence a direction of a particular decision.
- **Be clear**. Accounting standards should be clearly expressed after careful consideration.
- **Carry out research** to determine which aspects should be included in accounting standards.
- **Ensure regular communication** takes place and that any accounting standards take notice of international regulations.
- **Ensure that consistency exists** between accounting standards, accounting standards and company law and accounting standards and international developments.
- Only issue standards when the expected benefits exceed the costs of implementing the standard.

Statement of Principles

In December 1999 the ASB published its Statement of Principles for Financial Reporting. The statement is based on the International Accounting Standards Committee's *Framework for the Preparation and Presentation of Financial Statements* and sets out standard-setters views on:

- the activities which should be reported on and the particular aspects which should be highlighted;
- the attributes that information needs to have if it is to be included in financial statements;
- the type of information to be expressed;
- how the information should be presented in financial statements.

The Statement of Principles is not an accounting standard, and does not contain details on how financial statements for profit-making enterprises should be prepared. It simply sets out the principles which underpin how financial statements should be prepared or presented.

The main purpose of the Statement of Principles is to provide a framework under which the ASB will develop new or review existing standards.

Development of an accounting standard

The development and issuing of a new accounting standard can take a long period of time and will evolve from the following processes:

- **Internal research** is carried out or the ASB will receive a request highlighting a topic which requires to be standardised.
- A **period of consultation** and research takes place which includes the consideration of UK, Republic of Ireland and overseas procedures.
- A **discussion draft** is issued to interested groups who will comment on its appropriateness and feasibility.
- After discussion, a **Financial Reporting Exposure Draft (FRED)** is published and all parties can comment and suggest amendments.
- **FRED's** may be modified as a result of the consultation process.
- After consultation and revision a new **Financial Reporting Standard** (**FRS**) will be issued.

Once the Financial Reporting Standard is issued and is put into practice by accountants its effectiveness is monitored. A review will take place as necessary and further modifications made and revised standards issued.

 Now do Worksheet 13.1

SECTION TWO

Management Accounting

Chapter 14 Classification of costs

Chapter 15 Inventory control procedures

Chapter 16 Pricing stock issues

Chapter 17 Labour costs

Chapter 18 Overhead analysis

Chapter 19 Job costing

Chapter 20 Service costing

Chapter 21 Process costing

Chapter 22 Break-even analysis

Chapter 23 Marginal costing for decision making

Chapter 24 Budgetary control and preparation of budgets

Chapter 25 Information Technology in Accounting

Chapter 26 Spreadsheets in Accounting

Classification of costs

This chapter includes material from Int 2 level Management Accounting Outcome 1

I2
☆ **Describe the different elements of cost and classify them as direct, variable or fixed.**

☆ **Explain the procedures used to control the principal elements of costs – material, labour and overheads.**

This chapter includes material from Higher level Management Accounting Outcome 1

H
☆ **Explain the theory and relevance of costs to an organisation.**

What is costing?

Costing involves a detailed analysis of costs and allows budgets, standard costs, costs of operations, processes or activities to be established and compared with actual costs to permit the analysis of any variances.

Costing is the measure of the cost of material, labour and all other expenses. It allows an enterprise to estimate the cost of a particular operation, process or activity and to allow the selling price to be set depending on the profit required.

What is a cost unit?

A cost unit is an activity, product or operation for which a cost can be calculated. Examples of cost units are the manufacture of a table, a computer monitor, hair cut, canteen meal.

What is a cost centre?

A cost centre may be a production department, service, function, or item of equipment for which a cost can be calculated. Examples of cost centres are machine shop, canteen, power press, canning department.

Costs are classified as either a direct cost or an indirect cost.

Direct costs

Direct costs are associated with the actual unit of production and include direct labour, materials and expenses.

Direct labour is the cost of the direct operating labour – the wages of those employees actually involved in the manufacturing process, such as an assembly worker on car assembly line.

Direct materials is the cost of the actual material which forms part of the product being manufactured such as the seats for the car being made.

Direct expenses are special costs for a particular part of a product. For example, a royalty might have to be paid to another firm to allow a particular product to be made under licence, or there might be direct power plant costs of operating the machinery.

Indirect costs

All other costs are indirect and are usually known as overheads. The costs are associated with, but are not part of, the actual unit of production and include indirect labour, materials and expenses.

Indirect labour includes the wages of employees who do not manufacture the product but whose services are necessary to allow production to take place. Examples of indirect labour costs include the salary of the factory manager, factory supervision costs, storekeeper, fork-lift truck driver.

Indirect materials include the cost of any material used in the factory which is not part of the end product. Examples of indirect materials are oil for machinery used by the maintenance engineers or stationery used in the factory office.

Indirect expenses include the running costs of the factory. Examples of these costs include rent and rates, insurance, repair costs of the factory.

Variable and fixed costs

Costs can also be classified as variable costs or fixed costs.

Variable costs are costs which vary, in the short term, in proportion to output. Variable costs include direct material, direct labour and direct expenses. Figure 14.1 shows the relationship between variable costs and units produced. The variable costs are 0 when no units are produced, and are $8,000 when 10,000 units are produced.

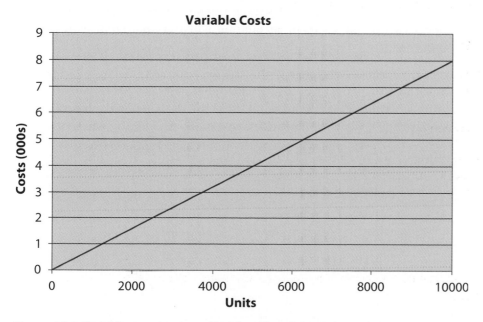

Figure 14.1 Variable costs increase directly with increased units produced

Fixed costs are all the other indirect costs involved in running a business. They are known as overheads. Fixed overheads are incurred on a time basis. In the short term they will not change with output and include such costs as rent, rates, and insurance. Figure 14.2 shows the relationship between variable costs and units produced.

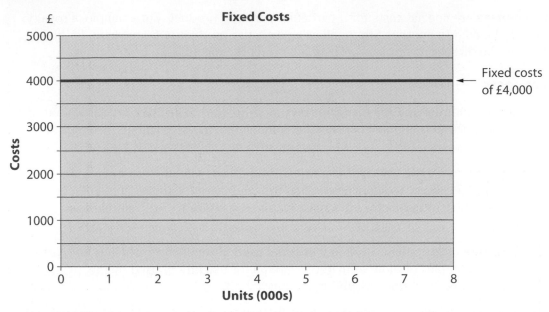

Figure 14.2 Fixed costs do not vary with increase in units produced

Semi-variable costs

Semi-variable costs contain both a fixed and variable element. Semi-variable costs are partly affected by the level of production. For example, the cost of electricity contains a fixed element (the standing charge) and a variable element (the cost of the actual electricity used).

Why calculate costs?

Detailed costs are calculated to estimate the total cost and allow for the setting of the selling price of a product. Comparisons can then be made between the actual costs and the estimated costs. Should a discrepancy arise the management accountant will carry out an investigation into the reasons for the differences.

A business does not necessarily calculate the selling price by determining the costs and then adding a profit. It may work the other way, by deciding what customers are likely to pay for a product and then calculating whether or not they can produce the item and make a profit at that price. With detailed analysis of costs the enterprise may be able to identify where savings can be made.

Task 1

1 Define a fixed cost and name two examples.

2 Define a variable cost and name two examples.

3 Explain the difference between a direct and indirect cost.

4 Copy and complete the following table by putting a tick in the appropriate column to identify the type of cost:

Cost	Variable Cost	Fixed Cost
Direct labour		
Factory rent		
Factory insurance		
Raw materials		
Vehicle licence		
Repairs to machinery		
Salary of Factory manager		
Storekeeper's wages		
Direct power		
Electricity		
Royalties for canteen		
Depreciation of plant		

5 Explain what a semi-variable cost is and give an example.

6 In the long term all costs are variable. Explain this statement.

MANAGEMENT ACCOUNTING

CHAPTER 15

Inventory control procedures

MANAGEMENT ACCOUNTING

Intermediate 2 Level Outcomes:

I2

This chapter includes material from Int 2 level Management Accounting Outcome 1

☆ **Explain the procedures used to control the principal elements of costs.**

It also includes material from Int 2 level Management Accounting Outcome 2

☆ **Direct materials and labour costs are recorded consistently from the information supplied.**

Higher Level Outcomes:

H

This chapter includes material from Higher level Management Accounting Outcome 2

☆ **Direct materials and labour costs are recorded consistently from the information supplied.**

I2
H

Why is inventory control important?

Of the three cost elements, materials will often account for the highest proportion of the cost of manufacture and as such it is essential that a business enterprise controls these costs. Adequate procedures must be set up within the organisation to monitor and control material costs.

Purchasing

Purchasing includes the procurement of materials, machines, supplies, services and tools on the most favourable terms consistent with maintaining a desirable standard of quality and continuity of service. Many factors influence the purchasing policy of a firm:

- price, price trends, quantity discounts and inflation;
- quality;
- reliability of delivery;
- storage costs;
- interest rates.

Duties of the buyer

It is the duty of the buyer working in the enterprise to:

- obtain materials of the correct quantity, quality and price within the time schedule set;
- record particulars of sources of supply, reliability of suppliers and prices;
- arrange for the disposal of scrap;
- keep up-to-date with the latest prices and trends;
- interview salesmen, obtaining and comparing quotations, placing orders and following up orders.

Before buying goods an enterprise must decide on what kind of purchasing procedure to adopt. For example, a large enterprise with many factories may allow each factory to purchase their own materials, or they may carry out the purchasing procedure from one centralised location.

Centralised and decentralised buying

Centralised buying is where all the buying is carried out from one office. A firm may have several branches throughout the country but all the buying is carried out from the one central office.

A centralised purchasing procedure has several benefits for an enterprise:

- **Economies of bulk buying**. Discounts may be offered because of the quantity being purchased.
- **Reduction in paper work**. Processing one order is much simpler and cheaper than processing several.
- **Uniformity of purchases**. The quality of the goods being purchased is standardised.
- **Specialisation of purchasing staff**. Purchasing staff become highly skilled and knowledgeable about the various suppliers they use.

However the creation of specialised department may lead to higher administration costs.

Purchasing procedures and documentation

Figure 15.1 shows the procedures and documentation required for a manual system of purchasing and recording. There are a number of steps to go through before the purchase is made, and it is important to ensure that proper records are kept to compare what has been ordered, what is delivered, and what is invoiced for.

Purchase requisition

The **purchase requisition** is the formal authority for the buyer to purchase goods. Requisitions can come from different departments, depending on the goods being purchased. For example, purchases of production materials will be raised by production department; the storekeeper will raise requisitions when the reorder levels of items are reached, production control will raise requisitions for new materials, the maintenance department will raise requisitions for spare parts, and the office manager will request the purchase of stationery items.

Figure 15.2 shows a purchase requisition form, detailing the quantity and description of the goods required, the supplier and order number.

Purchasing Procedures and Documentation

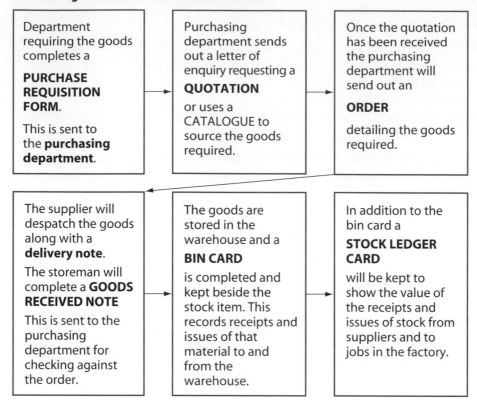

Department requiring the goods completes a **PURCHASE REQUISITION FORM**. This is sent to the **purchasing department**.	Purchasing department sends out a letter of enquiry requesting a **QUOTATION** or uses a CATALOGUE to source the goods required.	Once the quotation has been received the purchasing department will send out an **ORDER** detailing the goods required.
The supplier will despatch the goods along with a **delivery note**. The storeman will complete a **GOODS RECEIVED NOTE** This is sent to the purchasing department for checking against the order.	The goods are stored in the warehouse and a **BIN CARD** is completed and kept beside the stock item. This records receipts and issues of that material to and from the warehouse.	In addition to the bin card a **STOCK LEDGER CARD** will be kept to show the value of the receipts and issues of stock from suppliers and to jobs in the factory.

The supplier will send a **statement** for the goods sold to the firm and the firm will pay for the goods using a **cheque**

Figure 15.1 Purchasing procedures and documentation

Date: 1 June Year 1		**Requisition No**: 77362		
Date items required by: 21 June Year 1		**Department requesting items**: Central Stores		
Quantity	**Description**	**Stock Code**	**Supplier**	**Order No:**
300	25 mm x 50 mm steel carriage bolts	SB23	United Steel plc	CS4652
Requisitioned by:		**Approved by**		
Alan Wells, Supervisor		*John King, Purchasing Manager*		

Figure 15.2 A purchase requisition form, detailing the quantity and description of the goods required, the supplier and order number

No orders can be placed unless an authorised purchase requisition is received and signed by a person authorised to request the goods. To control purchase costs there will normally be a cash limit set for the value of items which a particular level of responsibility can purchase.

Copies of the purchase requisition will be sent to:

- the purchasing department who will place the order;
- production control informing them of the goods being ordered
- the storekeeper so he knows what has been ordered.

Purchase order

Before placing an order the buyer should consider:

- **Quantity**. The buyer must equate the economies of large scale orders against the costs of storage.
- **Quality**. British Standard Specifications should be used to ensure quality.
- **Price**. In addition to prices quoted the buyer must consider the following:
  - discount and credit terms;
  - quality and suitability;
  - spare parts and after sales service.
- **Delivery**. How long will it take for the goods to be delivered?

The purchases order consists of several copies and these will be distributed as follows:

1st Copy	Supplier
2nd Copy	Accounts department
3rd Copy	Warehouse or Stores department
4th Copy	Department raising the requisition
5th Copy	Production department
6th Copy	Retained in purchasing department

Receipt of goods

Materials should be unloaded at special receiving centres. This is normally the warehouse. The following procedure may be used in checking the goods:

- an **advice/delivery note** will either be forwarded at the time the goods are dispatched or will accompany the goods;
- stores department will **check the quantity** of goods received with the delivery note and normally sign it as being correct;
- **quality inspection** will vary according to type of material being received. Some materials will only require a brief inspection while other materials may require chemical analysis to check for quality;
- Where insufficient time is available to check quantity of delivered goods the delivery note will be **endorsed unexamined**;
- Goods received note is made out and **distributed** as follows;

1st Copy	Stores department
2nd Copy	Purchasing
3rd Copy	Accounts
4th Copy	Department raising the requisition
5th Copy	Retained in receiving department

```
ORDER NO:  CS4652

ERJ PLC
17 High Street
BOLTON
BL3 6TT

Account No 27354

UNITED STEEL PLC                          1 June Year 1
27 WINDYHILL ROAD
MOTHERWELL
ML5 6TK
```

Please supply, in accordance with instructions the following:

Qty	Description	Price	Total
300	25 mm x 50 mm steel carriage bolts Delivery – to Central Stores at the above address Terms: 5% Nett monthly Delivery by: 21 June Year 1	£0.50 each	£150.00

Signed *John King*
       Purchasing Manager

Figure 15.3 A purchase order form, issued by the buyer to the supplier

GOODS RECEIVED NOTE

From	United Steel plc		GR No 234		
Date	20 June Year 1				
Goods	Qty	Packages	Order No	**For official use only**	
				Rate	£
25 mm x 50 mm steel carriage bolts	300	1	CS4652		
Carriage	Received by		Goods Inspection Report No		
Trans World Shipping	Alan White		SB2256		
Purchase Requisition No	Noted on progress chart	Bin No	Stores ledger No	Invoice No	Ref No
77362	20 June	72	301	65643	P86

Figure 15.4 A goods received note, detailing actual goods received

The goods received note is used to:

- provide a record of material received;
- inform the storekeeper of material to be stored;
- provide a means of checking suppliers invoices;
- notify interested departments that the materials have been received.

Storage of materials

As well as centralised purchasing a centralised store may be used.

Advantages of centralised storage

- economy in staff and the concentration of specialised staff in one department;
- reduction in clerical costs and economies in records and stationery;
- better supervision is possible;
- staff become acquainted with many different types of stores and this can be useful if anyone is absent from work;
- better layout of stores;
- easier to carry out inventory check;
- stocks are kept at a minimum thus reducing storage space and costs;
- fewer cases of obsolescence;
- reduction in capital invested in stock;
- improved security can be achieved.

Disadvantages of centralised storage

- increased transportation costs;
- inconvenience to users where stores may be some distance away;
- breakdown in transport or hold-ups in central stores may result in production stoppages;
- greater risk of loss by fire.

The storekeeper

The storekeeper is in control of the stores department. He/she must be able to organise stores operations, be of great integrity and capable of controlling subordinates. His main duties will be:

- **maintaining stores** in a tidy manner and positioning all materials in stores correctly;
- **checking delivery notes**, accepting material into stores and completing goods received notes
- **issuing stores** on receipt of requisition;
- **requisitioning further supplies** from purchasing department;
- **completing and checking bin cards** to ensure physical quantities tie up with figures on the bin cards;
- **preventing fraud, theft and unauthorised access** to the stores department.

Stock control

It is important that the level of stock maintained is adequate for the needs of the firm and that problems are not created by either overstocking or understocking.

Overstocking occurs when too much stock is held by the firm. This has several disadvantages:

- overstocking ties up capital needlessly;
- risk of deterioration or evaporation of stock;
- risk of loss by theft is increased;
- unnecessary storage costs are incurred;
- greater risk of obsolescence. Production methods may change requiring material of a different grade or fashions may change;
- where prices changes occur frequently overstocking may result in the failure to buy at the best price.

Understocking occurs when too little stock is held in the stores. This can create problems for the firm:

- understocking may mean that material is not available when needed and result in production delays;
- risk of losing custom if delivery dates are not maintained;
- failure to take advantage of quantity discounts;
- frequent ordering may result in increased clerical costs;
- wages and fixed costs incurred without any compensating income from output.

It is important that details of all materials received into the stores or warehouse or issues from stores or warehouse are recorded by the storekeeper. The physical movement can be recorded on bin cards.

BIN CARD				
Part No: 25 mm x 50 mm steel carriage bolts				
Bin No 72				
Date	Reference	Receipts	Issues	Balance
18 June Year 1				25
20 June Year 1	GR No 234	300		325

Figure 15.5 A bin card, showing the items stored in the bin, receipts, issues and balances

The bin card is normally kept beside or attached to the material being stored. It will show the items stored in the bin, receipts (dates and quantities), issues (dates and quantities) and balances.

The receipt into stores of the steel carriage bolts will be recorded on the bin card, as shown above. The use of bin cards is on the decline in many enterprises because of the introduction of computerised stock control systems.

Control of stock levels

A **maximum stock level** is set for each item held. This represents the maximum quantity of the item which should be in the store at one time. Factors determining this level include storage costs, rate of usage, lead time for delivery, economic ordering quantity and possible deterioration and obsolescence.

A **minimum stock level** should be set for each item stocked. This represents the lowest level to which the item should be permitted to fall at any one time. This is determined by rate of usage and the lead time between ordering and receiving goods.

A **reorder level** should be set for each item. When this figure is reached a purchase requisition is prepared. The reorder level is set sufficiently far above the minimum level to allow time for deliveries to take place.

Stocktaking

All stock should be counted at least once a year to ensure that the stock quantities shown on the stock ledger cards or bin cards are correct. There are three main methods of stocktaking:

Annual stocktaking. All stocks are counted and valued on one particular day during the year. This method is administratively simple but it has the disadvantage that production will probably have to be halted during the stocktaking period.

Continuous stocktaking involves the counting of some items of stock on a cyclical basis throughout the year. It does not disrupt production, but it needs careful administration. It has the advantage of revealing stock losses earlier than the annual stocktaking.

Perpetual inventory. With this system the stores record card shows the quantity of receipts, issues and balances on hand. Information about stock is always available as the balance is known after each receipt or issue. However a physical check must be carried out at least once a year to check the accuracy of the stores record card and the bin card.

Issuing stock

Materials are issued to the factory by the storekeeper on receipt of a signed material requisition form. The storekeeper records the issues on the bin card. The stock record card is completed showing quantity, cost and department receiving the material.

Just In Time

The **Just in Time (JIT)** system was developed by Taiichi Ohno in Japan at the Toyota car assembly plant. Material is ordered to arrive at the factory in time to be used in production. Stock levels are practically non-existent. Materials delivered are of 100% quality and there are normally no rejects. The reliability of suppliers is very important to the firm.

The advent of the computer has made this system even more possible and was introduced into firms in Britain in the 1970s using assembly line production systems such as car manufacturers.

Advantages of JIT:

- reduction in storage costs;
- less capital tied up in stocks;
- quicker turn round of capital;
- lower stock inventory costs.

Disadvantages of JIT:

- transport costs could increase;
- delays in delivery resulting in delayed production.

Computerised stock control and inventory procedures

The introduction of information technology and computerised systems has revolutionised stock control procedures. Many firms now use computerised systems for their stock control and order processing systems such as *OrderWise* which can be used as a standalone system or linked to *Sage Line 50* and other leading accounts packages.

This system and other software packages can allow an enterprise to group products, forecast seasonal trends, find stock quickly, value issues using First In First Out (FIFO) and Last In First Out (LIFO), keep track of multiple stock and bin locations.

Task 1

1   List 5 factors which will influence which supplier of goods a business enterprise will use.

2   Explain the duties of a buyer in a business enterprise.

3   Explain the use of the following documents:

   a) Purchase requisition
   b) Quotation
   c) Order
   d) Goods received note
   e) Bin card
   f) Stock ledger card

4   Explain the benefits to a business enterprise of a centralised storage system for materials.

5   Explain the terms understocking and overstocking and explain the disadvantages of each.

6   What is Just in Time?

7   Explain the following terms associated with controlling stock levels:

   a) Maximum stock level
   b) Minimum stock level
   c) Reorder level

8   Explain the different methods of stocktaking a business enterprise may use.

CHAPTER 16

Pricing stock issues

Intermediate 2 Level Outcomes: ▐▐▐▶

I2
This chapter includes material from Int 2 level Management Accounting Outcome 1
☆ **Complete a partially prepared stock valuation card using Last in First out (LIFO) method.**

Higher Level Outcomes: ▐▐▐▶

H
This chapter includes material from Higher level Management Accounting Outcome 1
☆ **Complete a partially prepared stock valuation card using Average Cost (AVCO) method of valuation.**

I2
H

Pricing stock issues

The problem in placing a value on the stock being issued to a particular job or process is that the material used may have been purchased at different times and at different prices.

There are a number of methods of pricing stock issued to a particular job, process or operation. We will look closely at three methods:

1　First In First Out (FIFO)

2　Last In First Out (LIFO)

3　Weighted Average (AVCO)

First In First Out

In the First In First Out (FIFO) method, the price of the stock issued is based on the assumption that issues are made in strict order of receipt. The first stock received is the first stock issued. Issues to production will be charged at the first price paid until all the units at that price are used up. Then the next price paid will be used until all stocks from that receipt are issued to production.

Advantages of FIFO stock valuation

- It is a satisfactory method when prices are relatively stable.
- The balance of stock is a *true and fair* valuation for financial accounting purposes.
- Stock valuation is accepted by the Inland Revenue for taxation purposes.
- Conforms to SSAP9 and the Companies Acts regarding the valuation of stock.
- It is an easy method to operate.
- No profit or loss can arise in the accounts when this method of pricing is used.

Disadvantages of FIFO stock valuation

- Product cost does not reflect current values.
- Much clerical work required for the calculations and errors are possible.
- It is said to inflate profits, causing needless tax payments and a run down of assets if the residue is paid out in dividends.
- Comparison of the price of one job to another can be misleading.

Example 1 First In First Out

The following receipts and issues of Material Y were made during the first week in January.

- Jan 1 Balance in store   100 units at £5
- Jan 2 Received into store   100 units at £6
- Jan 3 Issued to Job 123   75 units
- Jan 4 Returned to supplier   25 units received into store on 2 January
- Jan 5 Issued to Job 124   30 units

The above information will be recorded on a stock ledger card which will show the physical movement of the materials and the costs of receipts and the value of issues from stores to the various jobs in the factory.

STEP 1 – Set-up stock record card and calculate and enter opening balance in stock record card and stock in the working notes

Jan 1 The balance of 100 units represents the stock held in the stores on that date.

The value of the stock held is 100 units × £5 = £500

STOCK LEDGER CARD Material Y								FIFO		
		Receipts			**Issues**			**Balance**		
Date	**Details**	**Quantity**	**Price £**	**£**	**Quantity**	**Price £**	**£**	**Quantity**	**Price £**	**£**
Jan 1	Balance							100	5	500

Working Notes:

Physical stock movement	
Price paid	£5
Units received	100

continued ➤

Example 1 First In First Out continued

STEP 2 – Calculate the value of the material received and the new balance

Jan 2: Stock of 100 units has been received. The value is: 100 units × £6 = £600

STOCK LEDGER CARD Material Y								FIFO		
		Receipts			Issues			Balance		
Date	Details	Quantity	Price £	£	Quantity	Price £	£	Quantity	Price £	£
Jan 1	Balance							100	5	500
Jan 2	Receipts	100	6	600				200		1,100

Physical stock movement			
Price paid	£5		£6
Units received	100	Jan 2	100

Calculate the new balances for quantity and stock value:

The unit balance is recalculated = 100 units + 100 units = 200 units

The new value balance is calculated = £500 + £600 = £1,100

STEP 3 – Calculate the value of the materials issued from store to Job 123

Jan 3: 75 units × £5 (the first price paid) = £375.

STOCK LEDGER CARD Material Y								FIFO		
		Receipts			Issues			Balance		
Date	Details	Quantity	Price £	£	Quantity	Price £	£	Quantity	Price £	£
Jan 1	Balance							100	5	500
Jan 2	Receipts	100	6	600				200		1,100
Jan 3	Job 123				75	£5	375	125		725

Physical stock movement			
Price paid	£5		
Units received	100	Jan 2	£6
Issues Jan 3	<u>75</u>		100
	25		

continued ➤

Example 1 First In, First Out continued

Calculate the new quantity and value balance:

Quantity balance of 200 – 75 issued = 125 new balance

Value balance of £1,100 – £375 value issued = £725 new balance

STEP 4 – Calculate value of materials purchased on 2 January, returned to supplier

Jan 4: Units returned are always entered in the stock ledger card at the purchase price paid – in this case £6.

The value of the returns will be 25 units × £6 = £150.

STOCK LEDGER CARD Material Y		Receipts			Issues			Balance		FIFO
Date	Details	Quantity	Price £	£	Quantity	Price £	£	Quantity	Price £	£
Jan 1	Balance							100	5	500
Jan 2	Receipts	100	6	600				200		1,100
Jan 3	Job 123				75	£5	375	125		725
Jan 4	**Returns**				**25**	**£6**	**150**	**100**		**575**

Physical stock movement			
Price paid	£5		£6
Units received	100		100
Issues Jan 3	75	**Returns Jan 4**	**25**
	25		**75**

The units and the value of the returns are deducted from the balances:

New quantity balance = 125 – 25 = 100

New value balance = £725 – £150 = £575

Note. Returns to suppliers are charged at the price paid (i.e. £6 per unit).

STEP 5 – Calculate the value of the units issued to Job 124

Jan 5. Units issued to Job 124. These units issued will be made up from materials purchased at different times and at different prices.

Jan 5. Job 124 needs 30 units. 25 units are left from the materials in stock at 1 January valued at £5 each.

These are charged at the first price paid of £5 = 25 × £5 = £125.

All of the units received at the price of £5 have now been issued so the next issue price paid is used to calculate the value of remaining stock to be issued to this job.

continued ➤

Rotated sidebar text: MANAGEMENT ACCOUNTING

Example 1 First In, First Out continued

The additional 5 units are charged at the next price of £6 = 5 units × £6 = £30.

The total cost for Job 124 will be £125 + £30 = £155.

The units and the value of the issues are deducted from the balances:

New quantity balance = 100 − 30 = 70

New value = £575 − £155 = £420

STOCK LEDGER CARD Material Y		Receipts			Issues			Balance			FIFO
Date	Details	Quantity	Price £ £	£	Quantity	Price £	£	Quantity	Price £ £	£	
Jan 1	Balance							100	5	500	
Jan 2	Receipts	100	6	600				200		1,100	
Jan 3	Job 123				75	£5	375	125		725	
Jan 4	Returns				25	£6	150	100		575	
Jan 5	Job 124				30	25 @ £5 5 @ £6	155	70	£6	420	

Physical stock movement				
Price paid	£5			£6
Units received	100			100
Issues Jan 3	75	Returns Jan 4		25
	25			75
Issues Jan 5	25	Issues Jan 5		5
	0			70

STEP 6 – Check the closing value of stocks

The stock value at the end can be easily checked. There are 70 units left at a value of £6 = £420.

Now do Worksheet 16.1

Last In First Out

In the **Last In First Out (LIFO)** method, the price of stock issued is based on the assumption that issues are made from the stock most recently purchased. Each time a new batch of stock is received the issue price changes until that batch is used up or a new batch is received. This is an 'accounting fiction' because it does not relate to the **physical movement** of stock in the store but to the price of the newest material in the store. When issuing stock the oldest material in stock should be issued first to production.

Advantages of LIFO stock valuation

- Costs are more nearly related to current price levels, so they are better for pricing and estimating purposes.
- Profit determination is much more conservative.
- There is less risk of running down assets via disposable income in the form of profits distributed to owners/shareholders.
- The cost is more realistic and gives management an indication of current costs.

Disadvantages of LIFO stock valuation

- Stock balances are not acceptable for tax purposes by the Inland Revenue.
- Balance of stock not realistic in current terms.
- Stock valuation using this method does not conform to SSAP9.
- Much clerical work required for calculations.
- If issues have to be accounted for from oldest category of stock the figure would be unrealistic, especially for slow-moving stock.
- It is difficult to compare the cost of different jobs.

Example 2 Last In First Out

The following receipts and issues of Material Y were made during the first week in January. The firm uses the Last In First Out method of valuing issues from stock.

- Jan 1 Balance in store   100 units at £5
- Jan 2 Received into store   100 units at £6
- Jan 3 Returned to supplier   25 units received into store on 2 January
- Jan 4 Issued to Job 123   75 units
- Jan 5 Issued to Job 124   30 units

The above information will be recorded on a stock ledger card which will show the physical movement of the materials and the costs of receipts and value of issues from stores to the various jobs.

STEP 1 – Set-up stock record card and calculate and enter opening balance in stock record card and stock in the working notes

Jan 1: The balance of 100 units represents the stock held in the stores on that date. The value of the stock held is 100 units × £5 = £500

STOCK LEDGER CARD Material Y								FIFO		
		Receipts			Issues			Balance		
Date	Details	Quantity	Price £	£	Quantity	Price £	£	Quantity	Price £	£
Jan 1	Balance							100	5	500

continued ➤

Example 2 Last In First Out continued

Working Notes:

Physical stock movement	
Price paid	£5
Units received	**100**

The value of materials issued and received into stores will be calculated as follows:

STEP 2 – Calculate the value of the material received and the new balance

Jan 2: Stock of 100 units has been received. The value is: 100 units × £6 = £600

STOCK LEDGER CARD Material Y											FIFO
		Receipts			Issues			Balance			
Date	Details	Quantity	Price £	£	Quantity	Price £	£	Quantity	Price £	£	
Jan 1	Balance							100	5	500	
Jan 2	Receipts	100	6	600				200		1,100	

Physical stock movement			
Price paid	£5		£6
Balance	100	**Received Jan 2**	100

Calculate the new balances for quantity and stock value

The unit balance is recalculated = 100 units + 100 units = 200 units

The value balance is recalculated = £500 + £600 = £1,100

STEP 3 – Calculate value of materials purchased on 2 January, returned to supplier

Jan 3: Units returned are always entered in the stock ledger card at the purchase price paid – in this case £6.

The value of the returns will be 25 units × £6 = £150.

STOCK LEDGER CARD Material Y											FIFO
		Receipts			Issues			Balance			
Date	Details	Quantity	Price £	£	Quantity	Price £	£	Quantity	Price £	£	
Jan 1	Balance							100	5	500	
Jan 2	Receipts	100	6	600				200		1,100	
Jan 3	Returns				25	£6	150	175		950	

continued ➤

Example 2   Last In First Out continued

Physical stock movement			
Price paid	£5		£6
Balance	100	Received Jan 2	100
		Returns Jan 3	<u>25</u>
			75

The units and the value of the returns are deducted from the balances:

New quantity balance = 200 – 25 = 175

New value balance = £1,100 – £150 = £950

STEP 4 – Calculate the value of the materials issued from store to Job 123

Jan 4: 75 units × £6 (the last price paid) = £450

STOCK LEDGER CARD Material Y											FIFO
		Receipts			**Issues**			**Balance**			
Date	**Details**	**Quantity**	**Price £**	**£**	**Quantity**	**Price £**	**£**	**Quantity**	**Price £**	**£**	
Jan 1	Balance							100	5	500	
Jan 2	Receipts	100	6	600				200		1,100	
Jan 3	Returns				25	£6	150	175		950	
Jan 4	**Job 123**				75	£6	450	100		500	

Physical stock movement			
Price paid	£5		£6
Balance	100	Received Jan 2	100
		Returns Jan 3	<u>25</u>
			75
		Issued Jan 4	<u>75</u>
			<u>0</u>

Calculate the new quantity and value balance:

Quantity balance of 175 – 75 issued = 100 new balance

Value balance of £950 – £450 value issued = £500 new balance

continued ➤

Example 2 Last In First Out continued

STEP 5 – Calculate the value of the material issued to Job 124

Jan 5: Job 124 needs 30 units

There are no units left at a cost of £6 so all the units needed for Job 124 must be issued from the units held at the start of the period at a price of £5 per unit.

Value = 30 units × £5 = £150

STOCK LEDGER CARD Material Y					FIFO						
		Receipts			Issues			Balance			
Date	Details	Quantity	Price £	£	Quantity	Price £	£	Quantity	Price £	£	
Jan 1	Balance							100	5	500	
Jan 2	Receipts	100	6	600				200		1,100	
Jan 3	Returns				25	£6	150	175		950	
Jan 4	Job 123				75	£6	450	100		500	
Jan 5	**Job 124**				**30**	**£5**	**150**	**70**	**£5**	**350**	

Working notes:

Physical stock movement			
Price paid	£5		£6
Balance	100	Received Jan 2	100
Issued Jan 5	<u>30</u>	Returns Jan 3	<u>25</u>
	70		75
		Returned Jan 4	<u>75</u>
			<u>0</u>

The units and the value of the issues are deducted from the balances:

New quantity balance = 100 – 30 = 70

New value balance = £500 – £150 = £350

STEP 6 – Check the closing value of stocks

The stock value at the end can be easily checked. There are 70 units left at a value of £5 = £350.

Now do Worksheets 16.2 and 16.3

Average Price method

The Average Price (AVCO) method of pricing issues of materials to the factory is based on a perpetual weighted average system. The price to be used to value issues to the factory from stores is recalculated each time material is received into the stores or when materials have been returned to the supplier because of a problem. The weighted average price of the material is used to record the issues from stores to the factory for production. This method takes into account both the quantity and the value.

As with the Last In First Out method of pricing issues, the physical movement of materials will be based on the first material being received into store will be the first material issued from store, regardless of cost.

Advantages of AVCO

- Average price method accepted by the Inland Revenue.
- One of the methods of stock valuation recommended by SSAP9.
- Simpler to calculate and easier to administer than FIFO or LIFO.
- All units are given equal value making it easier to compare the costs of different jobs.
- Where prices fluctuate often it gives a more even price than either FIFO or LIFO methods.
- No unrealised profits or losses occur because it is based on actual cost.

Disadvantages of AVCO

- Where prices are rising rapidly the average cost will be lower than actual replacement cost.
- Each time materials are received or returned to supplier the average must be recalculated.
- The price charged to production per unit may not reflect any of the actual prices paid.

Example 3 AVCO (Weighted Average)

The following receipts and issues of Material X were made during the first week in January.

- Jan 1 Balance in store   100 units at £5
- Jan 2 Received into store   100 units at £6
- Jan 3 Returned to supplier   25 units received into store on 2 January
- Jan 4 Issued to Job 123   75 units
- Jan 5 Issued to Job 124   30 units

The above information will be recorded on a stock ledger card which will show the physical movement of the materials and the costs of receipts and the value of issues from stores to the various jobs in the factory.

continued >

MANAGEMENT ACCOUNTING

Example 3 AVCO (Weighted Average) continued

STEP 1 – Calculate the value of the stock on hand at the start of the period and its average price

Jan 1: The balance of 100 units represents the stock held in the stores on that date.

The value of the stock held is 100 units × £5 = £500

The weighted average price is £5

STOCK LEDGER CARD Material X										AVCO	
		Receipts			Issues			Balance		
Date	Details	Quantity	Price £	£	Quantity	Price £	£	Quantity	Price £	£
Jan 1	Balance							100	5	500.00

STEP 2 – Calculate the value of the material received, the new balance and the new weighted average

Jan 2: Stock of 100 units has been received. The value is: 100 units × £6 = £600

STOCK LEDGER CARD Material X										AVCO	
		Receipts			Issues			Balance		
Date	Details	Quantity	Price £	£	Quantity	Price £	£	Quantity	Price £	£
Jan 1	Balance							100	5.00	500.00
Jan 2	Receipts	100	6.00	600.00				200	5.50	1,100.00

Calculate the new balances for quantity and stock value and the weighted average:

The unit balance is recalculated = 100 units + 100 units = 200 units

The value balance is recalculated = £500 + £600 = £1,100

Calculate the weighted average of the stock held = £1,100 ÷ 200 = £5.50

STEP 3 – Calculate the value of goods returned on 3 January

Jan 3: Twenty-five of the units purchased on 2 January were returned because they were faulty.

STOCK LEDGER CARD Material X										AVCO	
		Receipts			Issues			Balance		
Date	Details	Quantity	Price £	£	Quantity	Price £	£	Quantity	Price £	£
Jan 1	Balance							100	5.00	500.00
Jan 2	Receipts	100	6.00	600.00				200	5.50	1,100.00
Jan 3	**Returns**				25	6.00	150.00	175	5.43	950.00

continued ➤

Example 3 AVCO (Weighted Average) continued

Any returns made are returned at the price paid (i.e. £6).

Calculate the new balances for quantity and stock value and the weighted average:

The unit balance is recalculated = 200 units – 25 units = 175 units

The value balance is recalculated = £1,100 – £150 = £950

Calculate the weighted average of the stock held = £950 ÷ 175 = £5.43 (rounded to 2 decimal places).

The new weighted average must be calculated when goods are returned to suppliers. Units issued from store will be charged at the new AVCO price of £5.43.

STEP 4 – Calculate the value of the materials issued from store to Job 123

Jan 4: Issued 75 units to Job 123

75 units × £5.43 = £407.25

STOCK LEDGER CARD Material X								AVCO		
		Receipts			**Issues**			**Balance**		
Date	**Details**	**Quantity**	**Price £**	**£**	**Quantity**	**Price £**	**£**	**Quantity**	**Price £**	**£**
Jan 1	Balance							100	5.00	500.00
Jan 2	Receipts	100	6.00	600.00				200	5.50	1,100.00
Jan 3	Returns				25	6.00	150.00	175	5.43	950.00
Jan 4	**Job 123**				**75**	**5.43**	**407.25**	**100**	**5.43**	**542.75**

Calculate the new quantity and value balance:

Quantity balance of 175 – 75 issued = 100 new balance

Value balance of £950 – £407.25 = £542.75

The weighted average of stock held will only be re-calculated when items are received into stock or returns are made from stock.

continued ➤

Example 3 AVCO (Weighted Average) continued

STEP 5 – Units issued to Job 124 are issued at the new weighted average price of £5.43 per unit

Jan 5: Job 124 needs 30 units

Value = 30 units × £5.43 = £161.90

STOCK LEDGER CARD Material X									FIFO		
		Receipts			**Issues**			**Balance**			
Date	**Details**	**Quantity**	**Price £**	**£**	**Quantity**	**Price £**	**£**	**Quantity**	**Price £**	**£**
Jan 1	Balance							100	5.00	500.00
Jan 2	Receipts	100	6.00	600.00				200	5.50	1,100.00
Jan 3	Returns				25	6.00	150.00	175	5.43	950.00
Jan 4	Job 123				75	5.43	407.25	100	5.43	542.75
Jan 5	**Job 124**				**30**	**5.43**	**162.90**	**70**	**5.43**	**379.85**

The units and the value of the issues are deducted from the balances:

New quantity balance = 100 − 30 = 70

New value balance = £542.75 − £162.90 = £379.85

  Now do Worksheets 16.4 and 16.5

 # Inventory control procedures

Inventory control procedures are used by an enterprise to control the amount of money invested in stock. The control procedures will involve:

- monitoring stock levels;
- recording stock levels;
- forecasting future demand;
- setting reorder quantities to help determine when to order.

The overall aim of an inventory control procedure is to minimise the total costs associated with the stock. These costs can be divided in **carrying costs**, **ordering costs** and **costs of being without stock**.

Carrying costs include:

- interest on the capital invested in the stock;
- storage and staffing costs;
- handling costs;
- audit costs;
- insurance and security costs;

- obsolescence and deterioration;
- pilferage.

Ordering costs include:

- clerical and administrative costs;
- transport costs.

Costs of being without stock include:

- loss of sales resulting in lost contribution;
- loss of customers because of the unavailability of goods;
- production stoppages because of material shortages;
- additional costs of placing small orders or for urgent delivery.

Before looking at how an enterprise can ensure material is available when required, while incurring minimum costs, it is necessary to understand the terms associated with the inventory control procedures.

Lead time	The time between ordering the goods and the goods becoming available for production.
Economic order quantity	The reorder quantity which minimises ordering costs and the carrying costs of the stock.
Minimum stock level	The stock level below which the units held should not fall. It is calculated by taking into consideration the demand during the lead time and builds in an allowance for any errors in the forecasting of the lead time. If this level is reached it should act as a warning to management that stock usages are above the normal level.
Maximum stock level	This is the maximum desirable stock level. If stocks rise above this level the enterprise will incur additional carrying costs.
Reorder level	This is the stock level at which an order should be placed with the supplier. This level depends on the lead time and the demand for the materials during the lead time.
Reorder quantity	This is the number of units to be ordered and is usually the same amount as the economic order quantity.

Calculating stock control levels

In order to minimise stock costs an enterprise must ensure that materials are available when required. To achieve this they will calculate several different stock levels:

- Reorder level
- Minimum stock level
- Maximum stock level

Example 4

Brown plc provide the following information relating to the material required to manufacture Product X:

- Average daily usage   500 units
- Minimum daily usage   300 units
- Maximum daily usage   650 units
- Lead time   20-26 days
- Economic order quantity (previously calculated)   20,000 units

This information is used to calculate the reorder level, and the minimum and maximum stock levels.

STEP 1 – Calculate the reorder level

The reorder level is calculated using the formula:

Reorder level = Maximum usage × maximum lead time
= 650 units × 26 days = 16,900 units

STEP 2 – Calculate the minimum stock level

The minimum stock level is calculated using the formula:

Minimum stock level = Reorder level – (average usage during average lead time)
= Reorder level – (average usage × average lead time)
= 16,900 units – (500 units × 23 days)
= 16,900 units – 11,500 units
= 5,400 units

STEP 3 – Calculate the maximum stock level

The maximum stock level is calculated using the formula:

Maximum stock level = (Reorder level + Economic order quantity) – (minimum usage during minimum lead time)
= 16,900 + 20,000 – (300 × 20)
= 36,900 – 6,000
= 30,900 units

  ⊙ *Now do Worksheet 16.6*

Computerised stock control

The advent of information technology has enabled computerised stock control and order processing systems to be introduced into many business enterprises. The type of system adopted will depend on the size and perceived needs of the company.

Such systems are advantageous and will enable the company to:

- value stock using FIFO and LIFO methods;
- keep track of expiry dates and multiple stock and bin locations;
- allow flexible customer pricing (such as discount structures, price lists, special prices/offers, quantity breaks, global discounts etc);
- product audit trail;
- batch and serial number traceability.

These systems will link with other computerised accounting tools. Examples of such systems are *Sage Line 50* (a computerised ordering and stock control system) and *OrderWise*.

Labour costs

Intermediate 2 Level Outcomes:

 This chapter includes material from Int 2 level Management Accounting Outcome 1

☆ **Calculate the gross wages where basic, time, piece, bonus and overtime rates are applied consistently with the information or times sheets and/or clock cards supplied.**

It also includes material from Int 2 level Management Accounting Outcome 2

☆ **Direct materials and labour costs are recorded consistently with the information supplied.**

Higher Level Outcomes:

H This chapter includes material from Higher level Management Accounting Outcome 2

☆ **Direct materials and labour costs are recorded consistently with the information supplied.**

Controlling labour costs

Labour can be one of the biggest direct costs incurred in the manufacturing process. It is important that careful control is kept of labour costs.

Methods used to record the gate, or factory, time of workers vary considerably. Most modern works use time-recording clocks, which can be linked with a computerised wage control system, but other older methods may still be found.

The check or disc method

Metal **discs bearing the workers' numbers** are placed on hooks on a board kept at the entrance of the works. On entering the worker removes his disc and places it in a box provided. The box is removed at starting time and a 'late' box is substituted. The timekeeper uses the discs to record attendances and details of late comers.

Time recording clocks

Time recording clocks are more accurate than the disc method. The presence of a timekeeper is still necessary to prevent fraud and irregularities.

Card time recorders

Card time recorders give a daily and weekly printed and tabulated record of the times or arrival and departure of employees using a separate card for each employee.

Racks are installed near each recorder, the cards are removed from the *Out* rack, inserted into the clock and the time the worker enters is printed, then the card is placed in the *In* rack. When he leaves the factory the card removed from the *In* rack, inserted into the clock and placed in the *Out* rack, the time is again printed.

The times recorded on the cards along with the hourly rate to be paid is used to calculate the wages due for the week.

Clock card

Figure 17.1 shows an example of a clock card. It is designed so it is easy to see the hours worked and the rates of pay for those hours.

No ......5...... Wk Ending ...4 September Year 1...					
Name		JOHN McPHERSON No 72139			
EXTRA TIME	RATE		REGULAR TIME		
		1st Day	IN	4.30	07.00
			OUT		11.30
16.00	2		IN	4	12.00
18.00			OUT		16.00
		2nd Day	IN	4.30	07.00
			OUT		11.30
16.00	3		IN	4	12.00
19.00			OUT		16.00
		3rd Day	IN	4.30	07.30
			OUT		11.30
			IN	3.30	12.30
			OUT		16.00
		4th Day	IN		
			OUT		
			IN		
			OUT		
		5th Day	IN		
			OUT		
			IN		
			OUT		
		6th Day	IN		
			OUT		
			IN		
			OUT		
		7th Day	IN		
			OUT		
			IN		
			OUT		
TOTAL			TOTAL		

Figure 17.1 An example of a clock card showing hours and days worked

Daily or weekly time sheets

In addition to a clock card, a worker may be required to keep a **daily** or **weekly time sheet**. This gives details of the time spent on each separate job by each worker during the day or week in the factory. The times recorded are compared with the clock cards and any discrepancies should be explained.

Daily and weekly time sheets can be used in the building industry, decorators and civil-engineering contractors or where workers move to various locations in a factory such as cleaners and maintenance staff.

Time sheets are useful but times can be approximated and there can be a tendency for employees to forget periods of idle time (times when no job was to be done) or wasted time. If a conscientious foreman is in charge greater accuracy may be achieved.

DAILY TIME SHEET				Date ...1 Sept...	
Name ....J.McPherson....................		Work No ..72139..		Week No	5
Works Order No	Work completed	Time Started	Time Finished	Rate £	£
RM 163	MAINTENANCE	09.00	10.30	20	30.00
Employee's Signature		Foreman's signature			
For Office Use					

Figure 17.2 An example of a time sheet showing times started and finished, pay rates and work order numbers

Job tickets

Job tickets are used for recording the time worked on a particular job. One job ticket will be issued to an employee giving details of work to be completed. When the work is finished the employee returns the job ticket to the foreman and the length of time taken is recorded on the ticket.

If an employee cannot start work immediately, because he has to wait for material, or there is a machine breakdown, an **idle time card** should be used to record the waiting time.

Methods of remuneration

Time-based systems

In **time-based systems** of pay, payment is made by the hour, week or month irrespective of the level of output achieved. Different systems exist to encourage high performance while keeping the simplicity of time rates. For example, workers who agree to a high standard of output and efficiency receive a high hourly rate. This method is used where:

- it is difficult to measure output;
- all workers are doing the same type of work;
- quality rather than quantity of working is wanted;
- speed of work is determined by the actual process (such as a chemical reaction);
- where the output is difficult to measure (such as clerical work).

Example 1

Flat time rate where a set rate is paid for each hour worked.

Employees work a 35 hour basic week for which they are paid £5 per hour. Earnings are calculated as follows:

Earnings = clock hours worked × rate per hour
         = 35 hours × £5 per hour = £170

Task 1

From the following information calculate the basic wages to be paid to each employee:

Name	Basic Hours worked	Hourly Rate
James Smith	35	£8
Alan Wilson	40	£10
Lynn Thomson	38	£6
Richard Bryson	35	£12
Calum Mackay	38	£7

Overtime rate

The **overtime rate** is an extra amount paid for each hour worked over the basic working week. The amount of overtime pay will depend on when the extra hours are worked. It is usual for overtime worked on a Saturday and Sunday to be paid at a higher rate than if worked on a weekday.

Example 2

In a firm the basic hours worked are 38 hours per week. Workers are paid a basic rate of £9 per hour.

In the first week in September, J Singh worked 47 hours. The overtime hours were made up as follows:

- 4 hours on Sunday;
- 3 hours on Saturday;
- 2 hours during the week.

The **overtime** rate is the **basic** rate of pay **plus** a **fraction** of the basic rate. The fraction to be added to the basic rate will depend on when the overtime is worked.

During the week overtime is paid at **time and a third** (basic rate plus one third of the basic rate)

= £9 + (£9 × ⅓)
= £9 + £3
= £12 per hour

continued ➤

Example 2 continued

On **Saturday** overtime is paid at **time and a half** (basic rate plus half of the basic rate)

$= £9 + (£9 × ½)$
$= £9 + £4.50$
$= £13.50$ per hour

On **Sunday** overtime is paid at **double time** (basic rate plus basic rate)

$= £9 + £9$
$= £18$ per hour

The amount earned by J Singh during the first week in September would be calculated as follows:

Basic rate	= 38 hours × £9	= £342.00
Sunday overtime	= 4 hours × £18	= £72.00
Saturday overtime	= 3 hours × £13.50	= £40.50
Week day overtime	= 2 hours × £12	= £24.00
Total wage due		**£478.50**

Task 2

Copy and complete the following table to calculate the various overtime rates to be paid for each of the following basic rates of pay:

Basic Rate	Time and a third	Time and a half	Double Time
£4			
£6			
£12			
£15			
£21			

Task 3

1 R Smith's basic working week is 38 hours. His basic rate of pay is £6 per hour. Overtime is paid at time and a half for week day and Saturday working double time for Sunday working.

During the first week in August he worked a total of 50 hours, 5 hours overtime during the week and the remainder on Sunday.

Using the above information calculate his weekly wage.

continued ➤

2 From the following information calculate the wages to be paid to machine shop operators from the following information

Basic hours: 40   Basic Rate: £9 per hour

Overtime is paid at time and a third for weekdays and Saturdays and double time on Sunday

Name	Total Hours worked	Weekday/ Saturday hours	Sunday
C Lei	48	5	3
H Emerson	52	8	4
D Taylor	43	3	
S Fergusson	45		5
G Singh	46	3	3

3 J Johnston owns a house-building business. The basic working week for his joinery employees is 35 hours at a basic rate of £18 per hour. The first 6 hours of overtime worked are paid at time and a half, and any hours above that are paid at double time.

One of his joiners is currently working on building a new house and he submits the following timesheet.

WEEKLY TIME SHEET		R Simpson Joiner	Work No J21
Day	Start Time	Finish	Hours worked
Monday	0800 hours	1600 hours	
Tuesday	0800 hours	1800 hours	
Wednesday	0800 hours	1800 hours	
Thursday	0800 hours	1800 hours	
Friday	0800 hours	1700 hours	
Saturday	0800 hours	1200 hours	
Sunday	0800 hours	1600 hours	

You are required to calculate:

a) The total hours worked by Simpson

b) His wages for the week.

Advantages of using a time-based system

- an appropriate rate can be set where a high degree of skill is required;
- can be used for indirect labour where no output is measurable (such as sweepers, cleaners, night watchman);
- easy to understand for both employee and employer;
- provides steady rate of earnings each week;
- easy to calculate wages, with no need to refer to output;
- wage costs can be accurately predicted for budgeting purposes.

Disadvantages of using a time-based system

- no incentive for workers to increase output
- workers may suffer from low moral where no reward is obtainable for working harder or achieving higher productivity
- management and supervision must be good to ensure all workers are pulling their weight
- wages have to be paid even if no work available for workers to do.

Payment by Results

Payment by results is at the opposite end of the scale from time rates. With time rates the worker receives a fixed weekly wage and labour cost per unit of output will vary. Under the payment by results system the worker receives a variable weekly wage which is dependent on his production output achieved and the variable cost per unit will be the same. Payment by results requires less supervision than time rates but a higher standard of inspection.

Straight Piece-Work/Rate

In the piece-work system, the employer pays a specified amount for each unit produced. The wage earned by the employee depends on the amount of work carried out during the week. This method is suitable for production where large quantities of an identical product are produced.

Example 3

Department A produces component X. Workers in this department are paid 15p per component produced.

Employee 123 produces 1,250 components in Week 33. His wage for that week will be:

Wage = Number of components × 15p per component.
= 1,250 × 15p = £187.50

Task 4

From the following information calculate the wages to be paid to the following employees who all work in the Assembly department and are paid 30p per unit completed.

Name	Units Produced	Wage earned
A Brown	1,000	
W Quinn	1,250	
S Delaney	900	
R Grierson	1,100	
M Bennie	1,350	

MANAGEMENT ACCOUNTING

Advantages of piece-work systems
- simple to operate and calculate;
- strong individual incentive;
- exact cost of each unit is known;
- allows worker to build up expertise;
- fixed cost per unit will fall with higher outputs.

Disadvantages of piece-work systems
- accurate rate must be set as it cannot constantly be revised;
- comprehensive inspection system necessary;
- workers tend to take time off - having reached their goal they may go home early;
- opposed by trade unions;
- earnings liable to fluctuate widely;
- workers may sacrifice quality to increase output (wages);
- boredom and other problems related with repetitive work can adversely affect quality of output.

Bonus schemes

With time-based payments, any increase in production levels benefits the employer, whilst with piece-work payments, any increase in production levels benefits the employee. Bonus schemes share the benefits of increased production levels between employer and employee.

With bonus schemes the time saved in relation to the standard set by the employer is shared between the employer and the employee so that as the time saved increases, the labour cost per unit decreases. The employer will benefit in the form of reduced labour costs per unit.

Incentive/premium bonus scheme

With Incentive/premium bonus schemes a standard time is set for a job to be completed and the work is paid at a rate per hour. If the employee takes less than the standard time set he will be paid a bonus based on the time he saves.

Example 4

It is estimated that it will take 15 hours to paint the games hall in the school. The painter will be paid £10 per hour. A bonus of one third the time saved × the time rate will be paid.

If the painter completes the work in the 15 hours his wage will be:

Wage = Number of hours × hourly rate
       = 15 × £10 = £150

If the painter completed the job in 12 hours (saving 3 hours) his wage will be:

12 × £10 + (one third of the 3 hours saved × £10)
12 × £10 + ((3 × ⅓) × £10) = £130

Task 5

From the following information calculate the amount to be paid to each employee if the bonus is paid of half the time saved:

Name	Job No	Standard Time	Actual time taken	Hourly rate
J Ball	Job 23	10 hours	8 hours	£10
K Noakes	Job 24	12 hours	11 hours	£12
S O'Brien	Job 25	25 hours	22 hours	£15
K Gallacher	Job 26	6 hours	5 hours	£12
P Gibson	Job 27	10 hours	9 hours	£10

There are many different incentive/premium bonus schemes which can be operated but they all basically follow the same system where workers receive (in addition to the hourly rate) an amount for the time they save in completing a job. Two examples of premium bonus schemes are the Halsey premium bonus scheme and the Rowan premium bonus scheme.

Halsey premium bonus scheme

In the Halsey scheme, the employee is paid the **time taken for the job** plus **half of the time saved** at the normal time rate.

(Time taken × time rate) + (0.5 of time saved × time rate)

Example 5

K Moncrieff works for ABC Builders plc and has been given Job 71 to complete. The standard time for this job is 8 hours and he is paid an hourly rate of £10 per hour. Moncrieff completes the job in 6.5 hours.

Calculate the amount to be paid to him for Job 71.

The time saved by Moncrieff = 8 − 6.5 = 1.5 hours

The amount to be paid = (6.5 hours × £10) + (0.5 × 1.5 hours × £10)
= £65 + £7.50
= £72.50

Task 6

JB Builders uses the Halsey Premium Bonus system to pay their employees. From the following information calculate the wage to be paid for each of the jobs completed:

Name	Job No	Standard Time	Actual time taken	Hourly rate
A Green	Job 47	15 hours	12 hours	£10
L Whitelaw	Job 48	8 hours	7 hours	£12
X Kirkwood	Job 49	30 hours	26 hours	£15
R Smith	Job 50	26 hours	18 hours	£12
S Veer	Job 51	9 hours	6 hours	£10

Rowan premium bonus scheme

In the Rowan scheme, a standard time is set for the completion of a job and a **bonus is paid for the time saved**. The bonus is a **percentage of the time rate** equal to the **proportion of the time saved**.

$$\text{(Time taken} \times \text{time rate)} + \frac{\text{(time taken} \times \text{time saved} \times \text{time rate)}}{\text{time allowed}}$$

Example 6

L Warburton is paid £8 per hour and has completed Job 56X in 6 hours. The standard time set for the job was 8 hours. Calculate the wage to be paid to Warburton for Job 56X.

$$\text{Wage to be paid} = (6 \text{ hours} \times £8) + \frac{(6 \times 2 \times £8)}{8}$$

$$= £48 + £12 = £60$$

Task 7

Lee Manufacturing plc uses the Rowan premium bonus scheme to pay their employees. From the following information calculate the wage to be paid for each of the Jobs completed:

Name	Job No	Standard Time	Actual time taken	Hourly rate
A Govan	Job 102	10 hours	8 hours	£8
L Hamilton	Job 103	12 hours	8 hours	£8
J G Stewart	Job 104	15 hours	12 hours	£10
S Holloway	Job 105	8 hours	6 hours	£6
J McKechnie	Job 106	6 hours	4 hours	£6

Group bonus schemes

In cases where it is impossible to measure the output of individual workers it may be possible to measure the work of a group and to apply a bonus scheme on this basis. This may be applied where:

- individual output cannot be measured;
- output is dependent on the work of a group in which all members are interdependent;
- members of the group are of approximately equal skill;
- it is desired to overcome jealousy due to different earnings on individual piece rates;
- it is desired to give a bonus to indirect workers.

Payslips

At the end of the week or month each employee will receive a payslip giving details of wages/salaries earned, and total deductions (tax, National Insurance, and voluntary deductions like pension contributions). These can be computerised or prepared manually. The total information can be extracted from these for costing purposes.

Now do Worksheets 17.1 and 17.2

CHAPTER 18

Overhead analysis

Why do we need to analyse overheads?

I2 H

Overhead analysis is the process whereby an amount for each overhead is included in the total cost of the product.

Before preparing an overhead analysis you must understand what is meant by the terms **cost centre** and **cost unit**.

Cost centres

Cost centres may be a department, group of machines, method process or operation for which a cost may be calculated. Examples of cost centres include:

• cutting department	• finishing department
• plant	• steam plant
• machine shop	• material store
• hand labour	• personnel department
• canteen	• repairs and maintenance

These cost centres may be classified as production cost centres, process cost centres or service cost centres.

A **production** (or **process**) **cost centre** is a department (or group of machines) where production takes place resulting in a product which may be completely finished and ready for sale or a product which requires to be further processed before it is ready for sale. For example, the manufacture of light bulbs will take place in several production (or process) departments.

A **service cost centre** is department which provides a service to the production areas of the factory. Without the existence of this cost centre the production cost centres would find it difficult to manufacture the goods. Examples of service cost centres are maintenance department, canteen, human resources, factory management etc.

Cost unit

A cost unit is the product, service or time period which finally absorbs all costs including overheads from cost centres. Examples of cost units are:

• loaf of bread	• canteen meal
• tin of beans	• tonne-mile
• tyre	• litre of beer

There are two objectives in carrying out an overhead analysis;

- to enable cost control;
- to ascertain product costs.

These objectives are carried out through three successive stages of analysis:

1   Allocation of overheads

2   Apportionment of overheads

3   Absorption of overheads

Allocation of overheads

Where an item of overhead expenditure **can be directly identified** with one particular cost centre the **overhead is allocated (charged)** to that cost centre. For example, the salary of the supervisor working in Department A will be charged to Department A.

Another example of overheads being allocated is where metered consumption of an overhead takes place. For example, the electrical power might be metered for each cost centre so the cost centre is charged for the electricity on the basis of the number of kW hours used by the cost centre.

> **Cost centre charge = Department kW hours × rate per kW hour**

Apportionment of overheads

Where an overhead **cannot be directly identified** with one particular cost centre the **overhead will be apportioned (divided)** between each cost centre on the basis of the use made of that overhead by each cost centre. For example, the rent of the factory will be divided between each cost centre in the factory according to the area occupied by each cost centre.

Apportionment of overheads is carried out in two stages, primary apportionment and secondary apportionment.

Primary apportionment

The rate per unit of apportionment is calculated using the formula:

$$\text{Calculation} = \frac{\textbf{Total factory overheads}}{\textbf{Total units for apportionment}} = \textbf{Rate per unit}$$

The overhead to be charged to each cost centre is calculated by multiplying the rate per unit by the number of those units in each cost centre.

$$\textbf{Overhead apportioned} = \textbf{Rate per unit} \times \textbf{Cost centre units}$$

Methods of overhead apportionment

Units of apportionment have to be based on measurable quantities related to each part of the enterprise. The most common methods of apportioning overheads are:

- floor area;
- number of employees;
- value of fixed assets;
- labour hours;
- machine hours;
- metered consumption;
- direct labour costs;
- maintenance hours.

Floor area. Overheads are apportioned to cost centres according to the amount of floor space occupied by each cost centre. Examples of where floor area may be used as a basis for apportionment of an overhead are:

- rent and rates;
- building expenses;
- property insurance;
- fire precautions;
- lighting (where metered electricity consumption does not take place);
- cleaning.

$$\text{Rate of overhead apportionment} = \frac{\text{Total factory overheads (£)}}{\text{Total factory area (m}^2)}$$

$$= \text{Rate £ per m}^2$$

Example 1

World Wide Enterprises operates a small factory in Wick consisting of three production departments and two service departments.

Factory rates are estimated to amount to £50,000 per annum. The departments occupy the following areas within the factory:

Department	Area occupied (m²)
Cutting	25,000
Machining	15,000
Finishing	45,000
Maintenance	10,000
Canteen	5,000
Total area	100,000

Factory rates

$$\text{Rate of apportionment} = \frac{£50,000}{100,000 \text{ m}^2} = 50\text{p per m}^2$$

The following formula is used to calculate the overhead to be charged to each cost centre:

Overhead charged = Area of cost centre × rate per m²

So, for the Cutting department with an area of 25,000 m², the overhead charged is:

Overhead charged = 25,000 m² × 50p per m² = £12,500

Overheads charged to each department will be:

Department	Area occupied (m²)	Rate per m²	Overhead to be apportioned – Rates
Cutting	25,000	50p	£12,500
Machining	15,000	50p	£7,500
Finishing	45,000	50p	£22,500
Maintenance	10,000	50p	£5,000
Canteen	5,000	50p	£2,500
Total area	100,000		£50,000

After apportioning the overhead always check your arithmetic – make sure the total of the overheads apportioned agrees with the estimated overhead!

Task 1

Calculate the overhead apportionment rate and the amount for rent which will be charged to each cost centre:

Factory	Total Area m²	Department			Overhead to be apportioned Rent
		Department A	Department B	Department C	
A plc	100,000	40,000	25,000	35,000	£10,000
B plc	60,000	20,000	30,000	10,000	£12,000
C plc	50,000	10,000	15,000	25,000	£50,000
D plc	200,000	60,000	40,000	100,000	£50,000
E plc	75,000	25,000	30,000	20,000	£150,000

Number of employees. Overheads are apportioned to cost centres according to the number of employees who work in that cost centre. Examples of where the number of employees may be used as a basis for apportionment of an overhead are:

- personnel and welfare costs such as first aid;
- canteen costs;
- sports and social activities;
- wages of gatemen;
- administration costs.

$$\text{Rate of overhead apportionment} = \frac{\text{Total factory overheads (£)}}{\text{Total number of employees}}$$

$$= \text{Rate per employee}$$

Example 2

World Wide Enterprises estimates that the administration costs for the factory for the year will be £75,000. The number of employees working in each cost centre is:

Department	Number of employees
Cutting	20
Machining	15
Finishing	20
Maintenance	5
Canteen	15
Total number of employees	75

continued ➤

Example 2 continued

> **Administration costs**
>
> Rate of apportionment = $\dfrac{£75,000}{75 \text{ employees}}$ = £1,000 per employee

The following formula is used to calculate the overhead to be charged to each cost centre:

Overhead charged = Number of employees × rate per employee

So, for the Cutting department with 20 employees, the overhead charged is:

Overhead charged = 20 employees × £1,000 per employee
= £20,000

Overheads to be charged to each department will be:

Department	Number of employees	Rate per employee	Overhead to be absorbed
Cutting	20	£1,000	£20,000
Machining	15	£1,000	£15,000
Finishing	20	£1,000	£20,000
Maintenance	5	£1,000	£5,000
Canteen	15	£1,000	£15,000
Total number of employees	**75**		**£75,000**

Task 2

Calculate the overhead apportionment rate and the amount for personnel costs which will be charged to each cost centre:

Factory	No of Employees	Department			Overhead to be apportioned Personnel costs
		Department A	Department B	Department C	
A plc	100	50	30	20	£50,000
B plc	70	10	30	30	£140,000
C plc	500	200	150	150	£80,000
D plc	300	150	25	125	£90,000
E plc	2,000	700	1,000	300	£200,000

MANAGEMENT ACCOUNTING

Capital value of fixed assets. Overheads are apportioned to cost centres according to the value of the fixed asset used in the cost centre. This method of apportionment is most suitable for the apportionment of depreciation and insurance of machinery.

$$\text{Rate of overhead apportionment} = \frac{\text{Total factory overheads}}{\text{Value of fixed assets}} \times 100$$

$$= \% \text{ depreciation}$$

Example 3

World Wide Enterprises estimates that £30,000 depreciation will be written off the cost of the machinery during the year. The value of machinery in each department is as follows:

Department	Cost of machinery
Cutting	£90,000
Machining	£110,000
Finishing	£25,000
Maintenance	£45,000
Canteen	£30,000
Total cost of machinery	£300,000

Percentage depreciation

$$\text{Rate of apportionment} = \frac{\$30,000}{\$300,000} \times 100$$

$$= 10\% \text{ of cost}$$

The following formulae is used to calculate the overhead to be charged to each cost centre

Overhead charged = Value of fixed asset × % depreciation

So, for the Cutting department with assets valued at £90,000, the overhead charged is:

Overhead charged = £90,000 × 10% = £9,000

continued ➤

Example 3 continued

Overheads charged to each department will be:

Department	Cost of machinery	Percentage Depreciation	Overhead to be absorbed
Cutting	£90,000	10%	£9,000
Machining	£110,000	10%	£11,000
Finishing	£25,000	10%	£2,500
Maintenance	£45,000	10%	£4,500
Canteen	£30,000	10%	£3,000
Total cost	£300,000	10%	£30,000

Task 3

Calculate the overhead apportionment rate and the amount of depreciation costs to be charged to each department:

Factory	Cost of machinery	Department			Overhead to be apportioned Depreciation
		Department A	Department B	Department C	
A plc	£50,000	£20,000	£15,000	£15,000	£10,000
B plc	£30,000	£20,000	£5,000	£5,000	£15,000
C plc	£50,000	£10,000	£15,000	£25,000	£10,000
D plc	£400,000	£200,000	£140,000	£60,000	£50,000
E plc	£150,000	£60,000	£40,000	£50,000	£15,000

Direct labour hours. Overheads are apportioned to cost centres according to the number of direct labour hours recorded for each cost centre. Examples of where the number of direct labour hours may be used as the basis for apportionment are:

- indirect materials;
- inspection;
- quality control;
- indirect labour;
- holiday pay;
- internal transport;
- supervision;
- management expenses.

MANAGEMENT ACCOUNTING

MANAGEMENT ACCOUNTING

$$\text{Rate of overhead apportionment} = \frac{\text{Total factory overheads}}{\text{Total direct labour hours}}$$

$$= \textbf{Rate per direct labour hours}$$

Example 4

World Wide Enterprises estimate that the following indirect labour costs of £100,000 will be incurred in the coming year.

Department	Direct labour hours
Cutting	50,000
Machining	30,000
Finishing	90,000
Maintenance	20,000
Canteen	10,000
Total direct labour hours	200,000

Direct labour costs

$$\text{Rate of apportionment} = \frac{£100,000}{200,000 \text{ hours}} = \textbf{50p per hour}$$

The following formula is used to calculate the overhead to be charged to each department:

Overhead charged = Direct labour hours × rate per direct labour hours

So, for the Cutting department with 50,000 direct labour hours, the overhead charged is:

Overhead charged = 50,000 × 50p = £25,000

Overheads charged to each department will be:

Department	Direct labour hours	Rate per labour hour	Overhead apportioned Direct labour costs
Cutting	50,000	50p	£25,000
Machining	30,000	50p	£15,000
Finishing	90,000	50p	£45,000
Maintenance	20,000	50p	£10,000
Canteen	10,000	50p	£5,000
Total direct labour hours	**200,000**		**£100,000**

Task 4

Calculate the overhead apportionment rate and the amount of indirect labour costs to be charged to each department:

Factory	Total Direct labour hours	Department			Overhead to be apportioned Indirect labour costs
		Department A	Department B	Department C	
A plc	200,000	80,000	50,000	70,000	£20,000
B plc	120,000	40,000	60,000	20,000	£30,000
C plc	100,000	20,000	30,000	50,000	£25,000
D plc	400,000	120,000	80,000	200,000	£100,000
E plc	150,000	50,000	60,000	40,000	£15,000

Machine hours. Overheads are apportioned to cost centres according to the number of direct machine hours recorded for each cost centre. Examples of where the number of direct machine hours may be used as the basis for apportionment are:

- power;
- repairs.

$$\text{Rate of overhead apportionment} = \frac{\text{Total factory overheads}}{\text{Total machine hours}}$$

$$= \text{Rate per machine hour}$$

Example 5

World Wide Enterprises estimate that the following repair costs of £750,000 will be incurred in the coming year.

Department	Machine hours
Cutting	25,000
Machining	100,000
Finishing	10,000
Maintenance	14,000
Canteen	1,000
Total machine hours	150,000

continued ➤

Example 5 continued

> **Repairs**
>
> $$\text{Rate of apportionment} = \frac{\text{£}750,000}{150,000 \text{ hours}} = \text{£}5\text{p per machine hour}$$

The following formula is used to calculate the overheads to be charged to each cost centre:

Overhead charged = Number of machine hours × rate per machine hour

So, for the Cutting department with 25,000 hours of repairs, the overhead charged is:

Overhead charged = 25,000 hours × £5 per hour = £125,000

Department	Machine hours	Rate per Machine Hour	Overheads apportioned Repairs
Cutting	25,000	£5	£125,000
Machining	100,000	£5	£500,000
Finishing	10,000	£5	£50,000
Maintenance	14,000	£5	£70,000
Canteen	1,000	£5	£5,000
Total machine hours	**150,000**		**£750,000**

▶▶▶ Task 5

Calculate the overhead apportionment rate and the amount of machine repair costs to be charged to each department:

Factory	Total Machine hours	Department			Overhead to be apportioned Machine repairs
		Department A	Department B	Department C	
A plc	200,000	80,000	50,000	70,000	£40,000
B plc	120,000	40,000	60,000	20,000	£60,000
C plc	100,000	20,000	30,000	50,000	£50,000
D plc	400,000	120,000	80,000	200,000	£200,000
E plc	150,000	50,000	60,000	40,000	£30,000

Metered Consumption. Where it is possible to meter the consumption of a particular overhead this can be charged on that basis to the cost centre. Examples of where overheads are charged to each cost centre on the basis of metered consumption are:

- electricity;
- gas;
- water;

- steam;
- compressed air.

$$\text{Rate of overhead apportionment} = \frac{\text{Total factory overheads}}{\text{metered consumption}}$$

$$= \text{Rate per kW hour}$$

Example 6

World Wide Enterprises estimates that the power used in the factory during the year will be £100,000. The number of kW hours used in each cost centre is:

Department	kW hours
Cutting	5,000
Machining	5,000
Finishing	5,000
Maintenance	1,000
Canteen	4,000
Total	20,000

Power

$$\text{Rate of apportionment} = \frac{£100,000}{20,000 \text{ kW hrs}} = \text{£5p per kW hour}$$

The following formula is used to calculate the overhead charged to each cost centre:

Overhead charged = Department kW hours × Rate per kW hour

So, for the Cutting department with 5,000 kW hours, the overhead charged is:

Overhead charged = 5,000 kW hours × £5 per kW hour = £25,000

Department	kW hours	Rate per kW hour	Overhead apportioned Power
Cutting	5,000	£5	£25,000
Machining	5,000	£5	£25,000
Finishing	5,000	£5	£25,000
Maintenance	1,000	£5	£5,000
Canteen	4,000	£5	£20,000
Total	20,000		**£100,000**

Task 6

Calculate the overhead apportionment rate and the amount of power to be charged to each department:

| Factory | kW hours | Department | | | Overhead apportioned |
		Department A	Department B	Department C	
A plc	400,000	160,000	100,000	140,000	£100,000
B plc	300,000	60,000	90,000	150,000	£45,000
C plc	1,000,000	200,000	300,000	500,000	£100,000
D plc	400,000	120,000	80,000	200,000	£200,000
E plc	200,000	50,000	60,000	90,000	£50,000

Make a habit of showing all your workings for each exercise. This will benefit you in your final examination where a wrong figure with no working will gain no marks. A wrong figure using the correct method of calculation will only lose an arithmetic penalty.

Preparation of overhead analysis statements

Having studied the methods of allocation and apportionment of overheads you are now ready to undertake the preparation of an overhead analysis statement, prior to the secondary apportionment.

World Wide Enterprises uses the following layout when carrying out their analysis of overheads for their Dundee factory. This analysis may be carried out manually or using a spreadsheet where a template would be set up, the data added and the allocation and apportionment automatically calculated.

An example of an overhead analysis statement is shown here:

Overhead Analysis Statement – Dundee factory Year 2							
Overhead item	Apportionment basis	Total	Production Cost Centres			Service Cost Centres	
			Cutting	Assembly	Finishing	Canteen	Maintenance
		£	£	£	£	£	£
Allocation:							
Indirect Material	Directly allocated	30,250	5,000	10,000	3,000	3,750	£8,500
Apportionment							
Rent	Floor Area	50,000	20,000	7,500	12,500	7,500	£2,500

continued

Example 7 Allocation and Apportionment

World Wide Enterprises provide you with the following information and ask you to allocate and apportion the overheads to the production and service cost centres for their Dundee factory for Year 2.

The factory consists of 3 production and 2 service departments. The following information about each department is provided:

	Cutting	Assembly	Finishing	Canteen	Maintenance	Total
Floor area (m²)	20,000	7,500	12,500	7,500	2,500	50,000
Employees	50	30	10	5	5	100
Machinery (cost)	£75,000	£10,000	£75,000	£5,000	£35,000	£200,000
Labour hours	150,000	200,000	100,000	20,000	130,000	600,000
kW hours	150,000	190,000	50,000	4,000	70,000	500,000

Estimated overheads for the year are allocated as follows:

Overhead item	Total	Production Cost Centres			Service Cost Centres	
		Cutting	Assembly	Finishing	Stores	Maintenance
Indirect Material	£30,250	£5,000	£10,000	£3,000	£3,750	£8,500

Overheads to be apportioned are:

Overhead	Estimate	Basis of apportionment
Rent	£50,000	Floor area
Supervision	£200,000	Employees
Depreciation	£40,000	Value of assets
Heat and light	£100,000	Floor area
Power	£100,000	kW hours
Total	£490,000	

STEP 1 – Enter allocated overheads onto the overhead analysis sheet

On the overhead analysis sheet enter any overheads which have to be directly allocated to a particular cost centre. In this case the indirect material costs have already been divided between the cost centres.

continued ➤

Example 7 Allocation and Apportionment continued

STEP 2 – Calculate overheads to be apportioned to the cost centres using an appropriate basis

Apportion the overheads between the various cost centres on a suitable basis. The basis of apportionment may not be given, so apportion according to the use made of the overhead by each cost centre.

Rent	Cost Centre	Apportionment	Amount
Rate/m^2	Cutting	$20,000 \times £1 =$	£20,000
	Assembly	$7,500 \times £1 =$	£7,500
$= \dfrac{£50,000}{50,000 \text{ m}^2}$	Finishing	$12,500 \times £1 =$	£12,500
	Stores	$7,500 \times £1 =$	£7,500
$= £1/\text{m}^2$	Maintenance	$2,500 \times £1 =$	£2,500
	Totals	**50,000 m^2**	**£50,000**

Supervision	Cost Centre	Apportionment	Amount
Rate per employee	Cutting	$50 \times £2,000 =$	£100,000
	Assembly	$30 \times £2,000 =$	£60,000
$= \dfrac{£200,000}{100 \text{ employees}}$	Finishing	$10 \times £2,000 =$	£20,000
	Stores	$5 \times £2,000 =$	£10,000
$= £2,000$ per employee	Maintenance	$5 \times £2,000 =$	£10,000
	Totals	**100 employees**	**£200,000**

Depreciation	Cost Centre	Apportionment	Amount
Value of machinery	Cutting	$£75,000 \times 20\% =$	£15,000
	Assembly	$£10,000 \times 20\% =$	£2,000
$= \dfrac{£40,000}{£200,000} \times 100$	Finishing	$£75,000 \times 20\% =$	£15,000
	Stores	$£5,000 \times 20\% =$	£1,000
$= 20\%$	Maintenance	$£35,000 \times 20\% =$	£7,000
	Totals	**£200,000**	**£40,000**

Heat and Light	Cost Centre	Apportionment	Amount
Rate per m^2	Cutting	$20,000 \times £2 =$	£40,000
	Assembly	$7,500 \times £2 =$	£15,000
$= \dfrac{£100,000}{50,000 \text{ m}^2}$	Finishing	$12,500 \times £2 =$	£25,000
	Stores	$7,500 \times £2 =$	£15,000
$= £2/\text{m}^2$	Maintenance	$2,500 \times £2 =$	£5,000
	Totals	**50,000 m^2**	**£100,000**

continued ➤

Example 7 Allocation and Apportionment continued

Power	Cost Centre	Apportionment	Amount
kW hours	Cutting	150,000 × 20p =	£30,000
= £100,000	Assembly	190,000 × 20p =	£38,000
500,000 kW hr	Finishing	50,000 × 20p =	£10,000
	Stores	40,000 × 20p =	£8,000
= 20p/kW hr	Maintenance	70,000 × 20p =	£14,000
	Totals	**500,000 kW hrs**	**£100,000**

STEP 3 – Enter apportioned overheads into the Overhead Analysis statement and calculate total cost centre departmental overheads

Overhead analysis statement for the Dundee factory – Year 2

Overhead item	Apportionment basis	Total £	Production Cost Centres			Service Cost Centres	
			Cutting £	Assembly £	Finishing £	Stores £	Maintenance £
Allocation:							
Indirect Material	Directly allocated	30,250	5,000	10,000	3,000	3,750	8,500
Apportionment							
Rent	Floor Area	50,000	20,000	7,500	12,500	7,500	2,500
Supervision	Employees	200,000	100,000	60,000	20,000	10,000	10,000
Depreciation of machinery	Value of machinery	40,000	15,000	2.000	15,000	1,000	7,000
Heat and Light	Floor area	100,000	40,000	15,000	25,000	15,000	5,000
Power	kW hours	100,000	30,000	38,000	10,000	8,000	14,000
Total Cost Centre Overheads		520,250	210,000	132,500	85,500	45,250	47,000

 Now do Worksheet 18.1

Secondary apportionment of service cost centre overheads

Secondary apportionment is the division of service cost centre overheads between production and other service cost centres according to the use made of that service cost centre.

When the allocation of direct departmental overheads has been followed by the primary apportionment of common overhead costs to all production and service cost centres the service cost centre overheads must be reapportioned to the user departments (including other service costs centres) on the basis of the use made of that service.

Service cost centres also derive benefit from other service cost centres. Therefore, each service department cost must be apportioned amongst its users. However, once a service department's cost has been reapportioned that cost centre is **eliminated from any subsequent reapportionment**.

The first service department cost to be reapportioned should be that of the department serving the greatest number of other cost centres.

The basis used for reapportioning service cost centre overheads, in many cases, will be the same as those used to apportion the overhead costs

For example, personnel overheads could be divided between production and other service departments using the number of employees in each department, the basis for dividing up the overheads for the maintenance service centre costs may be on the number of machine hours.

Example 8

The following total overheads have been allocated and apportioned to each cost centre of the Dundee branch of World Wide Enterprises.

Overhead analysis statement – Dundee factory Year 2							
			Production Cost Centres			**Service Cost Centres**	
Overhead item	Apportionment basis	Total £	Cutting £	Assembly £	Finishing £	Canteen £	Maintenance £
Cost Centre Overheads		520,250	210,000	132,500	85,500	45,250	47,000

The following additional information is supplied:

	Cutting	Assembly	Finishing	Canteen	Maintenance	TOTAL
Labour hours	150,000	200,000	100,000	20,000	130,000	600,000
Number of employees	50	30	10	5	5	100

Service cost centre overheads are to be reapportioned to production and service cost centres in the following order:

- Maintenance department first on the basis of labour hours
- Canteen on the basis of the number of employees.

*The main problem experienced by students when attempting this is that they fail to realise that the cost centre overhead will not be shared by all cost centres and that the total machine hours or number of employees will **not** be used to calculate the rate of apportionment. Only the machine hours or number of employees for the **cost centres** sharing the overheads will be used.*

continued ➤

Example 8 continued

STEP 4 – Reapportion service cost centre overheads

The Maintenance department's overheads are to be shared between Cutting, Assembly, Finishing, and Canteen.

Department	Labour hours
Cutting	150,000
Assembly	200,000
Finishing	100,000
Canteen	20,000
Total labour hours	**470,000**

> **Rate of overhead reapportionment = Maintenance dept's overhead costs**
> **────────────────────────────────**
> **Labour hours for Cutting,**
> **Assembly, Finishing and Canteen**
>
> **= Rate per labour hour**

The basis for apportionment is 470,000 labour hours.

> **Maintenance department's overheads:**
>
> **Rate of reapportionment = £47,000**
> **──────────────**
> **470,000 labour hours**
>
> **= 10p per labour hour**

The overhead to be reapportioned to each cost centre will be:

Reapportioned overhead = Number of department labour hours × rate per labour hour

So, with 150,000 labour hours, the Cutting department's share of the Maintenance department's overhead costs will be:

Reapportioned overhead = 150,000 hours × 10p = £15,000

Department	Labour hours	Rate per labour hour	Overhead reapportioned
Cutting	150,000	10p	£15,000
Assembly	200,000	10p	£20,000
Finishing	100,000	10p	£10,000
Canteen	20,000	10p	£2,000
Total labour hours	**470,000**		**£47,000**

Always check that the total of the overheads reapportioned equals the total overhead allocated and apportioned to the service cost centre.

continued ➤

Example 8 continued

These figures are then entered in the overhead analysis statement and a new total overhead will be calculated for the Canteen.

The overhead amount reapportioned for the Maintenance department is shown in brackets to indicate that the overhead has been reapportioned between the other cost centres. The line underneath the figure shows that **no other costs** should be allocated or apportioned to this cost centre.

Overhead analysis statement – Dundee factory Year 2							
			Production Cost Centres			Service Cost Centres	
Overhead item	Apportionment basis	Total £	Cutting £	Assembly £	Finishing £	Canteen £	Maintenance £
Cost Centre Overheads		520,250	210,000	132,500	85,500	45,250	47,000
Reapportion- ment of service department costs							
Maintenance Department	Labour Hours		15,000	20,000	10,000	<u>2,000</u>	<u>47,000</u>
						47,250	

The reapportionment of the Canteen department's overheads will be between Cutting, Assembly and Finishing only.

Department	Number of employees
Cutting	50
Assembly	30
Finishing	10
Total	**90**

The basis for re-apportionment to the production cost centres will be 90 employees:

Rate of overhead reapportionment = $\dfrac{\text{Canteen overhead costs}}{\substack{\text{No of employees in Cutting,} \\ \text{Assembly and Finishing}}}$

= Rate per employee

Canteen overheads

Rate of apportionment = $\dfrac{£47,250}{90 \text{ employees}}$

= £525 per employee

continued ➤

continued ➤

Example 8 continued

The overhead to be reapportioned to each cost centre will be:

Reapportioned overhead = Number of department employees × rate per employee

So, with 50 employees, Cutting department's share of Canteen overhead costs will be:

Reapportioned overhead = 50 employees × £525 = £26,250

Overheads reapportioned to production cost centres are:

Department	Number of employees	Rate per employee	Overheads reapportioned
Cutting	50	£525	£26,250
Assembly	30	£525	£15,750
Finishing	10	£525	£5,250
Total	90		£47,250

Overhead analysis statement – Dundee factory Year 2							
Overhead item	Apportionment basis	Total £	**Production Cost Centres**			**Service Cost Centres**	
			Cutting £	Assembly £	Finishing £	Canteen £	Maintenance £
Cost Centre Overheads		520,250	210,000	132,500	85,500	45,250	47,000
Reapportion-ment of service department costs							
Maintenance Department	Labour Hours		15,000	20,000	10,000	2,000	47,000
						47,250	
Canteen	No of employees		26,250	15,750	5,250		
Total production cost centre overheads			251,250	168,250	100,750		

Once the overhead have been allocated to the production cost centres an Overhead Absorption Rate can be calculated. This is Step 5.

Now do Worksheet 18.2

Absorption of overheads

Once all overheads have been charged to production departments and a total overhead cost has been ascertained, the **overhead absorption rate** can be calculated.

Overhead absorption rates are established for each production cost centre within a factory to enable an equitable charge for overhead to be made against each product. Application of the overhead absorption rate allows an amount to be added to the cost of the product to allow for the recovery of the overheads

Selecting the best absorption rate

There are many different items of overhead expenditure which makes up the aggregate overhead for a given cost centre. This fact precludes any possibility of using a basis of absorption which is the same as the incidence of cost. For practical purposes a single rate to embrace all items of overhead cost rather than several rates is considered to be more suitable.

Fortunately there is one common factor for all overhead expenditure, which is **time**. Rent, rates, and insurance are paid for an agreed period of time, depreciation depends on the life of the asset, power consumption will vary with production time, and wages and salaries are paid on a time basis.

Therefore, the best method of calculating an overhead absorption rate will be on a time-related basis, if the results are to be equitable, between one product and another.

Production department overhead absorption rates

The cost accountant may decide that an equitable charge for overhead absorption can be made using a departmental overhead absorption rate.

To calculate the overhead absorption rate, the budgeted overheads for the Production department are taken from the overhead analysis sheet, and one of 6 methods of calculating the absorption rate will be used for that department.

For all overhead absorption rates the following formula can be applied:

$$\text{Rate per unit} = \frac{\text{Production department overheads}}{\text{Production department basis of absorbtion}}$$

For example, if the Production department's overhead costs are £50,000 and the overhead absorption rate is to be based on the number of machine hours (100,000 machine hours) worked in the department the overhead absorption rate would be calculated as follows:

$$\text{Production department} \\ \text{Overhead absorption rate} = \frac{£50,000}{100,000 \text{ machine hours}}$$

$$= 50\text{p per machine hour}$$

This rate can than be applied to production costs. If a firm asked the factory to carry out a machining job for them which took 3 hours, in addition to material, labour and variable overheads, the cost would be increased by the charge for overheads to be absorbed. In this case, the overhead absorbed would be:

Overhead absorbed = 3 hours × £0.50 = £1.50.

Methods of calculating overhead absorption rates

There are 6 commonly used methods of calculation an overhead absorption rate:

1 Machine hours

2 Units produced

3 Direct labour hours

4 Percentage of direct wages

5 Percentage of prime cost

6 Percentage of direct materials

Rate per machine hour. The incidence of most indirect costs is time-based and some, such as power, are only incurred while the machines are running. In many instances therefore the only satisfactory basis for the absorption of overhead is a machine hour, particularly where the cost centre is machine intensive.

Rate of overhead absorption = $\dfrac{\textbf{Production department overheads}}{\textbf{Total department machine hours}}$

= **Rate per machine hour**

Example 9

Calculate the overhead absorption rate for Production department from the following information:

- Production department overhead: £50,000
- Production departmental machine hours: 100,000

Machine hours

Rate of overhead absorption = $\dfrac{£50,000}{100,000 \text{ machine hours}}$

= **50p per machine hour**

Rate per unit of production. This is an easily applied basis of absorption but can only be adopted in the very rare example of single product output.

Rate per unit of production

Rate of overhead absorption = $\dfrac{\text{Production department overheads}}{\text{Total Production department unit output}}$

= Rate per unit

Example 10

Calculate the overhead absorption rate for Department C from the following information:

- Department C overhead: £75,000
- Units produced by department C: 37,500

Rate per unit of production

Rate of overhead absorption = $\dfrac{£75,000}{37,500 \text{ units}}$

= £2 per unit

Rate per direct labour hour. As a time based method of absorption, this basis is generally preferred to the percentage of direct wages method. It has the possible disadvantage of requiring the collection of additional data – the hours worked – but in most factories the direct labour hours are recorded for the calculation of wages.

Rate per direct labour hour

Rate of overhead absorption = $\dfrac{\text{Departmental overheads}}{\text{Total departmental direct labour hours}}$

= Rate per direct labour hours

Example 11

Calculate the overhead absorption rate for Department D from the following information:

- Department D overhead: £75,000,
- Departmental direct labour hours for D: 7,500 hours.

Rate per direct labour hour

Rate of overhead absorption = $\dfrac{£75,000}{75,000 \text{ direct labour hours}}$

= £10 per direct labour hour

Percentage of direct wages. Direct wages are obviously time-related regardless of the method of remuneration used. Where time wages are paid, earnings will vary directly with hours worked, so that direct wages are a useful method of overhead absorption.

> **Percentage of direct wages**
>
> Rate of overhead absorption $= \dfrac{\text{Departmental overheads} \times 100}{\text{Total departmental direct wages}}$
>
> $= \%$ Direct wages

Example 12

Calculate the overhead absorption rate for Department B from the following information:

- Department B overhead: £75,000,
- Direct wages for Department B: £150,000

> **Percentage of direct wages**
>
> Rate of overhead absorption $= \dfrac{\pounds 75,000 \times 100\%}{\pounds 150,000}$
>
> $= 50\%$ of direct wage cost

Percentage of prime cost. This is not a particularly good method of absorbing overheads as it is not purely time based.

> **Percentage of prime costs**
>
> Rate of overhead absorption $= \dfrac{\text{Departmental overhead} \times 100}{\text{Total prime cost}}$
>
> $= \%$ of prime cost

Example 13

Calculate the overhead absorption rate for Department E from the following information:

- Department E overhead: £50,000
- Prime cost: £100,000

Percentage of prime costs

Rate of overhead absorption = $\dfrac{£50,000 \times 100}{£100,000}$

= 50% of prime cost

Percentage of direct materials costs. This is not a particularly good method of absorbing overheads as it is not time based however it is useful where department activity is related to material usage.

Percentage of direct material costs

Rate of overhead absorption = $\dfrac{\text{Departmental overhead}}{\text{Total direct material cost}} \times 100$

= % of direct material cost

Example 14

Calculate the overhead absorption rate for Department F from the following information:

- Department F overhead: £250,000
- Direct material cost: £500,000

Percentage of direct material costs

Rate of overhead absorption = $\dfrac{£250,000 \times 100}{£500,000}$

= 50% of direct material cost

Example 15

STEP 5 – Calculation of overhead absorption rates

Once World Wide Enterprises have completed their overhead analysis, they will use the production department overheads to calculate the overhead absorption rates to be applied to production for the next year.

The following production overheads have been calculated for the Dundee Factory for Year 2:

World Wide Enterprises – Dundee factory Year 2			
	Cutting	Assembly	Finishing
	£	£	£
Production department overheads	251,250	168,250	100,750

The following additional information is available:

Production department information	Cutting	Assembly	Finishing
Machine hours	150,000	190,000	50,000
Labour hours	150,000	200,000	100,000
Units produced			403,000

The cost accountant decides that the overheads will be absorbed into production using the following bases:

Cutting: machine hours
Assembly: labour hours
Finishing: units produced

*When calculating the overhead absorption rate for each production department figures will normally be given for all three production departments. You must calculate only **one** overhead absorption rate for each department using the base given.*

Overhead absorption rates for World Wide Enterprises:

Cutting: machine hours	Assembly: labour hours	Finishing: units
Production Department Overhead Basis of apportionment £251,250 150,000 machine hours = £1.68 per machine hour	Production Department Overhead Basis of apportionment £168,250 200,000 labour hours = £0.84 per direct labour hour	Production Department Overhead Basis of apportionment £100,750 403,000 units £0.25 per unit

In examination questions answers are usually rounded to 2 decimal places.

 Now do Worksheets 18.3 and 18.4

Over- and underabsorption of overheads

Recovery of overheads is based on an estimate – a pre-set rate based on estimated production and overhead levels, such as a rate per direct machine hour etc. This results in the amount of overhead recovered being different from the actual overheads incurred for the period.

The overhead absorbed may differ from the actual overhead incurred because of the difference in the estimated and actual output resulting in, for example, fewer machine hours being worked.

Example 16

It is estimated that during year 100,000 units of product X will be produced requiring 50,000 direct machine hours. Budgeted overheads for the year are estimated to be £100,000.

The overhead absorption rate is based on direct machine hours worked:

$$\text{Rate per direct machine hour} = \frac{\textbf{Estimated overheads}}{\textbf{Direct machine hours}}$$

$$= \frac{\text{£100,000}}{\text{50,000 machine hours}}$$

$$= \text{£2 per machine hour}$$

Actual production resulted in 49,500 machine hours being worked

Actual overhead incurred amounted to £98,000.

Overhead absorbed = 49,500 × £2 = £99,000
Actual overhead incurred   = £98,000
Difference   = £1,000 overabsorbed

Underabsorption occurs when the **overheads absorbed** are **less** than **actual overheads** incurred.

Overabsorption occurs when the **overheads absorbed** are **more** than the **actual overheads** incurred.

Under- or overabsorbed overheads will affect the profit calculation.

Any **underabsorbed** overheads should be **added** to the total costs before calculating the profit.

Any **overabsorbed** overheads should be **deducted** from the total costs before calculating the profit.

Factory-wide overhead absorption rates

On occasions a cost accountant may decide that it is more equitable to have a Factory-wide overhead absorption rate which is applied to all departments rather than departmental overhead absorption rates. This rate makes no allowances for the fact that different departments use up overheads at different rates.

Example 17

If total factory overheads are £30,000 and the total direct labour hours for the factory are 30,000 the factory wide overhead rate would be calculated as follows:

Rate of overhead absorption = $\dfrac{\text{Total factory overhead}}{\text{Total direct labour hours}}$

$= \dfrac{£30,000}{30,000 \text{ hours}} = £1$ per direct labour hour

If a firm then asked the factory to carry out a particular job for them which took 16 direct labour hours, in addition to material, labour and variable overheads, the cost would be increased by the charge for overheads to be absorbed 16 hours × £1 = £16.

Now do Worksheet 18.5

CHAPTER 19

Job costing

Intermediate 2 Level Outcomes: ⓘ▶

This chapter includes material from Int 2 level Management Accounting Outcome 2

- ☆ **Describe the uses of job costing.**
- ☆ **Complete a range of cost statements to calculate the cost from information supplied.**
- ☆ **The cost for a job is accurately calculated.**
- ☆ **The profit for a job is calculated using mark-up.**

Higher Level Outcomes: ⓘ▶

This chapter includes material from Higher level Management Accounting Outcome 2

- ☆ **Describe the uses of job costing.**
- ☆ **Complete a job cost statement including the application of overhead absorption rates consistent with information supplied.**
- ☆ **The total or unit cost for a job is accurately calculated.**
- ☆ **The profit for a job is accurately calculated using mark-up or margin.**

The aims of job costing

Job or **specific order costing** is a method of costing used where work consists of a number of separate jobs, each of which is completed to a customer's specific requirement.

The most common use of job costing is by small factories in the engineering industry which produce one-off components or tools to order.

The principle of job costing is straightforward. Direct costs are collected and charged to each job, which is then charged to the customer plus a percentage for profit. The only problems are in estimating and cost collection, particularly in respect of overheads.

Steps in job costing

The customer asks the factory to tender an estimate for a piece of work. The items of cost are generally material, labour, factory overhead and selling and administration overheads.

- **Material** can be costed accurately.

- **Labour** costs must be approximated as there are no standard times set for unique jobs.

- **Factory overheads** will be estimated using one of the six pre-determined overhead absorption rates, such as machine hours, labour hours etc. **Selling and distribution overheads** will also have to be estimated.

The main problem with overheads is to ensure that all overhead expenses incurred in a year will be absorbed by jobs completed.

To keep a record of all costs incurred in completing a specific job for a customer a **job cost card** will be used. Workers will complete time sheets or job tickets for each job they are working on. Materials records from stores will show the quantity and value of the materials used for the job

A job cost card is shown in Figure 19.1. More complex cards will be used in industry, particularly with the increasing use of computers making it easier to record information.

JOB COST CARD			Job No	
Customer			Customer Order No	
Job Description			Start date	
			Delivery date	
MATERIALS	Quantity	Price per unit	Cost	Total Cost
LABOUR	Hours	Rate Per hour	Cost	
OTHER VARIABLE COSTS				
	Quantity	Price per unit	Cost	
Prime Cost				
FACTORY OVERHEADS	Overhead Absorption Rate	Cost		
FACTORY COST				
Selling and Distribution				
Administration				
Total Costs				
Profit				
Invoice Price				

Figure 19.1 Job cost card

For examination purposes a simplified job cost statement will be used.

Example 1

From the following information calculate the price to be charged to J and B Plc, who have placed an order for a special machine tool.

Job No 674

Material costs:

- Material X: £150
- Material Y: £305

Direct labour

- Machine shop: 80 hours at £10.00 per hour
- Finishing department: 20 hours at £8.00 per hour

Hire of special machine: £300.

Factory overheads are to be absorbed at £1.50 per machine hour for the machine shop and £0.75 per direct labour hour in the finishing shop. Selling and distribution overheads are estimated to be 10% of factory cost.

Calculate the invoice price of the job for the customer if profit is calculated at a mark-up of 50% of the total cost of the job.

STEP 1 – Calculate the material cost for the job and insert into the job cost statement

Direct material

Material X	£150.00
Material Y	£305.00
	£455.00

JOB COST STATEMENT		Job No 674
	COST £	Total £
DIRECT MATERIAL		
Material X	150.00	
Material Y	305.00	455.00

STEP 2 – Calculate the labour cost

Direct labour

Machine shop:	80 hours @ £10.00	£800.00
Finishing shop:	20 hours @ £8.00	£160.00
		£960.00

continued ➤

Example 1 continued

JOB COST STATEMENT	Job No 674	
	COST £	Total £
DIRECT MATERIAL		
Material X	150.00	
Material Y	<u>305.00</u>	455.00
DIRECT LABOUR		
Machine Shop – 80 hours @ £10.00	**800.00**	
Finishing Shop – 20 hours @ £8.00	<u>**160.00**</u>	**960.00**

STEP 3 – Add any special cost for the job

Hire of special machine: £300.00

JOB COST STATEMENT	Job No 674	
	COST £	Total £
DIRECT MATERIAL		
Material X	150.00	
Material Y	<u>305.00</u>	455.00
DIRECT LABOUR		
Machine Shop – 80 hours @ £10.00	800.00	
Finishing Shop – 20 hours @ £8.00	<u>160.00</u>	960.00
OTHER DIRECT COSTS		
Hire of special machine		<u>**300.00**</u>

STEP 4 – Calculate the prime cost of the job by adding all the direct costs together

Material	£455.00
Labour	£960.00
Special costs	<u>£300.00</u>

Prime cost   £1,715.00

JOB COST STATEMENT	Job No 674	
	COST £	Total £
DIRECT MATERIAL		
Material X	150.00	
Material Y	<u>305.00</u>	455.00

continued ➤

MANAGEMENT ACCOUNTING

Example 1 continued

JOB COST STATEMENT		Job No 674
	COST £	Total £
DIRECT LABOUR		
Machine Shop – 80 hours @ £10	800.00	
Finishing Shop – 20 hours @ £8.00	160.00	960.00
OTHER DIRECT COSTS		
Hire of special machine		300.00
Prime Cost		**1,715.00**

STEP 5 – Calculate the overheads to be absorbed by the job

Overheads will be added to the job for each production department the job passes through.

In the machine shop overheads are absorbed on the basis of machine hours:

80 machine hours × £1.50 per hour = £120.00

In the finishing shop overheads are absorbed on the basis of labour hours:

20 labour hours × £0.75 = £15.00

JOB COST STATEMENT		Job No 674
	COST £	Total £
DIRECT MATERIAL		
Material X	150.00	
Material Y	305.00	455.00
DIRECT LABOUR		
Machine Shop – 80 hours @ £10.00	800.00	
Finishing Shop – 20 hours @ £8.00	160.00	960.00
OTHER DIRECT COSTS		
Hire of special machine		300.00
Prime Cost		1,715.00
FACTORY OVERHEADS		
Machine Shop 80 machine hours @ £1.50	**120.00**	
Finishing Shop 20 labour hours @ £0.75	**15.00**	**135.00**

continued ➤

Example 1 continued

STEP 6 – Calculate the factory cost of Job No 674

Prime cost	£1,715.00
Factory overheads	£135.00
Total factory cost	**£1,850.00**

JOB COST STATEMENT	Job No 674	
	COST £	Total £
DIRECT MATERIAL		
Material X	150.00	
Material Y	305.00	455.00
DIRECT LABOUR		
Machine Shop – 80 hours @ £10.00	800.00	
Finishing Shop – 20 hours @ £8.00	160.00	960.00
OTHER DIRECT COSTS		
Hire of special machine		300.00
Prime Cost		1,715.00
FACTORY OVERHEADS		
Machine Shop 80 machine hours @ £1.50	120.00	
Finishing Shop 20 labour hours @ £0.75	15.00	135.00
TOTAL FACTORY COST		**1,850.00**

STEP 7 – Add other administration, selling and distribution overheads to the job

This figure is usually based on a percentage of the factory cost or one of the elements of cost. The amount to be added for Job 674 is to be 10% of factory cost.

Selling and distribution overhead = 10% of £1,850 = £185

JOB COST STATEMENT	Job No 674	
	COST £	Total £
DIRECT MATERIAL		
Material X	150.00	
Material Y	305.00	455.00
DIRECT LABOUR		
Machine Shop – 80 hours @ £10.00	800.00	
Finishing Shop – 20 hours @ £8.00	160.00	960.00
OTHER DIRECT COSTS		
Hire of special machine		300.00
Prime Cost		1,715.00

continued ➤

Example 1 continued

JOB COST STATEMENT		Job No 674
	COST £	Total £
FACTORY OVERHEADS		
Machine Shop 80 machine hours @ £1.50	120.00	
Finishing Shop 20 labour hours @ £0.75	15.00	135.00
DIRECT MATERIAL		
Material X	150.00	
Material Y	305.00	455.00
DIRECT LABOUR		
Machine Shop – 80 hours @ £10.00	800.00	
Finishing Shop – 20 hours @ £8.00	160.00	960.00
OTHER DIRECT COSTS		
Hire of special machine		300.00
Prime Cost		1,715.00
FACTORY OVERHEADS		
Machine Shop 80 machine hours @ £1.50	120.00	
Finishing Shop 20 labour hours @ £0.75	15.00	135.00
TOTAL FACTORY COST		1,850.00
Selling and Distribution		185.00

STEP 8 – Calculate the total cost of Job 674

Factory cost	£1,850.00
Selling and distribution	£185.00
Total Cost	**£2,035.00**

JOB COST STATEMENT		Job No 674
	COST £	Total £
DIRECT MATERIAL		
Material X	150.00	
Material Y	305.00	455.00
DIRECT LABOUR		
Machine Shop – 80 hours @ £10.00	800.00	
Finishing Shop – 20 hours @ £8.00	160.00	960.00
OTHER DIRECT COSTS		
Hire of special machine		300.00
Prime Cost		1,715.00

continued ➤

Example 1 continued

JOB COST STATEMENT		Job No 674
	COST £	Total £
FACTORY OVERHEADS		
Machine Shop 80 machine hours @ £1.50	120.00	
DIRECT MATERIAL		
Finishing Shop 20 labour hours @ £0.75	15.00	135.00
TOTAL FACTORY COST		1,850.00
Selling and Distribution		185.00
Total Job Cost		2,035.00

STEP 9 – Calculate the profit required for this job

For this particular job profit is calculated as a percentage of cost:

Profit = 50% of £2,035
= **£1,017.50**

STEP 10 – Calculate the invoice price for the customer and enter onto the job sheet

Total job cost	£2,035.00
Profit	£1,017.50
Invoice price	**£3,052.50**

JOB COST STATEMENT		Job No 674
	COST £	Total £
DIRECT MATERIAL		
Material X	150.00	
Material Y	305.00	455.00
DIRECT LABOUR		
Machine Shop – 80 hours @ £10.00	800.00	
Finishing Shop – 20 hours @ £8.00	160.00	960.00
OTHER DIRECT COSTS		
Hire of special machine		300.00
Prime Cost		1,715.00
FACTORY OVERHEADS		
Machine Shop 80 machine hours @ £1.50	120.00	
Finishing Shop 20 labour hours @ £0.75	15.00	135.00

continued ➢

Example 1 continued

TOTAL FACTORY COST		1,850.00
Selling and Distribution		<u>185.00</u>
Total Job Cost		2,035.00
Profit required		<u>**1,017.50**</u>
Invoice Price		**3,052.50**

Profit mark-up or margin?

Profit can be expressed in 2 ways, in terms of the mark-up, or in terms of the profit margin.

The **mark-up** is the amount of profit added to the cost of a job, and is expressed as a percentage:

> **Profit = Mark-up % × Cost of job**

For Job 674 the mark–up was 50% of the cost, so the profit is:

> **Profit** = 50% of £2,035 = **£1,017.50**

*In many questions, particularly at Higher level you will be asked to calculate the profit for a job using the **profit margin**. This is the profit as a fraction or percentage of the selling price. This does give candidates problems so the following method should help eliminate these problems.*

Example 2

If a profit margin of 33⅓% of the selling price instead of a mark-up of 50% of the cost price is used for calculating the profit in Example 1, how could we calculate the profit using the margin when we do not know the actual selling price?

What we do know is that the cost of the job is £2,035, and the profit margin is to be 33⅓%.

> **Cost of job + Profit = Selling price**

We express the selling price as 100%, and we know the profit margin is 33⅓% of the selling price. From this we can calculate the cost of the job as a percentage of the selling price:

> Cost of job = Selling price − Profit margin

so:

> Cost of job = 100% − 33⅓% = 66⅔%

We can now express the profit margin as a percentage of cost of the job:

> **Profit margin** = $\dfrac{33⅓\% \times 100\%}{66⅔\%}$
>
> = **50% of cost**

continued ➤

Example 2 continued

The profit can now be calculated:

Profit = 50% of £2,035 = **£1,017.50**

Check the accuracy of your calculation by substituting the values back into the Cost + Profit = Selling price equation.

£2,035 + £1,017.50 = £3,052.50

Calculate the profit margin:

= 33⅓% of £3,052.50 = £1,017.50

There is a relationship between the mark-up and the margin. Both refer to the same profit figure. However in the case of the **mark-up** the **profit** is expressed as a **percentage** or fraction of the **cost** whereas in the case of the **profit margin** it is expressed as a **percentage** or fraction of the **selling price**.

Now do Worksheets 19.1, 19.2, 19.3, 19.4 and 19.5

MANAGEMENT ACCOUNTING

CHAPTER 20

Service costing

Intermediate 2 Level Outcomes: ⫸

I2

This chapter includes material from Int 2 level Management Accounting Outcome 2

☆ **Describe the uses of service costing.**

☆ **Complete a range of cost statements to calculate the cost from information supplied.**

☆ **The cost for a service is accurately calculated.**

☆ **The profit for a service is calculated using mark-up.**

Higher Level Outcomes: ⫸

H

This chapter includes material from Higher level Management Accounting Outcome 2

☆ **Describe the uses of service costing.**

☆ **Complete a service cost statement including the application of overhead absorption rates consistent with information supplied.**

☆ **The total or unit cost for a service is accurately calculated.**

☆ **The profit for a service is accurately calculated using mark-up or margin.**

Costs of providing services

I2 H

Service costing is the method of costing used when a specific service or function is provided rather than the actual tangible product sold. Examples of where service costing techniques may be used are:

- canteen;
- human resources;
- public transport;
- removal firm;
- haulage firm;
- hotel, hospital;
- restaurants;
- colleges;
- tourism;
- computing and IT services.

An estimate of the total cost of the service will be calculated for a specific period (often a year) and this will be used to calculate the selling price for the service.

Cost units which can be calculated include:

Service	Cost Unit
Canteen	meals served
Human resources	per employee
Public transport	passenger mile
Taxi firm	passenger mile
Removal firm	removal
Haulage firm	tonne-mile
Hotel	occupied bed night
Hospital	patient days, number of operations
Restaurants	meals served
Colleges	full time equivalent units
Tourism	per visitor
Computing and IT services	help desk calls, computer repairs

The benefits of preparing a service cost statement include:

- **cost comparison**. These can be made between one period and another;
- checking that the **price charged** for the service adequately **covers the costs** and **allows for a profit**;
- ensuring an adequate charge is made to the various departments for the service provided.
- allowing comparisons to be made between the cost of using their own fleet of vehicles or using an outside contractor.

Costs incurred in service costing can still be divided into **running costs** and **standard costs**. These are equivalent to variable costs and fixed costs.

Examples of direct running costs

Service provided   **Variable costs**

Transport   driver's wages, petrol or diesel, tyres

Canteen   food, wages, gas for cooking

Hospitals   patient's drugs, medical salaries

Examples of indirect or standard costs

Service provided   **Fixed costs**

Transport   maintenance costs, licences, MOT, insurance, other administration costs

Canteen   supervisor's salary, electricity, insurance, rent

Hospital   cleaning, general support

Steps in service costing

Two problems in tackling a service costing question are:

- the large number of calculations which are required to be made;
- the period an expense is being incurred and should therefore be charged to the costing statement.

It is essential that you provide full working notes for each calculation.

Example 1

Highland Hospitality Coaches operates five 50-seater luxury coaches which operate between London and their hotels in the Highlands. You are given the following information:

1 The coaches were purchased at a cost of £100,000 each. They estimate that the coaches will have an optimum life of eight years and will have a trade-in value of £20,000.

2 Coaches operate 52 weeks per year averaging 1,500 miles per week.

3 Fuel costs are 90p per litre and on average the coach travels five miles per litre.

4 Each coach has two drivers, each working a basic 35 hours a week. Their basic wage is £8 per hour and they work 48 weeks per year. In addition, all drivers work four hours overtime per week and are paid double time for this. Holiday pay is paid at the basic rate.

5 The coaches are serviced every 15,000 miles at a cost of £300 per service.

6 Each coach has six tyres which require to be replaced every 40,000 miles at a cost of £100 per tyre.

7 Insurance costs are £1,200 per coach.

8 Licences cost £330 per coach.

9 Administration costs per coach are estimated to be 10% of drivers' wages.

10 When calculating the charge per mile for transport for their holidays, Highland Hospitality Coaches add 50% of the cost to the annual mileage running costs.

You are required to calculate:

a) the annual running cost for each bus.

b) the annual running cost per mile.

c) the annual mileage charge for holidays.

STEP 1 – Set up a service cost statement and calculate the annual depreciation for each coach and record on statement

$$\text{Annual depreciation} = (\text{Cost of coach} - \text{trade-in value}) \div \text{life of coach}$$
$$= (£100,000 - £20,000) \div 8$$
$$= £80,000 \div 8 = £10,000 \text{ per annum}$$

continued ➤

MANAGEMENT ACCOUNTING

Example 1 continued

HIGHLAND HOSPITALITY COACHES SERVICE COST STATEMENT	Annual Running costs of one coach £
Depreciation	**10,000.00**

STEP 2 – Calculate the annual mileage for each coach

You must make sure you use the correct number of weeks the coach will be operating.

$$\text{Annual mileage} = \text{Weekly mileage} \times \text{number of weeks operated}$$
$$= 1{,}500 \times 52 = 78{,}000 \text{ miles}$$

STEP 3 – Calculate the annual fuel cost for each coach

$$\text{Annual fuel cost} = \text{Annual mileage} \div \text{miles per litre} \times \text{cost per litre}$$
$$= 78{,}000 \div 5 \times 90\text{p} = £14{,}040$$

HIGHLAND HOSPITALITY COACHES SERVICE COST STATEMENT	Annual Running costs of one coach £
Depreciation	10,000.00
Fuel costs	**14,040.00**

STEP 4 – Calculate the drivers' wages

Care must be taken here to ensure that the correct number of working weeks are used in calculating the annual pay. An added complication here is that each bus has two drivers.

It is better to show full workings for basic pay, overtime and holiday pay:

$$\text{Basic pay per driver} = \text{basic hours} \times \text{basic rate} \times \text{weeks worked}$$
$$= 35 \times £8 \times 48 \text{ weeks}$$
$$= \mathbf{£13{,}440}$$

$$\text{Overtime per driver} = \text{overtime hours} \times \text{double time} \times \text{weeks worked}$$
$$= 4 \times (£8 \times 2) \times 48 \text{ weeks}$$
$$= \mathbf{£3{,}072}$$

$$\text{Holiday pay} = \text{basic hours} \times \text{basic rate} \times \text{holiday weeks}$$
$$= 35 \times £8 \times 4$$
$$= \mathbf{£1{,}120}$$

Drivers annual pay:

Basic pay	£13,440
Overtime	£3,072
Holiday pay	£1,120
Total pay	**£17,632**

Annual drivers' pay for one coach $= £17{,}632 \times 2 = £35{,}264$

continued ➤

MANAGEMENT ACCOUNTING

Example 1 continued

HIGHLAND HOSPITALITY COACHES	
SERVICE COST STATEMENT	Annual Running costs of one coach £
Depreciation	10,000.00
Fuel costs	14,040.00
Drivers' wages	**35,264.00**

STEP 5 – Calculation of servicing costs

To calculate this figure you need to use the annual mileage figure

Number of services required = annual mileage ÷ service interval
= 78,000 ÷ 15,000
= **5.2** services per annum

Each coach requires five complete services during the year which is equivalent to 75,000 miles. When calculating the true service cost the additional 3,000 miles travelled must charged to the costs.

Cost of services = Number of services × cost per service
= 5.2 × £300
= **£1,560**

HIGHLAND HOSPITALITY COACHES	
SERVICE COST STATEMENT	Annual Running costs of one coach £
Depreciation	10,000.00
Fuel costs	14,040.00
Drivers' wages	35,264.00
Servicing costs	**1,560.00**

STEP 6 – Calculation of tyre costs

Again the annual mileage figure must be used to calculate how many tyre changes are needed during the year.

Number of tyre changes required = annual mileage ÷ tyre change interval
= 78,000 ÷ 40,000
= **1.95** tyre changes

Each coach requires one complete tyre change and is just 2,000 miles short of a second tyre change. The total cost of the tyre wear must be charged to the costs.

Cost of tyres = number of tyre changes × number of tyres × cost per tyre
= 1.95 × 6 × £100
= **£1,170**

continued ➤

Example 1 continued

HIGHLAND HOSPITALITY COACHES	
SERVICE COST STATEMENT	**Annual Running costs of one coach £**
Depreciation	10,000.00
Fuel costs	14,040.00
Drivers' wages	35,264.00
Servicing costs	1,560.00
Tyres	**1,170.00**

STEP 7 – Charging of individual costs

Some costs will simply be added into the service cost statement.

- Coach insurance   £1,200
- Licence   £330

STEP 8 – Calculation of administration costs

Administration costs are charged on the basis of 10% of the drivers' annual wage for each coach.

Administration costs   = Drivers' annual wages × 10%
                                   = £35,264 × 10%
                                   = £3,526.40

HIGHLAND HOSPITALITY COACHES	
SERVICE COST STATEMENT	**Annual Running costs of one coach £**
Depreciation	10,000.00
Fuel costs	14,040.00
Drivers' wages	35,264.00
Servicing costs	1,560.00
Tyres	1,170.00
Insurance	**1,200.00**
Licence	**330.00**
Administration costs	**3,526.40**

STEP 9 – Calculate the total cost for one coach

HIGHLAND HOSPITALITY COACHES	
SERVICE COST STATEMENT	**Annual Running costs of one coach £**
Depreciation	10,000.00
Fuel costs	14,040.00
Drivers' wages	35,264.00

continued ➤

Example 1 continued

HIGHLAND HOSPITALITY COACHES	
SERVICE COST STATEMENT	**Annual Running costs of one coach £**
Servicing costs	1,560.00
Tyres	1,170.00
Insurance	1,200.00
Licence	330.00
Administration costs	3,526.40
TOTAL RUNNING COSTS	**67,090.40**

STEP 10 – Calculate the running cost per mile

To do this divide the total running cost by the annual mileage

$$\text{Running cost per mile} = \text{Total running cost} \div \text{Annual mileage}$$
$$= £67,090.40 \div 78,000$$
$$= \textbf{£0.86 per mile (rounded to 2 decimal places)}$$

This information can now be used to calculate the travel costs they will build into their holiday package charges.

STEP 11 – Calculate the mileage charge to be made

$$\text{Mileage charge} = \text{Annual mileage cost} + 50\% \text{ of annual mileage cost}$$
$$= £0.86 + (50\% \text{ of } £0.86)$$
$$= £0.86 \times £0.43$$
$$= \textbf{£1.29 per mile}$$

Each passenger will not be charged this figure per mile. The cost will be divided between the average number of passengers taking the holidays over the year.

Highland Holiday Coaches estimate that the average number of passengers carried each week to be 40.

STEP 12 – Calculate the passenger mile charge to be made by Highland Holiday Coaches for the holiday journey

$$\text{Charge per passenger mile} = \text{Mileage charge} \div \text{average number of passengers}$$
$$= £1.29 \div 40$$
$$= \textbf{£0.03 per passenger mile}$$

This charge will then be used to calculate the travel element of the holiday cost:

Cost of coach travel for average holiday per passenger

$$= \text{Average weekly miles} \times \text{cost per passenger mile}$$
$$= 1,500 \times £0.03$$
$$= \textbf{£45 per passenger}$$

Cost units

There are a number of cost units which are used to calculate service charges. The tonne-mile or tonne-kilometre is used by haulage firms to calculate the cost of carrying freight per mile. Alternatively, the passenger-mile or passenger-kilometre is used by coach and passenger transport firms to calculate the service cost per passenger mile.

Example 2 Tonne-mile units

ABC Haulage estimate the following data

Annual running costs	£175,000
Annual mileage	700,000

Maximum tonnes carried per journey: 5 tonnes

STEP 1 – Calculate cost per mile

Cost per mile = Annual running costs ÷ annual mileage
= £175,000 ÷ 700,000 miles
= **25p** per mile

STEP 2 – Calculate the cost per tonne mile carried

Cost per tonne-mile = 25p/mile ÷ 5 tonnes
= **5p** per tonne mile

Task 1

From the following information calculate the cost per tonne-mile for each carrier.

Carrier	Annual Costs	Annual Mileage	Average Tonnes per journey
ABC Carrier	£100,000	400,000	10
DEG Carrier Ltd	£125,000	500,000	20
FHJ Carriers	£300,000	600,000	10
LXC Carriers	£200,000	500,000	8
TRS Transport Ltd	£500,000	2,000,000	20

Example 3

Akeland Passenger Transport provides you with the following estimates:

- Annual running costs £1,000,000
- Annual mileage 2,000,000
- Average passengers per journey 42

continued >

Example 3 continued

STEP 1 – Calculate cost per mile

$$\text{Cost per mile} = \text{Annual running costs} \div \text{annual mileage}$$
$$= £1,000,000 \div 2,000,000 \text{ miles}$$
$$= \textbf{50p} \text{ per mile}$$

STEP 2 – Calculate the cost per passenger mile

$$\text{Cost per passenger mile} = 50p \div 42 \text{ passengers}$$
$$= \textbf{0.012p} \text{ per passenger mile}$$

Task 2

Passenger mile

From the following information calculate the cost per passenger mile for each branch of Country-Wide Coaches plc:

Name	Annual Running costs	Annual Mileage	Average number of passengers per journey
West Coaches	£220,000	880,000	40
North Coaches	£500,000	200,000	35
East Coaches	£1,000,000	2,000,000	40
Central Coaches	£1,500,000	5,000,000	50
South Coaches	£750,000	1,500,000	40

Now do Worksheets 20.1 and 20.2

Process costing

Intermediate 2 Level Outcomes:

This chapter includes material from Int 2 level Management Accounting Outcome 2

☆ **Describe the uses of process costing.**

☆ **Complete a range of cost statements to calculate the cost from information provided.**

☆ **The cost for a process is accurately calculated.**

Higher Level Outcomes:

This chapter includes material from Higher level Management Accounting Outcome 2

☆ **Describe the uses of process costing.**

☆ **Complete a process cost statement including the application of overhead absorption rates consistent with information supplied.**

☆ **The total or unit cost for a process is accurately calculated.**

What is Process costing?

Process costing is a method of costing used to calculate the cost of a product at each process, operation or stage of manufacture, where processes being carried out have one or more of the following features:

- the product is produced in one single process;
- the product of one process becomes the material of another process or operation;
- there is simultaneous production, at one or more processes, of different products, with or without by-products;
- during one or more processes or operations the finished products are not distinguishable from one another except in the final shape or form.

Process costing is used by firms which have a **continuous flow of identical products** where it is not possible to distinguish one unit from another. Process costing is used in many industries, such as:

- chemical works, oil refining, soap making, distillation processes, coking works;
- food processing, canning factories, biscuit works, meat products, milk, dairy;
- textiles, weaving, spinning;
- box making, paper mills, paint, ink and varnishing.

In process costing the terms **by-product**, **joint product**, **scrap** and **wastage** frequently occur and need to be understood.

By-product

A **by-product** is a product which is produced **in addition to the main product** from the material being processed. The value of the by-product is relatively low compared to that of the main product. By-products may be further processed to increase their saleable value.

A typical example of the production of by-products is in the oil refining industry where crude oil is processed and refined oil might be the main product. The by-products will include sulphur, bitumen and chemical fertilisers.

Joint products

A **joint product** is produced when two or more **products are separated during the manufacturing process**. Each has a sufficiently high saleable value to be considered as a main product.

In a process where two or more products are inevitably produced, and each one earns approximately the same profit as the other, these products would be considered joint products. The term can also be used to describe various qualities of the same product.

Scrap

Scrap is defined as **discarded material** which has **some recoverable value** and which is usually either disposed of without further treatment (other than reclamation and handling costs), or reintroduced into the production process in place of raw materials (such as cullet in glass making).

Products which are found to be defective, or raw material which proves not to be up to standard may be used in other departments of the firm or sold at a much lower price than they cost. In many firms off-cuts are unavoidably produced, such as when can lids are pressed out of a sheet of aluminium. The remaining aluminium can be collected and returned to the supplier for reprocessing. The supplier will credit the firm for returning the material.

It is important to keep the quantity of scrap produced to a minimum and where it occurs, to make it more profitable by further processing (such as metal turnings being made into pan scrapers).

Waste

Waste can be defined as **discarded substances** which have no **value**. For example, if broken glass fell into a tank of soup, the soup would be considered unfit for consumption and would have to be destroyed.

Steps in process cost accounting

In process costing the factory is divided into departments or processes and an account is kept for each. Materials, labour and overheads are charged to the account and by-products and scrap values are deducted from the costs. The material modified in the first operation is passed to the next process. In process costing the finished product of one process becomes the raw materials of the next and so on until the finished goods are produced

Standard costs may be used in process costing. A standard cost provides a measure against which actual costs may be compared and this gives management an excellent measure of the efficiency of production.

Figure 21.1 shows the elements of process costs. The diagram shows the passage of materials through the various processes.

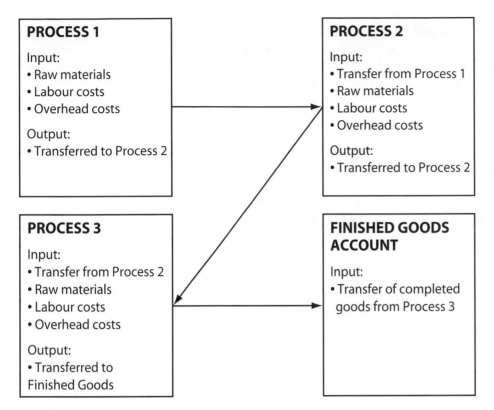

Figure 21.1 The elements of process costing

Raw materials

Raw materials are the basic materials used in the manufacture of the product. The material output from one process is the material input of the next. At any stage new material may be added to the process.

Labour

Generally speaking direct labour costs in process costing are relatively small. For example, in one large chemical firm the direct labour cost represents only 4 per cent of total costs. The charging of labour costs to the various processes is relatively easy as the workers usually spend all their time working on the one process, so costs are charged directly to that process.

Direct expenses

Each item of expenditure which can be attributed to a process will be charged to that process account.

Production overhead

In process costing the overhead element of total cost is normally very high. Great care should be taken in ensuring that each process is charged with a reasonable share of the production overhead. An overhead absorption rate will be used to calculate the amount to be added to the process costs.

Example 1 Simple process accounts

The manufacture of product Wye requires three distinct processes numbered 1-3. On completion, the product passes from Process 3 into finished stock.

During the month of May 1,000 kg of material X were introduced into Process 1. Throughout all 3 processes no losses of material occurred.

Process costs	Process 1	Process 2	Process 3
Inputs:	£	£	£
Direct materials (1,000 kg)	1,500		
Direct labour	250	300	2,100
Direct expenses	100	200	500

Fixed overheads absorption rate of 300% of direct labour costs.

STEP 1 – Enter the input costs incurred in the process into the input columns of the account

This will include the calculation of the overhead to be absorbed by Process 1:

Overhead to be absorbed = Direct labour cost × 300%
= £250 × 300% = £750

PROCESS 1 ACCOUNT

Input	Quantity	Cost per Unit £	£	Output	Quantity	Cost per unit £	£
Direct material	1,000	1.50	1,500				
Direct labour			250				
Direct expenses			100				
Fixed overheads			750				
	1,000		2,600				

STEP 2 – Calculate the cost per unit of output and enter in the output section of the process account

The Process 1 **output cost per unit** is calculated by dividing the total input cost by the number of units produced.

Output cost per unit = £2,600 ÷ 1,000 units
= £2.60 per unit

This figure is recorded in the **cost per unit** column in the output section of the account along with the total cost of the output and output units.

For each process account the quantity column and the money column for both the input and output section should be totalled and they should agree.

continued ➤

Example 1 Simple process accounts continued

PROCESS 1 ACCOUNT

Input	Quantity	Cost per Unit £	£	Output	Quantity	Cost per unit £	£
Direct material	1,000	1.50	1,500	**Transfer to Process 2**	1,000	2.60	2,600
Direct labour			250				
Direct expenses			100				
Fixed overheads			750				
	1,000		2,600		1,000		2,600

STEP 3 – Complete the Process 2 account

This will begin with the transfer of the **output quantity** and **cost** from Process 1.

The other input costs are entered into the account including the calculation of the fixed overhead (£300 × 300% = £900).

The Process 2 output cost per unit is calculated by **dividing** the **total output cost** by the **number of units** produced.

$$\text{Output cost per unit} = £4,000 \div 1,000 \text{ units}$$
$$= £4.00 \text{ per unit}$$

This figure is recorded in the cost per unit column in the output section of the account.

PROCESS 2 ACCOUNT

Input	Quantity	Cost per Unit £	£	Output	Quantity	Cost per unit £	£
Transfer from Process 1	1,000	2.60	2,600	**Transfer to Process 2**	1,000	4.00	4,000
Direct labour			300				
Direct expenses			200				
Fixed overheads			900				
	1,000		4,000		1,000		4,000

continued >

Example 1 Simple process accounts continued

STEP 4 – Complete the Process 3 account

This will begin with the transfer of the output quantity and cost from Process 2. The other input costs are entered into the account including the calculation of the fixed overhead (£2,100 × 300% = £6,300).

The Process 3 output cost per unit is calculated by dividing the total output cost by the number of units produced.

$$\text{Output cost per unit} = £12,900 \div 1,000 \text{ units}$$
$$= £12.90 \text{ per unit.}$$

This figure is recorded in the cost per unit column in the output section of the account.

PROCESS 3 ACCOUNT							
Input	Quantity	Cost per Unit £	£	Output	Quantity	Cost per unit £	£
Transfer from Process 2	1,000	4.00	4,000	Transfer to Finished goods	1,000	12.90	12,900
Direct labour			2,100				
Direct expenses			500				
Fixed overheads			6,300				
	1,000		12,900		1,000		12,900

STEP 5 – Now record the transfer from Process 3 to the Finished Goods account

FINISHED GOODS ACCOUNT							
Input	Quantity	Cost per Unit £	£	Output	Quantity	Cost per unit £	£
Transfer from Process 3	1,000	12.90	12,900				

Task 1

From the following information prepare the Process Account and show the transfer to the finished goods at the end of the month.

Process Costs	Process A	Process B	Process C
Inputs	£	£	£
Direct materials (3,000 kg)	3,000	-	-
Direct labour	1,000	1,200	900
Direct expenses	500	790	1,200

Fixed overheads are absorbed at the rate of 50% or direct labour costs in each process. No losses are expected or incurred in any of the processes.

Normal loss

With a process costing operation it is expected that there will be a loss of material quantity caused by the actual production process. Some losses will be scrap while other losses will be waste. This loss is inevitable in process industries, and it is essential that accurate records are maintained to enable control of these losses to be effected. This normal loss quantity can be calculated in advance, either by using a formula or based on previous processing experience.

Normal loss is the loss that is expected to occur under **normal operating procedures**. It may be caused by evaporation or off-cuts of material. The cost of this loss is simply absorbed into normal production costs and increases the cost per unit of the good output.

Example 2 Normal loss considered to be waste

The manufacture of product Alpha required 3 distinct processes, Cooking, Bottling, and Packaging. On completion, the product passes from Packaging to finished stock.

During the month of June 2,000 litres of raw material were introduced into the Cooking process. The company expects a normal material loss of 5% on the Cooking process. As this normal loss is due to evaporation it is considered to be waste with no saleable value.

Show the Cooking process account for June and the transfer to Process 2:

Inputs	Cooking process
	£
Direct materials (2,000 litres)	4,000
Direct labour	500
Direct expenses	200

Total factory fixed overheads of £8,000 are to be absorbed into each process at the rate of 200% of direct labour costs.

continued ➤

Example 2 Normal loss considered to be waste continued

STEP 1 – Record the inputs in the Cooking process account

Remember to add the fixed overheads to the total inputs.

$$
\begin{aligned}
\text{Fixed overheads} &= \text{Direct labour costs} \times 200\% \\
&= \pounds500 \times 200\% \\
&= \pounds1,000
\end{aligned}
$$

COOKING PROCESS ACCOUNT

Input	Quantity	Cost per Unit £	£	Output	Quantity	Cost per unit £	£
Direct materials	2,000	2.00	4,000				
Direct labour			500				
Direct expenses			200				
Fixed overheads			1,000				
	2,000		5,700				

STEP 2 – Calculate normal loss quantity of material and enter this figure in the output section of the Cooking process account

$$
\begin{aligned}
\text{Normal loss} &= \text{Input material} \times \text{normal loss \%} \\
&= 2,000 \text{ litres} \times 5\% \\
&= 100 \text{ litres}
\end{aligned}
$$

COOKING PROCESS ACCOUNT

Input	Quantity	Cost per Unit £	£	Output	Quantity	Cost per unit £	£
Direct materials	2,000	2.00	4,000	Normal Loss	100	-	-
Direct labour			500				
Direct expenses			200				
Fixed overheads			1,000				
	2,000		5,700				

STEP 3 – Calculate the normal output quantity

Normal output is the quantity of material the manufacturer expects to transfer into the next process when production is operating efficiently.

$$
\begin{aligned}
\text{Normal output} &= \text{Input quantity} - \text{normal loss} \\
&= 2,000 \text{ litres} - 100 \text{ litres} \\
&= 1,900 \text{ litres}
\end{aligned}
$$

continued ➤

Example 2 Normal loss considered to be waste continued

STEP 4 – Calculate the cost per unit of normal output

Once calculated the normal output quantity is used to calculate the cost per unit of normal production. This is the most important figure to be calculated in process costing.

$$\text{Cost per unit of normal output} = \frac{\text{Input cost} - \text{scrap value}}{\text{Normal output quantity}}$$

$$= \frac{\pounds5,700 - 0}{1,900 \text{ litres}}$$

$$= \pounds3 \text{ per litre}$$

Note: The normal loss in this example is actually waste with no re-saleable value. If the normal loss could have been sold as scrap this would have reduced the cost per unit of normal output.

STEP 5 – Show the transfer from the Cooking process account to the Bottling process account

COOKING PROCESS ACCOUNT							
Input	Quantity	Cost per Unit £	£	Output	Quantity	Cost per unit £	£
Direct materials	2,000	2.00	4,000	Normal Loss	100	-	-
Direct labour			500	Transfer to Process 2	1,900	3	5,700
Direct expenses			200				
Fixed overheads			1,000				
	2,000		5,700		2,000		5,700
Transfer from Cooking Process	1,900	3	5,700				

Now do Worksheet 21.1

Example 3 Normal loss considered to be scrap

Sometimes normal loss material can be sold for scrap. The income from this sale will reduce the cost of each normal unit.

Master plc manufacture aluminium cans from sheet aluminium in 3 processes. The provide you with the following information for the month of December:

Inputs	Pressing process
	£
Direct materials (6,000 kg)	24,000
Direct labour	5,000
Direct expenses	1,350

Fixed overheads are absorbed into production at the rate of 50% of direct labour costs.

Normal loss is expected to be 10% of input materials and can be sold as scrap at 75p per kg.

Show the Pressing process account and the transfer to the Flanging department.

STEP 1 – Record input costs into the Pressing process account

Remember to include the fixed overheads

$$\text{Fixed overheads} = \text{Direct labour costs} \times 50\%$$
$$= £5,000 \times 50\%$$
$$= £2,500$$

PRESSING PROCESS ACCOUNT							
Input	Quantity	Cost per Unit £	£	Output	Quantity	Cost per unit £	£
Direct materials	6,000	4.00	24,000				
Direct labour			5,000				
Direct expenses			1,350				
Fixed overheads			2,500				
	6,000		32,850				

STEP 2 – Calculate the normal loss

$$\text{Normal loss} = \text{Input quantity} \times \text{normal loss }\%$$
$$= 6,000 \text{ kg} \times 10\%$$
$$= 600 \text{ kg}$$

This normal loss can be sold for scrap at 75p per kg.

$$\text{Income from sale of normal loss as scrap} = \text{Normal loss quantity} \times \text{price per kg}$$
$$= 600 \text{ kg} \times 75p$$
$$= £450$$

continued ➤

Example 3 Normal loss considered to be scrap continued

These figures are entered into the output section of the Pressing process account:

PRESSING PROCESS ACCOUNT

Input	Quantity	Cost per Unit £	£	Output	Quantity	Cost per unit £	£
Direct materials	6,000	4.00	24,000	Normal Loss	600	0.75	450
Direct labour			5,000				
Direct expenses			1,350				
Fixed overheads			2,500				
	6,000		32,850				

STEP 3 – Calculate the cost of normal output

$$\text{Normal output} = \text{Input quantity of material} - \text{scrap quantity of material}$$
$$= 6,000 \text{ kgs} - 600 \text{ kgs}$$
$$= 5,400 \text{ kg of normal output}$$

Enter this quantity in the output quantity column.

$$\text{Cost per unit of normal output} = \frac{\text{Input costs} - \text{scrap sale}}{\text{Normal output}}$$

$$= \frac{£32,850 - £450}{5,400 \text{ kg}}$$

$$= \frac{£32,400}{5,400 \text{ kg}} = £6 \text{ per kg}$$

Enter the cost per kg and the total cost of normal output into the appropriate output columns.

PRESSING PROCESS ACCOUNT

Input	Quantity	Cost per Unit £	£	Output	Quantity	Cost per unit £	£
Direct materials	6,000	4.00	24,000	Normal Loss	600	0.75	450
Direct labour			5,000	**Transfer to Flanging Process**	5,400	6.00	32,400
Direct expenses			1,350				
Fixed overheads			2,500				
	6,000		32,850		6,000		32,850

continued ➢

Example 3 Normal loss considered to be scrap continued

STEP 4 – Show the transfer of the output to the Flanging process account

FLANGING PROCESS ACCOUNT							
Input	Quantity	Cost per Unit £	£	Output	Quantity	Cost per unit £	£
Transfer from Process 3	5,400	6.00	32,400				

  Now do Worksheet 21.2

 # Work-in-progress

As with all manufacturing processes at the end of the period there will be some material in each process which is partly finished. These partly-completed products need to be valued and the quantity accounted for. These materials are called **work-in-progress** and consist of direct materials, labour and overheads.

Example 4 Work-in-progress

Country Chemicals plc manufactures a number of chemicals used in the engineering industry. The chemicals pass through three processes before being transferred to finished goods.

They provide you with the following information for the month of March:

Process 1 involves the mixing two parts of Zeon to one part Aron.

- Material Zeon   5,000 kg at £4 per kg
- Material Aron costs   £3 per kg
- Direct labour   £5,000
- Direct expenses   £8,575

Fixed overheads are absorbed into production at the rate of 50% of direct labour costs.

Normal loss is expected to be 10% of input materials and can be sold as scrap at £3 per kg.

At the end of March there was 300 kg of work-in-progress valued at £5 per kg.

Prepare the Process 1 account and show the transfer of output to the Process 2 account.

continued ➤

Example 4 Work-in-progress continued

STEP 1 – Record the input costs in the Process 1 account

The total material cost and quantity needs to be calculated. Before doing this you need to calculate the quantity of Aron which has to be introduced into Process 1.

5,000 kg of Zeon was introduced into the process. For every 2 kg of Zeon introduced 1 kg of Aron should be introduced. To calculate the kg of Aron to be added divide Zeon material quantity by 2:

$$\text{Quantity of Aron} = 5,000 \text{ kg} \div 2$$
$$= 2,500 \text{ kg of Aron}$$

It is now possible to calculate the materials costs:

$$\text{Zeon} = 5,000 \times £4 = £20,000$$
$$\text{Aron} = 2,500 \times £3 = £7,500$$

Total material cost = £27,500

Other costs are entered into the input section of the process account.

Remember to calculate the fixed overheads to be charged to this process.

Fixed overheads = 50% of £5,000 = £2,500

PROCESS 1 ACCOUNT							
Input	Quantity	Cost per Unit £	£	Output	Quantity	Cost per unit £	£
Material Zeon	5,000	4.00	20,000				
Material Aron	2,500	3.00	7,500				
Direct labour			5,000				
Direct expenses			8,575				
Fixed overheads			2,500				
	7,500		43,575				

STEP 2 – Calculate the normal loss and its scrap value

$$\text{Normal loss} = 5\% \text{ of input weight}$$
$$= 5\% \text{ of } (5,000 + 2,500)$$
$$= 375 \text{ kg}$$

$$\text{Scrap value of normal loss} = 375 \text{ kg} \times £3 \text{ per kg}$$
$$= £1,125$$

continued ➤

Example 4 Work-in-progress continued

PROCESS 1 ACCOUNT							
Input	**Quantity**	**Cost per Unit £**	**£**	**Output**	**Quantity**	**Cost per unit £**	**£**
Material Zeon	5,000	4.00	20,000	**Normal Loss**	375	3.00	1,125
Material Aron	2,500	3.00	7,500				
Direct labour			5,000				
Direct expenses			8,575				
Fixed overheads			2,500				
	7,500		43,575				

STEP 3 – Calculate the total cost of normal output and enter in the process account

Calculation of normal output:

$$\text{Normal output} = \text{Input} - (\text{Scrap} + \text{work-in-progress})$$
$$= 7,500 - (375 + 300)$$
$$= 6,825 \text{ kg}$$

Now enter the work-in-progress figure in the process account and then calculate the total cost per unit of normal output.

$$\text{Cost per unit} = \frac{\text{Input costs} - (\text{scrap sale} + \text{work-in-progress})}{\text{Input material} - (\text{scrap material} + \text{work-in-progress material})}$$

$$= \frac{£43,575 - (£1,125 + £1,500)}{7,500 - (375 \text{ kg} + 300 \text{ kg})}$$

$$= \frac{£40,950}{6,825 \text{ kg}} = £6.00 \text{ per kg}$$

Enter the cost per kg and the total cost of normal output into the appropriate output columns.

PROCESS 1 ACCOUNT							
Input	**Quantity**	**Cost per Unit £**	**£**	**Output**	**Quantity**	**Cost per unit £**	**£**
Material Zeon	5,000	4.00	20,000	Normal Loss	375	3.00	1,125
Material Aron	2,500	3.00	7,500	**Work-in-progress**	300	5.00	1,500
Direct labour			5,000	**Transfer to Process 2**	6,825	6.00	40,950
Direct expenses			2,290				
Fixed overheads			2,500				
	7,500		43,575		7,500		43,575

Now do Worksheet 21.3

Abnormal loss

An **abnormal loss** is caused by **unexpected** or **abnormal conditions**, such as inferior material, or carelessness by workers. All losses under this category must be thoroughly investigated and steps taken to prevent any recurrence.

With the normal loss the cost is simply absorbed into the cost of production, but when an abnormal loss occurs a **separate abnormal loss account** must be opened and the total cost of the abnormal loss (the value of the material, wage, direct and production expenses incurred by the units lost) charged to an abnormal loss account. The enterprise has fewer units to transfer to the next process or finished goods than expected and the value of this loss must be calculated.

Example 5 Abnormal loss

Satin Soft produce fabric softeners, as own label brands, in three processes, for a number of supermarkets. They provide you with the following information for Process 1 for the month of June:

Process 1
Raw material	10,000 litres at £2 per litre
Direct labour	£14,000
Direct expenses	£1,500

Fixed overheads are absorbed into production at the rate of 40% of direct labour costs.

Normal loss is expected to be 10% of input materials and this can be sold for reprocessing at £1 per litre.

There was no work-in-progress at the end of the period and actual output amounted to 8,500 litres.

Prepare the Process 1 account and the abnormal loss account.

Example 5 Abnormal loss continued

STEP 1 – Calculate and enter the input values into the appropriate columns in the Process 1 account

Remember to take into account fixed overheads to be absorbed.

PROCESS 1 ACCOUNT							
Input	Quantity	Cost per Unit £	£	Output	Quantity	Cost per unit £	£
Material	10,000	2.00	20,000				
Direct labour			14,000				
Direct expenses			1,450				
Fixed overheads			5,600				
	10,000		41,050				

STEP 2 – Calculate the normal loss and its scrap value and enter the figures in the output section of the Process account

$$\text{Normal loss} = 10\% \text{ of input materials}$$
$$= 10\% \text{ of } 10,000 \text{ litres} = 1,000 \text{ litres}$$

$$\text{Scrap value of normal loss} = 1,000 \times £1$$
$$= £1,000$$

PROCESS 1 ACCOUNT							
Input	Quantity	Cost per Unit £	£	Output	Quantity	Cost per unit £	£
Material Zeon	10,000	2.00	20,000	**Normal Loss**	**1,000**	**1.00**	**1,000**
Direct labour			14,000				
Direct expenses			1,450				
Fixed overheads			5,600				
	10,000		41,050				

STEP 3 – Calculate the normal output quantity

$$\text{Normal output} = \text{Input quantity} - \text{normal loss}$$
$$= 10,000 - 1,000$$
$$= 9,000 \text{ litres}$$

STEP 4 – Calculate the total cost of normal output

$$\text{Total cost of normal output} = \text{Input costs} - (\text{scrap sale} + \text{work-in-progress})$$
$$= £41,050 - (£1,000)$$
$$= £40,050$$

Remember to take into account any work-in-progress when calculating this figure.

continued ➤

Example 5 Abnormal loss continued

STEP 5 – Calculate normal unit cost price

$$\text{Normal unit cost price} = \frac{\text{Cost of normal output}}{\text{Normal output}}$$

$$= \frac{£40,050}{9,000}$$

$$= £4.45$$

This figure is used to value good output from a process **and** any units lost in production.

STEP 6 – Calculate the cost of actual output and enter into outputs section of the process account

$$\text{Cost of actual output} = \text{Actual output} \times \text{cost per unit of normal output}$$
$$= 8,500 \times £4.45$$
$$= £37,825$$

PROCESS 1 ACCOUNT							
Input	Quantity	Cost per Unit £	£	Output	Quantity	Cost per unit £	£
Material Zeon	10,000	2.00	20,000	Normal Loss	1,000	1.00	1,000
Direct labour			14,000	**Transfer to Process 2**	8500	4.45	37,825
Direct expenses			1,450				
Fixed overheads			5,600				
	10,000		40,500				

STEP 7 – Compare actual output quantity with normal output quantity (taking into account any work-in-progress)

$$\text{Abnormal loss} = \text{Actual output} - (\text{input quantity} - (\text{normal loss} + \text{work-in-progress}))$$
$$= 8,500 - (10,000 - (9,000 + 0))$$
$$= 8,500 - 9,000$$
$$= 500 \text{ units of abnormal loss}$$

Output should have been **9,000**, but the firm only achieved **8,500**, so they have **lost 500 units** from production.

Enter the 500 units of abnormal loss in the outputs section of the Process 1 account and label it abnormal loss.

The quantity columns now agree, but the money column totals do not.

continued ➤

Example 5 Abnormal loss continued

PROCESS 1 ACCOUNT							
Input	Quantity	Cost per Unit £	£	Output	Quantity	Cost per unit £	£
Material Zeon	10,000	2.00	20,000	Normal Loss	1,000	1.00	1,000
Direct labour			14,000	Transfer to Process 2	8500	4.45	37,825
Direct expenses			1,450	**Abnormal loss**	**500**		
Fixed overheads			5,600				
	10,000		41,050		10,000		

STEP 8 – Calculate the value of the units lost from production

These are valued at the same cost per unit as normal output.

$$\text{Abnormal loss value} = \text{Cost per unit of normal output} \times \text{abnormal loss units}$$
$$= £4.45 \times 500$$
$$= £2,225$$

Enter the cost per unit and the value of the abnormal loss in the Process account.

The quantity column and the value column on both for input and output quantities should agree.

PROCESS 1 ACCOUNT							
Input	Quantity	Cost per Unit £	£	Output	Quantity	Cost per unit £	£
Material Zeon	10,000	2.00	20,000	Normal Loss	1,000	1.00	1,000
Direct labour			14,000	Transfer to Process 2	8500	4.45	37,825
Direct expenses			1,450	Abnormal loss	500	**4.45**	**2,225**
Fixed overheads			5,600				
	10,000		41,050		10,000		**41,050**

The most common problem candidates experience with an abnormal loss is that they do not value this loss at the cost per unit of normal output.

continued ➤

Example 5 Abnormal loss continued

STEP 9 – Transfer of abnormal loss to an abnormal loss account

Open an abnormal loss account and enter the values for the abnormal loss on the Input side.

PROCESS 1 ABNORMAL LOSS ACCOUNT							
Input	Quantity	Cost per Unit £	£	Output	Quantity	Cost per unit £	£
Abnormal loss from Process 1	500	4.45	2,225				
	500		2,225				

The abnormal loss account shows a total loss of £2,225. However as losses can be sold for scrap, the income from the scrap sale of the abnormal loss will reduce the total loss on this process.

STEP 10 – Calculate the income from the sale of abnormal loss for scrap

$$\text{Abnormal loss scrap income} = \text{Abnormal loss units} \times \text{unit scrap price}$$
$$= 500 \times £2$$
$$= £1,000$$

Enter this figure into the output side of the abnormal loss account.

The remaining abnormal loss is transferred to the costing profit and loss account and will be written off against profits.

PROCESS 1 ABNORMAL LOSS ACCOUNT							
Input	Quantity	Cost per Unit £	£	Output	Quantity	Cost per unit £	£
Abnormal loss from Process 1	500	4.45	2,225	Scrap sales	500	2.00	1,000
				Profit and Loss			1,225
	500		2,225		500		2,225

  Now do Worksheet 21.4

CHAPTER 22

Break-even analysis

Intermediate 2 Level Outcomes: ➤

This chapter includes material from Int 2 level Management Accounting Outcome 3

I2

☆ **Describe briefly the benefits to an organisation of using the break-even technique.**

☆ **Division of cost between variable and fixed is consistent with information supplied.**

☆ **Identification of contribution per unit is consistent with information supplied.**

☆ **Identification of break-even units is consistent with information supplied.**

☆ **Calculation of profit is consistent with information supplied.**

☆ **Conclusions drawn on the effect of increasing fixed and/or variable costs on profit and/or break-even point are accurate.**

Higher Level Outcomes: ➤

This chapter includes material from Higher level Management Accounting Outcome 3

H

☆ **Explain the assumptions, uses and limitations of break-even analysis.**

☆ **Apply correct break-even analysis and decision making formulae to information supplied.**

☆ **Calculate the effect of changes to a given situation relating to break-even analysis.**

What is break-even analysis?

Break-even analysis is an important tool in short term planning because it shows the relationship between costs, revenue, output levels and resulting profit.

To **break-even** means that the enterprise is **making neither a profit or a loss** – their total sales revenue is equal to their total costs.

The term **break-even** is commonly used but it can be misleading. It implies that the only concern is with that level of production which produces neither a profit nor a loss - the **break-even point**. Because of this, an alternative term can be used, and gives a better understanding of the technique, the **cost-volume-profit** analysis.

All business organisations incur costs and receive income. The **break-even chart** will show the **relationship** between **cost** and **income**.

The costs are all the expenses incurred in production. You are already familiar with these terms. Costs can be either **fixed** or **variable**, and added together they give the **total cost**.

Fixed costs do not depend on output. They remain constant at changing levels of output (in the short term).

Variable costs, on the other hand, are **directly related to output**. When production increases, variable costs will normally increase in proportion to output.

The **variable costs** will include the cost of **direct material, direct labour** and any other **direct expenses** incurred in the manufacture of the product.

Total costs are the total expenses incurred by a company in manufacturing its products. The **total cost** represents the total of the **fixed** and **variable costs**. As variable costs increase with output, so total costs will also increase with output.

A **break-even chart** can be prepared to show the relationship between fixed and variable costs, and revenue. We need to know how to use the information provided to prepare a break-even chart.

Example 1

Solsun plc provide you with the following information for production of their sunbed goggles for the month of March.

Fixed costs for the month	£5,000
Variable costs per unit	£2.50 per Unit
Selling price per unit	£5 per Unit
Maximum production	5,000 units

STEP 1 – Decide on the scale for the chart

The **X scale** is the horizontal scale of the chart. For this example, the X scale we are going to use for production is thousands. This means we will show production levels of 1,000, 2,000, 3,000, 4,000 and 5,000 in the chart.

The **Y scale** is the vertical scale of the chart. For this example, the Y scale we are going to use for costs and revenue is £5,000. We will show income and costs at the following levels – £5,000, £10,000, £15,000, £20,000 and £25,000.

STEP 2 – Set out the above information in a table and enter the output levels

Units	Variable Costs £	Fixed Costs £	Total Cost £	Sales Revenue £
0				
1,000				
2,000				
3,000				
4,000				
5,000				

continued ⮞

Example 1 continued

STEP 3 – Calculate the variable cost for each output level shown and enter in table

Variable costs are £2.50 per unit, therefore variable costs at each output level will be:

$$\text{Variable cost} = \text{Number of units} \times \text{variable cost per unit}$$
$$= 1{,}000 \times £2.50 = £2{,}500$$

Units	Variable Costs £	Fixed Costs £	Total Cost £	Sales Revenue £
0	0			
1,000	2,500			
2,000	5,000			
3,000	7,500			
4,000	10,000			
5,000	12,500			

STEP 4 – Enter the fixed cost for each output level

Remember fixed costs will remain the same (in the short term) regardless of output. Therefore £5,000 will be entered opposite each output level.

Units	Variable Costs £	Fixed Costs £	Total Cost £	Sales Revenue £
0	0	5,000		
1,000	2,500	5,000		
2,000	5,000	5,000		
3,000	7,500	5,000		
4,000	10,000	5,000		
5,000	12,500	5,000		

STEP 5 – Calculate the total cost for each output level and add to table

$$\text{Total cost} = \text{Variable costs} + \text{fixed costs}$$

At 1,000 units this will be £2,500 + £5,000 = £7,500. You can then calculate the total costs for the remaining levels of output.

Units	Variable Costs £	Fixed Costs £	Total Cost £	Sales Revenue £
0	0	5,000	5,000	
1,000	2,500	5,000	7,500	
2,000	5,000	5,000	10,000	
3,000	7,500	5,000	12,500	
4,000	10,000	5,000	15,000	
5,000	12,500	5,000	17,500	

continued ➤

Example 1 continued

STEP 6 – Calculate the sales revenue for each output level and enter in table

Selling price per unit is £5 per unit, so the sales revenue at 1,000 units will be:

Revenue = £5 × 1,000 units = £5,000

Units	Variable Costs £	Fixed Costs £	Total Cost £	Sales Revenue £
0	0	5,000	5,000	**0**
1,000	2,500	5,000	7,500	**5,000**
2,000	5,000	5,000	10,000	**10,000**
3,000	7,500	5,000	12,500	**15,000**
4,000	10,000	5,000	15,000	**20,000**
5,000	12,500	5,000	17,500	**25,000**

STEP 7 – Plot the data onto a graph

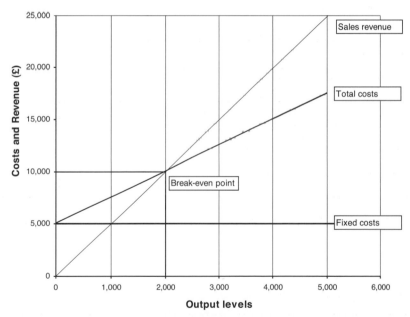

Figure 22.1 Break-even chart showing fixed and variable costs, and sales revenue

The chart shows the fixed costs, the variable costs (to give the total costs), and the sales revenue:

The **fixed costs** remain constant regardless of output and are shown by the horizontal line.

continued ➤

Example 1 continued

The **variable costs** vary with output. Note that this line starts at the fixed cost point. Even if no units are being produced the enterprise will still have to pay its fixed costs. The variable cost line also indicates the **total costs.**

The **sales revenue** is directly related to the levels of sales up to the point of maximum production (assuming all units are sold). Production may be limited because of plant capacity, skilled labour or raw material shortages.

The **break-even point** on the chart is where the **total cost line** and the **revenue line** cross. At this point **revenue is equal to total costs**. No profit or loss is made at this point.

Margin of Safety

Although an enterprise can produce a certain number of units, the market may be such that it cannot sell all of the units. The **difference** between the **break-even point** and the **sales level** achieved is called the **margin of safety**. The margin of safety can be calculated in units and in sales revenue.

Example 2

Solsun plc only sell 4,000 pairs of goggles during the month of March.

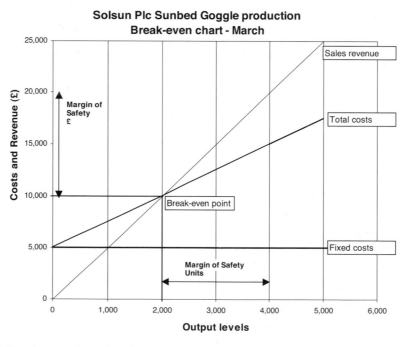

Figure 22.2 Break-even chart showing the margin of safety in units and in sales revenue

continued ➤

Example 2 continued

The chart shows the margin of safety in units and in sales revenue.

Margin of safety (in units) = Sales level – break-even level
= 4,000 – 2,000 = 2,000 units

Margin of safety (in revenue) = Sales revenue at 4,000 units – break-even revenue at 2,000 units

= £20,000 – £10,000 = £10,000

Task 1

a) The cost accountant provides you with the following information and asks you to prepare a table to show costs and revenues and a break-even chart for each product for presentation to the Board of Directors at his next meeting:

Product	Selling price per Unit £	Variable Cost per Unit £	Fixed Costs £	Maximum production level
Star	20	10	40,000	8,000
Mercury	10	5	20,000	6,000
Saturn	40	30	100,000	20,000
Jupiter	50	30	200,000	30,000
Sun	12	10	20,000	20,000

b) For each product state:

   (i)   Break-even point in units and in sales revenue

   (ii) Sales revenue at 5,000 units

   (iii) Point of maximum production

   (iv) Margin of safety in units and sales revenue if the following units of each product were sold:

Product	Units sold
Star	7,000
Mercury	4,000
Saturn	15,000
Jupiter	20,000
Sun	18,000

In your exams, in addition to drawing a chart you may be given one and asked to interpret the chart to provide specific information.

Interpretation of a break-even chart

Example 3

Study the break-even chart of Omega plc for the month of February.

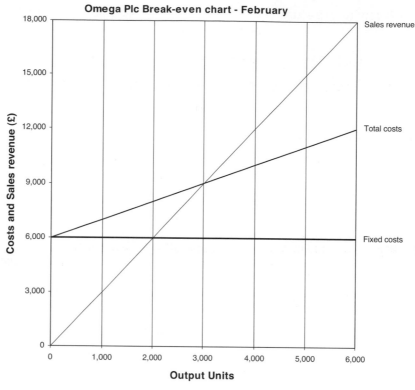

Figure 22.3 Break-even chart for Omega plc for February

From the chart calculate:

a)   The variable cost per unit

b)   The selling price per unit

c)   The profit earned when 6,000 units are sold

STEP 1 – Identify the break-even point and fixed cost amount

Identify the Break-even Point in £ and Units.

    Break-even point in £   = £9,000
    Break-even point in units =   3,000
    Fixed costs   = £6,000

Remember that at the break-even point the total costs are made up from fixed and variable costs.

continued ➤

Example 3 continued

STEP 2 – Calculate the variable cost per unit

$$\text{Variable cost per unit} = (\text{Total costs} - \text{fixed costs}) \div \text{break-even units}$$
$$= £9,000 - £6,000) \div 3,000 \text{ units}$$
$$= £3,000 \div 3,000$$
$$= £1 \text{ per unit}$$

STEP 3 – Calculate the selling price

At the break-even point, total costs and total sales revenue are equal.

Sales revenue at break-even point = £9,000

Units sold at break-even point = 3,000

$$\text{Selling price per unit} = \text{Sales revenue at break-even point} \div \text{units at}$$
$$\text{break-even point}$$
$$= £9,000 \div 3,000$$
$$= £3 \text{ per unit}$$

STEP 4 – Calculate the profit earned at 6,000 units

From the graph read off the sales revenue and the total costs:

Sales revenue at 6,000 units = £18,000

Total costs at 6,000 units = £12,000

$$\text{Profit} = \text{Sales revenue} - \text{total costs}$$
$$= £18,000 - £12,000$$
$$= £6,000$$

Contribution margin in break-even analysis

Using a break-even chart is not the only method of finding the break-even point. This figure may be calculated arithmetically.

Example 4

Anytown High School is considering installing a drinks vending machine. The fixed cost of this would be the machine rental of £50 per month. The school can purchase health drinks at 40p per bottle and sell them at 60p per bottle.

Before deciding whether or not to install the machine the school must know how many bottles must be sold to cover the cost of the rental – or to break-even.

One approach in calculating the break-even sales volume is the **contribution margin** approach.

From the sales proceeds of each bottle, the first 40p represents the variable cost of purchasing the drink. The amount remaining after paying the variable costs is the **contribution margin or marginal income**.

continued ➤

Example 4 continued

STEP 1 – Calculate the contribution per bottle

The following formula can be used to calculate the contribution per bottle

Contribution = Sales price per bottle – Variable cost per bottle

Sales price per bottle	60p
Less variable cost per bottle	40p
Contribution per bottle	**20p**

From the sale of each health drink 20p is available to pay for the fixed costs of hiring the machine and earning a profit.

STEP 2 – Calculate the break-even point in units

We need to know how many bottles with the contribution of 20p we need to sell to make £50. (Fixed costs amount to £50 for the hire of the machine. The contribution is 20p. This is the difference between the selling price and the variable cost per bottle.) To calculate the break-even point in units the following formula is used:

$$\text{Break-even point (in units)} = \text{Fixed costs} \div \text{Contribution per bottle}$$
$$= £50 \div 20p$$
$$= 250 \text{ bottles of health drink}$$

If we sell 251 bottles we will cover our fixed costs of £50 and make a profit of 20p. The income from this extra bottle is termed the **marginal income**.

Task 2

Zoltan manufacture five different products in five separate factories in Scotland. Calculate the break-even point for each product from the following information:

Product	Alpha £	Beta £	Gamma £	Delta £	Omega £
Variable costs	20	30	40	60	120
Selling price	25	40	70	100	190
Fixed costs	25,000	30,000	60,000	40,000	140,000

   Now do Worksheet 22.1

Profit forecasting using break-even analysis

Break-even analysis is useful for more than simply calculating the break-even point. It can be used to **calculate the profit for a given level of output**.

Example 5

Anytown High School estimates that they will sell 1,000 bottles of health drink every week. The head teacher wants to know how much profit the school will earn from these sales.

STEP 1 – Calculate the total contribution from the sales of 1,000 bottles

$$
\begin{aligned}
\text{Total contribution} &= \text{Units sold} \times \text{Contribution per bottle} \\
&= 1,000 \times 20\text{p} \\
&= \pounds 200
\end{aligned}
$$

STEP 2 – Deduct fixed costs from total contribution to calculate estimated profit

$$
\begin{aligned}
\text{Estimated profit} &= \text{Contribution} - \text{Fixed costs} \\
&= \pounds 200 - \pounds 50 \\
&= \pounds 150
\end{aligned}
$$

Task 3

Alpha Toys plc manufactures and sell a wide variety of toys. The following are estimates for sales for the next period.

Product	Soft toys £	Board Games £	Action Games £	Hand Held Games £	Card Games £
Contribution per toy	10	5	25	20	10
Estimated sales units	1,000	500	2,500	3,000	1,500
Fixed Costs	12,000	1,000	40,000	30,000	9,000

Calculate the estimated **profit** or **loss** made for the period for each range of toy.

Profit/Volume ratio or Contribution margin

The contribution is sometimes expressed as a percentage of the selling price. This is known as the **contribution margin** or the **Profit/Volume ratio (P/V ratio)**

Calculation of P/V ratio $= \dfrac{\text{Contribution}}{\text{Sales}} \times 100$

For the health drinks for Anytown School the P/V ratio would be:

P/V ratio $= \dfrac{20\text{p}}{60\text{p}} \times 100$

$= 33\frac{1}{3}\%$

This figure can be used to calculate the contribution for any sales revenue.

You must remember that, in the short term, the variable cost will remain constant and be the same percentage of the selling price.

Obviously the break-even computation can never be an exact figure, but it is sufficiently accurate to serve as a basis for managerial planning.

 Task 4

A plc manufacture five products in their Lenzie factory and provide you with the following information:

Product	A £	B £	C £	D £	E £
Sales Revenue	10	30	25	60	100
Variable Costs	5	10	15	20	40

a) Calculate the P/V ratio for each product.

b) Calculate the contribution for each product for the following sales levels:

Product	A £	B £	C £	D £	E £
Sales Revenue	100,000	90,000	75,000	120,000	200,000

c) Calculate the overall profit or loss made by the Lenzie factory if fixed costs amounted to £250,000 for Year 1.

Profit planning

Often an enterprise plans its sales, costs and activity and then computes the profit. In profit planning this is reversed; the enterprise decides what profit it wants and then works backwards to see what sales, costs and activity need to be to produce that profit.

In practice certain factors are usually fixed before the planning begins. Production capacity, materials or labour may be limited or selling price may be determined by the activities of competitors.

Example 6

Sharp plc manufactures a single product with a variable cost of £3 per unit. Fixed costs are £48,000. The market is such that up to 40,000 units can be sold at £6 per unit, but any additional sales must be made at £4 per unit. The planned profit is £80,000. How many units must be made and sold?

STEP 1 – Calculate the planned contribution

The planned contribution is the fixed costs plus the profit required

$$\begin{aligned}\text{Planned contribution} &= \text{Planned profits} + \text{fixed costs}\\ &= \pounds 80{,}000 + \pounds 48{,}000\\ &= \pounds 128{,}000\end{aligned}$$

STEP 2 – Calculate the contribution per unit

As the contribution will be different for the quantities to be sold two calculations will need to performed.

Contribution per unit for sales up to 40,000:

$$\begin{aligned}\text{Contribution per unit} &= \text{Selling price} - \text{variable costs}\\ &= \pounds 6 - \pounds 3\\ &= \pounds 3\end{aligned}$$

Contribution per unit for any sales over 40,000

$$\begin{aligned}\text{Contribution per unit} &= \text{Selling price} - \text{variable costs}\\ &= \pounds 4 - \pounds 3\\ &= \pounds 1\end{aligned}$$

STEP 3 – Calculate the contribution from the first 40,000 units sold

$$\begin{aligned}\text{Contribution per unit} &= \text{Contribution per unit} \times \text{units}\\ &= \pounds 3 \times 40{,}000\\ &= \pounds 120{,}000\end{aligned}$$

This is £8,000 short of the planned contribution. We know that any units sold in excess of 40,000 will only bring in a contribution of £1 per unit.

continued >

MANAGEMENT ACCOUNTING

Example 6 continued

STEP 4 – Calculate the additional units to be sold

$$\text{Additional units} = \frac{\text{Shortfall in planned contribution}}{\text{Contribution per unit from sales over 40,000}}$$

$$= \frac{£8,000}{£1}$$

$$= 8,000 \text{ units}$$

STEP 5 – Calculate the total unit sales to achieve the planned contribution of £128,000

$$\text{Total unit sales} = 40,000 + 8,000$$

$$= 48,000 \text{ units}$$

I2
H

Task 5

a) A plc manufactures a single product with a variable cost of £5 per unit. Fixed costs are £70,000. The market is such that up to 50,000 units can be sold at £12 per unit, but any additional sales must be made at £10 per unit. The planned profit is £400,000. How many units must be made and sold?

b) B PLC manufactures a single product with a variable cost of £4 per unit. Fixed costs are £40,000. The planned profit is £1,000,000. If the market is such that up to 150,000 units can be sold at £7 per unit, but any additional sales must be made at £5 per unit, calculate the number of units to be made to bring in the planned contribution.

c) C PLC manufacturers a single product with a variable cost of £4 per unit. Fixed costs are £40,000. The planned profit is £150,000. If the market is such that up to 25,000 units can be sold at £10 per unit, but any additional sales must be made at £5 per unit, how many units must be made and sold?

d) D PLC manufactures a single product with a variable cost of £8 per unit. Fixed costs are £80,000. The market is such that up to 48,000 units can be sold at £20 per unit, but any additional sales must be made at £15 per unit. The planned profit is £1,000,000. How many units must be made and sold?

e) E plc manufactures a single product with a variable cost of £3 per unit. Fixed costs are £100,000. The market is such that up to 100,000 units can be sold at £10 per unit, but any additional sales must be made at £6 per unit. The planned profit is £750,000. How many units must be made and sold?

I2
H

Now do Worksheet 22.2

Assumptions and limitations of break-even analysis

Break-even analysis assumes that:

- **all costs** are classified as either **fixed** or **variable**;
- **fixed** and **variable costs** are correctly separated over the **whole range of output**;
- **variable costs vary directly** with output;
- **fixed costs remain constant** for all levels of output
- **selling price per unit is constant** regardless of the level of output or demand;
- there is only **one product**, or, if there is more than one product, a **constant sales mix** exists over the whole range of output;
- **production and sales are equal** and there is no change in finished product stock level;
- there are **no changes in material prices or wage rates** and no design changes in the product or method of manufacture;
- **volume is the only factor** which affects costs and revenue;
- all estimated **data relates to a given range of output** within a **given time period**.

Limitations of break-even analysis

- Some **costs cannot be identified as fixed or variable** as with semi-variable costs which have a fixed plus a variable element.
- At higher levels of output, **variable costs** such as labour (overtime), or other costs **may increase faster than output**.
- Increased purchases may attract favourable discounts such as bulk buying from suppliers, resulting in **lower material price per unit**.
- At lower levels of output the **loss of bulk discounts** on raw materials or the need to **maintain basic wages** will affect the cost per unit.
- Higher activity levels may result in some **fixed costs increasing**. For example, the purchase of machinery or the increased supervision costs may result in costs being 'stepped up'.
- To achieve higher sales levels, **prices may have to be decreased** by way of discounts to bulk customers or promotional offers.
- **Sales mix may change** with changing tastes or fashion.
- Cost may also be affected by **external influences**. The price of oil may affect production or delivery costs.
- Production may be affected by strikes.
- New technology may affect the balance between fixed and variable costs.

Despite these limitations break-even analysis (or cost-volume-profit analysis) is still a useful tool. Provided the assumptions on which the analysis is made are understood, break-even analysis provides valuable information for the guidance of management. The greatest value comes from the analysis of the underlying relationship of volume, costs and profits and not from the location of the break-even point.

Task 6

Break-even analysis is a useful tool for management. Outline the main assumptions and limitations of the break-even analysis technique.

MANAGEMENT ACCOUNTING

CHAPTER 23

Marginal costing for decision making

> **Intermediate 2 Level Outcomes:**
>
> **I2** This chapter includes material from Int 2 level Management Accounting Outcome 3
>
> ☆ **Decision-making techniques are applied accurately where a limiting factor is applied.**
>
> ☆ **Conclusions drawn on the effect of increasing fixed and/or variable costs on profit and/or break-even point are accurate.**

> **Higher Level Outcomes:**
>
> **H** This chapter includes material from Higher level Management Accounting Outcome 3
>
> ☆ **Prepare a profit maximisation statement consistent with information supplied.**
>
> ☆ **Make appropriate recommendations consistent with information supplied.**

What is marginal costing?

Marginal costing is a technique of presenting costs in a different way. Economists define **marginal cost** as the **cost of producing one additional unit** or the **variable cost per unit**. In business, however, it is usually the total variable cost involved in a project that is relevant rather than variable cost per unit. Consequently the term **marginal cost** can relate to either a single unit or the entire production.

Importance of marginal costing

The importance of marginal costing in decision making lies in the fact that in the short term the only extra costs involved in a project are the variable costs.

Marginal costing can be used to analyse a given situation and may be of valuable assistance in formulating decisions such as:

- which product is the most or least profitable?
- which product should be manufactured when there is a limiting factor?
- what will the sales need to be to earn a given profit?
- what profit will be earned for a given volume of sales?
- which, of 2 machines is the best to use from the point of view of profitability?
- what will be the effect of changing the selling price or variable cost of a product?
- should they retain or close a factory?
- should a company manufacture or make a component?
- should they accept or reject a special order?

MANAGEMENT ACCOUNTING

In the previous chapter we looked at break-even analysis and the basic knowledge gained there will be used in marginal costing.

We used the terms **variable costs** in break-even analysis and it is useful just to remind ourselves what we mean by variable costs. These are the direct cost of making the product:

- **Direct materials.** The materials used in the product.
- **Direct labour.** The labour cost of the workers who actually makes the product.
- **Direct expenses.** Expenses incurred on components which become part of the product.

Marginal costs statements

Marginal cost statements are designed to bring out the contribution, and the overall profit. For example:

- **Total contribution = Total sales income – Total variable costs**
- **Total profit = Total contribution – Fixed costs**

Example 1

Zion plc provides you with the following information and ask you to prepare a marginal cost statement for their range of products A, B and C which are manufactured in the same factory.

Factory fixed costs amounted to £30,000 for the year.

	Product A £	Product B £	Product C £
Sales Revenue	24,000	16,000	50,000
Variable Costs:			
Material	7,000	3,000	7,000
Labour	5,000	2,000	9,000
Direct expenses	2,000	1,000	4,000

STEP 1 – Decide on the layout of a marginal cost statement

The statement needs to show the **sales revenue**, **variable costs** and **contribution** for each product and in total. It must allow for the fixed costs to be deducted from the total contribution and the total profit to be shown.

	Product A		Product B		Product C		Total
	£	£	£	£	£	£	£

STEP 2 – Enter the sales revenue in the second money column for each product and enter the total revenue in the end money column

	Product A		Product B		Product C		Total
	£	£	£	£	£	£	£
Sales		24,000		16,000		50,000	90,000

continued ➤

Example 1   continued

STEP 3 – Enter the individual variable costs in the first column and totals in the end column

	Product A		Product B		Product C		Totals
	£	£	£	£	£	£	£
Sales		24,000	16,000			50,000	90,000
Less Variable costs							
● **Material**	7,000		3,000		7,000		
● **Labour**	5,000		2,000		9,000		
● **Direct expenses**	2,000		1,000		4,000		
Total variable costs		14,000		6,000		20,000	40,000

STEP 4 – Calculate the contribution

Contribution = Sales revenue – Variable costs

	Product A		Product B		Product C		Totals
	£	£	£	£	£	£	£
Sales		24,000		16,000		50,000	90,000
Less Variable costs							
● Material	7,000		3,000		7,000		
● Labour	5,000		2,000		9,000		
● Direct expenses	2,000		1,000		4,000		
Total Variable costs		14,000		6,000		20,000	40,000
Total Contribution		10,000		10,000		30,000	50,000

STEP 5 – Enter fixed costs in the end money column

	Product A		Product B		Product C		Totals
	£	£	£	£	£	£	£
Sales		24,000		16,000		50,000	90,000
Less Variable Costs							
● Material	7,000		3,000		7,000		
● Labour	5,000		2,000		9,000		
● Direct expenses	2,000		1,000		4,000		
Total Variable costs		14,000		6,000		20,000	40,000
Total Contribution		10,000		10,000		30,000	50,000
***Less* Fixed costs**							30,000

continued ➣

Example 1 continued

STEP 6 – Calculate the profit

Profit = Total contribution – Total fixed costs

	Product A		Product B		Product C		Totals
	£	£	£	£	£	£	£
Sales		24,000		16,000		50,000	90,000
Less Variable Costs							
• Material	7,000		3,000		7,000		
• Labour	5,000		2,000		9,000		
• Direct expenses	2,000		1,000		4,000		
Total Variable costs		14,000		6,000		20,000	40,000
Total Contribution		10,000		10,000		30,000	50,000
Less Fixed costs							30,000
Total Profit							**20,000**

In many questions using the marginal costing technique you will be required to prepare marginal cost statements.

Task 1

Smith plc manufactures five different products, A, B, C, D and E in their Bathgate factory. Calculate the total contribution for each of the products from the following information:

PRODUCTS	A	B	C	D	E
	£	£	£	£	£
Sales	50,000	25,000	250,000	300,000	75,000
Variable costs	30,000	12,250	125,000	180,000	37,500

If fixed costs are £100,000 what will be the total profit earned be from the five products?

Task 2

From the following information prepare a marginal cost statement for Jones plc.

Product	A	B	C	D	E
	£	£	£	£	£
Sales	150,000	125,000	850,000	600,000	175,000
Variable costs:					
• Direct material	55,000	20,000	350,000	200,000	75,000
• Direct labour	45,000	50,000	220,000	305,000	40,000
Variable overheads	10,000	20,000	100,000	20,000	20,000

Fixed costs amounted to £250,000 per annum.

Example 2

In this example, we are given the number of units sold of each product, the unit sales value, unit variable costs for each individual variable cost. Before preparing the marginal cost statement you will need to calculate the individual total revenues and costs for each element.

The following data relates to three products S, T and U produced by a manufacturer.

Unit Data	S	T	U
Selling price	£10.00	£25.00	£40.00
Variable costs:			
• Direct material	£4.00	£12.00	£12.00
• Direct labour	£2.00	£12.00	£10.00
• Direct expenses	£0.50	£2.00	£6.00
Sales Volume (units)	20,000	5,000	10,000

Fixed costs for the factory are £165,000.

STEP 1 – Set up the columns for your marginal cost statement

Marginal Cost Statement				
	S £	T £	U £	Total £

continued ➤

Example 2 continued

STEP 2 – Calculate the sales revenue for each product

$$\text{Sales revenue} = \text{Selling price of S} \times \text{Sales units for S}$$
$$= \pounds10 \times 20{,}000$$
$$= \pounds200{,}000$$

Calculate the sales revenue for T and U using the formula above and enter all three figures into the marginal cost statement.

Marginal Cost Statement				
	S £	T £	U £	Total £
Sales	200,000	125,000	400,000	725,000

STEP 3 – Calculate the variable costs for each product

$$\text{Direct material for S} = \text{Material cost per unit for S} \times \text{Sales units for S}$$
$$= \pounds4 \times 20{,}000$$
$$= \pounds80{,}000$$

$$\text{Direct labour for S} = \text{Labour cost per unit for S} \times \text{Sales units for S}$$
$$= \pounds2 \text{ per unit} \times 20{,}000 \text{ units}$$
$$= \pounds40{,}000$$

$$\text{Direct expenses for S} = \text{Direct expenses cost per unit for S} \times \text{Sales units for S}$$
$$= 50\text{p per unit} \times 20{,}000$$
$$= \pounds10{,}000$$

Calculate the direct material, labour and expenses for T and U.

	S £	T £	U £	Total £
Sales	200,000	125,000	400,000	725,000
Variable costs:				
• Direct material	80,000	60,000	120,000	
• Direct labour	40,000	60,000	100,000	
• Direct expenses	10,000	10,000	60,000	
Total Variable costs	130,000	130,000	280,000	540,000

Complete the marginal cost statement.

continued ➤

Example 2 continued

STEP 4 – Calculate the total contribution for each product and the overall contribution

Marginal Cost Statement				
	S £	T £	U £	Total £
Sales	200,000	125,000	400,000	725,000
Variable costs:				
● Direct material	80,000	60,000	120,000	
● Direct labour	40,000	60,000	100,000	
● Direct expenses	10,000	10,000	60,000	
Total Variable costs	130,000	130,000	280,000	540,000
Contribution	**70,000**	**(5,000)**	**120,000**	**185,000**

From the **statement** it can be clearly seen that Product T is the least profitable of the three products producing a negative contribution. This information may be used to decide whether or not to continue to make this product.

STEP 5 – Calculate the profit and/or loss for all three products

Profit/(loss) = Total contribution – fixed costs

	S £	T £	U £	Total £
Sales	200,000	125,000	400,000	725,000
Variable costs:				
● Direct material	80,000	60,000	120,000	
● Direct labour	40,000	60,000	100,000	
● Direct expenses	10,000	10,000	60,000	
Total Variable costs	130,000	130,000	280,000	540,000
Contribution	70,000	(5,000)	120,000	185,000
Less Fixed costs				165,000
Profit				20,000

Management will be disappointed with these results and will wish to carry out an investigation as to how these figures can be improved.

Task 3

Easdale Enterprises plc produce three products A, B and C in their factory. From the following information prepare the marginal cost statement for the period January to June Year 3.

Unit information:

Products	A £	B £	C £
Selling price	100	150	200
Variable costs:			
• Direct material	20	40	60
• Direct labour	10	15	40
• Direct expenses	5	10	20
Sales units	7,000	6,000	4,000

Fixed costs for the period amount to £350,000.

Contribution per unit

The term **contribution** may relate to the contribution from the **whole project** or the contribution from **one unit**. Contribution will be the same at all given levels of activity because in the short-term the selling price and the variable cost of a unit will not alter.

Often in marginal costing and decision making you will be working with unit figures to calculate the contribution per unit.

Contribution per unit = **Sales price** per unit – **Variable costs** per unit

Example 3

The Statement below shows the unit contribution for the three products A, B and C.

	Project A		Project B		Project C	
	£	£	£	£	£	£
Sales		24		26		25
Variable costs:						
• Direct material	7		3		2	
• Direct labour	5		2		9	
• Direct expenses	2	14	1	6	4	15
Contribution		£10		£20		£10

continued ➤

Example 3 continued

For each product, the contribution is calculated by subtracting the total variable costs from the sales, so the contribution for Product A is:

Contribution A = £24 – £14 = £10

and similarly for Products B and C.

Task 4

Calculate the contribution per unit for each of the following products:

Unit Information:

Products	A £	B £	C £	D £	E £
Selling price	5	25	250	250	75
Variable costs: • Direct material • Direct labour • Direct expenses	1 1 1	6 4 2	60 30 35	100 50 30	20 10 7

Understanding contribution

Contribution is probably the most important word in decision-making terminology. When making a short-term decision between several alternatives the only relevant figures are the **variable costs** and the **income** of **each alternative**, as the **fixed costs** are the same, whichever alternative is selected.

The **difference** between the **income** and the **variable cost** – the **contribution** – measures the net gain to the business that will arise from selecting that alternative which gives the greatest contribution. Consequently the **profits** of the business **are maximised** by selecting the alternative that gives the **greatest contribution**. This principle is the basis for many decisions, but it must be qualified in two respects:

* Fixed costs must not alter. (In short-term decisions this qualification usually holds)
* No key factors are involved.

Contribution and profitability

Many people worry about the total disregard of the fixed costs in marginal costing and decision making. Essentially fixed costs represent an unalterable flow of money out of the business. To counter this outflow the business must find a project that brings into a business the maximum contribution. Usually, in business, there will be a number of projects all in operation at one time. Their combined contributions will be well in excess of the fixed cost. The difference is the profit to the business.

The essential point to note, however, is that when one must choose between a number of alternatives, the alternative which gives the **largest contribution** must **increase** the **profit most**. **Contribution** is a **measure of profitability**.

More about the Profit/Volume ratio

In the previous chapter we looked at how we can use the P/V ratio to calculate the contribution for any given sales revenue. Sales and contribution are in direct proportion to each other. If sales are increased by 20% so the contribution will increase by 20%.

Example 4

Chippin & Dale plc manufacture reproduction furniture. The following information relates to their Regency Range of chairs:

	Unit Price	10 Chairs	12 Chairs	% increase
Sales	£250	£2,500	£3,000	20%
Variable costs	£150	£1,500	£1,800	20%
Contribution	**£100**	**£1,000**	**£1,200**	**20%**

The increase in the output by two chairs from 10 to 12 shows a production increase of 20%. Sales revenue, variable costs and contribution have also increased by 20%.

The percentage increase in sales and contribution can be clearly seen. Since sales and contribution are always in direct proportion, then dividing one by the other will always give the same figure, so from the table above:

$$\text{P/V Ratio} = \frac{\text{Contribution}}{\text{Sales}}$$

Unit Price	10 chairs	12 Chairs
20	1,000	1,2000
50	2,500	3,000

All three figures cancel down to ⅖. You have already calculated this ratio as a percentage.

$$\text{P/V Ratio} = \frac{20 \times 100}{50}$$

$$= 40\%$$

Task 5

Calculate the P/V ratio from the following products:

Products	A	B	C	D	E
Sales	10,000	12,000	15,000	30,000	25,000
Variable costs	8,000	6,000	10,000	15,000	10,000

Contribution for any given sales revenue

The P/V ratio is useful because it enables the contribution to be calculated quickly for any given sales revenue figure:

Contribution = Sales × P/V ratio

Task 6

For Chippin & Dale calculate the contribution for the following sales levels using the P/V ratio of ⅖ calculated in Example 1.

Sales Revenue
£10,000
£30,000
£150,000
£50,000
£160,000

Fixed costs amount to £200,000 for the chairs

Calculation of sales break-even point using P/V ratio

In addition to calculating profit, the P/V ratio can be used to calculate the sales at break-even point when only the fixed costs are known.

Example 5

Micro plc's fixed costs for their Aberdeen factory amount to £100,000. Their P/V ratio for the product produced there is 25% or ¼. The manager wishes to know what sales he needs to break-even.

The formula used to calculate this is:

$$\text{Sales at break-even} = \text{Fixed costs} \times \frac{1}{\text{P/V ratio}}$$

$$= \frac{£100,000 \times 100\%}{25\%}$$

$$= £400,000$$

MANAGEMENT ACCOUNTING

Task 7

Calculate sales at break-even from the following information:

Fixed costs	P/V ratio
£20,000	⅖ or 40%
£50,000	⅕ or 20%
£90,000	⅓ or 50%
£80,000	¼ or 25%
£60,000	⅛ of 12.5%

Summary of break-even and marginal costing formulae

Using the break-even technique and marginal costing we can now build up a series of formulae which link **total costs**, **variable costs**, **fixed costs**, **break-even** points and **profits** with the volume of activity:

	Formulae
Total costs =	Fixed costs + variable costs
Contribution =	Sales – Variable costs
Profit =	Contribution – Fixed costs
Break-even point in units =	$\dfrac{\text{Fixed costs}}{\text{Contribution per unit}}$
Break-even point in £ Sales =	Break-even units × Selling price per unit
Total contribution =	Number of units × Contribution per unit
Profit =	Number of units × Contribution per unit – Fixed costs
Sales at break-even =	Fixed costs × $\dfrac{1}{\text{P/V ratio}}$
P/V ratio =	$\dfrac{\text{Contribution}}{\text{Sales}}$

These formulae will be used as we look at marginal cost applications.

Marginal cost applications

Limiting factor and profit maximisation

There is always something which prevents an enterprise from achieving an unlimited profit. Usually this is the sales quantity when the enterprise cannot sell all that it can produce.

However sometimes an enterprise could sell more but they cannot actually produce the units. Factors which limit output are scarcity of materials, shortage of labour, and limited machine capacity. Such a factor is called a **limiting** or **key factor**.

If a limiting factor is operating, it is important that the enterprise makes as much profit as it can each time it uses up one of the scarce units of key factor.

Since fixed costs do not alter, this means the enterprise needs to maximise the contribution per unit of limiting factor.

Example 6

Moncrieff plc makes products to customer's specific requirements. They have been asked to quote for three separate jobs which use ingredients X. Materials of ingredient X are limited. Moncrieff plc have sufficient material to complete two of the jobs. Therefore, a choice must be made as to which two jobs should be undertaken.

The following information is available for each job.

	Job A	Job B	Job C
Selling price	£3,000	£2,000	£2,800
Less Variable costs	£1,000	£1,200	£1,000
Tonnes required	4	1	3

STEP 1 – Calculate the contribution from each job

Contribution = Sales price – Variable costs

	Job A	Job B	Job C
Selling price	**£3,000**	**£2,000**	**£2,800**
***Less* Variable costs**	**£1,000**	**£1,200**	**£1,000**
Contribution	**£2,000**	**£800**	**£1,800**

Looking at contribution alone Job A appears to be the most profitable, followed by Job C then Job B. However, contribution per unit does not take into account the limiting factor of material available.

STEP 2 – Calculate the contribution per tonne (the unit of limiting factor)

$$\text{Contribution per unit of limiting factor} = \frac{\text{Contribution}}{\text{Tonnes required}}$$

	Job A	Job B	Job C
Contribution	£2,000	£800	£1,800
Tonnes required	4	1	3
Contribution per tonne	£500	£800	£600

The contribution per tonne indicates that the jobs should be undertaken in a different order from that suggested by the contribution calculations shown above.

continued ➤

Example 6 continued

STEP 3 – Rank the jobs in the order in which they should be produced

Where a limiting factor applies you will be asked to state the order in which jobs or products should be manufactured in order to maximise profits. This is known as **ranking**.

From the contribution per tonne Job B will be the most profitable followed by Job C then finally Job A. B and C will bring in higher contributions of £800 and £600 per tonne compared with £500 from Job A.

Ranking the order of production:

	Job A	Job B	Job C
Contribution per tonne	£500	£800	£600
Order of production	**(3)**	**(1)**	**(2)**

The next step would be to prepare a marginal cost statement for the two jobs undertaken. Often this is referred to as preparing a **profit maximisation statement**.

Example 7

Mitchell plc manufactures three products, Super and Deluxe and Elegance, on the same machine. Machine hours are limited to 80,000 hours per annum. Fixed costs are £180,000 per annum. Demand for each product is such that they estimate they can sell the following quantities:

	Super	Deluxe	Elegance
Sales units	20,000	6,000	5,000

The following unit information is available for each product:

	Super	Deluxe	Elegance
Selling price	£25	£40	£50
Variable costs	£10	£20	£30
Machine hours	2	5	4

You are required to calculate:

a) The contribution per unit for each product
b) The contribution per machine hour.
c) The order of production to maximise profits.
d) The number of units of each product which can be made.
e) Prepare a marginal cost statement to show the maximum profit to be made.
f) Calculate the change in profit if the sales mix requires that 5,000 units of Deluxe must be made and sold.

continued ➤

Example 7 continued

STEP 1 – Calculate the contribution per unit for each product

	Super	Deluxe	Elegance
Selling price	£25	£40	£50
Variable costs	£10	£20	£30
Contribution per unit	£15	£20	£20

STEP 2 – Calculate the contribution per machine hour (the limiting factor) and rank in order of production

	Super	Deluxe	Elegance
Contribution per unit	£15	£20	£20
Machine hours	2	5	4
Contribution per machine hour	£7.50	£4	£5
Order of production	(1)	(3)	(2)

Where a limiting factor applies it is likely that the enterprise will not be able to make all of the units it can sell. You therefore need to calculate the number of hours available to each product.

Normally you will be able to produce all of two of the products but only some of the third product. It is helpful to use a table to set out your calculations. Look at the example below.

STEP 3 – Set up a table to show the calculation of hours allocated to each product

Enter the products into your table in the order of production, along with the hours per unit required for each product.

			Maximum hours available =	80,000
Product	Hours per unit	Unit sales	Hours required	Hours left
Super	2			
Elegance	4			
Deluxe	5			

STEP 4 – Calculate the number of hours required for the maximum sales of Super of 20,000 units

Super was ranked first for production. The maximum hours required for Super are:

Maximum hours for Super = 20,000 units × 2 hours
= 40,000 hours.

continued ➤

Example 7 continued

The number of hours available is 80,000. We need 40,000 for Super, so we can produce all the units of Super.

Enter the hours into the table and calculate the hours left for production of the other two products.

			Maximum hours available =	**80,000**
Product	Hours per unit	Unit sales	Hours required	Hours left
Super	**2**	**20,000**	**40,000**	**40,000**
Elegance	4			
Deluxe	5			

STEP 5 – Calculate the hours required for the number of units we are going to make of Elegance

The next product to be made is Elegance. We can sell 5,000 units of this product.

$$\text{Maximum hours for Elegance} = 5,000 \text{ units} \times 4 \text{ hours}$$
$$= 20,000 \text{ hours}$$

Look at the number of hours left and consider whether you have sufficient hours available for this product. There are 40,000 hours are left, and we need 20,000 for Elegance, so we can produce all of Elegance.

			Maximum hours available =	**80,000**
Product	Hours per unit	Unit sales	Hours required	Hours left
Super	2	20,000	40,000	40,000
Elegance	**4**	**5,000**	**20,000**	**20,000**
Deluxe	5			

STEP 6 – Calculate the number of units which can be made of Deluxe

We can sell 6,000 units of Deluxe, but can we make them all? Calculate the hours required to make 6,000 units of Deluxe:

$$\text{Maximum hours for Deluxe} = \text{Units} \times \text{hours per unit}$$
$$= 6,000 \times 5 \text{ hours}$$
$$= 30,000 \text{ hours}$$

There are only 20,000 hours available for production, so we cannot make all of Deluxe. The number of units of Deluxe which can be produced is calculated as follows:

$$\text{Number of units} = \text{Hours available} \div \text{hours per unit}$$
$$= 20,000 \text{ hours left} \div 5 \text{ hours per unit}$$
$$= 4,000 \text{ units}$$

continued ➤

Example 7 continued

This information is entered in the hours and production table:

			Maximum hours available =	**80,000**
Product	Hours per unit	Unit sales	Hours required	Hours left
Super	2	20,000	40,000	40,000
Elegance	4	5,000	20,000	20,000
Deluxe	5	**4,000**	**20,000**	nil

STEP 7 – Prepare a profit maximisation statement

Calculate the total contribution from each product.

Total contribution = Units produced × Contribution per unit.

PROFIT MAXIMISATION STATEMENT				
	Super	**Deluxe**	**Elegance**	**Total**
Production units	20,000	4,000	5,000	
Contribution per unit	£15	£20	£20	
Total contribution	£300,000	£80,000	£100,000	£480,000
Less **Fixed costs**				£180,000
Maximum profit				£300,000

Sometimes it is necessary to produce a minimum number of each unit. This will affect the maximum profit the enterprise can make.

STEP 8 – Calculate the change in profits if 5,000 units of Deluxe must be made and sold

Production of Deluxe must increase by 1,000 units.

The hours required for the extra units of Deluxe means that we cannot product all units of the second most profitable product Elegance.

Hours required for 1,000 units of Deluxe = 1,000 units × 5 hours
= 5,000 hours

Additional contribution from Deluxe = Additional hours × Contribution per hour
= 5,000 × £4
= £20,000

Production hours lost from Elegance = 5,000

Loss in contribution from Elegance = Hours lost × Contribution per hour
= 5,000 × £5
= £25,000

continued ➤

Example 7 continued

Calculate the reduction in contribution:

Lost contribution from Elegance	£25,000
Increased contribution from Deluxe	£20,000
Reduction in contribution and profit	£5,000

Any reduction in contribution will result in a reduction in overall profits.

Change in Profits Statement:

Original profit	£300,000
Less reduction in contribution	£5,000
Decrease in profit	£295,000

Now do Worksheet 23.1

Accept or reject a special contract (short-term tactical decision)

One type of decision which often has to be made is whether or not to accept a special contract under which units will be sold below their normal selling price. In such circumstances the contribution is the relevant figure, since the whole of any contribution must be extra profit if the enterprise is over the break-even point, or a reduction of the loss if it is below the break-even point. Either way the enterprise is better off by the amount of the contribution.

But there are two important qualifications to the above:

- It is assumed that accepting the contract **will not** affect normal sales. Nothing is gained from selling units at £4 which otherwise would be sold at £5.
- It is also assumed that nothing better is likely to come along. If a business fills its orders with many low-contribution contracts and then has to turn away high-contribution contracts it is not making the best decision. Judging whether or not anything better is likely to come along is the responsibility of the management.

Example 8

Nilcal plc manufactures and sells a slimming drink to their customers by mail order at 80p per can. Variable costs are 30p per can and fixed costs are £40,000 per month.

The factory is currently working at 80% of capacity to produce 400,000 cans per month. Nilcal have an opportunity to utilise their surplus capacity by accepting an order from Dirmar plc, a chain of low price chemists, for 100,000 cans. The price per can to Dirmar plc would be 60p. Dirmar plc will market the product as an own label brand.

Advise the Board of Directors whether they should accept or reject this contract.

What other factors should Nilcal take into consideration before accepting or rejecting this order?

continued ➤

MANAGEMENT ACCOUNTING

Example 8 continued

STEP 1 – Calculate the contribution per unit for normal sales and special order

	Without special order	From special order
Selling price	80p	60p
Less **Variable costs**	30p	30p
Contribution per unit	50p	30p

STEP 2 – Calculate total contribution from normal and special order

Total contribution = Sales units × contribution per unit

Normal production contribution = 400,000 × 50p
= £200,000

Special order contributions = 100,000 × 30p
= £30,000

	Without special order	From special order
Sales units	200,000	100,000
Total Contribution	£200,000	£30,000

Accepting the special order would increase the contribution and profit of the enterprise by £30,000.

STEP 3 – Decided whether to accept the special order

From the above figures it looks as though it would be a good move for Nilcal to accept the special order. However, in addition to contribution, Nilcal plc will need to consider the following and balance the increased contribution against a number of factors:

- Whether they can sell more of their own product at 80p per can in the future.

- The effect on their own sales if their existing customers switch to Dirmar's own label brand because it is cheaper.

- Whether they are they likely to increase their sales of the higher contribution product?

- What happens if Dirmar's launch of their own brand label is successful and they want to order more cans. Will Nilcal fulfil the increased demand without affecting their production and sales of the their own higher contribution cans?

- Whether Nilcal are in a position to increase production without subsequent increased fixed costs?

- Accepting this order from Dirmar is it more likely that Dirmar will continue to trade with Nilcal?

Nilcal will make the decision after considering all these factors.

Retain or close a factory, or continue with or drop a product

Marginal costing can be used to help an enterprise to decide whether to keep or drop a product which appears to be making a loss or to keep a factory open when it is losing money.

You will often be asked to prepare the marginal costing statement for either the products or the factories and then to make a decision.

Example 9

Byo plc manufactures three products, in three different factories, for which the following profit statement has been produced:

BYO PLC PROFIT STATEMENT				
Product	A	B	C	Total
Sales	32,000	50,000	45,000	127,000
Variable costs	24,000	25,000	22,000	71,000
Contribution	8,000	25,000	23,000	56,000
Less Fixed costs	10,000	12,000	11,000	33,000
Profit/(Loss)	(2,000)	13,000	12,000	23,000

Factory A shows an operating loss of £2,000. The Board of Directors must do something to reduce this loss. In making the decision, they must consider whether:

- another product can be made in factory A which could increase the contribution of the whole organisation;

- to sell the factory and invest in new machinery at the other plants;

- the product produced in Factory A is connected to products produced in B and C and if discontinued will it affect their sales.

Make or buy decisions

Make or buy decisions arise when the product being manufactured has a component part that can either be made within the factory or bought from an outside supplier.

It appears that since the only extra cost to make the part is the variable cost, then the amount by which it falls below the purchase price of the component is the saving that arises.

However, this is deceptive because consideration must be given to the value of the other work which would not be completed because the component was being made instead of being purchased.

This is necessary since if making the part involves putting aside other work the business will lose the contribution this work would have earned. Such a loss must be added to the marginal cost of the part.

In economics such a cost is called an **opportunity cost**. This is a cost that is represented not by money being paid out, but by the loss in income that would otherwise have been obtained.

Therefore when an enterprise is faced with a make or buy decision it should compare the supplier's price with the variable cost of making the component, **plus** the loss of contribution from any displaced work.

Example 10

Product Exe takes 20 hours to process on machine Z. It has a selling price of £100 and a variable cost of £60. Product Wye (a component part of Exe) could be made on machine Z in 3 hours for a marginal cost of £5. The supplier's price is £10.

The firm is currently working at full capacity. Should the firm make or buy Wye?

STEP – 1 Calculate the contribution and contribution per hour from Exe

Selling price	£100
Less Variable costs	£60
Contribution per unit	£40

Contribution per hour from Exe = Contribution per unit ÷ number of hours
= £40 ÷ 20 hours
= £2 per hour

This means that if we produce Wye we will be losing £2 per hour from Exe.

STEP 2 – Calculate cost of making Wye

If we make Wye, then we lose production time from Exe and consequently the contribution earned by Exe will be reduced.

Cost of making Wye:

Variable cost	£5
Plus Loss in contribution from Exe = £2 × 3 hours =	£6
Total cost of making Wye	£11

STEP 3 – Compare the cost of purchasing Wye with making Wye

Cost of making Wye	£11
Cost of purchasing Wye	£10

It is therefore £1 cheaper to continue to purchase Wye than to use factory capacity to make it.

  Now do Worksheets 23.2, 23.3 and 23.4

Budgetary control and preparation of budgets

Intermediate 2 Level Outcomes:

This chapter includes material from Int 2 level Management Accounting Outcome 4

☆ **Explain the importance of budgetary control and describe the techniques available.**

☆ **Prepare a cash budget for a three month period.**

☆ **Cash and credit sales income is correctly calculated and applied to the correct month.**

☆ **Other incomes are correctly dealt with and applied to the correct month.**

☆ **Payments to creditors are correctly calculated and charged to the appropriate month**

☆ **Other payments are correctly calculated and charged to the appropriate month.**

☆ **Closing balance is correctly calculated and transferred to the correct month.**

Higher Level Outcomes:

This chapter includes material from Higher level Management Accounting Outcome 4

☆ **Evaluate the usefulness of budgeting as a means of planning and control.**

☆ **Complete a partially prepared sales or production budget.**

☆ **Complete a partially prepared cash budget.**

Why budgeting is important

Every business enterprise needs to plan to achieve its goals. One of the first plans an enterprise may make is to estimate its potential sales and from that, its income and expenditure for a period. It will do this using a **budget**.

A **budget** is a **plan**, expressed in quantities, and then converted to **monetary values**. The budget will be prepared for a particular period of time and will show the expected incomes and expenditures.

A budget may be prepared for the whole business, a department or for specific functions such as cash, sales or production. Budgets are used to plan, co-ordinate and control the activities of an enterprise.

Using budgetary control an enterprise can:

- plan its activity level for all areas of the business – production, labour, sales, plant etc;
- review proposed budgets to identify areas where targets may not be met;

- take action and revise proposed budgets;
- identify staff responsible for each area of the budget;
- set clear targets for staff.

During the budget period an enterprise will:

- compare actual performance against budgeted performance;
- analyse any variances (differences between budget and actual performance);
- take corrective action.

When preparing the budgets management must be careful to ensure that they are not too easy or difficult to achieve. This is referred to as the **tightness** of the budget.

A **'tight' budget** is one which would generally be achieved only under the most favourable conditions and is difficult to achieve. A **'loose' budget** is one which can be easily achieved but will result in managers becoming complacent.

If budgets are too tight staff will become demotivated and performance will fall as they know they cannot achieve them. If budgets are too loose inefficiencies will occur.

Steps in preparing a budget

The essentials of budget preparation are clear thinking and common sense. A Budget Committee is usually given the responsibility for the preparation of a the budget.

The five steps in preparing a budget are:

1 **Prepare a forecast**. A forecast is a prediction of what will happen as a result of a given set of circumstances.

2 **Determine enterprise policy** (such as product range, normal working hours, channels of distribution, stocks, research and development, investments etc)

3 **Calculate requirements** in terms of quantities required to meet the forecasts and policies (e.g. staff, machines, material) and convert quantities to money values. This results in the **initial budget**.

4 **Review the forecast**, policies or budget, or both, until an acceptable budget emerges.

5 **Accept the budget**. This then becomes the **Master Budget** and as such becomes an executive order.

Always remember that in budget preparation it is **quantities** which are budgeted, not monetary figures. The money is simply a way of expressing quantities in a common form.

Budget period

A **budget period** is the period of time for which a budget is prepared and employed. Several factors will influence the budget period. For example, if there is a natural cycle time (usually one year for trading) then it is logical to use the cycle time as the budget period. The budget periods for the main budgets are usually as follows:

- Trading budget - one year.
- Capital budget - several years.
- Research and development budget - several years.

MANAGEMENT ACCOUNTING

Budgets and financial needs

Budgets will show what sort of financing is going to be needed. The **operating budgets** will show the need for **short-term finance**, while the **capital budget** will show the need for **long-term finance**.

Operating budgets

An **operating budget** is one that sets out the planned requirements for the day-to-day operations of an enterprise over the normal trading period, usually one year.

It details the sales and expenditure plans. Capital receipts and expenditure relevant to the budget period are included but these are extracts from the actual capital budget.

There is always some factor which will prevent an enterprise from expanding its production and sales. This is called the **principal budget factor**. This factor is usually sales. The enterprise cannot sell all it can produce. There are other possible factors which may limit enterprise activity - shortage of machinery, skilled labour, cash, space, materials or management ability.

This principal budget factor must be considered before any other factors can be budgeted. Part of the art of management is to make plans so that the use of the principal budget factor is maximised.

The principal budget factor does not remain constant. If the limitations imposed by one factor are removed then another will take its place, becoming the principal budget factor. In practice, it is important that an enterprise is aware when the principal budget factor is about to change.

Functional budgets

Functional budgets are a series of inter-related budgets, prepared for specific departments or activities within the organisation by the departmental managers.

Budget	Features
Sales units and revenue	<ul><li>this is thought to be the most important budget functional budget;</li><li>usually the first, and most difficult, budget to prepare;</li><li>based on estimated customer demand, reports from sales force, market research and past performance;</li><li>prepared first in terms of estimated sales units and then converted to sales revenues;</li><li>sales manager is responsible for the preparation of this budget;</li><li>budget may be classified according to products, salesmen, customers, territories and periods.</li></ul>

Budget	Features
Production units and Production costs	<ul><li>prepared by the production manager and takes account of material, labour and other direct expenses required to meet sales output;</li><li>based on the sales budget, production capacity and budgeted stock requirements;</li><li>prepared in production units taking account of manufacturing capacity and budget period;</li><li>production budget may show that the firm cannot produce the anticipated sales units and result in the sales budget being revised;</li><li>production units will be converted into costs for the production cost budget;</li><li>the buyer in the purchases department will use this budget to plan and source material required for production levels.</li></ul>
Plant utilisation	<ul><li>identifies how much machine time will be required to meet production levels;</li><li>gives details of machine time in each manufacturing department;</li><li>highlights periods of over- or under-use of machines;</li><li>allows for planned overtime, change in working practices.</li></ul>
Capital expenditure	<ul><li>shows details of any anticipated capital expenditure for the period;</li><li>takes account of requests from various departments including production for new capital equipment.</li></ul>
Selling and distribution	<ul><li>based on the sales budget and estimates the cost of selling the budgeted sales.</li></ul>
Cash	<ul><li>very important budget for the enterprise and prepared from the information contained in the other functional budgets;</li><li>shows anticipated receipts and payment for the budget period;</li><li>highlights periods of cash surplus or shortages;</li><li>allows for bank overdraft or loans to be arranged or for short term investments to be made.</li></ul>

Once all the budgets have been compiled they are grouped together in the **Budgeted Profit and Loss Account** and **Balance Sheet** and they become the **Master Budget**. This Master Budget may be revised several times until an overall satisfactory budget is produced. At that point it ceases to be a plan and becomes an **executive order**. Departmental managers will be striving to achieve the targets set in this Master Budget throughout the budget period.

Budget administration

The preparation of annual budgets is a difficult and sometimes stressful job. An enterprise requires a good organised structure to ensure that budgets are completed by the dates set. There are a number of components required for successful budget administration:

Component	Features
Budget Committee	• consists of Chief Executive, Budget Officer and Departmental Managers; • the role is to oversee and co-ordinate the preparation of the budget.

Budget Officer	• senior management accountant responsible for ensuring that:
	  • budget committee instructions are passed onto appropriate departments;
	  • a **budget timetable** is kept to by managers;
	  • the **budget committee** receive appropriate data when required;
	  • the work of the committee is co-ordinated;
	  • administrative tasks relating to budget are carried out on time.

Budget Timetable	• prepared to ensure that all the budgets are prepared on time. • smaller budgets must meet deadlines to allow Master Budget to be prepared.
Budget Manual	• sets out the duties and responsibilities of those preparing the budgets; • includes copies of all forms and records which will be used in budget preparation; • provides the information necessary to ensure the budget is prepared on time.

Any delay in issuing the Master Budget will have a detrimental affect on the budget period and the performance of the enterprise. If the budget is not completed until after the start of the budget period its effectiveness will be reduced and may even result in a project not being started.

Fixed and flexible budgets

A **fixed budget** is one which is designed to remain **unchanged regardless of the volume** of output or turnover achieved.

A **flexible budget** is one designed to **adjust the cost levels to suit the level of activity** actually achieved. A flexible budget recognises the differences in behaviour between fixed and variable costs in relation to output or turnover. The flexible budget is based on the actual output at standard costs and is compared to actual cost of actual output.

Task 1

1 What is a budget?

2 What are the benefits to an enterprise of preparing budgets?

3 Explain the difference between a forecast and a budget.

4 List the five steps to be followed when preparing a budget.

5 Explain the difference between functional and operating budgets.

6 Name three functional budgets.

7 What is a principal budget factor and why it important?

8 What is the master budget and why is it important?

9 Explain the difference between fixed and flexible budgets.

continued ➤

10 Explain the purpose of the following:

a) Budget Committee

b) Budget Officer

c) Budget timetable

d) Budget manual

Preparation of the cash budget

The **cash budget** is probably one of the most important budgets prepared by an enterprise. The cash budget is used to calculate the amount of estimated cash available from sales and other incomes and the total estimated expenditure each month.

Any surplus or deficit of cash can be planned for, either by the enterprise deciding on short term investments or by arranging an overdraft or loan to cover any of the deficits.

The firm can also plan for any expenditure on capital equipment – purchase of machinery and any other substantial payments such as debenture interest or shareholders dividends.

The cash budget is prepared each month divided into four separate sections:

1 Opening balance: This figure represents the cash and bank in hand at the start of the month.

2 *Add* income: All monies received during the month are shown. For example, income from sales, sale of assets, interest received etc. You need to calculate the total income received each month. Note that this **will not** include the opening balance.

3 *Less* Expenditure: This section details all the monies actually spent during the month. For example cash paid to creditors for materials, expenses for heating and lighting, payment of debenture interest, or dividends, purchases of assets etc. The total expenses are then calculated.

4 Closing balance: This represents the amount of cash/bank the enterprise has at the end of the budget period, usually one month.

The closing balance is calculated as follows:

Closing balance = (Opening balance + Total income) – Total expenditure

The closing balance at the end of one month is the opening balance at the start of the next month.

Example 1 Preparing a cash budget

Arch plc provide you with the following information for the six month period January – June Year 1:

a   Opening balance on 1 March was £6,000.

b   Selling price per unit will be: Credit customers £18 per unit and Cash customers £17.10.

continued ➤

Example 1 Preparing a cash budget continued

c Credit customers pay one month after delivery.

d Estimated sales units:

	January	February	March	April	May	June
Credit sales	4,500	4,320	4,950	5,400	4,860	5,850
Cash sales	500	480	550	600	540	650

e Estimated production to meet sales demand will be:

January	February	March	April	May	June
4,410	4,950	5,400	4,960	5,850	4,860

f Material costs will be £8 per unit payable in the month after purchase.

g In May Arch plc estimate that they will receive £2,000 interest from investments.

h Labour costs are £3 per unit and employees are paid in the month of production.

i Variable overheads are £1 per unit and are paid in the month following production.

j Monthly fixed costs amount to £6,000. Included in the fixed costs is depreciation of £1,500.

k Debenture interest of £8,000 is due to be paid in April.

l Shareholder's dividends of £3,000 are due to be paid in May.

m Arch plc plan to purchase new machinery costing £200,000 in March. This will be paid for in four monthly instalments starting in April.

You are asked to prepare the cash budget for the months of March, April and May.

STEP 1 – Prepare the cash budget layout

You have been given information for sales and production figures relating to six months, but you have only been asked to prepare the budget for a three month period.

Arch plc CASH BUDGET FOR 3 MONTH PERIOD MARCH – MAY			
	£	£	£
	March	April	May

continued ➤

Example 1 Preparing a cash budget continued

STEP 2 – Enter the opening balance into the cash budget (Note a)

Once entered add the heading for the income section.

Arch plc CASH BUDGET FOR 3 MONTH PERIOD MARCH - MAY			
	£	£	£
	March	April	May
Opening balance	**6,000**		
Add Income			

STEP 3 – Calculate cash sales revenue for March, April and May (Notes b and d)

Cash sales = Unit selling price × monthly sales units

Unit sales and cash received	March	April	May
Cash sales (units)	550	600	540
Cash price per unit	£17.10	£17.10	£17.10
Sales revenue – cash	£9,405	£10,260	£9,234

STEP 4 – Calculate credit sales revenue (Notes b and d)

The cash budget is being prepared for March, April and May. Credit customers pay one month after they have received the goods. This means that we will receive payment from our customers for goods we sold in:

- February in March
- March in April
- April in May

So, to prepare the cash budget for March to May, we need to use the credit sales figures for February to April.

Credit sales = Credit sales price × units sold

Month units sold	February	March	April
Credit sales (units)	4,320	4,950	5,400
Credit selling price	£18	£18	£18
Cash received	£77,760	£89,100	£97,200
Month cash received for credit sales	March	April	May

continued ➤

Example 1 Preparing a cash budget continued

STEP 5 – Enter the cash and credit sales revenues into the cash budget

Any other sources of income should be entered into the income section at this time. For example, Arch plc expects investment income of £2,000 in May (Note g).

Arch plc
CASH BUDGET FOR 3 MONTH PERIOD MARCH - MAY

	£	£	£
	March	April	May
Opening balance	6,000		
Add Income			
Cash sales	9,405	10,260	9,234
Credit sales	77,760	89,100	97,200
Investment income			2,000
Total income	87,165	99,360	108,434

The total income for the three months is calculated by adding together all the income figures.

STEP 6 – Calculate the expenditure during the three months and enter into the cash budget (Notes e and f)

Material costs are paid one month after being used in production. The amount is based on the **production units for the previous month**. It is important to remember that the majority of the expenditure costs will be based on the **production budget**. Enter the material cost figures into the cash budget.

Material costs = Unit purchase price × monthly production units

Production month	February	March	April
Total units produced	4,950	5,400	4,960
Cost per unit	£8	£8	£8
Cost of material	£39,600	£43,200	£39,680
Month cash paid for materials	March	April	May

continued ➤

Example 1 Preparing a cash budget continued

STEP 7 – Calculate labour costs (Notes e and h)

Labour costs are paid in the month the units are manufactured and are based on production units.

Labour cost per unit = Rate per unit × monthly production units

Production month	March	April	May
Total units produced	5,400	4,960	5,850
Cost per unit	£3	£3	£3
Total labour costs	£16,200	£14,880	£17,550

STEP 8 – Calculate variable overhead costs (Notes e and i)

Variable expenses of £1 per unit are paid in the month following production. Like materials the February variable expenses will be paid in for in March.

Production month	February	March	April
Total units produced	4,950	5,400	4,960
Variable expenses per unit	£1	£1	£1
Total variable expenses	£4,950	£5,400	£4,960

Arch plc CASH BUDGET FOR 3 MONTH PERIOD MARCH - MAY			
	£	£	£
	March	April	May
Opening balance	6,000		
Add Income			
Cash sales	9,405	10,260	9,234
Credit sales	77,760	89,100	97,200
Investment income			2,000
Total income	87,165	99,360	108,434
Less Expenditure			
Material	39,600	43,200	39,680
Labour	16,200	14,880	17,550
Variable overheads	4,950	5,400	4,960

continued ➤

Example 1 Preparing a cash budget continued

STEP 9 – Enter other estimated expenses into the cash budget (Notes j, k and l)

Fixed costs amount to £6,000 per month. However £6,000 will not be paid out each month. Included in the £6,000 is depreciation which is the reduction in the value of a fixed asset due to usage or obsolescence. No cash is paid out for depreciation, which is a 'paper transfer' and does not affect the Cash/Bank position of the enterprise.

The fixed costs actually paid by the enterprise each month is calculated in the following way (Note j):

> Fixed costs paid = Fixed costs – Depreciation charge
> $\quad\quad\quad\quad = £6,000 – £1,500$
> $\quad\quad\quad\quad = £4,500$

Each month £4,500 is paid out for overheads. This figure is entered in to the columns for March, April and May.

Amongst the other expenses there will be specific amounts for specific months and care must be taken to ensure these are entered into the correct monthly column.

Debenture interest due of £8,000 is to be paid in April and will be entered into that column (Note k).

Shareholder's dividend of £3,000 is due to be paid in May and will be entered into that column (Note l).

Arch plc CASH BUDGET FOR 3 MONTH PERIOD MARCH – MAY			
	£	£	£
	March	April	May
Opening balance	6,000		
Add Income			
Cash sales	9,405	10,260	9,234
Credit sales	77,760	89,100	97,200
Investment income	—	—	2,000
Total income	87165	99,360	108,434
Less Expenditure			
Material	39,600	43,200	39,680
Labour	16,200	14,880	17,550
Variable expenses	4,950	5,400	4,960
Fixed costs	**4,500**	**4,500**	**4,500**
Debenture Interest		**8,000**	
Shareholder's dividend			**3,000**

continued ➢

Example 1 Preparing a cash budget continued

STEP 10 – Calculate the amounts chargeable for fixed assets purchased each month (Note m).

Usually fixed asset purchases will be paid for over a period of time. In the example Arch plc are buying a new machine costing £200,000 which will be paid for over a four month period.

Monthly instalment = Total cost of machinery ÷ number of instalments
= £200,000 ÷ 4
= £50,000 per month

You need to be careful to ensure that you start the payments in the correct month. The machine is purchased in March, but they start to pay for it in April.

Arch plc CASH BUDGET FOR 3 MONTH PERIOD MARCH – MAY	£	£	£
	March	April	May
Opening balance	6,000		
Add Income			
Cash sales	9,405	10,260	9,234
Credit sales	77,760	89,100	97,200
Investment income	——	——	2,000
Total income	87,165	99,360	108,434
Less Expenditure			
Material	39,600	43,200	39,680
Labour	16,200	14,880	17,550
Variable expenses	4,950	5,400	4,960
Fixed costs	4,500	4,500	4,500
Debenture Interest		8,000	
Shareholder's dividend			3,000
Purchase of machinery	——	**50,000**	**50,000**
Total expenses	**65,250**	**125,980**	**119,690**

All the expenses have now been entered into the cash budget, and should now be totalled.

continued ➤

Example 1 Preparing a cash budget continued

STEP 11 – Calculate the closing balances

Closing balance = Opening balance + Total income – Total expenditure

This has been set out in the table below:

	March £	April £	May £
Opening balance	6,000	27,915	1,295
Add Total income	87,165	99,360	108,434
	93,165	127,275	109,729
Less Total expenditure	65,250	125,980	119,690
Closing balance	27,915	1,295	-9,961

The **closing balance** for **March** becomes the **opening balance** for **April** and is entered into the cash budget.

The closing balance for May results in a **negative balance**. This means the enterprise has **spent more** than it has **taken in**. The enterprise needs to make arrangements to cover the lack of cash either through arranging a loan, or deciding to obtain the machinery in another way. For example, it could try to lease the machine, or spread the payments over a longer period of time.

Arch plc CASH BUDGET FOR 3 MONTH PERIOD MARCH – MAY	£	£	£
	March	April	May
Opening balance	6,000	**27,915**	**1,295**
Add Income			
Cash sales	9,405	10,260	9,234
Credit sales	77,760	89,100	97,200
Investment income			2,000
Total income	87,165	99,360	108,434
Less Expenditure			
Material	39,600	43,200	39,680
Labour	16,200	14,880	17,550
Variable expenses	4,950	5,400	4,960
Fixed costs	4,500	4,500	4,500
Debenture interest		8,000	
Shareholder's dividend			3,000
Purchase of machinery		50,000	50,000
Total expenses	65,250	125,980	119,690
Closing Balance	**27,915**	**1,295**	**-9,961**

Task 2

1   Schubert plc started trading with a capital of £10,000 paid into the bank on
    1 March. From the following information prepare the cash budget for March, April,
    May and June.

	March	April	May	June
	£	£	£	£
Credit sales	1,500	1,800	2,000	2,500
Cash sales	1,500	500	600	800
Credit purchases	4,000	2,300	2,700	2,600

Notes:

a   All debtors are allowed one month's credit.
b   Creditors are paid one month after delivery.
c   On 1 April equipment was purchased for £3,000.
d   A proposed ordinary divided on £2,500 will be paid in June.
e   Wages of £300 are paid monthly.

2   Bach plc provides you with the following information and ask you to prepare their
    Cash Budget for November and December. Their cash balance on 1 November is
    £4,200.

	Sept	Oct	Nov	Dec
	£	£	£	£
Credit sales	19,500	20,800	22,000	19,500
Cash sales	5,500	5,500	6,600	4,800
Credit purchases	8,000	7,000	6,300	5,600

Notes:

a   All debtors are allowed one month's credit.
b   A motor vehicle was sold for £3,000 on 1 November.
c   Creditors are paid two month after delivery.
d   On 1 November debenture interest of £2,000 was to be paid.
e   A machine costing £10,000 was purchased in September. It is being paid for in
        five equal instalments.
f   Wages of £300 are paid monthly.
g   Monthly fixed costs including depreciation of £500 are to be £2,000.

continued ➤

3 From the following information prepare the three month cash forecast as for January- March for Verdi plc.

Projected Sales		Cost analysis of Sales per £:	
January	£16,000	Raw material	45p
February	£20,000	Wages	35p
March	£24,000	Expenses	7.5p

Notes:

a The balance at the bank on 31 December is estimated to be £2,400.
b December Sales debtors and creditors (for raw materials) were £22,000 and £9,000 respectively.
c New fixed assets will be purchased and paid for as follows:
  ● December £1,800, January £3,400, February £2,700; March £1,300.
d Wages and expenses are paid in the month in which they are incurred, while raw materials, creditors and sales debtors are settled in the succeeding month.

4 Williams plc provides you with the following information for the six month period July–December Year 1.

a Opening balance on 1 October was £12,000.
b Credit unit selling price will be £50. Cash customers pay £40.
c Credit sales account for 75% of total sales each month and customers pay two months after delivery.
d Estimated sales demand:

Sales units on:	July	Aug	Sept	Oct	Nov	Dec
Credit	7,500	7,950	8,250	9,000	8,100	9,750
Cash	2,500	2,650	2,750	3,000	2,700	3,250

e Estimated production units each month will be sufficient to meet the next months estimated sales figure.

July	Aug	Sept	Oct	Nov	Dec
10,600	11,000	12,000	10,800	13,000	12,600

Notes:

f In November Williams plc plan to sell two motor vehicles and expect to receive £10,000 for each of them.
g Material cost per unit is £15. We pay our creditors one month after the material is used in production.
h Labour costs are £8 per unit and employees are paid in the month of production.
i Variable expenses are £2 per unit and are paid in the month of production.
j Monthly fixed costs amount to £5,000. Included in the fixed costs is depreciation of £500.

continued ➤

k Debenture interest of £15,000 is due to be paid in December.

l Williams plc plan to purchase a new motor vehicle costing £50,000 in October. This will be paid for in five equal instalments starting in October

You are required to prepare the cash budget for the period October–December.

5 Mozart plc provides you with the following information for the six month period July–December Year 1.

a Opening balance on 1 October is estimated to be £8,000.

b Credit unit selling price will be £10. Cash selling price will be £9.

c Credit sales customers pay one months after delivery.

d Estimated sales demand:

Sales units on:	July	Aug	Sept	Oct	Nov	Dec
Credit	5,260	6,000	7,200	8,800	6,400	9,600
Cash	2,740	1,500	1,800	2,200	1,600	2,400

e Estimated production each month will be:

July	Aug	Sept	Oct	Nov	Dec
7,500	9,000	11,000	8,000	12,000	12,600

Notes:

f In November Mozart arranges a bank loan of £30,000.

g Interest of 5% per annum is payable on the loan. The loan interest is paid monthly starting in December.

h Material cost per unit is £3. We pay our creditors one month after delivery.

i Labour costs are £2 per unit and employees are paid in the month of production.

j Variable expenses are £1 per unit and are paid in the month of production.

k Monthly fixed costs amount to £1,000. Included in the fixed costs is depreciation of £200.

l Preference dividend of £3,000 is due to be paid in December.

m Mozart plc plan to purchase new machinery costing £40,000 in October. They will pay a deposit of £20,000 in the month of purchase and the remainder will be paid in five equal instalments starting in the month after purchase.

You are required to prepare the cash budget for the period October–December.

Sales budget

Usually the first budget prepared will be the **sales budget**, because the sales quantities often affects the preparation of the other budgets. To prepare the sales budget you will need the following information:

- Opening stock units
- Production units for each month
- Closing stock units

You may only be given either details of the opening or closing stocks. The closing stock for one month will be the opening stock for the next month.

Example 2

Alanson plc provides you with the following information for the 6 month period January to June.

Month	Production	Opening Stock	Closing Stock
January	5,000	750	800
February	5,500	800	780
March	6,000	780	920
April	8,000	920	650
May	4,800	650	700
June	5,000	700	650

To calculate the sales quantity in units:

STEP 1 – Set out the sales budget in a columnar table:

You will need one column for details and one column for each month.

SALES BUDGET FOR January to June						
	Jan	Feb	Mar	Apr	May	June

STEP 2 – Enter the opening stock balance for each month into the table

SALES BUDGET FOR January to June						
	Jan	Feb	Mar	Apr	May	June
Opening stock	750	800	780	920	650	700

STEP 3 – Calculate the total number of units available for sale

Number of units available for sale = Opening stock + Production units

SALES BUDGET FOR January to June						
	Jan	Feb	Mar	Apr	May	June
Opening stock	750	800	780	920	650	700
Add Production	5,000	5,500	6,000	8,000	4,800	5,000
	5,750	6,300	6,780	8,920	5,450	5,700

continued ➢

Example 2 continued

STEP 4 – Enter closing stock into your sales budget and calculate the sales units

Remember the closing stock for one month will be the opening stock for the next month. Closing stock for January of 800 units will be the opening stock for February of 800 units.

Deduct **closing stock** from **units available for sale**.

SALES BUDGET FOR January to June

	Jan	Feb	Mar	Apr	May	June
Opening stock	750	800	780	920	650	700
Add Production	5,000	5,500	6,000	8,000	4,800	5,000
	5,750	6,300	6,780	8,920	5,450	5,700
Less Closing stock	800	780	920	650	700	650
Sales in units	4,950	5,520	5,860	8,270	4,750	5,050

The sales units from this budget will be used to calculate the sales revenue figures and the unit selling and distribution expenses for inclusion in the cash budget.

Task 3

Calculation of sales budgets

1 From the following information prepare the sales budget for the six month period January–June for Year 1 for ABC plc:

	Jan	Feb	Mar	Apr	May	June	July
Production	5,000	2,300	4,500	6,000	3,900	4,200	6,000
Opening stock	230	450	600	390	420	500	650

2 From the following information prepare the sales budget for the six month period July December for Year 1 for DEF plc.

	July	Aug	Sept	Oct	Nov	Dec	Jan
Production	7,000	3,450	6,750	9,000	5,850	6,300	7,500
Opening stock	345	675	900	585	630	750	650

continued ➤

3 From the following information prepare the sales budget for the six month period January-June for Year 1 for GHI plc.

	Jan	Feb	Mar	Apr	May	June	July
Production	18,750	16,250	16,875	22,500	14,625	15,750	18,750
Opening stock	2,500	1,700	2,250	1,500	1,600	1,900	2,500

4 From the following information prepare the sales budget for the six month period July-December for Able plc.

	July	Aug	Sept	Oct	Nov	Dec	Jan
Production	10,000	8,000	9,500	7,500	8,000	7,600	5,400

Closing stock for each month will be 10% of the following month's sales.

5 From the following information prepare the sales budget for the six month period July-December for Beta plc.

	July	Aug	Sept	Oct	Nov	Dec	Jan
Production	11,250	9,000	10,600	8,500	12,000	11,400	8,100

Closing stock for each month will be 20% of the following month's sales.

Production budgets

The **production budget** will be prepared from the information contained in the sales budget. To prepare the production budget you will need the following information:

- Closing stock units;
- Sales units for each month;
- Opening stock units.

Example 3

Alanson plc provides you with the following information for the six month period January to June.

Month	Sales	Opening Stock	Closing Stock
January	4,000	550	600
February	6,500	600	700
March	5,000	700	820
April	7,000	820	650
May	3,800	650	750
June	4,000	750	650

continued ➤

Example 3 continued

To calculate the quantity produced during each month in units:

STEP 1 – Set out the production budget in a columnar table:

You will need one column for details and one column for each month, just as in the sales budget.

PRODUCTION BUDGET for January to June						
	Jan	Feb	Mar	Apr	May	June

STEP 2 – Enter the closing stock balance for each month into the table.

PRODUCTION BUDGET for January to June						
	Jan	Feb	Mar	Apr	May	June
Closing stock	600	700	820	650	750	650

This represents the stock produced during the month which is unsold.

STEP 3 – Calculate the total number of units produced during the month

This consists of the total of the unsold units plus the sales units.

Number of units produced = Closing stock + Sales units

PRODUCTION BUDGET for January to June						
	Jan	Feb	Mar	Apr	May	June
Closing stock	600	700	820	650	750	650
Add Sales	4,000	6,500	5,000	7,000	3,800	4,000
Units available for sale	4,600	7,200	5,820	7,650	4,550	4,650

STEP 4 – Enter opening stock into your production budget to calculate the production units

Remember the closing stock for one month will be the opening stock for the next month. Closing stock for January of 700 units will be the opening stock for February of 700 units.

Production units = Units available for sale – Opening stock

continued ➤

Example 3 continued

PRODUCTION BUDGET for January to June						
	Jan	**Feb**	**Mar**	**Apr**	**May**	**June**
Closing stock	600	700	820	650	750	650
Add Sales	4,000	6,500	5,000	7,000	3,800	4,000
Units available for sale	4,600	7,200	5,820	7,650	4,550	4,650
Less **Opening stock**	550	600	700	820	650	750
Production units	**4,050**	**6,600**	**5,120**	**6,830**	**3,900**	**3,900**

The production units from this budget will be used to calculate the material purchases, labour costs and variable overheads figures for inclusion in the cash budget.

Task 4

Calculation of production budgets

1   From the following information prepare the production budget for the six month period January–June for Year 1 for A plc.

	Jan	**Feb**	**Mar**	**Apr**	**May**	**June**	**July**
Sales	6,000	6,500	7,000	6,800	4,500	5,200	6,000
Opening stock	650	700	680	450	520	600	720

2   From the following information prepare the production budget for the six month period July December for Year 1 for B plc.

	July	**Aug**	**Sept**	**Oct**	**Nov**	**Dec**	**Jan**
Sales	9,000	9,750	10,500	10,200	6,750	7,800	9,000
Opening stock	975	1,050	1,020	675	780	900	650

3   From the following information prepare the production budget for the six month period January–June for Year 1 for C Plc.

	Jan	**Feb**	**Mar**	**Apr**	**May**	**June**	**July**
Sales	22,500	24,375	26,250	25,500	16,875	19,500	22,500
Opening stock	2,500	1,700	2,550	1,500	1,600	1,900	2,000

continued ➤

4 From the following information prepare the Production budget for the six month period July-December for D plc.

	July	Aug	Sept	Oct	Nov	Dec	Jan
Sales	13,500	14,600	15,750	15,300	10,100	11,700	13,500

Closing stock for each month will be 50% of the following month's sales.

5 From the following information prepare the production budget for the six month period July-December for E plc.

	July	Aug	Sept	Oct	Nov	Dec	Jan
Sales	20,500	21,900	23,650	22,950	15,100	17,550	20,250

Closing stock for each month will be 10% of the following month's sales

6 From the following information prepare the production budget for the six month period July-December for F plc.

	July	Aug	Sept	Oct	Nov	Dec	Jan
Sales	15,100	16,450	17,800	17,200	11,400	13,200	15,200

Opening stock for each month will be 20% of the current month's sales

More complex cash budget calculations

As your skills develop in preparing budgets you may be asked to calculate the selling price for cash and credit customers, taking into account possible doubtful debts.

Example 4

In the worked example Arch plc's unit selling price is £20. Credit customers are allowed a 10% trade discount and cash customers an additional 5% cash discount.

To calculate the unit selling price for credit and cash customers:

Credit customer's price

Unit selling price	£20.00
Less Trade discount of 10%	2.00
Credit selling price	18.00

All credit customers will pay **£18 per unit**.

Cash customers are given an **extra discount** of 5% off the **credit price**:

Credit price	£18.00
Less Cash discount 5%	0.90
	17.10

All cash customers will pay **£17.10 per unit**.

Task 5

The following information related to the credit and cash selling prices offered by the following firms.

	A plc	B plc	C plc	D plc	E plc
Unit selling price	£100	£50	£10	£2,000	£30
Trade discount	20%	50%	10%	40%	15%
Additional cash discount	5%	3%	2%	4%	6%

Calculate the credit and cash selling price for each firm.

Example 5

In the worked example Arch plc's unit sales are:

	Jan	Feb	Mar	Apr	May	Jun
Estimated sales	5,000	4,800	5,500	6,000	5,400	6,500

Credit sales represent 90% of all units sold. To calculate the credit sales units:

Credit sales units = Total sales × Credit sales %

For January

Credit sales units = 5,000 × 90% = 4,500

The credit sales units are shown in the table below for each month.

	Jan	Feb	Mar	Apr	May	Jun
Estimated sales	5,000	4,800	5,500	6,000	5,400	6,500
Credit sales = 90%	**4,500**	**4,320**	**4,950**	**5,400**	**4,860**	**5,850**

If 90% of sales are on credit then cash sales must account for 10% of total sales.

Cash sales units = Total sales × Cash sales %

For January

Cash sales units = 5,000 × 10% = 500

The cash sales units are shown in the table below for each month.

	Jan	Feb	Mar	Apr	May	Jun
Estimated sales	5,000	4,800	5,500	6,000	5,400	6,500
Cash sales = 10%	**500**	**480**	**550**	**600**	**540**	**650**

Task 6

1 From the following information calculate the cash and credit sales for each month. Credit sales represent 75% of all units sold.

	January	February	March
Estimated sales	10,000	12,000	14,000

2 From the following information calculate the cash and credit sales for each month. Credit sales represent 80% of all units sold.

	January	February	March
Estimated sales	6,000	7,000	9,000

3 From the following information calculate the cash and credit sales for each month. Credit sales represent 50% of all units sold.

	January	February	March
Estimated sales	9,000	8,000	11,000

4 From the following information calculate the cash and credit sales for each month. Credit sales represent 85% of all units sold.

	January	February	March
Estimated sales	5,500	4,800	6,000

5 From the following information calculate the cash and credit sales for each month. Credit sales represent 90% of all units sold.

	January	February	March
Estimated sales	120,000	110,000	115,000

Adding sales values into the cash budget

The credit and cash sales values need to be calculated for inclusion in the cash budget.

Using the information in Example 5, the cash budget is being prepared for March, April and May. Credit customers pay one month after they have received the goods. This means that we will receive payment from our customers for the goods we sold in:

February in March
March in April
April in May

Calculate the credit sales for the three months February – April

Month units sold	February	March	April
Credit sales	4,320	4,950	5,400
Credit selling price	£18	£18	£18
Cash received = Credit units × selling price	£77,760	£89,100	£97,200
Month cash received for credit sales	March	April	May

Cash customers pay for their goods at the time they receive them.

To calculate the cash sales for March April and May:

Unit sales and cash received	March	April	May
Cash Sales	550	600	540
Cash price per unit	£17.10	£17.10	£17.10
Sales revenue = Units × cash selling price	£9,405	£10,260	£9,234

Task 7

1   From the following information calculate cash and credit sales units and the sales revenues for inclusion in the cash budget for the three month period February-April for Alpha plc.

   - Unit selling price £50.
   - Credit customers receive trade discount of 30% and pay one month after delivery.
   - Cash customers receive an additional discount of 5%.

Estimated Sales amount to:

January	February	March	April
10,000	12,000	13,000	9,000

Alpha plc estimate that 75% of all sales will be on credit.

2   From the following information calculate cash and credit sales units and the sales revenues for inclusion in the cash budget for the three month period February-April for Beta plc.

   - Unit selling price £100.
   - Credit customers receive trade discount of 40% and pay two months after delivery.
   - Cash customers receive an additional discount of 5%.

continued ➤

Estimated sales amount to:

December	January	February	March	April
13,000	11,000	9,000	8,000	10,000

Beta plc estimate that 80% of all sales will be on credit.

3 From the following information calculate cash and credit sales units and the sales revenues for inclusion in the cash budget for the three month period February–April for Gamma plc.

- Unit selling price £200.
- Credit customers receive trade discount of 50% and pay two months after delivery.
- Cash customers receive an additional discount of 5%.

Estimated sales amount to:

December	January	February	March	April
20,000	18,000	12,000	14,000	16,000

Gamma plc estimate that 60% of all sales will be on credit.

4 From the following information calculate cash and credit sales units and the sales revenues for inclusion in the cash budget for the three month period July–September for Omega plc.

- Unit selling price £400.
- Credit customers receive trade discount of 25% and pay one month after delivery.
- Cash customers receive an additional discount of 10%.

Estimated sales amount to:

June	July	August	September
120,000	130,000	100,000	150,000

Omega plc estimate that 65% of all sales will be on credit.

5 From the following information calculate cash and credit sales units and the sales revenues for inclusion in the cash budget for the three month period May–July for Zeta plc.

- Unit selling price £150.
- Credit customers receive trade discount of 30% and pay two months after delivery.
- Cash customers receive an additional discount of 10%.

Estimated sales amount to:

March	April	May	June	July
10,000	11,500	13,000	12,000	14,000

Zeta plc estimate that 70% of all sales will be on credit.

When dealing with credit sales an enterprise must take into account the fact that some of their credit customers may not pay for the goods supplied. The concept of prudence ensures that when calculating the cash received from credit customers this is taken into consideration.

Example 8

Arch plc estimate that doubtful debts will be 5% of all credit customers.

When calculating the sales revenue from credit customers the 5% must be deducted from expected revenue so that a true and fair view of the cash situation can be ascertained.

The cash received from credit sales for the three months February – April, allowing for doubtful debts will be:

Month units sold	February	March	April
Credit sales	4,320	4,950	5,400
Credit selling price	£18	£18	£18
Cash received	£77,760	£89,100	£97,200
Less provision for doubtful debts 5%	£3,888	£4,455	£4,860
Expected receipts from credit sales	£73,872	£84,645	92,340
Month cash received for credit sales	March	April	May

These figures will be entered into the cash budget for the appropriate months.

Task 8

1   From the following information calculate the amount to be entered into the cash budget after allowing for doubtful debts of 4%.

Expected revenue before allowing for doubtful debts:

	Jan	Feb	Mar
Credit sales revenue	£50,000	£56,000	£48,000

2   From the following information calculate the amount to be entered into the cash budget after allowing for doubtful debts of 8%.

Expected revenue before allowing for doubtful debts:

	Jan	Feb	Mar
Credit sales revenue	£150,000	£156,000	£148,000

continued ➤

3 From the following information calculate the amount to be entered into the cash budget after allowing for doubtful debts of 10%.

Expected revenue before allowing for doubtful debts:

	Jan	Feb	Mar
Credit sales revenue	£75,000	£80,000	£66,000

4 From the following information calculate the estimated sales revenue to be entered into the cash budget after allowing for doubtful debts of 10%.

Credit selling price £20

	Jan	Feb	Mar	Apr	May	Jun
Credit units sold	10,000	12,000	9,600	8,500	11,300	10,250

5 From the following information calculate the estimated sales revenue to be entered into the cash budget after allowing for doubtful debts of 6%.

Credit selling price £3,000

	Jan	Feb	Mar	Apr	May	Jun
Credit units sold	500	550	400	475	600	890

  Now do Worksheet 24.1

Information Technology in Accounting

Intermediate 2 Level Outcomes:

I2

This chapter includes material from Int 2 level Management Accounting Outcome 5

☆ **Explain the benefits of using information technology in management accounting.**

Higher Level Outcomes:

H

This chapter includes material from Higher level Management Accounting Outcome 5

☆ **Explain the advantages and disadvantages to a business organisation of using information technology.**

I2
H

The use of IT in accounting

We live in an age where more and more information is available at the touch of a button. The accounting profession has had to keep pace with this and there are now many ready-made accounting software packages on the market which can be used in a wide variety of business enterprises. Some firms will have their own **accounting information system** which will **collect**, **process** and **transmit** financial information for the needs of their particular business enterprise. The accounting information system may be part of the organisation's **management information system**.

Many of the accounting software packages produced are integrated. This means that if the business enters details of a sale on credit to a customer into the system, the sales account and the customer's account are automatically updated. When the payment is made the bank and the customer's account is again updated.

Whether a firm uses a manual accounting system or a computerised system, the principles are the same. Information needs to be collected, processed and transmitted in a readily understandable and usable manner.

Accounting information passes through 3 stages:

Collect data

Data can be collected from an internal or external source such as:

Internal sources

- cash and credit sales invoices and receipts;
- cheque counterfoils or credit transfers/direct debits receipts;
- weekly time sheets for wage calculations;
- job cards.

External sources:

- invoices from suppliers;
- statements from suppliers;
- cheques;
- electricity or telephone accounts.

Process the data

Information is entered into the accounting software only once and processed. The information is grouped according to the needs of the enterprise.

Sales will be grouped according to regions, departments, or salesmen and split between cash and credit sales.

Sales will be recorded in sales account and in the debtors account at the same time, unlike many manual systems where different departments kept their own records.

Transmit the data

The output is produced in an appropriate form for each separate user. For example, the Sales Manager may want a breakdown of sales for different regions, the Financial Accountant may want to know the total of the debtors or creditors for a particular at the end of the financial period, or a list of accounts overdue from customers.

Accounting software packages

A search on the internet reveals a large number of accounting software packages for both Financial and Management Accounting. Below are some examples of what these accounting packages do.

Financial Accounting	Management Accounting
• Sales ledger - recording customers' accounts	• Costing for material, labour, overheads
• Purchase ledger – recording suppliers' accounts	• Budgeting and forecasting
• Nominal or Expense ledger – recording details of all expenses and the bank account	• Job costing and special order costing
• Recording details of stocks – updated with deliveries and issues	• Investment appraisal
• Wage calculations – payroll details	• Manufacturing concerns for production scheduling, tracing batches, etc
• Preparation of Trading and Profit and Loss Accounts	• Process costing
• Preparation of Balance Sheets	

Popular examples of accounting software packages are *Sage, Omni, Pegasus, Moneysoft*, etc.

Advantages of a computerised accounting system

- **Speed**: Transactions can be processed much faster than in a manual system.

- **Accuracy**: Computerised systems are more accurate, especially where the double entry is entered automatically.

- **Security**: A system of passwords can be used to restrict access to computerised records.

- **Space saving**: Computerised records take up much less space than manual records.

- **Reduction in costs**: A large number of transactions can be dealt with by a smaller number of employees thus reducing costs.

- **Access**: The information on a computerised system can be accessed from different locations – even world wide

- **User friendly**: The design of accounting software packages means that a detailed knowledge of accounting is not required. Non-specialist staff may be employed, again reducing costs.

- **Decision making**: This can be more effective as information can be produced and revised much more quickly than with a manual system.

Disadvantages of computerised accounting system

- **Cost of purchasing the software and hardware** can be expensive as can be staff training costs.

- **Operator error**: The information contained on the computerised system is only as good as the accuracy of the date entered by the operator.

- **Security**: Even although the enterprise uses a system of passwords, the computer system is still vulnerable from hackers, competitors and even current employees who feel aggrieved.

- **Technical problems**: Care has to be taken when purchasing the software and hardware necessary to run the system. The wrong choice of either can result in a costly mistake. Up-to-date virus protection systems must be employed to keep the system safe.

- **Industrial relations**: Industrial problems can result if reduction in staff occurs because of the implementation of the computer software system.

Task 1

1 Explain what the following terms mean when used in association with a computerised accounting packages:

a) Collecting

b) Processing

c) Transmitting

2 List three uses of a financial accounting software package

3 List three uses of a management accounting software package.

4 Explain how the introduction of an accounting software package will improve the efficiency of the decision making process in a business enterprise.

5 Outline the advantages and disadvantages to a business enterprise of introducing a computerised accounting system.

CHAPTER 26

Spreadsheets in Accounting

Intermediate 2 Level Outcomes: ⫸

This chapter includes material from Int 2 level Management Accounting Outcome 5

☆ **A spreadsheet is used to complete a range of cost statements.**

☆ **Entries in spreadsheet are consistent with information supplied.**

☆ **Use of spreadsheet formulae is comprehensive and consistent with information supplied.**

☆ **Data and formulae printouts are produced with gridlines, row and cell references**

Higher Level Outcomes: ⫸

This chapter includes material from Higher level Management Accounting Outcome 5

☆ **Prepare and update a range of cost statement consistent with the information supplied using a spreadsheet.**

☆ **Data entries in a spreadsheet are consistent with information supplied.**

☆ **Use of spreadsheet formulae is comprehensive and consistent with purpose.**

☆ **Spreadsheet printout for data and formulae is comprehensive and consistent with purpose and printout shows gridlines, row and cell references.**

Using spreadsheets

This chapter gives a brief overview of the use made of spreadsheets by business enterprises. It gives a basic introduction to the principles of using a spreadsheet – entering formulae, formatting cells, creating templates, producing data and formulae printouts. It does not give detailed instructions for any specific spreadsheet software package.

As well as using accounting software packages some firms rely heavily on the use of spreadsheets in preparing budgets, forecasts, carrying out decision making scenarios, preparation of final accounts etc. There are many different spreadsheet software packages available on the market for an enterprise to choose from, but the most common are *Microsoft Excel* and *Lotus 1-2-3*.

A spreadsheet consists of a grid of **rows** and **columns**. Where a row and column intersect this is called a **cell**. Each cell can contain **text**, **data** or a **formula**.

	A	**B**	**C**
1	Trading Account for year ended		
2		£	£
3	Sales		100,000
4			
5			
6			
7			
8			
9			

Column letter → C

data ← 100,000

Active cell → A4

Row number → 6

Cell → (C6)

Figure 26.1 An example of text and data in a spreadsheet

Formulae can be used to carry out a wide range of mathematical and arithmetical calculations add, subtract, multiply, divide, calculate percentage as well as deal with 'what if' scenarios.

There are advantages to using a spreadsheet:

- **Speed**: Calculations are carried out quickly.
- **Accuracy**: If the formula has been entered correctly there is no need to check the accuracy of the calculation.
- **Changes** can be made to different values and the results produced almost instantaneously.
- **Formula** and **data** can be copied from one part of the spreadsheet to another.
- A number of **'What if'** scenarios can be easily carried out and results achieved quickly.
- **Templates** can be prepared for various accounting scenarios such as job cost statements, cash budgets, overhead analysis etc.
- **Presentation of information**: Data can be presented in different ways. For examples, sales figures can be converted to graphs or charts for meetings.

The spreadsheet can be viewed in two ways. One view shows the data and labels as numbers and words, while the other view also shows the formulae which carry out the calculations (instead of the results of those calculations). You will need to be able to switch between the data view and the formulae view and print out copies of each with the gridlines and row and column heading showing.

Spreadsheet can be used throughout the Intermediate and Higher courses, although their use will only be assessed in the Management Accounting Unit.

Using formulae

This section will give a brief overview of the formulae you will need to know for the Intermediate 2 and Higher. Examples here are based on Microsoft Excel.

Example 1

To examine the use of the different formula we are going to create a spreadsheet template for a Trading Account.

The spreadsheet in Figure 26.2 shows the formulae view where the both data and formulae can be seen.

When entering formulae into a spreadsheet some of the recognised mathematical signs are changed. **Add** and **subtract** remain the same, but the **multiply** and **divide** symbols have been altered. These are shown below

Add	Subtract	Multiply	Divide
+	-	*	/

As in mathematics care must be taken in the use of brackets for parts of the calculation

Formatting spreadsheet cells

When using a spreadsheet you will want the data to be displayed in a particular way. This is called **formatting**.

In the spreadsheet in Figure 26.2, cells B5, B6, C7 and D3 show the data as whole numbers. Cells C6, D8 and D9 use this data in calculations, so the results in these cells will also show as whole numbers. You do not usually have to format these cells for this as the spreadsheet defaults to using whole numbers.

In cell B14, the answer should be displayed as a **percentage**, so we need to **format the cell** to automatically show the answer as a **percentage**. If this is done we do not need to multiply the gross profit figure by 100.

In cell B15, the **average stock** value should be displayed as **currency**. Usually when formatting for currency you are automatically offered 2 decimal places, but we may decide that we only want whole numbers to be displayed.

Cell B16 shows the **rate of stock turnover**. Normally we will be working to 2 decimal places for this calculation therefore we want to format this cell to show 2 decimal places.

continued ➤

Example 1 continued

	A	B	C	D
1	Trading Account for year ended 31 March Year 2			
2		£		£
3	Sales			100,000
4	Less Cost of Sales			
5	Opening Stock	7,000		
6	Add Purchases	52,000	=B5+B6	
7	Less Closing Stock		5,000	
8	Cost of goods sold			=C6-C7
9	Gross Profit			=D3-D8
10				
11				
12	Analysis of Trading Account Performance			
13				
14	Gross Profit Percentage	=D9/D3*100		
15	Average Stock	=(B5+C8)/2		
16	Rate of Stock turnover	=D8/B15	times	

Figure 26.2 Spreadsheet showing formulae in cells C6, D8 and D9, and B14, B15 and B16

Each formulae starts with the **=** sign. This is the 'flag' which tells the computer that the cell contains a formula and a calculation is required.

Cell Reference	Formula	Explanation of formula
C6	=B5+B6	Addition formula calculating **total value** of **Opening Stock + Purchases**
D8	=C6-C7	Subtraction formula calculating the **Cost of Goods Sold =** **Opening Stock + Purchases – Closing Stock**
D9	=D3-D8	Subtraction formula calculating the **Gross Profit**
B14	=D9/D3*100	This formula calculates the **Gross Profit Percentage**. If the cell is formatted as a percentage cell you will not need to multiply by 100.
B15	=(B5+C8)/2	This formula is used to calculate the **average stock**. It is in 2 parts and requires the use of brackets. The spreadsheet must first add the **Opening** and **Closing Stocks** together before **dividing by 2** to find the average.
B16	=D8/B15	This formula calculates the **Rate of Stock Turnover**. The result of the formula in D8 is the **Cost of Goods Sold** is **divided** by the result of the formula in **B15** which calculates the **Average Stock**.

The spreadsheet in Figure 26.3 is the same as in Figure 26.2, but shows the results of the formula calculations.

continued ➢

Example 1 continued

	A	B	C	D
1	Trading Account for year ended 31 March Year 2			
2		£		£
3	Sales			100,000
4	Less Cost of Sales			
5	Opening Stock	7,000		
6	Add Purchases	52,000	59,000	
7	Less Closing Stock		5,000	
8	Cost of goods sold			54,000
9	Gross Profit			46,000
10				
11				
12	Analysis of Trading Account Performance			
13				
14	Gross Profit Percentage	46%		
15	Average Stock	£6,000		
16	Rate of Stock turnover	9.00	times	

Figure 26.3 Spreadsheet showing results of calculations in cells C6, D8 and D9, and B14, B15 and B16

To help with your understanding of spreadsheets the above template should be keyed into your particular spreadsheet system. Enter the data and formulae in the appropriate cells. Save and print out the spreadsheet. Follow your teacher's instructions for your particular system.

Absolute cell reference and copying

If a number of calculations require figures to be multiplied by the same figure, (for example, sales units multiplied by the same sales price) the formulae can be set up as an **absolute cell reference**.

The cell reference uses the **$** sign which indicates to the software that this same figure should be copied into the adjacent cells .

Example 2

The spreadsheet in Figure 26.4 contains information about the sales units and sales income for a six month period.

	A	B	C
1	Sales analysis for January - June		
2			
3	Selling Price	£30	
4			
5	Months	Units Sold	Income
6	January	5,000	**B3*B6**
7	February	5,800	
8	March	5,600	
9	April	6,000	
10	May	6,500	
11	June	6,900	
12	Total		
13			

Figure 26.4 Spreadsheet showing sales information for a six month period

The **absolute cell reference** will be **B3** and in the cell reference formulae it will appear as **B3**.

The formula to calculate the monthly sales income appears in **C6** for January.

Sales income for January calculated on a calculator will be **5,000 units × £30**. The formula keyed onto your spreadsheet will be **B3*B6**.

The formula will be copied down the table and as each row advances the spreadsheet moves the row number for **Units Sold** down by one, but the cell reference for the **Selling Price** remains fixed.

Updating a spreadsheet

Any changes to the trading information will be entered into the appropriate cell and the spreadsheet will be automatically updated.

For example, if it was discovered that the purchases figure in cell C6 should have been **£55,000** instead of **£52,000**, it would be a simple matter to enter the correct figure into cell C6. As soon as this is done, the spreadsheet **updates** all the calculations that depend on this figure.

Cell Reference	Item	Original Figure	Updated Figure
B6	Purchases	£52,000	£55,000
C6	Opening Stock + Purchases	£59,000	£62,000
D8	Cost of goods sold	£54,000	£57,000
D9	Gross Profit	£46,000	£43,000
B14	Gross Profit Ratio	46%	43%
B16	Rate of Stock Turnover	9 times	9.5 times

Using conditional formula

Conditional formulae are used to test a cell for a certain condition, and depending on the result, one or two specific actions care taken.

Example 3

The salesmen working for JRG Co will receive a bonus of 2% of their sales figure if they reach or exceed their sales target of £50,000 in any one month. Salesmen not achieving their target receive no bonus.

Figure 26.5 shows sales for the first quarter of the year.

	A	B	C
1			
2		1st Quarter £	Bonus Due £
3	Alan Smith	47,500	
4	George Hamilton	52,500	
5	Douglas Macintyre	63,000	
6	Michael Rowes	45,000	
7	Total		

Figure 26.5 Sales for the first quarter of the year.

When dealing with conditional formula it is useful to actually write out what the actual conditions are. Start the statement with 'if'

If sales target is **greater than** or **equal** to **£50,000 then** salesmen receive **2% bonus**, **otherwise** they receive **nothing**.

This sentence is converted to the following formula which will be entered into C3:

=IF(B3>=50000,B3*2%,0)

- the **comma** after the 50000 represents the word **then**
- the **comma** between the % and 0 represents the word **otherwise**

so the formula can be understood as:

IF: B3 is greater or equal to £50,000
Then: B3 multiplied by 2%
Otherwise: 0

Once the formula is entered into the spreadsheet in cell B3 it is then copied down the column to calculate the commission for each salesmen, shown in Figure 26.6.

continued ➤

MANAGEMENT ACCOUNTING

Example 3 continued

	A	B	C
1			
2		1st Quarter £	Bonus Due £
3	Alan Smith	47,500	0
4	George Hamilton	52,500	1,050
5	Douglas Macintyre	63,000	1,260
6	Michael Rowes	45,000	0
7	Total		

Figure 26.6 Spreadsheet showing Bonus Due based on sales information for four salesmen for the 1st quarter of the year

Any of the exercises from the previous chapters can be completed using a spreadsheet. For these exercises you will need to prepare a spreadsheet template and enter the data provided before entering the formulae.

Now do Worksheets 26.1, 26.2, 26.3, 26.4 and 26.5

Index

A

abnormal loss 354–8
absolute cell references 428–31
absorption rates 313–20
accounting concepts 1
Accounting Standards Board
  (ASB) 246–8
accruals
  final accounts 34, 47, 56–7, 63–7
  standards 248
  subscriptions 183–5
accumulated funds 185–7
acid test ratio 205–6, 210, 223
adjustments to final accounts
  56–95
agreements, partnerships 112–14
amortization of leases 85
annual depreciation 80–4
apportioning overheads 295–312
  direct labour hours 300–302
  employee numbers 297–8
  fixed assets 299–300
  floor area 295–7
  machine hours 302–3
  metered consumption 304–5
  primary apportionment 295
appropriation accounts see profit
  and loss appropriation accounts
Articles of Association 148
ASB (Accounting Standards
  Board) 248–50
assets
  balance sheets 46–54, 168
  depreciation 79–95
  leasing 152
  new partners 136–45
  plc balance sheets 168
  see also current assets;
    fixed assets
authorised capital 153
Average Price (AVCO) method
  275–8
average stock turnover 194–5,
  210, 215–16

B

bad debts 67–78
balance sheets 46–55
  assets 46–54, 168
  equations 53–4
  final accounts 46–55
  liabilities 47–8, 50–4
  not-for-profit organisations
    185–9
  partnerships 127–32
  plcs 166–73
  preparation 48–53
  ratio analysis 201–10

balances 121–2, 400, 407
bank accounts 175–6
bank overdrafts 152
bank reconciliation statements
  241–6
bin cards 257, 263
bonus schemes 289–92
bonus shares 151
book-keeping 25–32, 90–5
break-even analysis 359–73
  assumptions 372
  charts 360–6
  contribution margin 366–7, 369
  fixed costs 359–62
  limitations 372
  margin of safety 363–4
  marginal costing 384–5
  profit 367, 370–1
budgets 395–422
  administration 398–9
  budget periods 396
  cash budgets 400–410, 416–22
  complex calculations 416–18
  control 395–422
  financial needs 397
  fixed budgets 399
  flexible budgets 399
  functional budgets 397–8
  operating budgets 397
  preparation 395–422
  production budgets 413–16
  sales budgets 410–3, 418–22
  sales values 418–22
business transactions 12–21
buying 258
by products 341

C

called-up capital 155
capital
  accounts 114
  expenditure 32
  interest on capital 118–27
  liabilities 48
  partnerships 114, 118–27
  plcs 151–4, 171
  return on capital employed
    201–3, 210, 222
  venture capital 153
card time recorders 282–3
cash accounts 175–6
cash budgets 400–410, 416–22
  complex calculations 416–18
  sales values 418–22
cash sale till receipts 22
centralised storage 262
charts, break-even analysis 360–6
check time-keeping method 282

cheques 23–4, 242
classification of costs 253–6
clearing 241
clock cards 283
closing balances 400, 407
commission errors 230–31
Companies Acts 79
compensation errors 233–4
computerised systems
  accounting 423–5
  stock control 265, 280–81
  stock pricing 280–81
conditional formulae,
  spreadsheets 432–3
consistency concept 247
contracts, special 391–2
contribution 381–6, 388
contribution margin method
  366–7, 369
control
  budgets 395–422
  computerised control 265,
    280–1
  inventory 257–65, 278–9
  labour costs 282–92
  stock 262–5, 278–81
copying formulae, spreadsheets
  430–31
cost cards 322
cost centres 253, 293–4, 308–12
cost units
  cost classification 253
  manufacturing 109
  overheads 294
  services 332, 338–9
cost-volume-profit analysis see
  break-even analysis
costing
  cost classification 253–6
  job costing 321–30
  marginal costing 374–94
  process costing 340–58
  service costing 308–12, 331–9
costs
  break-even analysis 359–60
  fixed costs 97, 254–5, 359–62,
    385
  indirect costs 97, 254
  manufacturing 96–110
  material costs 97–8, 254, 317,
    321–8, 342
  opportunity costs 393–4
  prime costs 97–101, 316
  semi-variable costs 255
  services costs 332
  stock of work in progress 102–4
  total costs 359–61, 363, 385
  trading accounts 37, 105–10

types of costs 96–7, 101, 253–4, 332
see also direct costs; labour costs; overheads; variable costs
counterfoils, cheques 23
credit cards 23
credit notes 19–20
creditors 2, 208–9, 211, 225
creditors' payment period 208–9, 211, 225
cumulative preference shares 150
current accounts 114, 116–18, 120–2, 125
current assets
final accounts 47, 50–3
partnerships 131
plc balance sheets 168
current liabilities
balance sheets 47, 50–3
not-for-profit organisations 189
partnerships 131
plc balance sheets 169
see also liabilities
current ratio 203–5, 210, 223
see also working capital

D
data systems 423–4
debentures 151–2
debit cards 23
debts 67–78
bad debts 67–78
debtors' collection period 206–7, 211, 224
doubtful debts 67–78
partial bad debts 69–70
recovery 71–2
decision-making 374–94
closing factories 393
dropping products 393
make or buy decisions 393–4
marginal costing 374–94
special contracts 391–2
deferred shares 150
depreciation 79–95
book-keeping entries 90–5
Companies Acts 79
fixed assets 79–95
methods 80–90
diminishing balance depreciation method 86–90
direct costs 96–7, 99–100, 253–4
expenses 97, 99–100, 254, 342
labour 99, 254, 342
material 96, 254, 317
wages 96, 316
see also variable costs
direct labour hours 300–302, 315
disc time-keeping method 282

discount 15
dishonoured cheques 23–4, 242
dividends, plcs 155–66
documents 12–24
business transactions 12–21
goods/services payments 22–4
plcs 148
purchasing 258–62
trade 12–24
trail diagram 12
double-entry book-keeping 25–32
doubtful debts 67–78
drawings accounts 114, 117–20, 121–5

E
efficiency ratios 192
balance sheets 206–10
formulae 210–11
performance analysis 221, 224–5
profit and loss accounts 200–201
trading accounts 195–8
equal instalment depreciation method 80, 83–4, 86
errors 226–40, 242
bank statements 242
suspense accounts 236–40
trial balance 226–40
estimated statements 213–20
expenditure
revenue expenditure 32
see also income and expenditure accounts
expenses
direct expenses 97, 99–100, 254, 342
expense ratios 200–201, 211, 224

F
factoring 152
factory overheads 319–21, 323, 325–8
see also overheads
factory-wide overhead absorption rates 319–20
fees 175
FIFO *see* First In First Out method
final accounts 33–55, 191–225
accruals 34, 47, 56–7, 63–7
adjustments 56–95
analysis 191–225
bad debts 67–78
balance sheets 46–55
comparing results 191–2
doubtful debts 67–78
fixed asset depreciation 79–95
performance analysis 221–5
plcs 154–73

preparation 33–55
prepayments 56–63
profit and loss accounts 34, 39–46
purpose 33
ratio analysis 191–225
trading accounts 34–9, 43–6
financial accounting 1–250
Financial Reporting Standards (FRSs) 250
financial year adjustments 57–63, 63–7
First In First Out (FIFO) method 265–9
fixed assets 46–7, 49–53
depreciation 79–95
fixed assets turnover 209–11, 225
overheads apportionment 299–300
partnerships 130, 132
fixed budgets 399
fixed costs
break-even analysis 359–62
cost classification 254–5
indirect costs 97, 254
manufacturing accounts 97
marginal costing 385
see also overheads
flexible budgets 399
forecasting
budgets 396
profit 368
formatting spreadsheet cells 428–30
formulae, spreadsheets 427–33
founder shares 150
FRSs (Financial Reporting Standards) 250
functional budgets 397–8

G
general partners 113
going concerns 247
goods
cost of goods 37
goods received notes 260–2
payment documents 22–4
goodwill 134–45
grants 152, 175
gross profit 38–41
profit and loss accounts 40–1
ratio 191–3, 210, 213–15, 222
trading accounts 38–9
see also profit
group bonus schemes 292

H
Halsey premium bonus scheme 290–91
hire purchase 152

I

incentive/premium bonus
    schemes 289–91
income and expenditure accounts
    178–83
    see also profit and loss
        accounts
indirect costs 97, 254
    see also fixed costs; overheads
Information Technology (IT) 423–5
Inland Revenue 3
interest on capital 118–27
    current account balances 121–2
    drawings 123–5
    loans 126–7
    partnerships 118–27
inventory control 257–65
    purchasing 257–62
    stock control 263–5
    stock pricing 278–9
invoices 14
issued capital 154
IT (Information Technology) 423–5

J

JIT (Just In Time) system 264–5
job costing 321–30
    aims 321–9
    cost cards 322
    labour 321, 323–8
    materials 321–8
    overheads 319–22, 323, 325–8
    profit mark-up/margin 329–30
job tickets 284
joint products 341
Just In Time (JIT) system 264–5

L

labour
    direct labour hours 300–302,
        315
    process costing 342
labour costs 282–92
    bonus schemes 289–92
    control 282–92
    direct costs 99, 255, 343
    job costing 322, 324–9
    payment by results 289–90
    remuneration systems 285–93
    time-keeping methods 283–5
Last In First Out (LIFO) 271–75
leases, amortization 85
leasing assets 152
ledger accounts 25–32
    example accounts 28–32
    real/personal/nominal
        accounts 27
    recording transactions 28
    trial balance 31
    types 26

letters of enquiry 13
liabilities
    balance sheets 47–8, 50–4
    long-term 48, 52, 130–1
    not-for-profit organisations 189
    partnerships 130–1
    plc balance sheets 169, 171
    see also current liabilities
life membership fees 175
LIFO *see* Last In First Out
limited companies 146–73
    accounts 146–73
    definitions 146–7
    private companies 147
    see also public limited
        companies
Limited Liability Partnership Act
    2000 113–14
limited partners 112
Limited Partnership Act 1907 112
limiting factors, marginal costing
    385–91
liquidity ratios 192
    balance sheets 203–5
    formulae 210
    performance analysis 221, 223
loans 127–8, 151, 175
long-term liabilities 48, 52, 130–1
loose budgets 396
loss
    abnormal loss 354–8
    normal loss 346–52, 355
    see also profit and loss
        accounts

M

machine hours 302–3, 314
make or buy decisions 393–4
management accounting 1–9,
    252–433
managers 4
manufacturing accounts 96–110
    costs 96–110
    overheads 101–2, 106–08
    preparation 96–110
    prime costs 97–101
    stock of work in progress
        102–4
    trading accounts 105–10
marginal costing 374–94
    applications 385–94
    break-even analysis 384–5
    contribution 381–4, 388
    decision making 374–94
    profit limiting factors 385–91
    statements 375–81
    variable costs 374–6, 379,
        381–2, 385
marginal income 366–7
mark-up 193, 210, 221–2, 329–30

matching concept 56–7, 63, 248
material costs
    cost classifications 254
    direct costs 96, 254, 317
    job costing 321–8
    manufacturing 96–8
    overheads 317
    process costing 342
materials, storage 262
membership fees 175
Memorandum of Association 148
mortgages 152

N

net assets 48, 51–3
net profit
    profit and loss accounts 39–42
    ratio 197–8, 210, 222
    see also profit
net sales 36
nominal accounts 27
non-cumulative preference shares
    150
normal loss 346–52, 355
not-for-profit organisations
    174–89
    accounts 175–89
    balance sheets 185–9
    financial sources 174–5
    income and expenditure
        accounts 178–83
    receipts and payments accounts
        176–7
    running clubs 174–5

O

omission errors 229–30, 238, 242
opening balances 400
operating budgets 397
opportunity costs 393–4
orders 13, 259–61
ordinary shares 149, 157–60, 161,
    163
original entry errors 227–9
over-capitalization 204
overcasting errors 239
overdrafts 152
overheads 293–320
    absorption 313–20
    allocation 294, 306–8
    analysis 293–320
    apportionment 295–312
    definitions 97
    job costing 319–21, 323, 325–8
    manufacturing 101–2, 106–8
    primary apportionment 295
    process costing 342
    secondary apportionment 295,
        308–12
    service cost centres 308–12

statement preparation 305–8
see also fixed costs
overtime rates 285–6
owners of businesses 4

P

paid-up capital 154
partial bad debts 69–70
participating preference shares 150
partnerships 111–44
  accounting 114–18
  agreements 112–14
  asset revaluation 136–45
  balance sheets 127–32
  definitions 111–12
  goodwill 134–45
  interest on capital 118–27
  limited partners 112
  new partners 134–45
  profit and loss accounts 114–19,
    122–6
  profit-sharing ratios 136–45
payment
  by results 288–9
  documents 22–4
  receipts and payment accounts
    176–7
payslips 292
performance analysis 221–5
personal accounts 27
piece-work rates 288–9
plcs *see* public limited companies
preference shares 149–50, 155–6,
  161, 163
premiums, shares 150
prepayments 34, 56–63, 183–5
pricing stock 266–81
primary overheads apportionment
  295
prime costs 98–102, 316
principle, errors of principle
  232–3
private limited companies 147
process costing 340–58
  abnormal loss 354–8
  accounting 341–51
  elements diagram 342
  normal loss 346–52, 355
  work-in-progress 351–4
production budgets 413–16
profit
  break-even analysis 368,
    370–71
  contribution 382
  forecasting 368
  job costing 329–30
  manufacturing accounts 109–10
  margin/mark-up 329–30
  marginal costing 382–91
  maximisation 385–91
  net profit 39–42, 197–8, 210, 222

partnership ratios 136–45
planning 370–71
profit and loss accounts 39–42
P/V ratio 369, 383–5
trading accounts 38–9
see also gross profit;
  profitability ratios
profit and loss accounts 34,
  39–46
  appropriation accounts 114–21,
    122–6, 155, 160–6
  income and expenditure
    accounts 178–83
  manufacturing 110
  preparation 40–2
  ratios 197–200
  trading accounts 43–6
profit/volume (P/V) ratio 369,
  383–5
profitability ratios 191
  balance sheets 201–3
  formulae 210
  performance analysis 221–2
  profit and loss accounts
    197–8
  trading accounts 191–3
provisions 34, 153
prudence 248
public limited companies (plcs)
  147–73
  balance sheets 166–73
  capital raising 151–4
  dividends 155–66
  features 147
  final accounts 154–73
  financial sources 152–3
  formation 147–54
  profit and loss accounts 155,
    160–6
  provisions 153
  reserves 153, 171
  shares 149–51, 155–6, 161, 163
purchasing 257–62
  buying 258
  documentation 258–62
  orders 13, 259–61
  procedures 258–62
  purchase requisition 258–60
  purchases figures 217–20
  receipt of goods 260–62
P/V ratio *see* profit/volume ratio

Q

quotations 13

R

rate of stock turnover 194–7, 210,
  215–16, 224
ratio analysis 190–225
  balance sheets 201–10
  estimated statements 213–20

final accounts 191–225
formulae 210–13
performance analysis 221–5
profit and loss accounts
  198–201
trading accounts 191–7
raw material costs 97–8, 342
real accounts 27
receipt of goods 260–62
receipts and payment accounts
  176–7
receipts for payments 22
recovery of bad debts 71–2
remuneration systems 284–92
reserves, plcs 153, 171
return on capital employed 201–3,
  210, 222
revaluation of assets depreciation
  method 90
revenue expenditure 32
revenue reserves 153, 171
reversal errors 234–6
rights issue, shares 151
Rowan premium bonus scheme
  291
running balance accounts 26
running costs, services 327,
  332

S

sales
  assets 91–5
  budgets 410–13, 418–22
  cost of sales 37
  net sales 36
  P/V ratio 384
scrap 341, 349–52, 355
scrip issue, shares 151
secondary apportionment,
  overheads 295, 308–12
semi-variable costs 255
services
  costing 308–12, 327, 331–9
  payment 22–4
shareholders 3
shares 149–51, 155–6, 161, 163
software packages 424–5
specific order costing *see* job
  costing
spreadsheets 426–33
  absolute cell references
    430–31
  formatting cells 428–30
  formulae 427–33
  updating 431
standard costs 332
standards 247–50
  accounting concepts 248–9
  ASB 248–9
  confusion avoidance 248–9
  developments 250